NOT
HERE,
BUT IN
ANOTHER
PLACE

NOT
HERE,
BUT IN
ANOTHER
PLACE

Ralph Barker

ST. MARTIN'S · New York

Library of Congress Cataloging in Publication Data

Barker, Ralph, 1917–
    Not here, but in another place.

1. Moluccans, South, in the Netherlands—History.
2. Terrorism—Netherlands. 3. Hijacking of trains—
Netherlands. 4. Hostages—Netherlands. 5. Nether-
lands—History—1945–   I. Title.
DJ92.I53B37   364.1'54'09492   80–10965
ISBN 0–312–57961–6

Contents

Part I 1975—The Train and the Consulate

Part II 1977—The Train and the School

Acknowledgments

IN THE COURSE OF MY RESEARCH for this book I spent several months in Holland, during which time I was fortunate in encountering a high degree of frankness and cooperation from Dutch and South Moluccan alike. This cooperation continued in the course of subsequent long and detailed correspondence. Personal interviews with many of those taken hostage during the various sieges, and contact with friends and relatives of the hijackers, helped immeasurably in establishing the principal characters and in reconstructing the course of events day by day. Official Dutch reports provided the framework of government action and reaction, and material provided by South Moluccans and their sympathizers gave an insight into their struggle for an independent South Moluccan Republic.

I am deeply indebted to all those who helped me, and in listing them by name I would like to stress that, although the responsibility for the text is of course mine, many of them helped very considerably. At the same time I would crave the same tolerance already shown to me if I have omitted someone whom I should have included.

There were four or five people and/or agencies whose contributions were decisive. First chronologically was the weekly Dutch newspaper *Vrij Nederland,* where the editor, Rinus Ferdinandusse, gave me unlimited access to the cuttings and files in his library, and authorized staff writer Mrs. Tessel Pollman to help me with background and introductions, a task she performed unstintingly. Gerhard Vaders, formerly editor of *Nieuwsblad van het Noorden* and a hostage on the first hijacked train, generously allowed me to use his own account as source material, besides providing an essential link with other hostages and helping in many other ways. George Flapper, a hostage in the second hijacked train, filled the same role on that incident with energy and enthusiasm. W.H.M. van Leeuwen, Chief Information Officer at the Ministry of Justice in The Hague, was a valued friend at court in government circles. Lastly Gerhard Knot, Secretary of the Dutch-Melanesian Aid Foundation, provided much material and arranged many contacts for me on the South Moluccan side.

R.B.

Sources

(All appointments are those held at the time of the sieges.)

Dutch Government

Joop den Uyl, Minister President (Prime Minister)

W.F. de Gaay Fortman, Minister for Internal Affairs

Henk Zeevalking, State Secretary for Justice

Government Officials and Agencies

Ministry of Defense, Public Information Branch, and especially Lt. Col. A.P. de Jong, Major George Struycker-Boudier, and T.H.F. van Hees

Ministry of Culture, Recreation, and Social Work, and especially Dr. G. Hendriks and Messrs. Hielkema and Koster

Ministry of Justice, and especially W.H.M. van Leeuwen, Chief Information Officer, Mrs. Toos Faber, Public Relations Consultant to the Judiciary, and Dr. Dick Mulder, District Psychiatrist for The Hague

Ministry of Foreign Affairs, and especially Mr. de Jong of the Indonesian Desk

Royal Netherlands Embassy, London, and especially C.F. Stork, Information Officer

Mrs. A.P. Schilthuis, Queen's Commissioner for the Province of Drenthe

Baron W.A. van der Feltz, Attorney General for South Holland and Zealand

A.A. Beckeringh van Rhijn, Burgomaster of Beilen

Ms. S. Somer-Dijstra, Secretary, Commission van Overleg Zuid-Molukkers (the Köbben Commission)

Various Dutch Authorities and Individuals

State Police (Rijkspolitie), and especially Lt. Col. L.P. Bergsma, Chief of State Police, Province of Drenthe, and Lt. A.A. Smeels, State Police, Assen District

Police Headquarters Amsterdam, and especially Mr. van Steenbergen

Nederlandse Spoorwegen (Netherlands Railways), and especially A.J. Meinsma and H. Meijer, Press Officers

Prof. Dr. J. Bastiaans, Chairman of the Department of Psychiatry at Leiden State University

Prof. Dr. W.K. van Dijk and Prof. Dr. R. Giel, Psychiatric Clinic, Academic Hospital, Groningen

Vrij Nederland, and especially Rinus Ferdinandusse, Tessel Pollman, Max van Weezel, and Guan Seleky

Dutch-Melanesian Aid Foundation, and especially the Secretary, Gerhard Knot

W.G.A. Kousemaker, and H.W.J. Droesen, lawyers acting at various times for the South Moluccan accused

Mrs. Hilda Verweij-Jonker

Dr. Henk Havinga, psychiatrist

M.H. Marien

Rick Wilson, of Anglotext

Paul Bakker, of the Landelijk Comité Zuid-Molukken

J. Ritzemar Bos

Chris van der Veen

Mrs. Ria Willemse

South Moluccans

J.A. Manusama, President, South Moluccan government-in-exile

P.W. Lokollo, Vice-President

J. Latumahina, Minister for Internal Affairs

Rev. S. Metiary, Chairman of Badan Persatuan

Etty Aponno, Chairman of the Pemuda Masjarakat (Free South Moluccan Youth)

Dr. H. Tan

Dr. F. Tutuhatunewa

Ruud Metekohy

Priscilla Metekohy

Pieter Tuny

Pieter Papilaya

Zeth Pessireron

Frieda Tomasoa
Willem Sopacua

Indonesians

The Indonesian Embassy, The Hague, and especially the Ambassador, General Sutopo Yuwono; Soerjadi Kromomihardjo, Head of the Political Department; and Alwi Alatas, Deputy Chief of the Information Section

Hostages

The 1975 Train—W. Albracht, H. Brinker, Mrs. Wientje Kruyswijk, L. Laurier, H. Prins, F. Santing, T. Stevens, W. Timmer, Mr. and Mrs. C. Ter Veer, G. Vaders, K. Wielenga. Also Willem Bulter, brother of Leo Bulter

The Indonesian Consulate

Mrs. V.P. Martron, Wessel van Pijlen, Heru Dharma, and Harsoyo Tjitrosubono

The 1977 Train

G. Flapper, J.W.B. Cuppen, C.J. (Kees) Huibregtse-Bimmel, J.W. Huismans, M. Hustinx, A.M.H. (Ton) Kroon, Miss W. Loman, Miss W. Mann, A.H. (Ton) Meulman, C.V. Nijmeijer, Mrs. S. Sein, Miss J. Winkeldermaat. Also Mrs. Coby Flapper, Mrs. Marie José Cuppen, Mrs. Marianne Kroon, and Mrs. Vera Nijmeijer

The School

Mrs. S. Abbink, S. van Beetz, André and Henny Penn, H. Ten Bosch, Mrs. M. Gerritsen, Mrs. Meursing

Translations

Mrs. T.W. Aserappa, Mrs. J. Dorrell, M.H.P. McCarthy

Books, Magazines, Newspapers, Pamphlets, Reports

Republik Maluku Selatan, by Dr. Gunter Decker (Verlag Otto Schwartz & Co., Gottingen, 1957)

Terrorism and the Liberal State, by Paul Wilkinson (Macmillan, 1977)

South Moluccan Radicalism in the Netherlands: Nationalist or Emancipation Movement, by M.H. Marien (Sociologia Neerlandica Volume IX, Number II, 1973)

Out of the Shadow of the Past: Myth and Reality of the Moluccan Problem, by J.Persijn (Internationale Spectator, February 1976)

United Nations Security Council, Official Records Sixth Year, Special Supplement No. 1 (Document S/2087, United Nations Commission for Indonesia: report on activities since the transfer of sovereignty, 13 April 1951)

Report of a Protest: An Open Appeal to World Opinion to Condemn the Immoral Policy of the Dutch Government Towards the People of the South Moluccas (Badan Persatuan, undated, circa 1970)

Confrontation (Department of Information Service of the Republic of the South Moluccas, 1975)

Principal Characters

THE HOSTAGES

Wijster Train Hostages, 1975, in order of seating

9. K. Wielenga (project leader)
10. L. Verver (real estate agent)
11. L.F. Butler (soldier)
12. Mrs. S.T. (Wientje) Kruyswijk (housewife)
17. L.F. Laurier (trade union official)
18. J. Bies (soldier)
19. Mrs. C.J. (Joanna) Jansen (housewife)
20. Mrs. T. Bakker (housewife)
25. Mrs. D. Ter Veer (housewife)
26. C. Ter Veer (shop proprietor)
27. H. Bos (maintenance technician)
28. F. Santing (student)
33. Mrs. M.H. (Riet) Overtoom (housewife)
34. E.J. (Bert) Bierling (economist)
35. J. van der Boon (biologist)
36. Mrs. G. van Giessen (housewife)
47. Mrs. M. (Bé) Barger

   (housewife)
13. Mrs. S.T. Sluiter (dietician)
14. R.H. de Groot (real estate agent)
15. Mrs. C. van Hille (former nurse)
16. Mrs. W.J. (Betle) van Overeem (housewife)
21. G.J. Foeken (district nurse)
22. P. Gruppelaar (administrator)
23. W. Timmer (teacher)
24. (Vacant)
29. J.H. Hoven (clerk)
30. T. Stevens (soldier)
31. A. Oosting (woodworker)
32. Irma Martens (student)
37. H. Prins (radiobiologist)
38. G. Vaders (newspaper editor)
39. D. Smit (pensioner)
40. W.O. Albracht (engineer)
48. Rev. G.A. Barger (retired clergyman)

NOTE: Seats 1–8 were left empty, for use by the hijackers. Similarly seats 49–56, while seats 41–46 were also available for them. (See diagram of interior of train on page 8.)

Hostages in the Indonesian Consulate, 1975

Teachers: Saka Datuk, A. Rustamadji, Mrs. Mariana, Mrs. K. Ruri

Officials of the Jakarta Raya Municipality Visiting the Consulate:
Messrs. Akhir, Mizar, and Sudradjad

Officials of the Consulate-General: Mrs. Etty Abdulkadir, Pandji Asaari, Heru
Dharma, Musni Iskandar, Mrs. Farida Sahupala Karim, J.P. Pardede, Ashadi S.
Prawirodirdjo, Mrs. Nunuk Moertsdji Rahardjo, K.R. Rasyid, Mrs. Astuti Saleh,
Miss Nies Sumarno, Harsoyo Tjitrosubono

Employees of Nitour Travel Agency:
Raden Suhirman, Miss Nies Sumarno, Arthur van Asdonck

Employees of Intras Travel Agency:
Anita Hoeboer, Mrs. Vera Martron, Wim Simon

Guests of the Consulate:
Dr. Fanggiday, Wessel van Pijlen

Those Who Escaped from the Building:
Hasan Wirasastra (Chief of the Chancellery), Messrs. Abedy, Bustomi, and
Hasan Tisnadibrata (members of the Chancellery), and Miss A. Mangundap
(Passport official)

Schoolchildren:
Fifteen elementary and junior high school students also held hostage for varying
lengths of time

De Punt Train Hostages, 1977

M.J. van der Aa (social worker)
M. (Rien) van Baarsel (architectural
    consultant)
P.R. Blankert (student dredger)
B. Boevink (administrative assistant)
Miss M.J. Bos (student)
A.L. Bramer (trainee civil engineer)
Miss R. Brinkman (student)
Mrs. A.H. Brouwers (housewife)
Miss H. Bruins (student teacher)
J.W.B. Cuppen (painter and art
    school teacher)
Miss M. Drost (medical student)

A.J. Dijkman (company official)
J.M. (Hans) Oude Elberink (official,
    Netherlands Railways)
Mrs. N. Ellenbroek (housewife)
J.W. Fakkert (social worker)
G. Flapper (student)
J. Franken (salesman)
Miss J. Fransen (student)
J.T.V.M. Geusgens (chemist)
T.J. van Hattem (helmsman,
    Merchant Service)
G.J. Hogervorst (social worker)
J.C. Hoogenboom (waiter)

C.J. (Kees) Huibregtse-Bimmel (student baker)

Miss Lubina Huinink (student)

J.W. Huismans (administrative assistant)

M. Hustinx (law student)

H. Koelma (student)

A.M.H. (Ton) Kroon (buyer, ladies' clothing)

M. Kuiper (engineer, Netherlands Railways)

Miss W. (Mini) Loman (clerical officer)

Miss H. Maat (student teacher)

Miss W. Mann (student teacher)

A.H. (Ton) Meulman (head conductor, Netherlands Railways)

Miss J.M.O. (Ansje) Monsjou (bank employee)

C.V. Nijmeijer (Rijkspolitie, State Police)

Miss R. Oostveen (medical student)

D.P. Pot (student)

P.J. Putker (student dredger)

P.G.M. de Ruyter (teacher, butchers' school)

Miss I. Rijstenberg (student)

F.A.H. Schager (student teacher, physical training)

Mrs. S. Sein (housewife)

J. Slachter (carpenter)

R.M. Smit (student baker)

J.H. Soetevent (student dredger)

Mrs. H. Stokvis (housewife)

B. van der Struik (art school teacher)

H.J. Tiemersma (student baker)

A. Tomas (administrator, construction)

A.J. Twigt (teacher, higher school of navigation)

Miss J.W. Wiegers (student teacher)

Miss J. Winkeldermaat (student dietician)

R.W.J. Woudenberg (social worker)

E.S.K. Yong (roof tiler)

Hostages in the School, 1977

E.E. van Vliet, headmaster

Mrs. S. Abbink

S. van Beetz

Miss D. Harkink

A.J. Weijnholt

Also 105 Dutch schoolchildren aged 6 to 12

OFFICIALS

On the Dutch Government Side

Joop den Uyl—Prime Minister or Minister President

Andreas van Agt—Minister of Justice

Henk Zeevalking—State Secretary for Justice

Willem de Gaay Fortman—Minister of the Interior

Max van der Stoel—Foreign Minister

Harry van Doorn—Minister of Culture, Recreation, and Social Work

Mrs. A.P. Schilthuis—Queen's Commissioner for the Province of Drenthe

A.A. Beckeringh van Rhijn—Burgomaster of Beilen

Lt. Col. L.P. Bergsma—Chief of State Police (Rijkspolitie), Drenthe Province

W.C. van Binsbergen—Attorney General for the Northern Provinces

Baron W.A. van der Feltz—Attorney General for the Southeastern Provinces

Dr. Dick Mulder—District Psychiatrist for The Hague, Ministry of Justice

Dr. Henk Havinga—psychiatrist called in by the Dutch Government

On the South Moluccan Side

J.A. Manusama—President of the self-styled government-in-exile

P.W. Lokollo—Vice-President

Mrs. Josina Soumokil—widow of former President Dr. Chris Soumokil

Rev. Samuel Metiary—Chairman of the Badan Persatuan (Body Unity)

General I.J. Tamaëla—South Moluccan delegate (self-appointed) to the United Nations

Theodoor Kuhuwael—civil servant in the Dutch Ministry of Education, and Minister of Education in Manusama's government

Dr. Frans Tutuhatunewa—general medical practitioner and Minister of General Affairs in Manusama's government

Zeth Pessireron—foreman in the Pemuda Masjarakat, the Free South Moluccan Youth Movement

Dr. J.J. de Lima—medical adviser and psychiatrist in the Dutch Ministry of Culture, Recreation, and Social Work

D. Manuputty and H.Z. Tahapary—staff members of the Korps Pendjaga Keamanan (KPK), a South Moluccan organization for keeping order in the camps and villages

Etty Aponno—Chairman of the Pemuda Masjarakat, the Free South Moluccan Youth Movement

Dr. Hassan Tan—sometime Minister of Health in Manusama's government

THE HIJACKERS

The Train at Wijster, 1975

Elija Hahury, Paul Saimima, Jacobus Tuny (Kobus), Cornelis Hetharia (Djerrit), Albert Sahetepy (Abbé), Jacob Metekohy (Joop), and Cornelis Thenu (Cor)

The Indonesian Consulate

Jacob Ririmasse (Jopie), Josef Huly (Otjek), Henkie Metekohy, Bob Solissa, Jan Lumalessil (Ottek), Johannes Sihasale, and Chris Kaihatu (Pablo)

The Train at De Punt, 1977

Max Papilaya, Marcus Lumalessil (Rudi), Ronnie Lumalessil, Junus

Ririmasse, Mattheus Tuny (Thys), George Matulessy (Kojak), Andreas Luhulima,

Domingus Rumamory (Mingus), and Hansina Oktoseja

The School at Bovensmilde

Willem Soplanit, Isaac Thenu, Guustav Tehupuring, and Tommy Polnaya

Maps and Diagrams

Papa and Mama, when you find this letter I shall not be at home any more, but with my friends. . . .

Now I want to be frank with you, Papa and Mama: I am afraid, because I don't know what's going to happen. I am rather a loud-mouthed and self-opinionated girl, but I am also afraid. The weapon I carry I carry with a belief in myself. Therefore, don't be afraid that I will use this weapon lightly. Don't regard me as a child that means to use this weapon to kill people.

I am asking you, Papa and Mama, to forgive me my many faults and the deeds I have done wrong. If I am killed it doesn't matter because it will not be for nothing. It is not a senseless goal. . . .

I know that although our road will be very long and difficult to get our liberty, with the help of God we shall reach it. I also want to say that with God's will, we will see each other again, perhaps not here but in another place. That is in God's hands.

Hansina

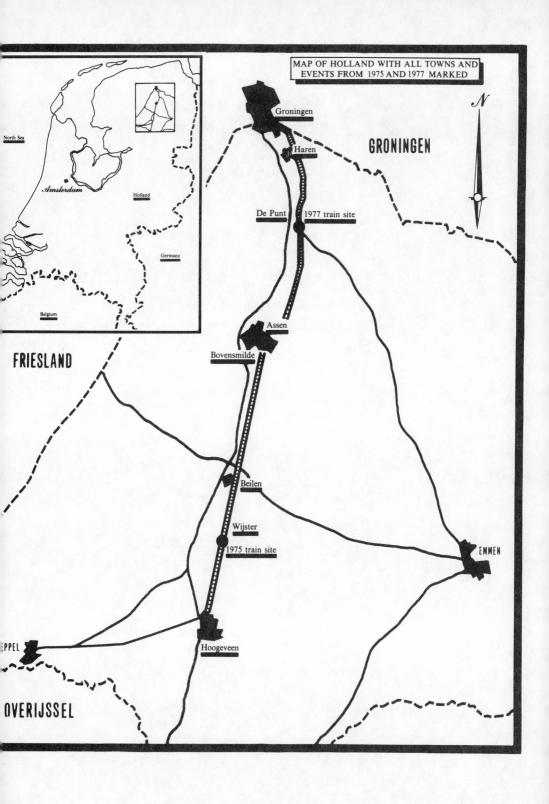

Part I
1975 — THE TRAIN AND THE CONSULATE

CHAPTER 1

"This Is a Hijacking!"

F OR THIRTY-YEAR-OLD Hans Braam, the task of driving the 9:33 AM
local train from Groningen in northeast Holland south through Assen
to Zwolle and then southwest through his hometown of Amersfoort to
Amsterdam—120 miles in all—was no more than routine. Perched on his
seat in the bullnosed cabin, neatly attired in the maroon jacket and cap
provided by his employers, Netherlands Railways, he was scheduled to
arrive at Amsterdam Central at 12 o'clock precisely.

It was a routine journey, too, for guard-conductor Herman Brinker, of
Zwolle. The fifty-three-year-old Brinker had started work on that wintry
morning, Tuesday, December 2, 1975, by joining Train 378 at Zwolle on
its northward run to Groningen, where he had teamed up with Braam.
A smart blue cap with a white band hid a well-preserved mop of fair hair,
and the company's livery for guard-conductors—blue jacket and gray
trousers—looked well on his compact, powerful frame. Not, one would
have said, an easy man to dupe over a suspect ticket, but the man's
essential good nature shone through.

For a good many of the passengers preparing to board the train, however, the journey ahead was not routine at all.

Hans Prins, a robust, handsomely bearded, forty-year-old biologist,
arrived that morning at his office in Assen, eighteen miles south of Groningen, to find that a box of blood samples had been wrongly delivered in the
mail. Prins was a director of a medical biological laboratory performing
specialized analyses for hospitals. His offices had recently been moved to
Assen, but the laboratory was still situated at Hoogeveen, thirty miles to
the south. Rather than see the work on the blood samples delayed, de-
stroying its value, he decided to go at once by train to Hoogeveen and

3

deliver the box himself. He would board the Groningen–Amsterdam local at Assen at 9:53 AM.

Waiting for the train on the southbound platform, he was aware of two groups of young South Moluccans, three quite near him and four more further down the platform. Stacked beside both groups were collections of bulky packages, wrapped in Saint Nicholas paper.

Saint Nicholas Day—December 5th, when the Dutch celebrate the traditions of Santa Claus—was only three days off. Christmas is a religious festival for the Dutch, and it is on the anniversary of Saint Nicholas that they give presents to children and to each other, wrapping them in colored paper. It is traditional to choose some small article that has special significance for the recipient, and camouflage it by wrapping it up to make it look huge.

Even allowing for tradition, Prins thought the packages were suspiciously bulky. Could these young men be members of some militant group from Assen or the nearby Moluccan quarter of Bovensmilde, on their way, perhaps, to Amsterdam or The Hague for some act of terrorism? He recalled some of the outrages already perpetrated by disgruntled young South Moluccans, mostly against representatives of the Indonesian Government, which they blamed for their exile in Holland.

It was in Prins's mind to go to station officials, or to the police, to give some kind of warning, but he hesitated. Eventually, for fear of making himself look ridiculous, he dismissed the idea.

At forty-seven, Wientje Kruyswijk, blonde and slender, was still a woman of almost ethereal beauty. A widow with three children, she was going shopping for Santa Claus presents in Amsterdam with her friend Bette van Overeem. She didn't go to Amsterdam very often, and when she did she always went by car. But on this chill, damp, misty December morning, with the threat of icy roads to come, she thought it would be wiser to go by train. After discussing it with her friend, she arranged to meet her at the station at Haren, the first stop south of Groningen, where Train 378 was due at 9:39 AM.

The motto of Netherlands Railways—"safe, quick, and cheap"—meant little to Wientje Kruyswijk. She hadn't been in a train for seven years.

Another Haren resident who normally traveled by car was thirty-six-year-old real estate agent Karel Wielenga. Wielenga had a business appointment in Arnhem to plan a new hotel development and would have gone by road but for his two associates, Luuk Verver and his son-in-law Robert de Groot, who wanted to discuss the plan on the way. They persuaded him that it would be easier to study the detailed models and blueprints they carried with them in the first-class compartment of a train than on the highway, with one of them absorbed in the driving.

Living in Groningen South, adjacent to Haren, were Cor and Dinie Ter Veer. At forty-nine, Cor Ter Veer was a successful men's outfitter, proprietor of three clothing shops in Groningen. Salesmen traveling the Common Market did not always get as far north as Groningen, and it was Ter Veer's habit to visit the big warehouses in Amsterdam. It was for an appointment at one of these warehouses, at 1:30 that afternoon, that he was now heading. As he had only the one visit to make, his wife Dinie decided to go with him—it would be interesting to see the warehouse, and there would be time for some St. Nicholas shopping. They set out from their house on the outskirts of Groningen by car and made for the highway.

Like Wientje Kruyswijk before them, the Ter Veers looked apprehensively at the weather. They too disliked the prospect of a night drive home on icy roads. Before they reached the highway, it began to rain. Soon every vehicle that passed them was spattering the windshield with mud, so thick that the wipers were unable to cope. At times the road ahead was completely obscured. Suddenly through the murk they saw a sign saying: ASSEN 1200 METERS. "I've had enough of this," said Ter Veer. "We'll turn off for Assen and take the train. We'll just about catch the intercity express." But as they drove into the station carpark, the express pulled out.

Ter Veer, less philosophic than his wife, slapped his thigh in annoyance. He had an uncomfortable feeling that the day had started badly. For a time they sat in the car, undecided what to do. But the fact that even the local train would get them to Amsterdam in good time, coupled with the thought of the drive back in darkness, soon convinced them.

Waiting on the platform, Ter Veer saw a group of colored youths and wondered who they were. There were a lot of foreign workers in Holland, many of them dark-skinned, as well as 300,000 Dutch Indonesians; but he did not identify them as South Moluccans. One of them was squatting on the platform, propping up a parcel wrapped in St. Nicholas paper. The party, he decided, must be on their way to some sort of celebration. As he strode by, striving to keep himself warm, a gust of wind blew the parcel clattering to the floor. Ter Veer bent down and retrieved it, delivering it back to an outstretched brown hand. For a split second it crossed his mind that it might be a rifle.

Eighty-two-year-old Diederik Smit was on his way to Hengelo, in eastern Holland, near the German border. He would be changing at Zwolle.

Troubled for years by a stomach ulcer, he was nevertheless a wiry old man of great resilience. But like the Ter Veers he had just missed the express, and he was fuming. He had set out from his home in Norg, seven miles northwest of Assen, in nice time, and would have caught the express comfortably if his bus had not been seven minutes late.

Already aboard Train 378 was an even older passenger, the Reverend G. A. Barger, a retired vicar, who was eighty-four. He and his eighty-two-year-old wife, whom he called "Bé," were on their way back to an old people's home at Zutphen, having been away for four days. They had driven by car to the Zwolle area, to see one daughter, then continued to Groningen by train for the christening of a grandchild by a second daughter, Mia.

Seventy-four-year-old Mrs. T. Bakker of Hilversum, in further contrast, had been visiting her sister-in-law at Assen, and before returning home planned to stop off at Hoogeveen to visit one of her sons, then do some St. Nicholas shopping for her grandchildren. She had not planned to catch anything as early as the 9:53, but she had awakened early and, finding herself with time to spare, set out for the station on the chance of getting the earlier train. Inclined to stoutness, she was of a querulous nature, and something of a pessimist. "I don't suppose I'll catch it," she called out as she waved good-bye. But she was a splendid walker for her age, and she caught the 9:53 with time to spare.

Trade union official Louis Laurier, fifty-three, of Haren, on his way to a conference in The Hague, had elected not to go by road for two reasons. One, his car was in dock, and two, although he borrowed his wife's car to drive to the station, he had been working late the night before and didn't feel like a long drive. Instead, he settled down in the train to read an article that had caught his eye in *Elseviers Magazine:*
FEARFUL UNREST AMONGST YOUNG SOUTH MOLUCCANS.

The slim, wiry Willem Albracht, looking much younger than his sixty-five years, in a cap that covered his gray-white hair, was chairing a meeting that afternoon at Utrecht. It was a special journey for him, the last such journey he expected to make. He was winding up his engineering business and looking forward with characteristic optimism to an active retirement.

Thirty-eight-year-old psychologist Walter Timmer, of Assen, traveled to Zwolle daily to lecture at the Social Academy there; every morning he caught the train from Assen at eight o'clock. But this morning he had had to visit a student in Groningen. He had driven there and back by car, then got his wife to run him from his home to the station to catch the 9:53. He had never caught a train as late as this before.

One man who felt himself a creature of habit was fifty-year-old Gerhard Vaders, editor for the past fourteen years of the Groningen newspaper *Nieuwsblad van het Noorden,* the biggest and most successful daily produced in northern Holland. Vaders was on his way to an editors' conference that afternoon in The Hague. From his home in the village of Paterswolde southwest of Groningen, he attempted to achieve some variety on these journeys by alternately driving north to board the train at Groningen, where he got in the first-class smoker at the rear of the train nearest to the barrier, or south to Assen, where it was more convenient to get in the first-class smoker at the front. This morning it was his day to drive south to Assen—a choice that was to prove of some significance. At Assen he strolled to his customary bench at the extreme south end of the platform, lit a cigar, and sat there waiting for the train. Either way he would have caught Train 378, but today he would sit in the front instead of the back.

Vaders, too, spotted the two groups with the St. Nicholas parcels, and having spent three years in Indonesia during his time in the armed services, he had a smattering of Malay and recognized them as South Moluccans. They seemed in good spirits and were laughing among themselves. They gathered up their parcels as the train came in.

Three more young men, carrying hand luggage only—their heavy equipment had gone on ahead of them—were waiting on the platform at Assen. They were soldiers serving their time in the armed forces and traveling in uniform. They were bound for Nunspeet, between Zwolle and Amersfoort, the departure point for the army transport that would take them to their post with NATO forces in Germany. All three were wearing army greatcoats. Jan Bies had traveled that morning from his home in Haulerwijk, Friesland, Thys Stevens from Nieuw-Buinen, to the east. Both were twenty. The third young soldier, Leo Bulter, twenty-two, came from the hamlet of Lonneker, north of Enschede, near the Dutch–German border, but he had traveled north to Assen to visit his girlfriend, Janet, a nurse in a home for handicapped children, and to say good-bye; she had come to the station to see him off. Of striking good looks, he was the youngest of seven children. His mother was a widow. Bies, tall, broad-shouldered, and flaxen-haired, and Stevens, slight and boyishly open-faced, had known each other for some months, but they met Bulter for the first time on the platform that morning. None of them carried arms. Soldiers don't tell each other very much about themselves, and the talk soon got around to the usual barracks subjects—cars, football, beer, and women.

1975 Wijster Train; Number 378   south

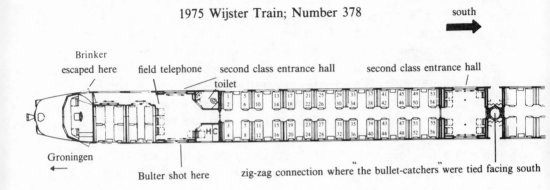

Train 378 (see diagram above) consisted of two identical sections coupled together, each train-set consisting of two carriages back to back, with a driver's cabin at each extreme. The carriages in each set were joined by a semiflexible, zigzag, concertina-type passageway. At the front of the first set, immediately behind the driver's cabin, was a spacious baggage compartment, with a double-door entry. Then came the first-class accommodation—two twelve-seat compartments, one smoking and one nonsmoking, separated by the first-class entrance platform, which housed five tip-up seats fitted to the partition walls. A toilet section was followed by a twenty-four-seat, second-class, nonsmoking compartment, and then came the zigzag connection.

Beyond the junction, the second carriage opened out into a second-class entrance platform, again with tip-up seats, and then came the main second-class compartment (smoking), consisting of fifty-six seats, eight seats to a row, made up of four seats facing each other on either side of a central aisle. There was then a toilet, another entrance platform with more tip-up seats, and finally two second-class compartments of minimum size, eight seats in each, hard against the rear, empty, driver's cabin.

Between the first and second train-sets, there was no passageway of any kind, just two bullnosed driver's cabins blindly facing each other. The only communication between the two sections was by public address system operated from the driver's cabin. The train was powered by electricity, by way of overhead cable. The "goal-posts" supporting the cable were sixty-five to seventy meters apart.

In the extreme front of the first-class passenger accommodation, with his back to the baggage compartment, Vaders put his briefcase on the rack, took off his coat, sat down and lit another half-corona. In the

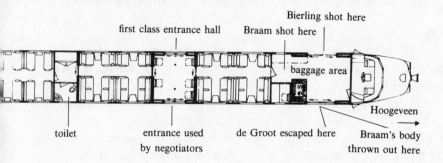

first class entrance hall

Bierling shot here

Braam shot here

baggage area

Hoogeveen

toilet

entrance used by negotiators

de Groot escaped here

Braam's body thrown out here

relaxing warmth of the compartment, he settled down to scanning his morning paper.

Across the aisle from Vaders, Karel Wielenga and his associates were already oblivious to their surroundings, deep in contemplation of a scale plan of the projected development. For ease of study and handling, the plan was pinned to a drawing board. Behind these three, the Ter Veers sat down opposite Wientje Kruyswijk and Bette van Overeem. The women were discussing a political meeting they had attended the previous evening, and Cor Ter Veer, always interested in politics, could not refrain from listening.

Walter Timmer found a window seat in the second-class carriage and settled down to prepare his lecture. This morning he would be teaching relaxation therapy, and the book he extracted from his briefcase was a manual on the subject that gave examples of successful therapy. It was entitled *Learn to be Free.*

Herman Brinker was quietly working his way through the front train-set inspecting tickets. He passed the time of day with the South Moluccans, who were standing on the second-class entrance platforms, still split into two groups. He had no difficulty in recognizing who they were—there was a concentration of them in the Assen area, and he often saw them on the trains. Some of them were apt to be aggressive, but these two groups were well-behaved. He eyed their parcels tolerantly. "Celebrating Santa Claus? Going to a party?" They grinned in apparent acquiescence. It did not occur to Brinker that it was a party at which he was to be a principal guest.

At Beilen, halfway between Assen and Hoogeveen, the train made its third scheduled stop. Braam as usual was punctual. The time was 10:03 AM. Among those joining the first train-set were two students, sixteen-year-old motor-mechanic trainee Frits Santing, on his way to technical college in Apeldoorn, and seventeen-year-old Irma Martens, who was looking forward rather nervously to an end-of-term exam at her college at Hoogeveen, where she was training to be a kindergarten teacher. Of a gentle nature, she was wearing a unisex hair style that made her look boyish.

Also getting on at Beilen were seventy-two-year-old Mrs. Joanna Jansen, an asthma sufferer, returning to her home in Hengelo; a thirty-year-old mechanic named Bos, a man of few words, bound for Hoogeveen; and forty-seven-year-old Albert Oosting, who had an appointment with his doctor in Hoogeveen. As the appointment was for ten o'clock that morning and it was already 10:03, he was going to be late; but Oosting hated waiting about in doctors' offices, and he knew his doctor was generally behind schedule. Catching the 10:03 from Beilen was a calculated risk. With any luck, he would be there before his name was called.

As the train pulled out of Beilen, some of the South Moluccans from the rear platform moved forward to join their friends. Two or three minutes later, when speed had been regained, the train braked with unaccustomed violence and came to a stop a quarter of a mile short of a level crossing. There was a moment of complete silence as the passengers looked out uncomprehendingly at the empty Drenthe landscape.

Karel Wielenga, his study of the development plan interrupted, looked for a station platform to reassure himself and was disturbed at seeing none. There must have been a breakdown, perhaps a signal failure. In fact, one of the Moluccans had pulled the emergency brake.

"Mena Muria!" This was the rallying cry of the South Moluccan independence movement.[1] "Hands up! This is a hijacking! Stay where you are or I'll shoot!"

The moment of silence exploded in a second into pandemonium, as though someone had suddenly turned up the volume full blast. Carriage doors were thrown open, rifles were pointed inside, shots were fired down through the floor and up through the roof. Passengers screamed; hijackers danced about excitedly and shouted instructions.

The intruders were wearing black wool balaclava helmets that obscured their features, but there were slits for their eyes and mouths. The hooded effect lent their eyes an evil magnetism. Only one of the hijackers had yet gone as far forward as the first-class smoker, and on impulse Wielenga

---

[1]"Fore—Aft," a call used by South Moluccan fishermen when drawing in their nets.

decided to act. The fellow's mad, he thought, probably an escaped lunatic, and he grabbed the barrel of the rifle that was pointed into the compartment and held on. He was used to firearms, and he thought he could cope with one man.

"Let go! Get away from the rifle!"

In the next second, as the gun went off, Wielenga relaxed his grip. The fellow was not alone. Two more hooded robbers, terrorists—he knew not what—were storming into the compartment, jerking up and down like marionettes, and firing their weapons indiscriminately as they came. One of them held an Uzi—an Israeli-made submachine gun. Even shorn of their St. Nicholas paper, the guns were gaily decorated, with strips of blue, white, green, and red paper circling the barrels in that order, imitating the colors of the South Moluccan flag.

Throughout the first train-set, the story was the same, and as passengers reacted slowly, immobile with shock and unable to grasp what was happening, more warning shots were fired. "Quick, quick! It's not a joke! It's deadly serious! Hands up! Keep out of the aisle! Anyone who moves will be shot."

Hans Braam realized that someone had applied the emergency brake, and he wondered what could have caused them to do so. Then he heard the shooting. He opened the door of his cabin to investigate, locked it behind him as a precaution, and crossed the baggage compartment leading to the first-class smoker. As soon as he opened the door, he saw the terrorists.

Two of the hijackers had been given the task of neutralizing the driver. They were Jacobus Tuny, known as Kobus, a tall, melancholy fellow who at twenty-six was the oldest of the group (he was carrying the Uzi), and Cornelis Hetharia, 23, known as Djerrit. Owing to a miscalculation, they had not been able to reach the driver's cabin as quickly as planned. Train 378 was unusual in that it had a first-class carriage at the front, and the two terrorists, holding second-class tickets, had not been able to work their way forward until the actual moment of the hijacking. As Braam emerged from the baggage compartment, they shouted "Stop! Stay put!" But Braam, taking in the situation at a glance, backed through the door and slammed it shut.

At this the tall hijacker Kobus panicked. The driver was going back to his cabin to raise the alarm—that was his fear. There would be some form of communication up there, linking him with the nearest station. It didn't suit the hijackers to have the outside world alerted just yet, not until they had matters fully under control, and Kobus's reaction was to fire several warning shots through the door with his Uzi, aimed to deter the driver from his purpose but not with the intention to kill.

In his panic, Kobus did more damage than he intended, and the groans of the driver were chillingly audible. Forcing their way forward, the two South Moluccans found Braam sprawled across the floor of the van, wounded in the leg and the jaw and lying in a pool of blood. Considerably shaken, they returned to the carriage.

"Come along. Everyone out."

The Moluccans began forcing the first-class passengers back through the leading train-set with guns at their backs. There was a moment of confusion as the first- and second-class passengers collided in the middle, but they were finally assembled in the main second-class smoker, the one that held fifty-six seats. There was no chance of escape—there was a hooded gunman at every door.

Stunned and incredulous as they were, some of the passengers could not contain their sense of outrage, or their curiosity. "What's it all about? What are you doing this for?" The more cautious whispered amongst themselves. "Are they Palestinians?" Union leader Laurier expected them to go around with a bag collecting jewelry, watches, and cash; he could think of no other motive than robbery. One of those who guessed who and what they were, and who remembered other acts of violence for which South Moluccans had been responsible, was Rob de Groot, and he asked, "Are you trying to get your friends out of prison?" That had been the motive of several international hijacks, and a number of South Moluccans were in prison after previous outbreaks of violence.

Resentment among some of the passengers was so strong that they taunted the hijackers with forecasts of rapid military intervention. "Talk like that and you'll get a bullet through your head," was one hijacker's response. "What about the antiterrorist squad?" asked a passenger. "Aren't you afraid of them?" "Afraid? Now is the time to hate." Another said, "If there's any shooting, you'll be the first to be killed. We'll see to that. Now, stand over there."

They hustled all the passengers over to one side of the carriage, then threw an assortment of plastic bags at their feet. "You'll find sheets of newspaper inside. Stick them over the windows. Quickly!" Rolls of cellophane tape were also thrown at them. Those who had been protesting most were pushed forward, and there was no option but to obey. Two of those singled out were Gerry Vaders and Rob de Groot; both had had the temerity to ask questions. Taking a bundle of papers, Vaders started in the middle of the compartment and worked toward the front.

As Vaders worked, he scanned his surroundings. The view from the top of the railway embankment was mist-laden and bleak. The flat, sodden meadows were patchworked by the bare winter earth of the fields; gaunt lines of straggly silver birch, scarcely taller than hedgerows, etched the horizon; the massive pylons of the electric grid ran parallel to the overhead cables, pushing up into a drab, featureless sky: all these combined to produce a landscape of forlorn desolation. Signs of human habitation were scant. All he could see was the pale red roof of a farmhouse to the east, perhaps half a mile distant, the washing on the line in the farmyard limp in the still air. Beyond it lay the unsightly litter of the provincial refuse dump and compost factory, rendered sinister by the mechanical hoists that planted their feet like monstrous giraffes among the rubbish, and the carpet of gulls that scavenged the long plateau of the surface. Thrusting into this dingy panorama, indistinct as a smudged pencil drawing, was the bold outline of the bright yellow train.

"Get on with it," chivvied the hijackers. Vaders and de Groot both came under their critical gaze. The hijackers suspected de Groot of being deliberately slow. "Hurry up! You can do better than that!" "I could do the job better," retorted de Groot angrily, "if you gave me better tape."

Already the hijackers had picked out de Groot as a man who asked too many questions. Now he had answered back. He had thus drawn attention to himself as a man who might be dangerous. More than that, in his tailor-made blue suit, white shirt, and orange tie, he was obviously the successful business executive, well-dressed but not overdressed, patently at the other extreme of Dutch society from the Moluccans. He was thus a marked man.

Another man marked by his clothing, though his preference was more for the functional, was Vaders. As he reached up to cover the window above the Ter Veers, his jacket dropped open, and Ter Veer noticed the tag of his own men's shop on the inside pocket. He studied the face. Good Lord, he thought, it's Mr. Vaders.

Having reached the front of the compartment, Vaders found himself near two of the Moluccans. He had seen one of them fire through the door of the baggage compartment, and he wondered what had happened to the driver.

"Has anyone been hurt?"

"Yes, the driver. He wanted to be a hero. He's been shot."

It seemed to Vaders that the voice was unsteady, betraying an emotional conflict beneath the staccato surface of the words.

"Shouldn't an ambulance be called?"

"That won't be necessary. He's dead."

In fact, Hans Braam, although mercifully unconscious, was not dead. His extremities were twitching, and he was still clearly alive. Twenty minutes after the initial attack, the hijackers went forward to look at him, and it was Kobus, unable to bear the sight of what he had done, who decided he must put an end to the man's suffering. The explosion that followed echoed with sickening finality throughout the train.

The only terrorist who took satisfaction from the shooting of the driver was the fanatical twenty-three-year-old Elija Hahury, known as Eli. Immediately distinguishable from the others because of his Afro-Asian hairstyle, Eli saw in the death of the driver the opportunity to bind the group together in corporate guilt. This, he sensed, would enable him to exercise a power over them that he might not otherwise gain, since in principle they all had equal status and there was no acknowledged leader. It was an essential part of their plan to use the hostages as a lever to force the government's hand, and they were all implicated in this. But if the government resisted, a degree of ruthlessness would be required that might be hard to sustain. Now that they had killed the driver, there could be no turning back.

After covering the windows on one side, the passengers were put to work on the other. When they had finished they were told to sit down. "Stay put. Don't move. If the train is attacked, you will stand at the windows." It was the tall hijacker Kobus speaking, and he motioned with his gun to command obedience. "That way, you'll catch the first bullets. And don't make any more complaints or objections. The train driver has already been shot. Anyone else who wants to play the hero should keep that in mind." His eye fell on the three soldiers, who had kept together. "You three, break it up. One at the front, one in the middle, one at the back."

Having singled out some of the men for special attention, the hijackers turned to the women, especially to Wientje Kruyswijk, who was staring at them keenly. "We are emancipated too," they warned her. "We also kill women."

Each passenger, in his or her own way, consciously or subconsciously, was facing a psychological dilemma. What were they up against, and what sort of behavior was most likely to result in survival? Was it best to assert oneself as a personality, a recognizable human being, or to shrink into one's shell, trusting to a faceless anonymity to escape notice? Most passengers instinctively adopted the latter course. Being inconspicuous seemed to offer the best chance of safety.

For most of them, it was a question they could mull over. They would adapt to circumstances. So long as the hijackers themselves chose anonymity in their balaclavas, no approach on a human level seemed possible. But for two men, Vaders and Prins, a clash of wills with the hijackers seemed inevitable: Vaders because, as a journalist, he felt impelled to record what was happening; Prins because of the blood samples. He must try to get those delivered without delay, and it was even possible that they might be a passport to early release from the train.

For the three soldiers, there was no choice at all. However much the other passengers might seek to submerge their identity in the crowd, such a blurring of outline was impossible for men in uniform. And since the hijacking must almost certainly be aimed at extracting concessions from the government, of which they were the uniformed representatives, they expected to be victimized.

While Vaders and Prins were considering what they would do, the soldiers' fears were intensified as they watched the only other person in uniform, guard-conductor Brinker, dragged forward unceremoniously to the driver's cabin. As for Brinker, his fears that he was about to be shot were heightened when he saw what had happened to Braam.

"Open the cabin," ordered the hijackers.

Brinker gave them his keys, and they opened the door. "Call the nearest station," they told him. "Tell them it's a hijack and that no other trains will be allowed on this track. If they are, they'll be shot at."

"That's not an outside telephone. That's the intercom for the train."

"Where's the telephone?"

"There isn't one."

The hijackers were clearly nonplussed. They had expected to be able to telephone their demands, whatever they were, from the train.

After a few moments of indecision, they switched on the intercom. "Attention, all passengers. This is a hijack. The driver is already dead. Stay in your seats. Anyone who tries to escape will be shot." To the passengers in the second train-set, this was the first explanation they had had of what was happening.

The hijackers turned back to Brinker. "Can you drive the train?"

"No."

Brinker's answer was instinctive. He didn't really know whether he could drive it or not. He supposed he could have had a try, but he was in no mood to cooperate. And his instinct was to say no.

The hijackers appeared to accept his denial. "Come with us."

They took him right through to the back of the first train-set, then opened the entrance door and motioned him out. All the way they were prodding him with their guns. This is it, he thought. They're going to shoot me now.

"Undo the coupling," they told him. And when he hesitated, they fired their guns, aiming between his ankles. With trembling hands he fumbled at the coupling. There was a button release, and he operated it. Although there was not much movement, the two sections were now disconnected.

"Have you done it?"

"Yes."

"Get back in the train."

Although the second train-set was superficially under guard, Brinker gathered that the hijackers were less interested in the people in that section. Probably they had as much as they could cope with in the front.

They took him back through the first train-set to the driver's cabin and began tying him up, feet together, hands behind his back. Then they propped him up against the driver's seat. "If there's an attack, you'll be the first to be shot."

In the second-class smoker, Gerry Vaders had not pondered his situation long. The moment the Moluccans came in, he had felt transported back to the atmosphere of the war. The action presented him with a unique opportunity, a once-in-a-lifetime scoop, the reporter's dream of "I was there!" The question was how to go about it, whether to take notes covertly or overtly. He knew that if he took them openly they might think he was plotting against them; they would almost certainly resent it. But to be caught in some subterfuge might be worse. In either case his anonymity might be destroyed, and that could be dangerous. Yet he could not pass up the opportunity without losing his self-respect.

He still had a sense of guilt left over from the war. He had done nothing to be ashamed of; it was just that he felt he hadn't taken enough risks, especially on behalf of the Jews. His sister had done more and had finished up in Dachau, and that rankled. This time he would choose to take risks. Calculated risks. He decided that the open approach was best.

In his briefcase he had a notebook, but when they had been herded back through the train, he had left his belongings where he was sitting. Rifling his pockets, he found two circulars that had recently been delivered from his daughters' school. He would scribble on the back of them.

He looked at his watch. 10:37 AM. Exactly half an hour since the train had been halted. He began his first entry.

10:07 AM. Just past Beilen. Door slammed open. The barrels of a rifle and a Sten gun are pointed inside. Shots are heard, hard and dry. In a reflex movement someone reaches for a gun barrel—an act of recklessness which goes unpunished. Another shot: it misses. The hijackers are extremely nervous. Black woollen balaclavas cover their faces so that only their eyes and nose can be seen. A lot of shouting and some more shots.

That was as far as he got. One of the Moluccans had seen him and was striding toward him. He looked away. Next moment he felt a tap on the shoulder. "Come with me." With the barrel of a gun poked into his neck, Vaders was propelled uncomfortably forward into the second-class entrance hall.

"Sit down. On the floor. If you try to get away we shall shoot without mercy."

He had no idea what they had in store for him, and he looked, as others had done, for some possible means of escape. But with the barrels of a rifle and a pistol pointed at his head, held by unsteady hands only inches away, that idea was stillborn. Perhaps it hadn't been a good idea to start writing so soon.

"Are you expert at handling those things?"

"You'll see."

He watched as two other hijackers secured the exit doors with chains and padlocks and then began taping sticks of explosives close to the floor where the doors met. They were doing this throughout the train. Anyone who tried to open those doors would blow themselves up.

When the job was finished, they turned their attention to him. Producing some rope, they began to tie him up, first his thumbs, then his wrists, then his feet. Then they made him stumble forward into the zigzag connection between the two carriages, where they roped his body to strong points to hold him steady.

"What's the idea?"

He guessed what they were up to. He knew they feared attack from outside. He was to be part of their protection against it, a bullet-catcher they called it, a human shield.

He was standing with his back to the passengers, looking forward through the empty carriages ahead. The door into the baggage area had been left open, perhaps deliberately, and he could see the legs of the dead driver as a constant reminder of his own likely fate. Behind, he was cut off from the passengers by a glass sliding door.

"As long as you don't try to get away, nothing will happen to you."

Then they left him. But he didn't place much reliance on their word. When he tried to look back through the door, a pistol was immediately leveled at him.

The rope chafed his wrists and ankles, and soon his feet felt like slabs of raw meat. The only relief from the macabre scene ahead was the view he had of the bare Drenthe countryside, stark as a van Gogh painting, visible because the windows in the forward carriage had not been covered.

Five miles down the line at Hoogeveen, where Train 378 was now overdue, a call was made to Beilen to confirm the time of departure. There was no alarm as yet—trains passing through the province of Drenthe were subject to delays from straying cattle. A woman from a farmhouse to the southwest (Farmhouse Etten) walked across the fields to the train and returned to report her suspicions, but this took some time, and it was not until 10:45 AM that Assen Police were notified that the train was "missing." A patrol car was alerted, but meanwhile two mechanics on their way by car to attend to a job at the refuse dump passed over the level crossing 400 meters to the south and saw the stationary train. They left the car and made their way northwards along the track to see what had happened. One of them tried to enter the first-class section of the first train-set but found the door was locked. He tried the door of the luggage van, but that too was locked. Raising himself onto the step, he peered through the window and saw the driver lying on the floor. Before he could do anything else, he came under fire from the train.

"Get the hell out of here, or I'll kill you!"

The mechanic raced back toward Farmhouse Etten, west of the level crossing, and from there reported by telephone to traffic control at Groningen. Meanwhile, his colleague ran north along the track towards Beilen to alert the railway staff there.

All this was unknown at Hoogeveen when the next northbound train arrived there. The driver was instructed to go carefully but to try to find out what was delaying Train 378. Seeing the stationary train ahead of him, Driver Hofland pulled up just before reaching it, hoping for a word with the driver.

The arrival of this train was glimpsed by Vaders from his post in the passageway. Help, it seemed, was at hand. But no posse of police or marines emerged from the train. Instead, one man, Conductor Laning, got down to investigate. He immediately came under fire from the hijackers. Vaders saw him race back to his train, and, as the hijackers fired several more warning shots, Driver Hofland quickly reversed out of range. Then he reversed all the way back to Hoogeveen to report.

CHAPTER 2

A Time to Kill

THE HIJACKERS HAD STOPPED THE train one and a half miles beyond the village of Wijster, halfway between Beilen and Hoogeveen. The line in this section ran almost dead straight north and south, and there was no fear of surprise attack by rail. The level crossing to the south accommodated a minor country road, which the hijackers hoped to use for their escape. Another level crossing lay 1,200 meters behind them to the north. The intention had been to stop the train halfway between the two crossings, but the hijacker chosen to pull the emergency brake, twenty-two-year-old Albert Sahetepy, known as Abbé, had got confused over the counting of the electricity pylons that were his landmarks and had pulled the cord two pylons too late, sixteen after Beilen instead of fourteen. Nevertheless, the hijackers were in a fine strategic position, difficult for both access and observation, with open ground all round them and no cover of any kind within 1,000 meters, apart from three isolated farmhouses, Farmhouse Staal (the one seen by Vaders), Farmhouse Etten, and Farmhouse Anton, to the southeast. None was less than 500 meters from the train. If the occupiers kept alert, it would be difficult for anyone to approach the train even at night without being seen.

However, the hijackers fully expected to be out of the train before nightfall. The seizure of the train was no more than a preliminary; had their expectations of telephonic communication not been disappointed, they would already have put their immediate demands to the authorities. These were: a jet aircraft to be made ready at Schiphol Airport, Amsterdam, and a bus to take them there. They planned to take their hostages with them.

These plans, and their own involuntary part in them, were as yet

19

unknown to the passengers. But there were few who did not feel a deadly fear of what was afoot and did not curse their ill fortune at choosing to travel on this particular train.

By this time, the hijackers had removed their grotesque helmets, and somehow this eased the passengers' terror. Gone was the robot, subhuman look; they were suddenly revealed as youths—boys even—nervous and insecure, more frightened perhaps than the passengers but, above all, individuals, differing one from another. While some seemed aggressive in character, fingering their guns with neurotic impatience and clicking the triggers, others seemed friendly.

Most threatening in appearance, although one of the smallest, was Eli Hahury. He wore no beard, and his moustache was neatly trimmed, but his moon-shaped, flue-brush hairstyle seemed an incongruous burden to his lithe, sinewy frame. Tinted glasses accentuated the sinister, inscrutable look he seemed out to achieve. His repellent exterior, however, hid an unhappy, tortured soul. Angry at the injustice that he felt had been done to his parents when they were brought to Holland, and perhaps exaggerating their discontent, he had become deeply involved in plots and demonstrations against what he conceived to be his Dutch "oppressors" and had eventually drifted into crime. "How can I change my life," he had asked a friend, "when every time something happens in Bovensmilde, and the police are called in, they come first to me?" He felt persecuted because of his color, and he gave up his job because he saw it as a temptation to integrate into Dutch life. Only moderately articulate, he preferred action to talking, and his religion only drove him further forward on the path to violence. "God created people with a place to live, a country. Why must we South Moluccans be denied one?"

More often than not, it was Eli who brandished the Uzi, and in addition he carried a pistol and a *klewang*—a long Indonesian knife—tucked in his belt. A black jacket set off the starkness of his appearance, and to the passengers he looked uncomfortably like the popular idea of a psychopathic killer. First impressions that he might be the leader, however, proved inaccurate: as noted, there was no appointed leader, though Eli and another young South Moluccan, Paul Saimima, were nominally in charge. If they disagreed, the group held a vote, and, since there were seven of them, they could always get a decision. The result was that there was often a great deal of talk before anything was done.

It had been Eli's idea to hijack a train, and three months earlier he had asked twenty-five-year-old Paul Saimima if he was willing to take part. Paul, a mechanic by trade, was one of a great many young South Moluccans indoctrinated from childhood with the ideal of RMS—Republik Maluku Selatan, a free South Moluccan republic independent of Indonesia —and he had agreed. No one had ever hijacked a train before, so the notion had a novel appeal, but it was not original. Eli had formed the idea from a newspaper report of a group of Palestinian terrorists whose plan to hijack a train—it was the Warsaw Express, taking Jewish emigrants on their way to Israel—had been frustrated.

The basis for South Moluccan unrest went back twenty-five years. This latest manifestation of it had been fertilized by government indifference and royal tactlessness. The Dutch had repeatedly brushed aside the political aspirations of the South Moluccans in Holland and insisted that they were a social problem. A week earlier, Queen Juliana, in a speech to mark the attainment of independence by the former Dutch colony of Surinam, had unwittingly ignited the fuse. "All peoples," she had said, "have a right to their own country."

Quite apart from the uniqueness of the train idea, it was, from the viewpoint of the hijackers, a practicable one. Living as this group did in the Assen area, the railway provided a convenient target, with its characteristics well known to them. Although their ultimate aim was a jet, which they believed would attract more publicity, as well as get them out of the country, they felt that direct intrusion into a heavily guarded international airport was beyond their resources. Instead, they borrowed from another planned hijack, this time a successful one, that of Japanese Red Army anarchists who laid siege to the French Embassy in The Hague in 1974, taking ten hostages, including the ambassador, and demanding the release of one of their group held prisoner in France. They wanted a bus to take them to Schiphol, where an airplane must be waiting for them, destination not stated, and they demanded a ransom of £130,000. The incident was not quite analogous, as some of the hostages had been foreign nationals, but the French had provided a Boeing 707, while a volunteer crew, two Dutch and one British, had come forward. The South Moluccans did not see why, having taken possession of a train and a number of hostages, they should not get the same cooperation.[2]

This was the plan that Eli put to Paul. In contrast to Eli, Paul was a young man with sensitive features that were often a mirror of his emotions. He was the thinker of the group, and his eyes more often radiated pity for his victims than anger or hatred. Yet he was equally dedicated,

[2]The plane flew via Aden to Damascus, where the terrorists gave themselves up to the Palestine Liberation Organization. Plane, crew, and ransom returned safely.

and it was he who had spoken the words, "Now is the time to hate," quoting deliberately from Ecclesiastes. Like all the other hijackers, he was a devout Christian and knew his Bible. But he had only agreed to take part on condition that the group were ready to go to the limit, to die for their cause. There was something of the desire for martyrdom in Paul; he did not expect to survive the action.

Vaders had already concluded that Paul might prove even more danger-ous than Eli. With sufficient intelligence for a degree of self-knowledge, he would be aware of his weaknesses and would strive to overcome them. He would be out to prove himself.

It was Paul who had produced the detailed plan. Working in the pro-duction department of the Philips Electronics Company at Hoogeveen, he had traveled by train daily from Assen and knew the line well. At Philips, he was known as a hard worker, but he had resigned some weeks earlier, giving no reason. At twenty-five he was the oldest of the hijackers, bar one.

Kobus, the one who had shot Hans Braam in a moment of panic, although the oldest, looked the most confused. The accident to the driver —he saw it as an accident, as did the other hijackers—had temporarily unnerved him. He was only just beginning to realize what he had got himself into. He displayed certain idiosyncracies of dress, and for no apparent reason wore black satin gloves day and night. For reading, and perhaps for reassurance, he consulted his Bible. For all his bluster at the start, he seemed a decent enough fellow.

The youngest and smallest was Cornelis Thenu, known as Cor, or *Ketjil* ("Shorty—the little one"), but although only 17, he betrayed none of the uncertainty of some of the others. He was not afraid of guns, which he handled devotedly, if at times carelessly; he was the one whose gun had clattered to the platform at Assen, to be picked up by Ter Veer. He seemed to be enjoying himself, and a talent for sick humor was manifested in an unpleasant habit of poking his gun into people's ribs without warning. Despite his apparent dexterity, there always seemed the danger of an accident.

Jacob Metekohy, until recently a student teacher, was twenty, but he had abandoned his studies to devote himself exclusively to the RMS ideal. Known to the others as Joop, he was something of an intellectual. Al-though shy and uncommunicative, he occasionally revealed an engaging, toothy grin. He numbered several Dutch youths at the academy amongst his friends.

Twenty-three-year-old Djerrit Hetharia, already mentioned, was another who displayed a sense of humor; but he had about him something of the pathos of the clown. In many ways he seemed the kindest and most helpful of the hijackers, and at times his manner was apologetic, as though he felt ashamed of what he was doing and did not entirely believe in it. But there were other times when he posed as a tough guy and revealed a tenacious streak. He had played his part in the planning and was fully committed.

Abbé, twenty-two, had trained as an electrician but never worked as one. Instead he had contented himself with repetitive tasks on factory production lines in Assen and Hoogeveen. He had long since become convinced that recourse to violence was the only way of propagating the RMS cause, and he had lost his latest job through involvement in a previous incident.

These were the seven young men who now sought to control the destinies of thirty-four hostages as well as their own. All were members of a Free South Moluccan Youth Movement called Pemuda Masjarakat, dedicated to furthering the RMS cause. Although consisting, as a group, of students who had dropped out and the unemployed, they were not in any sense the dregs of South Moluccan society. Rather they were typical of the best in that society, loyal to strong family ties, active in church youth groups, and of at least average educational standards, which amongst their kind were not high.

Things had gone wrong for them from the start. Killing was something they knew they would have to threaten, to get what they wanted; that was an essential part of the plan. But the reality of it was something they hadn't taken into account, not as a group. Now, right at the beginning, they had killed, and even Eli was beginning to have cause to regret it. Not only had it been unnecessary, it was also inconvenient. When the bus came, as they were confident it would, they had planned to move the train down to the crossing, since shepherding hostages along the line, perhaps under the surveillance of sharpshooters, would be a precarious process. The uneasiness they felt in their hearts, however, had to be quelled if they were going to succeed.

All right, so they had killed. There were no recriminations. If there was guilt, then they accepted it, as a group responsibility. The effect, as Eli had foreseen, was to draw them closer together. They would see this thing through to the finish. Every one of them had sworn his readiness to die for the cause.

The first necessity, now that they knew there was no telephone, was to communicate with the authorities by some other means. They had brought stenciled copies of their demands and manifestos, but for the present they intended to confine their requests to the provision of the bus and the plane. Not until they were safely aboard the aircraft with their hostages did they intend to reveal their political objectives. That, they felt, was the moment, the classic situation where the government must give in.

The hijackers were not alone in wanting to get something delivered. Hans Prins, too, was fretting about his blood samples. After a whispered conversation with some of the other passengers, he decided to approach the hijackers. Explaining about the blood samples, he asked whether it might be possible for him to take them off the train, or if there was any way to have them sent off the train and onward to Hoogeveen.

The South Moluccans stared at him, their suspicion and hostility obvious. They didn't believe him; he was up to some trick. He tried to reassure them, and they took the box from him gingerly, handling it as though it might contain explosives. Finally, after moving some distance away and arguing amongst themselves, they opened it cautiously.

After satisfying themselves that Prins's description of the contents was accurate, they returned to ask some questions. What kind of analysis was intended? For what sort of patient? Prins answered that the blood samples had been taken from pregnant women and that the purpose of analysis was so that the doctors could control the placental function. This seemed to impress them.

By drawing attention to himself, Prins knew he was taking a risk, just as Vaders had done. But he was unprepared for their next question.

"Are you a medical doctor?"

For a fraction of a second, he hesitated. If he said he was, they might let him off the train. But to lie to them might be fatal.

"Well, I . . ."

"Can you prove it?"

"No, I'm a . . ."

Before he could finish, they were talking animatedly amongst themselves. In the confusion, they had taken his denial as meaning that he *was* a doctor but that he had no papers with him to prove it. And when he realized they had misunderstood him, he decided to exploit their mistake. Even if they didn't let him go, he could play the part of doctor. It would establish him as a necessary part of their schemes, and perhaps afford him some protection, even help him to influence them.

The immediate result was that they agreed that the box could go off the train. This suited their plans. They were releasing two women passengers, one of them a South Moluccan, and a child. The released passengers would deliver the stenciled list of demands to the authorities, and the box could go with them.

"How much time will be needed," he asked, "to end the affair?"

The hijackers replied cautiously, "That depends on your government, and how soon they give in to our demands."

"I can't figure that out unless I know what your demands are."

They gave him one of the stenciled sheets, and he sat down to read it. As he did so, the muscles of his face tightened, and he found he was clenching the paper. The demands contained an ultimatum. If agreement wasn't reached quickly there would be more killings. He was glad he was sitting alone. There was no sense in alarming the others. In any case, he could hardly believe they would carry out their threat.

It was 11:00 AM when the passengers selected to take the demands and the box were set free. A woman and her child were released from the rear platform and another woman from the front. She had to crawl past Vaders's legs to get through. "She is pregnant," Vaders was told. "You see, we are not such devils." These exits were the only ones that had not been booby-trapped, and both were closely guarded. The freed passengers walked toward the northern of the two level crossings, away from the heavily guarded front part of the train, where they were picked up by a police patrol car.

Following the siege of the French Embassy in 1974, the Dutch Government had worked out a blueprint for action against future terrorist incidents, but by its very nature it had to be flexible. Because terrorism was classed as a crime, the minister responsible for dealing with outbreaks was the minister of justice, a forty-four-year-old lawyer and academic turned politician, named Andreas van Agt. A crisis center, where all policy decisions would be taken, would be established within his ministry, with van Agt himself in the chair. In his absence, the minister for internal affairs, elder statesman W.F. de Gaay Fortman, a man of wide academic and political experience, would deputize. In the absence of both men, the prime minister, or minister-president, as he was more correctly known, Socialist leader Joop den Uyl, would assume control. Staffed by a small team of civil servants, the crisis center would enlist the help of other ministers and of specialist advisers and would be able to call upon, through the Ministry of Defense, a specially formed commando unit of the Korps Mariniers.

Responsible for implementing policy decisions and for dealing with all matters of routine would be a management center near the site of the incident. There, the chairman would be the attorney general for the province (Holland has five attorneys general for its eleven provinces) who would act as the direct representative of the minister of justice. The hierarchy at this center, of more or less equal status, would include the Queen's Commissioner for the Province, the burgomaster of the nearest town, the district public prosecutor, and the area chief of the state police (Rijkspolitie). The latter, in exercising his responsibilities, could call in the assistance of the municipal police and the military. (Municipalities of more than 25,000 inhabitants qualified for their own police force.)

A third and final link in the communications chain, keeping the terrorists at arm's length, would be a command post as near as possible to the site of the incident, staffed by police who would establish and maintain direct contact with the terrorists where possible and channel information back to the management center.

The chief of the state police in the province of Drenthe was a tall, well-built, fair-haired Frieslander named Colonel L.P. Bergsma, and it was to his headquarters in Assen that the first reports of the incident at Wijster were telephoned. Almost simultaneously, in nearby Beilen, a township of some 13,000 people ten miles south of Assen and five miles north of the incident, the usual Tuesday morning meeting of the inner circle of the town council in the modern town hall was interrupted by a telephone call. "Burgomaster, there has been a shooting on a train near Wijster."

Soon afterward the news was confirmed by a call from Bergsma. "I think there has been a hijacking of a train." The burgomaster, the bald but slim and youthful-looking A.A. Beckeringh van Rhijn, in his early fifties, immediately abandoned the meeting, and the council chamber, a high-ceilinged and high-windowed upstairs room at one end of the building, oval-shaped and with a small public gallery, was rapidly converted into a management center. At 11:20 AM the woman and child who had been released from the train arrived with the hijackers' written demands.

Others who had been alerted by Bergsma were the attorney general, W.C. van Binsbergen, and the queen's commissioner for the province, Mrs. A.P. Schilthuis; they in turn informed the ministries at The Hague —Justice and Interior, respectively—to which they owed allegiance. But even at Beilen it was not until after midday that a quorum was assembled because the attorney general had to travel from Leeuwarden, a cross-country journey of forty-five miles. Since the hijackers were demanding an answer by 12:45, in default of which they were threatening to kill one of their hostages at 1:00 PM, some sort of temporizing reply had to be concocted.

While awaiting the arrival of his colleagues, Beckeringh van Rhijn studied the list of demands. This is what he was faced with:

DEMANDS

1. We demand a sixty-seat bus, supplied by the Raterink Travel Agency of Beilen. Seats must have been removed, curtains fitted. Plus a driver.
2. We demand that the Dutch Government arrange for an aircraft to be ready for our use at Schiphol Airport.
3. We demand sound police handcuffs, to avoid having to fire prematurely at passengers who think they can play tricks on us.
4. We must be informed before 12:45 PM that our demands will be satisfied. If not, we shall kill one of the hostages at 1:00 PM and, after that, one every half hour (so that three will be dead by 2:30).
5. The attitude of the police and the so-called terror brigade determines the fate of the hostages. They must therefore keep away and out of our sight. An attempt to recapture the train and free the hostages will be no use since they are surrounded by explosives. These have also been mounted on the doors.
6. You must realize that if we were not prepared to go to any lengths, we would not have started: in other words, the lives of the hostages, as well as our own, count for nothing.
7. The coach must be ready at the nearest level crossing on this railway line. We must be notified by telephone that our demands will be granted, or by one person who must be dressed in slacks and sports shirt and who must approach the train from the front. Our destination is none of your business, it is ours, of which we shall inform the crew of the aircraft when we are aboard. So you will be told over the aircraft radio—we shall depart one hour after that, to give you time to make your preparations. We will take some hostages with us to prevent being shot down above some airspace or other. We shall release the other hostages five minutes before departure, and also hand in our arms. The explosives and hand grenades we shall keep. We shall not exchange any other hostages. We do not release women hostages, as we grant men and women equal rights. We do not want to see police or something similar at the airport, otherwise things might turn out fatal for some hostages.

Free South Moluccan Youth
Mena Muria

An ultimatum that expired in little more than an hour after receipt at local level, with a killing to follow after a further fifteen minutes, gave no time for tactical maneuver, let alone for conferences on strategy with the Ministry of Justice at The Hague. Beckeringh van Rhijn knew well enough what his recommended courses of action were, but he knew too that he was going to have to improvise. Deceleration and delay—those were the watchwords. Don't hurry; try to slow things down. Try to establish a channel of communication. Experience had taught that, once contact was made, the danger diminished. Don't lie to them. Don't change the site if at all possible. Leave policy decisions to the minister. But first he had to buy time. And with no telephone link, he was going to have to find a volunteer to take his reply—when it was fashioned—to the train.

The difficulty was to guess how serious the terrorists were. Did they mean what they said? He could scarcely credit it, but he had to assume that they did. He began to scribble a rough form of reply.

Hearing of the communications problem, a twenty-seven-year-old police sergeant named Auke de Vries volunteered to deliver the message, and Beckeringh van Rhijn asked him if he was married. Receiving an affirmative, he told deVries: "Go and ask your wife if she agrees." The man had to go home anyway to collect slacks and sport shirt. "Yes," he said, when he got back, "my wife agrees." By this time, Piet Bergsma and the equally tall and appropriately regal Tineka Schilthuis had arrived, and between them a reply was hammered out. Designed to allow a respite for consultation with The Hague and the examination of possible alternatives, the message aimed at avoiding definite commitments while mollifying the terrorists, explaining the delay, and getting a dialogue going. It read as follows:

1. Your demands have been received at Beilen Town Hall at 12:15 PM. You will realize that a decision cannot be made in thirty minutes.
2. Your demands have been passed to the Dutch Government. We will contact you as soon as a reply is received.
3. Meanwhile I have contacted Raterink Travel for the preparation of the bus you require.
4. In view of the above, we request that you refrain from irresponsible moves, in order not to impair negotiations.

> (signed)
> Beilen, December 2, 1975,
> The Burgomaster.

This message, calm in tone although composed under pressure, was deliberately clothed in ambiguity, but it seemed to its authors to strike the right note. A bus was being prepared, and negotiations might be in prospect, but meanwhile the reaction of the government must be awaited. The illusion of flexibility, it was hoped, would persuade the terrorists to pause.

Unfortunately the level of the reply, from the local burgomaster, was interpreted by the hijackers, when de Vries approached the train on foot from the northern crossing and delivered it by megaphone at 1:10 PM, as an insult. Their bid for nationwide publicity was being treated as a village disturbance. A little rational thought would have convinced them otherwise; but the hijackers were not acting in a rational situation. Their whole psychology and motivation stemmed from a conviction that they had been humiliated and ignored by the Dutch Government over a period of twenty-five years. For all that time, the Dutch had been allowed to get away with temporizing replies that never came to anything. They weren't going to get away with them now.

"If we don't get an answer by half past one," the hijackers shouted back at de Vries, "we shall kill one hostage." This left a margin of twenty minutes for the management center to react—which meant, by the time de Vries had returned with the message, no time at all.

Of the passengers, only Prins had read the ultimatum. But several at the rear of the first train-set heard the shouted threat. As the margin narrowed and the hijackers were seen consulting their watches, the tension mounted. When the hijackers pulled on their balaclava masks, the fear that some new violence was imminent grew. Yet few of the passengers could bring themselves to believe that the Moluccans would carry out their threat. The situation was so farfetched that it seemed unreal.

The Moluccan given the task of singling out the first victim was Paul. As he walked toward the rear through the second-class smoker, the passengers averted their gaze, staring stolidly at their feet, heads slumped forward, in the submissive posture adopted under overwhelming threat by animals and birds. Eventually Paul came to the last occupied seats, where he stopped. This was where Karel Wielenga and his party were sitting, also a woman named Sluiter, on her way to Utrecht.

As Paul stopped, one man, scorning to be intimidated, looked him in the eye. It was Rob de Groot.

"What time is it?" asked Paul.

"Half past one."

Paul stood in front of de Groot and chucked him under the chin like a naughty child. "You're the next one. Will you kindly come with us?"

"Okay—so what?"

De Groot felt too angry to panic. He was in a killing mood himself. He had spent ten years in the army, and he was chafing at the frustration of being thoroughly trained in both armed and unarmed combat and yet helpless to act. The indignity of being ordered about at gunpoint, too, was something he bitterly resented. But he certainly didn't expect to be shot. Not at all. They would probably beat him up. Well, he was young and strong; he could take it. The army had toughened him, and if he was just a shade flabbier than in his army days, he was still in good condition. With the hijackers twirling their guns like cowboys in a bad movie, he murmured a farewell to his father-in-law and allowed himself to be coerced forward through the train.

Crawling between Vaders' legs in the zigzag connection, the Moluccans took de Groot through to the second-class nonsmoking section. Vaders, not realizing it was one of the passengers, thought it was a man named Pronk, minister for the underdeveloped countries, come to negotiate. Curiously enough, de Groot had been mistaken for Pronk before. Height, features, coloring, gold-rimmed glasses, were almost identical, and both men were immaculate dressers. But from the way the man was being treated, Vaders soon guessed his error.

"May we have your papers?"

Ahead of him, through the open door of the luggage van, de Groot could see the dead driver, lying in a pool of blood. Pale but outwardly calm, he handed over the documents he had on him.

The terrorists moved away, and he heard them arguing amongst themselves. He had a smattering of Malay from his army service, and he gleaned enough to know that they were disputing his execution. "Yes, but it's murder," said one. Another, the one with the Afro-Asian hairstyle, urged, "We can't go back now. Just look *there.*" And he pointed to the driver.

Up to now, it had all seemed to de Groot like a bad dream. Now it dawned on him that they really meant to kill him. Stepping fastidiously over the dead driver, they took him forward into the baggage area.

This curious progression, played absolutely silently, held a nightmarish quality for Vaders, watching from the passageway. He knew nothing of the ultimatum, yet he was certain that an execution was about to take place.

Half a mile from the train, support units of the state police, the army, and the marines were being assembled and the whole area was being cordoned off. It was the police west of the train—on Vaders' right, looking forward—who saw, at 1:47 PM, the door of the luggage compartment slide open. Then a body in a red maroon coat was thrown from the train like a sack of potatoes. It was not difficult to guess that it was the driver, killed presumably when the train was hijacked, as already feared from the report by the two mechanics.

The terrorists had threatened a killing at one o'clock and another at 1:30, so they were behind schedule. A certain reluctance to kill might be deduced from the use of Braam's body to make good the one-o'clock threat. But soon after the body was thrown out, the door was opened again.

"Okay," said Paul to de Groot. "You've got time for one quick prayer."

In the preceding minutes, de Groot had brought his emotions under control. No use to panic, and no place for heroics, such as trying to take one of the hijackers with him. He would simply hasten his own death.

"Why does it have to be me?" He was thinking aloud, not really intending any kind of appeal. "I've got a wife and three children. It's so *stupid,* for such a thing as this, to be killed. Why does it have to be me?"

In his heart he knew that he had as much courage as the next man, yet he was close to crying. It was not that he was afraid—he felt no fear in the sense that he had known fear in the past. The emotion he felt was pity, pity for himself and for his family. It was such a dreadful pity.

"It's not our fault." It was Paul who spoke. There were two other Moluccans with him, but they were silent. "We don't want to kill. Your government has driven us to it."

"What good does it do your cause, that you kill a man, and make three orphans and a widow? I was a child when you were brought here. It's got nothing to do with me."

"That doesn't matter." The South Moluccans believed in guilt by association. "You've had plenty of time to learn about it, in books and magazines, and you've done nothing. Come on, say your prayers."

He began to pray, silently but fervently. He prayed for his children, and he prayed for his wife. He bowed his head, but because of the blood on the floor he did not kneel. He stood near the door, facing forward with his back to a strong-point, so that they couldn't shoot him from behind while he prayed, and he kept his eyes open.

As soon as he started praying, he was astonished to see, over the rims of his glasses, that they put their guns down forward of the doorway, then stepped back against the far wall, folded their hands over their belts, and joined him in prayer.

He was a normal man, he had sinned as much as anyone, and he prayed now for himself, and for the forgiveness of his sins. Even as he prayed, the tragicomic aspect of the scene was not lost on him. But what amazed him most of all was that, while he prayed, his brain continued not only to work but to work at top speed.

When he had finished, he kept the same stance, head forward, hands together. "Okay," they were saying, "hurry, hurry." They couldn't shoot him, it seemed, while he maintained an attitude of prayer. "Amen," they prompted, "amen." They were waiting for him to signify that he had finished. He guessed that they wouldn't wait much longer.

During his prayers, he had weighed the chances of jumping from the train and rolling down the embankment into the dike at the bottom. It was not a feat he would normally care to attempt. The floor of the train stood several feet from the ground. There was about two feet of gravel beside the track, and then the embankment sloped down steeply for perhaps ten to fifteen feet in a tangle of thistles and brambles, while the ditch at the bottom, half covered in weeds, might be deep. The one piece of good fortune was that they had opened the door on the right-hand side of the track looking forward, and the northbound track lay on the opposite side of the train. A good jump, and he could clear the leveled area at the top of the embankment where Braam's body lay and roll down the slope.

Another thing that had occurred to him, in that flash of schizophrenia while he prayed, was that his executioners appeared to be right-handed. If he jumped forward, they would have to swing round rather awkwardly to get in a shot at him. By that time he would be rolling down the bank and at their mercy, but he would be a moving target, and in the excitement of the moment they might miss.

He sensed that he was leaving it late. They were moving forward. Just as he felt they were about to shoot, he leaped through the door.

De Groot's plea on behalf of his wife and children, and his prayers, had so weakened the resolve of the sensitive Paul that, unknown to de Groot, he had whispered to Cor, his fellow executioner: "If possible don't shoot to kill." But as de Groot jumped, the diminutive, 17-year-old Cor reacted involuntarily by firing at him almost point-blank. De Groot, certain he had been hit, rolled over and over down the bank and finished up at full stretch on his chest in the bottom of the dike. Half submerged in a mixture of water and mud, he avoided suffocation by stretching his arms out before him and turning his head to one side.

Playing dead was the oldest of tricks, but the leap and the roll down the bank had knocked all the wind out of his lungs, and he was gasping for breath. Yet he dared not attempt more than the shallowest of intakes, lest they see his back rise and fall and know that he was alive.

Paul was certain that de Groot had been mortally hit, but twice more Cor fired at the inert body. Then they closed the door of the van, leaving de Groot for dead.

The effect on the Moluccans was traumatic. When they came back through the carriage to where Vaders was standing, he saw that two of them, whom he now knew to be Paul and Djerrit, were weeping.

"Can you understand us, sir?" The question, posed in a voice husky with emotion, came from Paul. Vaders took some care with his reply.

"I can understand your case."

"We don't hate you, but we have no choice. The Bible says there is a time to kill. The time has come. We don't hate you as people." They were quoting Ecclesiastes again.

"How could I hate you?" said Djerrit. "My wife is Dutch."

Vaders wondered if this was true. Somehow he doubted it. A further indication that these young men might be living in a fantasy world was provided by Paul. "My father was beheaded by the Japs, just for hiding a photograph of Queen Wilhelmina." Paul looked no more than twenty-five and had in fact been born in 1950. His story could not possibly be true.

Yet the tears of the hijackers were genuine enough. They were still visibly upset as they turned to the task of covering the windows in the forward part of the train.

Nearly all the passengers had seen de Groot go forward with the hijackers, and then they had heard shots. When the hijackers returned, de Groot was not with them. Yet there were still some who were able to deceive themselves, to close their minds to what was going on around them. One who could not do so was Karel Wielenga. The agitation of de Groot's father-in-law, and his own dreadful suspicions, forced a question from him.

"What has happened to Mr. de Groot?"

"He's dead."

Most of the Moluccans believed this was true. But soon afterwards, Vaders, still lashed in the passageway, overheard a phrase in Malay that he thought he recognized, something like *"Tidah mati,"* meaning "Not dead." Someone, perhaps, had seen the body move. Then Wientje Kruyswijk thought she heard another Moluccan shout: "He's away!"

De Groot, lying immobile in the dike, heard the hijackers close the door of the luggage van and refasten the padlock and chain. It was some time before he could be sure of it, but he had not even been hit. When he judged that the hijackers had settled down again in the train, he began to crawl out of the ditch.

Just out of reach of his outstretched hands were his glasses, and the first thing he did was to drag himself forward to recover them. He didn't know whether they had fallen off when he rolled down the bank or as he crashed into the ditch. He would have liked very much to know the answer. There was a small, neat hole from a .22 bullet in the right-hand lens.

He put his glasses on again, crawled up the bank, stepped over the body of the driver, and ran across the fields toward Farmhouse Etten, southwest of the train. As he approached the farmhouse, he heard voices, and he jumped into another ditch, thinking they were Moluccans operating in support of the hijackers. Then the voices called to him, and he realized they were police. The time was 1:55 PM. From the moment when Paul had asked him the time, the whole episode, seemingly interminable, had lasted twenty-five minutes.

None of the passengers could see out of the train, even Vaders's view now being cut off, and the Moluccans, believing that it was to their advantage to cower the passengers, maintained the fiction that de Groot was dead. But they couldn't deceive the authorities. For the hijackers this meant that, if they were to retain their credibility as terrorists, the shooting of another hostage in de Groot's place was going to be necessary.

Vaders believed he would have been chosen before de Groot had he not already been trussed up. It had been too much trouble to untie him. Now he realized that, if de Groot had indeed gotten away as he suspected, another sacrifice might be demanded.

CHAPTER 3

Death of a Soldier

HOUR BY HOUR, as the ropes cut grooves in his wrists and ankles and burnt off the skin, Vaders tried to forget his pain and fatigue in constructive thought. All he succeeded in doing was taking stock of himself. He was not a man given to conceit or self-importance, but as the long-established editor of a successful newspaper, he inevitably had a certain opinion of himself. You think you're a big man, he heard himself ruminate, someone who matters in the world, but to these young people you are nothing.

He knew of no one apart from himself and de Groot who had issued any sort of challenge to the terrorists, and he had to anticipate being next on their list. He tried to prepare himself for it. What did his life amount to? He could not pretend he was altogether happy with it, yet in a way he was satisfied. His philosophy had always been that there was some plus and some minus to everyone's life, and that when the final balance sheet was struck, nearly everyone finished up close to zero. Some said that was pessimistic, but he had always thought it was realistic, and he thought so now.

Although he had formed the impression that the hijackers were not ruthless killers, he had seen how utterly unpredictable they could be. Eli, he was sure, had something basically unbalanced about him, a deeply disturbed young man, with a cruel streak, insensitive to suffering, always apt to be dangerous. Paul's ambivalence might be played on, yet it might take him in the wrong direction. The others he classed as immature. He had seen them hesitate over the shooting of de Groot, and he guessed that, if de Groot was still alive, it was their lack of resolution, even perhaps their humanity, that had saved him. He was ready to believe that the wounding

35

of the train driver had not been premeditated, but he had sensed their desperation as the fact of the killing sank in. Having killed once, as Eli had calculated, they had nothing to lose by killing again.

He still thought the best protection for them all was to get through to the hijackers on a human level. It was easy enough, in a mood of fanatical patriotism, to plot to hold a faceless group of people hostage and even threaten to kill them. But when it came to leveling a gun at an identifiable human being, he sensed that they had faltered.

The fact that they were already shooting hostages suggested to Vaders that they were in far too much of a hurry. They had barely given the government time to react. In a situation like this, without precedent so far as Vaders knew, it might be some time before the government decided what to do. He was not optimistic about the duration, but of one thing he was certain: the terrorists had to be slowed down. If a negotiating position could be established, the killings might stop.

"This could be a long-drawn-out affair," he told Paul, trying to sound casual. "Do you realize what they'll do? I mean the prime minister, den Uyl, and the minister of justice, van Agt. They'll try to wear you down, like they did last month with Dr. Herrema's captors in Ireland."

"We're prepared for that."

Vaders saw that he was on dangerous ground. Their situation was not comparable with Herrema's. If Eddie Gallagher and Marian Coyle had killed Tiedé Herrema, they would have lost their only protection.[3] But if the South Moluccans could steel themselves to it, they could go on killing hostages one by one until public opinion forced the government to give in.

What Vaders didn't know was that the hijackers had already decided, calmly and deliberately, that at 2:30 PM they would take another victim.

Vaders badly needed a smoke, and in pursuit of his policy of human contact, he asked Paul to get a cigar from his pocket. Then he asked for the lighter from his other pocket.

"Can we have your papers?"

It was precisely the same question they had asked de Groot as they took him forward to shoot him, and he could feel the sweat breaking out on

---

[3]Gallagher and Coyle, two fanatical members of the Provisional IRA, had kidnapped the Dutch industrialist Herrema and demanded the release of three IRA prisoners as ransom. The Irish police and military surrounded the house where Herrema was being held hostage, psychological pressure was applied, and eventually the terrorists, realizing the hopelessness of their situation, surrendered after an eighteen-day seige, allowing Dr. Herrema to go unharmed.

his brow. He decided to lie. His position was precarious enough already, and they might see a newspaper editor as a natural target.

"You've already got them."

In fact, all they had taken from him was his diary. His wallet, with his means of identification, was still in his pocket, the same pocket as the lighter. But they accepted his word.

"What's your profession?"

As a trained observer and recorder of events, he had just witnessed, or thought he had witnessed, the preliminaries to an execution. He answered as vaguely as he could.

"I work for a newspaper."

"Which one?"

"Nieuwsblad van het Noorden."

"I subscribe to that paper," said Djerrit. He added in explanation that he lived in Middelstum, a village ten miles north of Groningen. These statements, too, were untrue. But Vaders took him at his word, comment · ing drily, "I'm afraid we'll soon have one subscriber less." One editor less, too, perhaps—but he kept that thought to himself.

Their reception of the fact that he worked for a newspaper encouraged him to put a proposition that had occurred to him earlier. "What about letting me do an interview, making a written record of your aims and motives, to be delivered to the government?" But he could see at once that they had no intention of getting involved in lengthy explanations until their demands for a bus and a plane were met.

The other hostages, as they were slowly recognizing themselves to be, were getting more and more impatient at the apparent absence of government intervention. No one was more disturbed than Hans Prins, who knew the details of the ultimatum. Two people, as he thought, had already been killed, and, unless the government acted quickly, a third was due to be sacrificed in a few minutes.

So far, the ultimatum seemed to have reached no further than the local burgomaster. Didn't the government care that the lives of Dutch citizens were at stake? Why didn't they send a senior minister to the train? That, in the eyes of the hostages, was the crying need, the one thing that these trigger-happy youths might take notice of.

In fact the only move towards mediation came from a South Moluccan organization called the Badan Persatuan ("Body Unity"), the social unity movement of South Moluccans in Holland, which ordered two young staff members of another South Moluccan organization, the Korps Pendjaga Keamanan (KPK) to find out who the boys were in the train and what they wanted. (The normal task of the KPK was to keep order and guard the peace in South Moluccan villages and camps.) The two KPK staff members, D. Manuputty and H.Z. Tahapary, reported to the town hall in Beilen at 2:00 PM and offered to go to the train. Were they to be trusted, or would they merely reinforce the hijackers' resolve? This was the dilemma that faced the gray-haired attorney general van Binsbergen, now in the chair at the management center. But with no other delaying action available and any form of communication better than none, the offer was accepted.

The strain of waiting was affecting hijackers and hostages alike. The hijackers could not keep still; they shuffled and twitched as though suffering minor convulsions. First they sought the security of the group, then deserted it to fidget and fret on their own, tracing irrational patterns of movement. Peering briefly through cracks in the newspapers, looking for some last-minute government gesture or perhaps an attack, they redoubled their vigilance, ears cocked for the slightest sound. They checked their watches; they looked and listened; they fondled their guns; they pointed them sadistically at the passengers; they looked and listened again. Bound by the terms of their ultimatum as securely as Vaders was bound in the passageway, they knew they would have to kill soon.

In contrast, the passengers remained as statuesque as if they were in a waxworks, fearing that the smallest movement might be pounced on, as in a children's game. As the air in the compartment became impregnated with the imminence of death, they staked their all on keeping out of focus, ostrichlike, as though they could achieve invisibility by some supreme effort of will. Thus they sat with heads bent forward, staring fixedly at the floor, fearing to close their eyes, but not daring to meet anyone's gaze. Although few would admit to themselves that the missing Robert de Groot had been shot, the terms of the ultimatum had now filtered through to most of them, and their posture was eloquent of their misery. Emotionally exhausted by the events of the day, they were left with a single, primeval instinct, that of self-preservation. Please, God, don't let it be me.

The agony was further prolonged as the South Moluccans waited for some sign from the government. But the two young KPK staff members, Manuputty and Tahapary, had not yet left the town hall. Just before three o'clock, Paul walked down the aisle as before, to select the next victim. This time he stopped beside one of the soldiers. It was twenty-two-year-old Leo Bulter, the soldier from Enschede who had gone to Assen to say good-bye to his girl friend. As two other South Moluccans closed in, Paul tapped him on the shoulder.

"Come with us."

Finding some sort of role to play, as Hans Prins had done as "doctor," offered the best protection against morbid introspection and faltering morale, if not against the whims of the hijackers. But that kind of relief could never be available to Bulter, Stevens, and Bies. Although they were draftees, cut off from their civilian occupations for no more than fourteen months, they had completed their military training, and in principle their role was to fight. The humiliation of their helplessness was greatly magnified in consequence. Now their suspicions that they might be victimized because of their uniform seemed about to be confirmed.

The fear of what the hijackers might be about to do to him was in the young soldier's eyes. After three years at technical college following school, he had been trained in the army as a gun repairer, giving him expert knowledge of how deadly the weapons he was being threatened with could be. But he got up and accompanied the hijackers forward.

Not a soul in the carriage protested. They did not even look up. In spite of themselves, their reaction was one of relief. Survival, personal survival —nothing else mattered. To protest would be to invite the obvious remedy. Come and take his place.

Perhaps they were only going to tie the boy up. That must be it. They could not bring themselves to accept that these young men were such cold-blooded killers. Even Prins, who had read the ultimatum, could not believe it.

Instead of squeezing Bulter past Vaders and up to the luggage compartment, they took him to the entrance platform at the rear of the first train-set. There, to guard against another escape attempt, his hands were tied behind his back by Eli. Then Paul opened the door—on the same side of the train as for Braam and de Groot.

"Can I talk with you?"

In seeking to make a plea for his life, Bulter asked the question with dignity. Paul felt himself weakening at once, as he had with de Groot, but this time Eli was there to stiffen resolve, and he cut in at once, silencing Bulter. "We're sorry, but we've got to do it to get our demands met." Without giving Bulter a chance to say more, he pushed him through the door and fired at him with the Uzi as he fell.

Paul could not stand there and let Eli take sole responsibility for the killing, and, as Bulter sprawled face down beside the southbound track, he fired at him three times, then closed the door. So paradoxical was his nature that he missed every time.

All this was observed in horrific detail from a quarter of a mile away by police, military, and press. The time was 3:02 PM.

As Paul and Eli stooped to pick up the spent cartridges, they laid the blame for the shooting of Bulter on the Dutch Government, cursing them for ignoring their ultimatum and forcing their hand in this way.

It had seemed at first to the hostages that the hijackers were well-organized and professional. But the catalogue of their mistakes was mounting. They had botched the job of killing Bulter. Terribly wounded, he was writhing about on the gravel beside the track, crying like a child.

Vaders heard a sound like a dog howling. Djerrit was in the compartment in front of him, and he saw the South Moluccan fire out of the train through a small open window.

"What was that?"

"Nothing." But Djerrit had the grace to look ashamed.

Even now the young soldier's agonies were not ended. Inside the train, the passengers could still hear the displacement of gravel as he struggled to move, and the choking sobs of pain as he did so. Yet they dared not ask questions, not even of each other.

Bulter had lain there for five minutes when, at 3:07, the door opened again, and two figures jumped down from the train. They were Paul and Abbé. They each fired another burst, but even this was not well directed, and finally Abbé stood over the dying soldier, pointed a gun at his temple, turned his head away, and fired. Then he and Paul returned to the train.

When Vaders asked again what had happened, Djerrit lied a second time. "One of the soldiers slammed a door shut behind him and tried to escape."

Those who had seen Bulter led out by the hijackers, heard his piteous cries, and the shots that silenced them, experienced a kind of cerebral atrophy, their minds bludgeoned by horror and grief. For the other two soldiers, indeed, the anguish was insupportable. Faced with an obscene and pointless murder, a man might find some garment to clothe his naked terror; a boy could not. This, for the two young soldiers, added shame to humiliation.

Nine minutes after the shooting, but too late to save Bulter, Manuputty and Tahapary approached the train to make contact with their fellow countrymen. After a short delay, they were allowed to enter the first train-set at the rear, but the hijackers refused to negotiate with the KPK or any other South Moluccan organization, and the pleas of the two would-be mediators to stop the killing and start negotiations were rejected. The hijackers repeated their request for a bus, and they added two further demands—for a train driver and portable radios. They wanted the radios to keep in touch with news of the hijack.

By this time Farmhouse Anton, the farmhouse southeast of the train, had been commandeered as a police headquarters, and a command post was established there. At 3:30 PM, as the two would-be mediators left, Sergeant de Vries, dressed as before, paid a second visit to the train. His mission, requested by the management center after a hurried consultation with Andreas van Agt, now assuming overall command at The Hague, was to get as much information as possible and try to establish some form of communication. "Your further demands are awaited," was the burden of the verbal message delivered by de Vries. "Request speedy reply and details. Do you need communication aids or food?"

This transparent attempt to gain time did not deceive the hijackers, who reacted angrily. Ordering de Vries into the train, they told him, "There has to be a bus within an hour, with curtains and no seats. If the bus isn't here within the hour, we'll shoot two more men."

"No," interposed another hijacker, "we'll shoot five this time."

The whole exchange was overheard in trepidation by Conductor Brinker, who was still tied up in the driver's cabin. "Hurry up," he shouted to de Vries. "Can't you see it's serious?" For de Vries, white with tension, it was a prompting that was hardly needed. Before he was allowed to leave the train, he was shown the explosives the hijackers had planted. Then he was roughly handled. As he left the train, he was forced to step over both the dead bodies lying beside the line. "We want a bus, a train driver, and portable radios. If you return empty-handed again, we'll kill you as well."

"We'll give you till five o'clock."

"Don't forget the handcuffs either."

When the news of the failure of the Manuputty/Tahapary mission and of the belligerence of the hijackers towards de Vries reached the management center, they decided, after consultation with The Hague, to revert to communication by megaphone. As for the threat of further killings in little more than an hour, the difficulty again lay in evaluating how serious these threats were. If the hijackers were indeed bent on pursuing such a program, there was nothing anyone could do about it before five o'clock, short of abject surrender. Sitting tight, keeping their nerve, and waiting to see what happened was a staggering responsibility for the hierarchy at Beilen; but at least they had the support of the minister. Meanwhile, with the crisis center still not in operation, van Agt authorized them to compose another temporizing reply.

The passengers, still blind to the outside world because of the covering on the windows, knew nothing of this new ultimatum. And although many of them were suffering from shock and amnesia, and even behaved at times as though the delay to their journey might be normal, the pretense was a preposterous one. Yet even those who tried to face the truth could scarcely credit it. Could this really be happening to them? Was it possible, in the liberated Dutch society of the 1970s? Surely it couldn't last much longer?

The early assumption that the terrorists would quickly be overcome by government intervention, however, was crumbling, leaving a growing sense of isolation and abandonment. The government, it seemed, was ignoring them, and they resented it bitterly. While they suffered the most excruciating mental torture, the government did nothing. What if it had been den Uyl or van Agt who had been hijacked? That would have been a different story! Such was their conclusion, and they joined with the hijackers in cursing the government. Now, as their twilight world of blocked windows deepened into darkness, they faced the near-certainty of a night in the train.

Worst of all, perhaps, was the agony of those who simply could not reconcile themselves to their situation. These, mostly, were the people who had caught the train by chance. "Why didn't we stay on the highway?" bemoaned Ter Veer, over and over again, so inconsolably that his wife feared for his sanity. Some of the women, however, although aware of their danger ("We also kill women"), sought solace in a murmur of whispered conversation, keeping up their spirits with small talk.

Even those who got in at Beilen had now been in the train for six hours without food or drink, yet no one felt hungry. None of them had stretched their legs, none had even dared ask to go to the lavatory. But the worst physical sufferers were Vaders and Brinker, still harnessed in their bullet-catching positions.

Two of the male passengers, Wielenga and Timmer, had drawn the attention of the hijackers to the length of Vaders's vigil and offered to take his place. They didn't know about Brinker. Now, with darkness falling, they volunteered again.

"Is it possible to change the guard?"

"That's a reasonable question."

Vaders was released at last, and Timmer replaced him, while Wielenga was taken forward to replace Brinker. The hijackers were still treating Brinker roughly, and, although he was allowed to go to the toilet, he was marched back among the passengers and ordered to lie on the floor. To get out of the way of the hijackers, he dived under one of the passenger's feet. It turned out to be Laurier. "It's serious all right," whispered Brinker. "The driver's dead—and he's not the only one."

Some of the older passengers were still unable to grasp their situation. Seventy-four-year-old Mrs. Bakker, protesting at the delay, blamed the railway company. "Can I travel on this ticket tomorrow?" she asked Brinker.

"I've got a whole case of tickets," muttered Brinker, "but first let's get out of this train."

Vaders limped back from his six-hour vigil in the passageway and sat next to Prins. He was so stiff with cramp that Prins at once got to work massaging his limbs, while the hijackers looked on dubiously. Prins didn't care whether they objected or not. Soon beads of sweat were dripping from his brow, but he kept on for at least half an hour.

"They've given you a rough time," said Prins.

"Are you a physiotherapist?"

"Something like that."

It seemed to Vaders that, during his long absence, some diabolical change had taken place in his fellow passengers. With a single red emergency lamp for illumination, faces had changed color and contour, while voices, although lowered, were strangely resonant, as in a crypt. He felt he was in a ghost train, with his own tangible existence also in doubt. He was glad of the bodily contact with Prins as the biologist continued the massage.

Wielenga, in the driver's cabin, was one of those who had tried to face up to the fact of the killings. It might well, he thought, be his turn now.

"Can you drive the train?"

The question took him by surprise. What would they do if he said no? Fearing that his life might depend on it, he tried to make some sense of the controls. He had no engineering or technological experience or knowledge, but the problem must be soluble. He didn't know where they wanted to go, and he didn't ask, but he had a wild idea that if he could get the train rolling, not too fast, some of the passengers might have a chance to jump out.

His fingers fumbled at the controls. Somehow he had to get the train going. But the instruments stared back at him inscrutably.

"I can't do it."

They began tying his wrists behind his back, the preliminary, he feared, to another execution. He had to delay it somehow.

"Can I have a cigarette?"

The hijackers had threatened to kill two more hostages at five o'clock.

The time was nearly up. Wielenga had no knowledge of this, but even without it, the atmosphere was menacing enough.

They put a cigarette in his mouth and lit it, and the darkness outside the cabin intensified. Perhaps they were granting his last wish. As they tied his wrists together, they saw that his hands were trembling.

"Do you think we are murderers?"

How should he answer? How best to save his life? He resolved to try to shame them. He spoke in a whisper.

"Yes, you are murderers."

He didn't know what reaction to expect. A beating-up, perhaps a bullet. The phrase had slipped out. But they drew back.

"It's your government that's responsible. They are the murderers. They're the ones who've betrayed us. They've taken away our identity. They've forced us to kill."

They were trying to justify themselves. It seemed a good sign. The longer they talked, the less they might act. In the next few minutes, they sketched in the political background to their claims—the first time, so far as Wielenga was aware, that they had done so. "The Dutch Government brought us here. They promised us we should go back to Ambon, back to our country. We declared our independence. For twenty-five years they've done nothing. Now we act. Now we save our honor."

He took heart from their youthful earnestness. "It's no honor," he told them, "for an Ambonese to kill somebody who is unarmed, while the attacker has a weapon. Better to attack us outside the train, when both sides have weapons. You have a Colt, and I have a Colt, and we see who's best."

They were silent, and he felt he had shamed them, as he had hoped. He tried to follow up his advantage.

"Let me talk to your commander."

"We have no commander. We all have the same status."

"Then let me talk to the authorities." Wielenga believed, as the hijackers had done, that there must be two-way communication from the train.

"That's not allowed. And you can't anyway. There's no telephone."

They completed the job of tying him up, then left him. Whether they had intended to kill him or not, he didn't know. But it was now after five o'clock, and it seemed that, after the bungling of the Bulter shooting, the hijackers had no stomach for more killing that night. That, anyway, was the government's hope.

CHAPTER 4

"Holland Did Treat Them Badly"

F EARING THAT THE NOISE and vibration of the generator might mask the sound of an approaching attack or reconnaissance, the hijackers switched off the heating soon after dark, and with the outside temperature falling, the passengers shivered. But in the eerie glow of the emergency lamps, the whispered conversations, often on trivial matters, continued, interrupted at intervals by staccato threats and cajolings from the hijackers over the loudspeakers. "We advise against panic attempts to escape. Anyone who attempts to escape will be shot. There are already several dead, so it makes no difference to us if there are more." These threats were chiefly directed at the occupants of the second train-set, who were not being held at gunpoint and were not under any sort of guard. One passenger, a serviceman, had already escaped, and five others followed during the night, but sixteen more were sufficiently intimidated to stay. Otherwise the hijackers seemed in a quiescent mood; the loudspeaker threats were succeeded by a soft melodious voice singing a plaintive Ambonese song.

The melody reminded Wientje Kruyswijk of a cherished contact with the South Moluccan people when she was young, and she began recalling it. "Holland did treat them badly. I was with them when they were brought over from Indonesia in 1951. I was only twenty-two, not married then, and I was living with my parents in Java. I wasn't a nurse, but I asked for a job helping to bring the South Moluccan soldiers and their families—the men of the KNIL, the Royal Dutch Indonesian Army—back to Holland. They couldn't be demobilized in Indonesia because they'd fought on the Dutch side against Sukarno.

"The ship was an old troopship, the *Atlantis*. It was known as the stork ship. All the wives were pregnant, and eighty-six babies were born during the voyage. Some of these boys must have been among them. 'We have to go to Holland now,' the parents told us, 'but we go back to Ambon in half a year!' The attitude of the authorities was the same. 'We're bringing them over, but we'll be taking them back.' That's twenty-five years ago, and they're still here."

At 7:20 PM, a distorted, disembodied voice called to the hijackers out of the darkness by bullhorn, and, although only part of the announcement was understood, disillusion mounted as the message unfolded. Auka de Vries was passing on the management center's second temporizing reply. "We haven't been able to find a driver to move the train. In conjunction with Netherlands Railways, efforts to find a volunteer continue. The requested radios are available, and you can come and collect them. What is the destination of the aircraft? We want to establish contact with you. Then we can start negotiations about your demands. This message comes from the mayor of Beilen."

Start negotiations! Six hours earlier, at 1:10, the demands of the hijackers had been acknowledged. According to the burgomaster, they had already been passed to the Dutch Government. The bus company had been contacted, and the hijackers had been told that a bus was being prepared. The next move had lain with the government, and the people in the train, hijackers and hostages alike, had been waiting in a frenzy of impatience since then. In all that time, they had imagined that urgent talks were taking place to effect their release. Now it seemed that no progress whatever had been made.

The disappointment was numbing in its enormity. Possibly for that reason, the dominant reaction of both groups was one of cynicism and derision.

"At last a reply—from the mayor of Beilen!"

"We've been here all day, and we still haven't gotten further than the local burgomaster!"

"Mr. Mayor, you're a creep!"

The passengers joined in. "Why don't they send den Uyl and van Agt? If *they* were here with us, we'd be on the airplane by now."

The ridicule was so spontaneous that for a moment it became a shared intoxication, drawing the two groups together. But revulsion, if it came, thought Vaders, might be violent.

The truth was that, although the hijackers had planned sensibly and in some detail, they had not thought their action through to its logical end, other than a preparedness to die for their cause, nor did they have much in the way of contingency plans. The dumb intransigence of the government had confused them; they had not expected to be held up for so long. But now that they were beknighted, they accepted the delay fatalistically. They certainly didn't intend to risk collecting the radios in darkness; that could be a trap. As for the plane, they saw it as a secure and spectacular headquarters from which, protected by their hostages, they would dictate their political demands and attract attention to their cause. Amazingly, they hadn't thought seriously about a destination.

The South Moluccans as a people set great store by promises and the honoring of them. Complementing this altogether creditable characteristic lay a tenacity for justice. The hijackers had been told that a bus was being prepared for them. If this was not quite the same thing as a promise of a bus, they were in no mood to bother with such subtle distinctions. They believed in the bus. The only difficulty, they had been led to understand, lay in finding a driver.

Many of the passengers, by a form of osmosis, also believed in the bus. But some were not so sure. One man at least, sixty-five-year-old Willem Albracht, had consistently maintained, when he himself was not affected, that governments should never negotiate with terrorists. How did he feel now? He was pleased to find that he felt the same. But he was quite prepared to avoid the consequences, to find an excuse to escape selection for guard duty or worse. Although he was so cold that he kept his cap on all the time, he pushed it back clear of his temples at critical moments to expose his gray hair.

The passengers, too, were resigning themselves to a night in the train. Reflecting the mood of the hijackers, they experienced a slight relaxation. This brought a consciousness of their physical needs, and one by one they put their hands up, as they had not dared to do before, to go to the lavatory. Some of them had packed food for the journey, and they produced what they had and divided it up with their neighbors. Among the lucky ones were the Ter Veers, who were sitting opposite the soldier Thys Stevens, on his way to Germany. Stevens's mother had packed him a substantial snack for the journey. But the Ter Veers were not so lucky when Paul brought around a bottle of drinking water. The hijackers were now revising their ideas, preparing for a longer siege, and they had decided to conserve the water supply. By the time the bottle reached the Ter Veers, it was nearly empty. Ter Veer could not get a worthwhile sip without tipping the bottle almost vertical, and in doing so he earned a rebuke from Paul. "No, no—not too much."

Hans Prins, pursuing his role of doctor, toured the compartment asking the passengers if they were on any particular medical treatment, what medicines they carried, if any, and whether they could recall what they were, the quantities they were supposed to take, and the name of the doctor who had prescribed them. Then he compiled a list in the hope of transmitting it to the authorities next day.

While he was thus engaged, one of the hijackers came to him for medical advice. He thought his girl friend might be pregnant, and he was worried that the shock she would get on hearing of his part in the hijacking might harm the baby. The chance to weaken the resolve of this particular hijacker was obvious, but Prins, careful not to overplay his hand, did not exaggerate the danger. They had accepted him as a doctor, and they must learn that he could be trusted. That, in the long run, would be the best way to exert influence in his new role.

While the hijackers took turns to mount guard, the passengers prepared to settle down for the night. But sleep, on this bitter December evening, proved elusive. They had sat for twelve hours already, and the seats were not wide enough for them to stretch out. They had no blankets, and they were miserably cold. To conserve water, they were not allowed to wash, even after going to the lavatory, and they had no toothbrushes or towels. There was only one lavatory for the passengers' use, and it soon became choked and malodorous. The shock to the nervous system had increased the frequency of bowel movements, and some of the women had begun to menstruate.

Kobus, speaking very softly in Dutch so that they had to strain to hear him, came up with a verbal nightcap, bitter to the taste. They, the hostages, were the people who had to suffer for the misdeeds of the government. "If your government doesn't agree to our demands, we shall shoot at least one hostage every day."

With this as a bedtime story, they pulled their coats and other garments around themselves in a vain effort to keep warm and closed their eyes. Vaders's coat was still in the first-class compartment, and he asked Paul if he could get it. Paul made an apologetic gesture. "We used it to mop up the driver's blood." Vaders was left shivering, with no hope of sleep. Later someone gave him a coat, and he tucked it round himself thankfully.

Before they fell into an uneasy doze, some of the passengers caught a glimpse of the seventeen-year-old Cornelis, reading his Bible by the light of a torch, and praying.

The alternatives facing Andreas van Agt, when he assumed control that afternoon in the massive neogothic building in the center of The Hague that housed the Ministry of Justice, seemed stark and clear-cut: capitulation to the hijackers' demands, or an assault on the train, with all the risks that implied. Faced with a similar dilemma in 1974, when the French Embassy was seized, the government, although refusing to allow hostages to be taken out of the country, had compromised to a considerable extent. South Moluccan militants, van Agt realized, would have taken due note of that. But more recently a third option, pioneered by the New York police in criminal kidnappings, had emerged. The outstanding example in Europe of this method of dealing with a situation where hostages were involved was the handling by the Irish Government of the kidnapping by IRA terrorists of the Dutch industrialist Dr. Herrema. By standing firm, promising no concessions, and making no deals, the Dublin government had brought home to the kidnappers the hopelessness of their situation. An important bonus of this method was the human relationship that tended to develop between hijacker and hostage, making cold-blooded killing less and less likely as time passed.

Such a policy of attrition seemed callous and inhuman at first glance, bearing heavily on the hostages and their families. And in the mass hostage situation that now faced van Agt, it had one serious weakness, as Vaders had seen. If the South Moluccans went on killing hostages every few hours, as they threatened to do, the case for an attempt to save further bloodshed might become overwhelming. This, after careful consideration, was a bridge that van Agt decided to cross when he came to it.

A devout Catholic who had trained and practiced as a lawyer, van Agt had worked on the drafting of statutes and legislation at the Department of Justice before becoming Professor of Penal Law at his home university of Nijmegen. Then in 1971, the government, always a coalition in Holland, needed a new minister of justice, and van Agt, despite some misgivings, accepted the post. Although not seeing himself as a professional politician, and with few convictions outside religion and law reform, he enjoyed the glamour of public life, and he found himself leading the Christian Democratic Appeal, an amalgam of Christian parties of the center that included his own Catholic Peoples' Party and Willem de Gaay Fortman's Protestant Anti-revolutionary Party and commanded a place in any coalition. When Joop den Uyl, leader of the Parliamentary Labor Party and a dedicated and crusading politician, became minister-president in 1973 at the age of fifty-four, the balance was adjusted by appointing van Agt, then forty-two, his deputy.

Under the Dutch constitution, van Agt was the supreme commander in charge of the prevention and suppression of all criminal acts. The minister-president had a coordinating role but no executive responsibility.

Thus, there had been times, during the French Embassy siege and a jail meeting incident, when van Agt had resented what he saw as interference from "Uncle Joop." As political and intellectual opposites, the two men were bound to clash, but their attitudes to the South Moluccan problem coincided, and, whatever their differences in committee, they presented a united front on terrorism. Now, with den Uyl absent in Rome attending the European Council, the initial decisions would be van Agt's, supported by de Gaay Fortman, Minister for Internal Affairs.

Of less than average height, spare and extremely fit—he was an enthusiastic amateur racing cyclist—van Agt exuded an air of austerity that was contradicted by his love of good food and good wine and an addiction to long thin cigars. Living in a bachelor flat within walking distance of his ministry and returning to his home and family (a wife and three children) at Nijmegen on weekends, he was often seen dining at a favorite restaurant in The Hague during the week. Contradictions were a part of his nature; his preference for sober, unpatterned suiting was generally offset by a colorful tie. An unusually low forehead, from which the dark hair scarcely graying at the temples had not receded, a thin, hooked nose, and a small, sensitive mouth, in which the lips were often pursed into a cupid's bow, lent his face a masklike symmetry that aided his powers of concealment. Because few claimed to know what was going on in his mind, he was regarded as unpredictable. Entering politics, as he had, at the top, avoiding the rough and tumble, he was dismissed by some as a light-weight. But like many an irregular worker—he never appeared in his office before 11:00 AM and often worked far into the night—he was at his best in an emergency. By the time the crisis center was formed in embryo and he was in control, the terrorists' first ultimatum had expired and the young soldier, Leo Bulter, had been murdered. Thus he was faced with agonizing decisions from the start.

There were two immediate practical problems: establishing reliable communications with the hijackers, and finding suitable contact persons or mediators. Although the hijackers were refusing to negotiate and van Agt had no intention of negotiating in the true sense of the word, contact had to be established if government strategies and tactics were to be effective and lives were to be saved. Such contact, according to the blueprint that had been worked out beforehand, would be confined to command-post level, so that neither the management center nor the government itself could have their hand forced by the hysterical pleas of a terrified hostage. Saving the lives of hostages was the first objective, but not at any price.

A complication was that so far the gunmen had given no indication of their eventual purpose. Van Agt had no doubt that their action was the culminating phase in an escalating frustration amongst young South Moluccans, which had already manifested itself in several violent protests, but knowledge of their aspirations made him certain that the hijackers would have some long-term political goal.

Ending the hijacking by force—the military option, as it was known— was an alternative that he by no means ruled out; indeed, it was an essential factor in any successful strategy. But although troops had been called in and the whole area around the train had been cordoned off, a violent reply, he believed, was premature. In any case, there were no contingency plans in existence for an assault on a train. The possibility of giving the terrorists the road transport they asked for and then delivering a surprise attack on the bus was considered, but he dismissed it, partly because of the danger to the hostages, partly because it came under the heading of unfair play. He was realist enough to accept that when governments are faced with terrorism they must themselves be prepared to employ deception, and he did not reject the idea on moral so much as on pragmatic grounds. Once having played a trick of that kind, the government would forfeit the right to be trusted again.

That evening, as den Uyl flew back from Rome, van Agt went on television to assure the nation that under no circumstances would the hijackers be allowed to leave the country, with or without their hostages. This was a firm and uncompromising line, and it was well received by the Dutch public. Had there been no killings, van Agt might have left himself more room to maneuver, but now he committed himself to a policy of making no concessions and of seeking mediators who might persuade the hijackers to surrender, using stalling tactics to wear down the hijackers while preparing as quickly as possible for the worst.

The first man he approached was J.A. Manusama, the self-styled South Moluccan president-in-exile, and he was gratified by Manusama's response. Acknowledged by most South Moluccans as their political leader, Manusama also went on television and condemned the hijacking as a "horrible affair." To van Agt he offered to send his South Moluccan paramilitary force, the KPK, to the train to disarm the hijackers, but this was not a solution that van Agt felt the government could contemplate.

In his baroque, richly carpeted office on the first floor of the Department of Justice building overlooking the Plein, Minister van Agt sat at his baize-topped desk at one end of the room with his back to the full-length front windows, a single desk lamp, heavily shaded, confirming his aversion to strong light. From a mural above the veined marble fireplace at the far end of the room, he was attended by the mythological figure of Justice, blindfolded and balancing the scales. Along the top of the oak paneling facing him on the inside wall was an inscription with which he was temperamentally in sympathy: "One should consider slowly and with foresight and then act swiftly." In the center of the room a baize-topped table was surrounded by six high-backed, carved-oak, brocaded chairs, the minister's chair, facing the mural, being marginally more ornate than the others, without ostentation. It was around this table, in the course of the evening, that representatives of other ministries—Internal Affairs, Defense, Culture (with a special responsibility for minorities), and Transport—and officials of Netherlands Railways gathered to discuss the course of events, to express opinions, and to formulate plans. The main conference room, separated from the minister's room by an anteroom, was reserved for general meetings, the secretary general's office at the far corner of the facade was retained for direct liaison with the management center at Beilen. Other adjacent offices were commandeered for small teams of specialist advisers, while the library was adapted into a communications center.

When dealing with so mercurial an adversary, it seemed wise, during the hours of darkness, to let sleeping dogs lie, so further attempts to establish a reliable means of communication were postponed until daylight. An approach to the train at night might be misunderstood. Meanwhile the silence of the hijackers and the trickle of escaped hostages seemed to augur well. Since it was assumed that the hijackers were exhausted by the traumas of the day, the possibility of a sudden surprise attack spearheaded by the marines came under discussion, but there was general agreement that force should only be used as a last resort. The pressing need was to use the hours of darkness for consolidation and to examine clandestine methods of getting more information out of the train. For the latter, the latest surveillance techniques, including listening devices and infrared cameras, were available. Under the direction of Piet Bergsma, police, army marksmen, marine commandos from the recently formed antiterrorist unit, and an assortment of armored vehicles reinforced the double cordon that already encircled the train, one at 300 meters and another at 8 kilometers. These barriers had a dual purpose—to stop unauthorized persons getting near the train and to thwart any possible escape attempts by the hijackers, with or without the use of hostages for cover. But it was the hostages, those in the second train-set, who effected escapes.

While there were still passengers who remained blissfully or stubbornly ignorant of their peril, the majority were fighting a battle to keep some sort of composure. Few had been able to relax their minds sufficiently to read during the day, and few could now relax their bodies sufficiently for sleep. The atmosphere in the carriage was subterranean and spooky, with the hijackers passing continually to and fro in the aisle, flashing their torches at imaginary intruders, suspecting conspiracies in every movement. Worst of all was the uncertainty, the complete ignorance of what was going on. At any time, the peace might be shattered by gunfire as the marines moved in.

Everyone had their own method of keeping their mind on trivial things. Typical was Louis Laurier, who passed the time attempting endless sums, multiplying $2 \times 2 \times 2$ until he lost count and started again. Some, finding their neighbors as wakeful as themselves, played party games based on Dutch place names in fevered whispers. In these the player had to find a location starting with the last letter of the last named town. There was also the memory tester "I go traveling with a toothbrush," which had a nice irony to it, since nearly everyone was traveling without one. For most of them, though, it was the longest night of their lives.

Those who had been individually terrorized for hours on end, like Vaders and Brinker, suffered most. After standing for six hours, Vaders's stomach gave way, and he made frequent trips to the lavatory. Once, on his way back to his seat, he was intercepted by Paul. "Here's some medicine. Rub it on where it hurts. It will make it warm." Vaders massaged his stomach with the ointment and it soothed his pain. Its spicy aroma identified it as some traditional South Moluccan remedy: it smelled of coconut and nutmeg.

Laurier, during a three-hour spell at the bullet-catching post, felt a coat being draped over his shoulders. Then someone pressed a segment of orange into his mouth. After all that had happened, these acts of consideration from the hijackers seemed grotesque.

Next morning, when it was light enough to see, Vaders realized that his warmth had been provided by an army greatcoat. They had given him Leo Bulter's.

CHAPTER 5

Republik Maluku Selatan

T HE DUTCH FIRST ESTABLISHED their authority over the Indonesian
archipelago through the Dutch East India Company in the seven-
teenth century, the prize being a virtual monopoly of the spice trade. The
natural center of the spice region was the island of Amboina in the South
Moluccas, and it was here that the company established its headquarters.
In succeeding centuries, the commercial importance of the Spice Islands,
as the South Moluccas were popularly known, deteriorated, and during
the Napoleonic era, the Dutch temporarily lost control. But they soon
reestablished it, and, in the course of the nineteenth century, the Ambonese won for themselves a privileged position in the Dutch colonial
empire, serving in many areas as schoolteachers, clergymen, and public
servants, and above all as soldiers. They became the leaven of the Dutch
colonial army, the Koninklijke Nederlands Indische Leger, or KNIL
(pronounced k-nil), and they retained this special relationship right up to
the Second World War.

The South Moluccas lie south of the Phillipines and north of Timor,
between Celebes in the west and New Guinea in the east. Centered around
Ambon, the capital of Amboina, they include the larger island of Ceram,
the legendary "mother island," sparsely populated and about the size of
Belgium, and a multitude of islands of varying sizes scattered over many
thousands of square miles. (See map on page 55.)

The inhabitants of the South Moluccas, about 1.2 million in all, although of mixed origin, are predominantly Melanesian, and they have
preserved characteristics and qualities that make them markedly different
from the Malaysians of Java and Sumatra. Taller and bigger physically,
many of them have the darker skin and heavier features of the Papuans

54

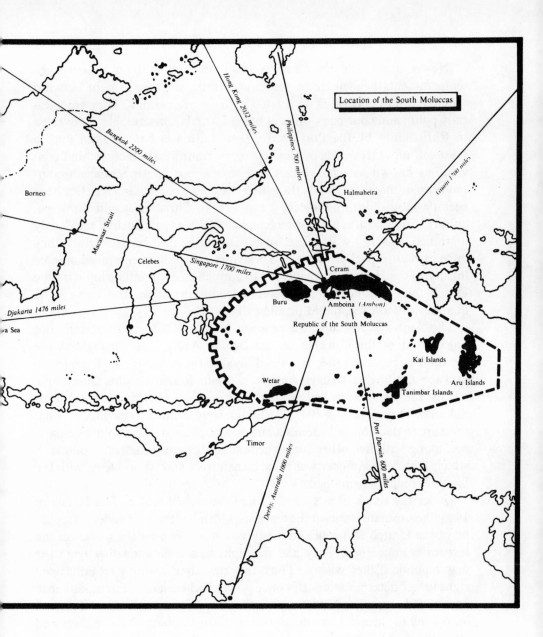

Location of the South Moluccas

Borneo

Hong Kong 2032 miles

Philippines 700 miles

Bangkok 2200 miles

Guam 1700 miles

Halmaheira

Macassar Strait

Celebes

Singapore 1700 miles

Ceram

Djakarta 1476 miles

Buru

Amboina (Ambon)

va Sea

Republic of the South Moluccas

Kai Islands

Aru Islands

Wetar

Tanimbar Islands

Timor

Derby, Australia 1000 miles

Port Darwin 600 miles

of New Guinea, and their hair is black and either frizzy or curly. In temperament, they tend to be open and volatile, and they lack the outward serenity and reserve often associated with eastern peoples. They are naturally polite and courteous without being formal or inscrutable. Converted to Christianity by the Portuguese, their faith has been grafted onto a mystical, unwritten code of local customs, traditional practices, and conventions known as *adat*, which still survives in South Moluccan communities in the Netherlands. But their most stubborn characteristics have been developed during their long exposure to Christianity and European culture. Such abstracts as independence, justice, and fidelity are deeply ingrained, and they will defend them with all the resilience for which they once earned respect as soldiers. These qualities, which embraced a fierce loyalty to the House of Orange, led to a much closer relationship with the Dutch than was normal in a colonial administration. But these same qualities posed exceptional problems later.

The Ambonese occupied a position in the Dutch military scene not unlike that of the Gurkhas in the British Army, and throughout the Japanese occupation, they remained loyal to the Allied cause. Even in the postwar nationalist struggle, many of them fought on the Dutch side against the Republic of Indonesia, the revolutionary Javanese republic of Sukarno. Thus, when, in 1949, the Dutch were compelled by international pressure to decolonize Indonesia and accept Sukarno's republic as a partner, along with five other constituent states, in a new federal republic to which Dutch sovereignty was to be transferred, special problems with the South Moluccans emerged.

Under the terms of a Round Table Conference held at The Hague in 1949, the ultimate status of the territories forming the new Federal Republic of the United States of Indonesia was to depend on the wishes of the territories concerned. They had the right to secede altogether from the new republic if they wished. Thus, they appeared to enjoy an unfettered right to self-determination. But once power had been transferred, Sukarno abandoned federalism and established a single, unitarian state. Regional autonomy for former constituent states, it was implied, could be discussed later. Since this policy was backed by Sukarno's army, the only organized armed force remaining, and since the Dutch were now powerless to intervene, territories that objected that federalism was sacrosanct in the terms of the transfer, and that a single state meant Javanese supremacy, were soon overpowered. The one exception was in the South Moluccas. It was around Ambon, where over 1,000 KNIL personnel were awaiting demobilization or transfer to the Indonesian army under the terms of the Round Table Conference, that discontent erupted. Some of the leaders of earlier uprisings took refuge there, and, although there had been no thought of seceding from federation, a political campaign developed against the absorption of the South Moluccas into a single Indonesian state.

Historically, the South Moluccas formed an autonomous province or *daerah* within East Indonesia, and East Indonesia was to have been a constituent state in the new republic. Ambonese influence in East Indonesia was considerable, and many of the state's leaders were South Moluccans. Now they saw their cherished independence, which the Dutch imagined they had protected, being submerged. It was against this background that fighting broke out in the city of Ambon, and on April 25, 1950, the county aldermen of the *daerah*, led by the president and vice-president, issued a proclamation forming a new South Moluccan Republic —Republik Maluku Selatan—or RMS. This was to be made up of Amboina, Buru, Ceram, and other adjoining islands. The new republic proclaimed its separation from the old East Indonesian state, "which was no longer capable of maintaining its status as a component state," and from the new Republic of the United States of Indonesia, "which had acted in contravention of the resolutions of the Round Table Conference and the Provisional Constiutution."[4]

Sukarno's government attempted to settle what they characterized as an internal rebellion by peaceful means, and they sent a mission to Ambon under the leadership of a member of the cabinet who was himself a South Moluccan (more South Moluccans live outside the territory than inside). But the leaders of the new RMS, incensed that the mission should arrive off Ambon in a war vessel, refused to negotiate. The mission later expressed the opinion that the proclamation of RMS did not represent the popular will, but was inspired by disgruntled members of the KNIL and the church, who had the most to lose by the Dutch departure; and it may be true that only a minority of South Moluccans were ever truly loyal to the Dutch crown. But whatever the inspiration, the majority seem to have rallied to the RMS cause.

"Grave anxiety," "deeply shocked," "cannot remain indifferent"— these were among the phrases of condemnation used by the Dutch prime minister in an official protest to Sukarno's government, and the United Nations Commission for Indonesia (UNCI) offered to intercede. But in

---

[4] The English text, broadcast at the time from Ambon, is at Appendix A.

what was ostensibly a police action to settle a domestic affair, Indonesian forces, transported by a Dutch shipping company,[5] landed on Buru and Ceram and, on November 3, 1950, entered the city of Ambon. Since the Indonesian Army, like the KNIL, was stiffened by troops of South Moluccan origin, the fighting was bitter, but the result was inevitable. Guerrilla warfare in the mountainous districts of Ceram continued throughout the 1950s and early 1960s under the leadership of a lawyer named Dr. Christian Soumokil, but the rebellion as such was over. The absorption of an indigenous group into a national society, with little regard for their feelings or sense of ethnic and cultural identity, was thus begun, and the great powers, anxious for good relations with the new Indonesian republic, acquiesced.

Soumokil, a convinced federalist, had been minister of justice in the government of the state of East Indonesia, and he now became the spiritual leader of the exiled RMS.

At the time of the transfer of sovereignty, there were 65,000 troops of the KNIL in Indonesia, of whom 8,000 were South Moluccans, and, under the terms of the transfer, this army was to be dissolved. By the time of the signing of the agreement, 26,000 of these troops had already joined the Indonesian army, as they were entitled to do if they wished, and a further 18,750 had been demobilized, either in their places of origin or in places of their choice, again in accordance with the terms of the transfer. But during the revolt in the South Moluccas, the further demobilization of troops of Ambonese origin became a matter of some delicacy. With the Indonesian army in control in Ambon, many of them wished to be demobilized on Ceram, where they could have joined the guerrilla forces under Soumokil, or in Dutch New Guinea. But for the Dutch to agree to either of these alternatives would have been to antagonize the new Republic of Indonesia at the outset, and they proposed to demobilize these troops within territory under Sukarno's control. This the remaining Ambonese soldiers resisted.

There were still some 3,500 of these troops awaiting demobilization under Dutch protection in Java, and, with their dependents, who traditionally accompanied them, they numbered about 12,500. Although several groups of ex-KNIL South Moluccans had been demobilized without discord, the fear that developed in the Java camps was that once Dutch protection was removed, they would be victimized and perhaps even slaughtered wherever they might elect to go.

---

[5]Koninklijke Nederlandse Paketvaart Maatschappij (KPM).

After a representative of the RMS had asked for an opinion on the legal position, the Netherlands branch of the International Law Association concluded on June 24, 1950, that the RMS had the right to proclaim its independence and that it might lawfully maintain that independence against all others. A similar ruling was given by the president of the district court of Amsterdam on November 2 of the same year, when the legitimacy of the RMS and its competence to act as plaintiff in a lawsuit were challenged by the Dutch shipping company that had transported the invading Indonesian troops and their weapons to the South Moluccas to put down the rebellion. The president ruled that the proclamation of the independent RMS was a lawful exercise of the right of self-determination by the people of the South Moluccas and that the RMS existed as a state according to both international and Netherlands law, and this judgement was later confirmed by the Amsterdam court of appeal. But the ruling came too late to redress the damage. Some 10,000 Indonesian troops and their weapons had been transported in an act of complicity which, whether inadvertent or not, was to cause lasting bitterness among South Moluccans.

Meanwhile, a group representing the South Moluccan soldiers immobilized on Java and led by a sergeant-major in the KNIL named F.A. Aponno asked the president of the district court of The Hague to forbid the Dutch Government to demobilize the Ambonese soldiers in territory of the Indonesian Republic or in South Moluccan territory occupied by the Indonesian army. (The soldiers only wished to be repatriated, it was reaffirmed, to the remaining free territory of the RMS—which for practical purposes meant the island of Ceram.) The Aponno group won their case, and neither the court of appeal, when the Dutch Government challenged the verdict, nor the high council of the Netherlands, similarly appealed to, would set the judgement aside. Despite all their efforts to rid themselves of an intractable problem, the Dutch found themselves obligated to safeguard the remnant of the South Moluccans against whatever dangers might face them on Amboina or elsewhere, while the soldiers were not to be transported from their secluded and guarded camps on Java without their consent.

Since the government had undertaken to demobilize these men by April 1, 1951, they were faced with a dilemma. To resolve it, they proposed that, if the alternatives of demobilization in the occupied Moluccas or on the spot in Java were rejected, an order would be issued for discharge in the Netherlands. Most of the South Moluccans on Java availed themselves of this opportunity, and shipping space had to be made available for some

12,500 people to be transported to Holland, there to await conveyance to their ultimate destination, whatever that might be. The Indonesian Government agreed to readmit any of those servicemen and their families who chose at a later date to return to Indonesia, but they would have to return as Indonesians.

There was no promise made that they could return to a free Ambonese Republic nor that the soldiers could retain their military status, but the payment of pensions or standoff pay as applicable was underwritten. The temporary nature of the transfer to the Netherlands was emphasized in the text of the order governing the terms of the discharge, which added that the refugees were to be accommodated in camps, where the costs of care et cetera would be deducted from their income.[6]

The first group of South Moluccans left Indonesia at the end of February, 1951, and evacuation continued over several months. It was in this period that Wientje Kruyswijk sailed with some of them on the "stork" ship, *Atlantis*. The men were illiterate and spoke poor Dutch, the women and children spoke only Malay. On their arrival, the soldiers were duly discharged from the army and housed in camps originally built in the 1930s to support construction schemes for the relief of the Dutch unemployed. In two cases, at Westerbork, near Beilen, and at Lunetten, near Vught, former German concentration camps were used after they had been converted for the purpose.

Having been accustomed to living in camps with their families all their lives, the South Moluccans settled in happily enough, continuing their traditional cultural activities and trusting implicitly in the Dutch and in eventual reinstatement in Ambon. But their pensions, which under the terms of the transfer of power were the responsibility of Indonesia, were not paid on the grounds that the men themselves, by rejecting the alternatives of transferring to the Indonesian Army or being returned to their places of origin as loyal citizens, had broken the agreement. Since the order governing dispatch to the Netherlands signed by the Dutch army chief of staff stated clearly and unconditionally that pensions would be paid, here was the first major disillusionment. Although for five years they were supported entirely—and not ungenerously—by the Dutch Government, and pensions were eventually paid by the Dutch when they reached pension age, they felt the affront to their dignity.

"There is pathos in the situation," wrote one commentator soon after the first families arrived in Holland, and he forecast trouble ahead.

---

[6]The full text of the order is in Appendix B.

As their stay in Holland is regarded as a temporary safeguard "until the sky has cleared," no attempts are made for their integration into the Dutch community. As the Netherlands, like all countries in the Atlantic Treaty, have to expand their army, it would seem sensible to use these Ambonese for the task they do so well—and enlist them in the army. This, however, is impossible as the Indonesian Government let them go on condition that they would not be used operationally or sent outside Holland. The optimists say that in Indonesia things are soon forgotten and in a short time there will be no trouble about sending the Ambonese back to their own country. Pessimists, who think that an historical antagonism can never be straightened out, fear that this Ambonese group will remain a sore spot in the overcrowded Netherlands.

This prescient appreciation appeared in the *London Observer* in March, 1951.

As the Indonesian Government had defaulted on the pensions, it might seem that the Dutch could reasonably have enlisted these men in the Dutch army, perhaps restricting them to the European theater. But they did not take this course—nor did they offer them any alternative place in Dutch society. The Ambonese joined the many thousands of displaced persons in Europe, while no firm plans were laid to rehabilitate them in their own country or to assimilate them in Holland.

The struggle for an independent South Moluccan republic was continued on two main fronts: in Ceram, where Dr. Soumokil was leading his guerrilla army and controlling much of the island; and in Holland, where South Moluccan politicians, led by Manusama, a civil engineer and mathematics teacher who had played an important role in the proclamation of independence and who had been a minister in the first cabinet, continued to maintain the legality of the proclamation and to seek recognition from the Dutch Government and the intervention of the United Nations. In neither of these quests was he successful.

Manusama's qualities of scholarly achievement, personal integrity, and faith in a righteous cause slowly became outdated, and although he was not in immediate danger of being superseded, his authority was sometimes challenged. A particular rival, the self-styled General Tamaëla, a former sergeant-major in the KNIL (virtually the highest rank a South Moluccan could reach), believed that Manusama was making a mistake in continuing to look for help from the Dutch; his policy had achieved nothing in twenty-five years and had no hope of doing so. Since 1968, Tamaëla, with minority backing from South Moluccans in Holland, but without status of any kind, had appointed himself as a special advocate and canvassed the South Moluccan cause in the corridors of the United Nations in New York, but he too had achieved nothing. One of the recurring problems over the years, outside as well as inside Holland, was that the Indonesian regime was regarded by the West as a friendly one, while the RMS lacked the revolutionary leftist aura that might have attracted the Marxists.

The Dutch had been in the Far East for 400 years, and it took them several more years after their exit to accept that they were out of Indonesia and deprived of all influence for good. During the years of adjustment, they found it equally difficult to reconcile themselves to the fact that there was nothing they could do for the territorial rehabilitation of the Ambonese. Eventually, as the impracticability of repatriation became apparent, the Dutch sought to begin the process of integration, and by the mid-fifties the Moluccans in Holland were expected to earn their own living wherever possible. By the end of the decade, Dutch policy was to assimilate them into the Dutch community, at the same time taking care to encourage and develop their natural skills and preserve their group life. Gradual evacuation of the camps was begun, the inhabitants being transferred to special residential areas in Dutch towns.

Had this policy been pursued with vigor in accordance with the detailed recommendations of the committee that inspired it, it might have succeeded.[7] The most serious omissions were in the fields of education and employment, where special facilities had been deemed essential by the committee. These omissions undoubtedly contributed to Moluccan resentment at what they saw as a disavowal of their claim to an independent republic and a repudiation of their desire to return to their country. If they did not often oppose the policy physically, they resisted it mentally. The loss of self-respect created by the discharge from military service, to which their lives had been dedicated, was aggravated by what they saw as a threat to their corporate identity. Despite a rising population, which had reached 33,000 by 1975, and dispersal to housing settlements in many parts of Holland, a sizable proportion, perhaps more than half, fearing cultural extinction, refused to integrate. Indeed, for the older generation, integration in any complete sense was impossible. Many of them still spoke little or no Dutch.

For the generation born and growing up in Holland, learning Dutch at school and becoming increasingly oriented toward Dutch society, the

---

[7] *Report of the Verweij-Jonker Committee: The Ambonese in the Netherlands.* The Hague, 1959.

problems of identity multiplied. Indoctrinated by their elders into the RMS ethos and the injustice of its overthrow, and coming to believe not only in Indonesian knavery but also in Dutch complicity and United Nations indifference, they interpreted Dutch treatment of their parents over the years as an insult and humiliation. And they became determined to avenge it. At the same time, they came to despise their parents for their obstinate loyalty to their former masters, thus widening the generation gap.

Obsession with the ideal of independence for their country, a country many of them had not been born in and few had seen, became a symbol of identification and a focus of radicalism. The dream of an Ambonese homeland, which at one point seemed to have faded, appealed with redoubled magnetism to these ardent young Moluccans. At the same time they saw that the era of the amalgamation of indigenous groups into national societies and federations, for reasons of economy, defense, or convenience, had gone out of fashion, giving way to a secessionist climate and the emergence of small independent or semi-independent nations. News of the struggles of these indigenous groups, in Spain, in Africa, and in the Pacific, was a source of inspiration to them. Familiarity with Western culture and Western political realism did little more than guide their steps toward violence.

In 1963 the guerrilla war waged by Dr. Soumokil in Ceram was finally put down, and in 1966 Soumokil was executed. In the same year, the anger this caused among the South Moluccans in Holland was manifested in the firing of the Indonesian Embassy in The Hague by twelve South Moluccan youngsters, most of them under twenty. Warnings by Manusama, who succeeded Soumokil as president-in-exile, that continued disregard of South Moluccan grievances would lead to tragic consequences were discounted or ignored, and this eventually led, in August, 1970, to the most militant action up to that time.

Suharto had succeeded Sukarno as president of Indonesia in 1965, and it was he who ordered the execution of Soumokil. When Suharto made the first Indonesian state visit to Holland in 1970, a group of young South Moluccans, demanding that Suharto confer with Manusama on the independence question, organized an armed occupation of the residence of the Indonesian ambassador at Wassenaar, a suburb of The Hague, with the intention of forcing the issue by keeping him and other residents of the house hostage. The ambassador escaped, but his wife and staff were held hostage for twenty-four hours, and a Dutch policeman on guard duty was shot dead. On the intervention of moderate South Moluccan leaders, the culprits surrendered, but pleas that the government's integration policy was putting intolerable pressure on the South Moluccan minority did not save thirty-three young representatives of it from a prison sentence.

The Moluccan leaders were not so naïve as to look to the Dutch Government for recognition of the RMS. "We are reasonable and realistic enough to understand that for the time being this is not among the political possibilities," said Manusama. What they asked for was respect and understanding for their political ambitions. But the government continued to view Moluccan unrest as having social rather than political roots, and their attitude, supported by public opinion, was uncompromising: integrate or be repatriated. The result was further outbreaks of violence.

In December, 1974, a group of demonstrators broke into and badly damaged the Peace Palace at The Hague. And then, on April 2, 1975, shortly before the twenty-fifth anniversary of the declaration of RMS, the Dutch police frustrated a plot to storm Soestdijk Palace and take Queen Juliana hostage. The plot was uncovered when two heavily armed youths were picked up in a routine traffic check.

Soon afterwards, action by Dutch police and security forces against South Moluccan residential areas in a search for weapons brought charges of racial discrimination, already a sensitive subject because of the undoubted disadvantages suffered by young South Moluccans in the employment market. Eventually, in August, 1975, after repeated warnings of catastrophe if the Dutch Government failed to open their minds to the political problem, Manusama, in an attempt to impress on the Dutch Government the seriousness of the situation, broke off the informal relations he had established with the Dutch prime minister, at the same time appealing to South Moluccans in Holland to keep calm. Then, in November, came the provocation of the queen's speech on the independence of Surinam.

CHAPTER 6

The Bullet-Catchers

S OON AFTER DAWN ON WEDNESDAY MORNING, December 3, 1975, Sergeant de Vries approached the hijacked train on foot for the fourth time and tried to contact the terrorists by megaphone. He could get no response. Not until it was fully daylight, when a police patrol car bumped along a rough track leading toward the train from Farmhouse Staal to the east, did the hijackers react, and then, at a range of several hundred meters, they fired on the car, forcing the police to withdraw. These incidents were duly reported from the command post to the management center and thence to The Hague, where van Agt ordered the suspension of attempts at establishing communication while further initiatives from the hijackers were awaited. He also vetoed the provision of radios, one of the cardinal rules being to isolate the terrorists as much as possible. Meanwhile he telephoned Manusama and invited him to come to the Ministry of Justice for talks.

It was a beautiful, crisp winter's morning, and the rays of the sun, baffled by the layers of newspaper on the carriage windows, still penetrated sufficiently to spread a warm glow. The busiest man aboard the train was biologist Hans Prins. Having made the decision the previous day to play an active role, he took the attitude, whenever the hijackers objected to the special privileges he claimed, that his job was to comfort the passengers and to take medical care of everyone, including the hijackers. Therefore, he must be allowed some freedom of movement. In adopting this role, he saw a further opportunity, that of infiltrating the hijackers themselves, isolating one from another, asking questions about their demands, and putting forward comments of his own. Perhaps because they had no single acknowledged leader, he found it was possible to involve

65

them individually in discussion, to suggest ideas to them, and to hint at a different approach. Getting them arguing among themselves had obvious dangers, especially for him personally; they might see him as a troublemaker. But if he could exert some influence on them it would be worth the risk.

One incident that morning gave him a minor psychological advantage. When the hijackers complained that the prime minister had not yet answered their demands and threatened that further killings might be necessary, he reminded them that den Uyl was in Rome; his visit had been reported in all the papers. This was apparently unknown to them, and for a time they were silent.

Vaders and Prins were sitting together in the middle of the carriage. No one but Prins was allowed to move without permission. Opposite them sat a couple in their early thirties, quite unknown to each other, thrown together by chance. The man, Bert Bierling, an economist, was married with two young children; he was known in his home town of Sappemeer, east of Groningen, as a particularly friendly and cheerful family man. The woman, Riet Overtoom, of Annen, northeast of Assen, was also married, and she too had two young children; she was on her way to Hillegom, south of Haarlem, to move her mother into an old people's home.

Those sitting near Prins noticed that his soft voice and gentle manner had a soothing effect on the hijackers. Whereas Vaders realized that he had been marked by the hijackers as an aggressive type, he saw that Prins, with a calm word here and there, even an occasional joke, handled them well. That he was walking a tightrope, however, Vaders was sure.

Prins had compiled a list of drugs needed by the hostages, and he was pressing to get it transmitted to the authorities. But the hijackers had other things on their minds.

Those hostages who were not still half-stunned by the events of yesterday were seeking the opportunity, in whispered conversations, to play some part as a group in the mediation that seemed the only way of bringing relief. Prins thought that with his list of medicines they should send an appeal to the government and to public opinion, urging that the hijackers' demands be met before there was further loss of life. There was a chorus of approval, almost if not quite unanimous, and several refinements were put forward, Laurier suggesting that the appeal ought to be addressed to the trade unions too. After some prompting by Vaders, Prins drafted and read out the following document:

APPEAL

Due to the fact that a Raterink coach was not available at the stated time of 1:30 PM on 3 December, 1975, three people have lost their lives. [It was still thought that de Groot was probably dead.] We are convinced that, in spite of the very good relationship with the young men who hold us hostage, more lives will be lost if a coach is not provided at the earliest possible moment. These boys now have nothing to lose. We appeal to the authorities to agree to the stated demands immediately. We also appeal to our families, parents, employers, trade union leaders, etc. to do all they can to persuade the government to give in. We take the view that responsibility for further loss of life rests entirely with the government. We are well treated by our captors. On behalf of all hostages . . .

Wednesday, 3 December 1975 (with general consent).

The justification for this appeal lay partly in the fact that no one protested against it. If some were dubious, others complained that it was "nothing like strong enough." Albracht, with his reservations about giving in to hijackers, did not like it, but he kept his disapproval to himself. One who was ambivalent towards it was Vaders, although he had had a hand in its compilation. He saw two points in its favor: it gave the hostages a sense of cohesion, of doing something positive together as a group, distracting their minds from purely selfish fears; and it allied them in some measure to the hijackers, drawing the two groups together. "We are not such bad people," the hostages seemed to be saying. "We are trying to understand you. We realize we can only get out of this situation together." Against this, it was an act of complicity with terrorism and would probably be interpreted as having been written under duress. How else could the authorities view it, with two dead bodies lying near the southbound track and threats of more killings to come? Vaders concluded that it was not a matter that called at the moment for deep analysis. He could see no harm in it externally, and he believed it had value inside the train.

The document was shown to the hijackers, and they approved it. They also approved what Prins had written beneath the appeal and on the reverse:

Medicines normally used by hostages, now running out: Hydergine, bronchodilatory tablets, valdispert, valium, laudanum or other constipating agent. Also needed: food, incl. milk, bread, rolls, drinking water, hot tea, oranges, apples, plastic mugs for 55 people.
Yesterday's list of seven demands.

Blankets, portophones, or mobilephones, lavatory paper, portable radio, newspapers. The refusal to provide the required coach at the set time has already claimed three lives. Help us by sending bus immediately. What is written on the reverse page must be taken seriously. The facts relating to the circumstances on the train are correct.

                                        Wednesday, 3 December 1975, 8:55 AM.

The hijackers, too, were in the throes of composition. They were preparing a further demand note, and they had selected a young Chinese passenger to deliver it to the farmhouse where the police had established their command post; he could deliver Prins's letters as well. After the delivery, he was to return to the train with the government's answer.

Prins asked to see the latest demands of the hijackers, and they showed the note to him. Its contents, as before, dismayed him.

Because our demands have not been satisfied, we have killed three people. We now repeat our demands: We want a train driver to take us to the nearest level crossing, where a coach must be waiting. We want handcuffs to manacle the passengers. We want the bus to go to Schiphol. If these demands are not satisfied by one hour after the bearer arrives at the police station, we shall kill another person.

What frightened Prins was the deadline, and he stressed to the hijackers the communication problems that must exist outside the train. The police command post, which had been identified from the train, was nearly half a mile away, and there was no direct connection with it. The police in turn would have to contact the government. The Chinese passenger might never reach the police post—he might even elect to escape. A further complication was that he spoke little or no Dutch; he was a seaman-cook with a British passport. Surely, argued Prins, it would be better to send a responsible Dutchman? Both he and Vaders volunteered to go, with the solemn promise to return. But the hijackers refused.

Prins next suggested that he should accompany the Chinese youth halfway, to control the direction he took. He himself could be controlled by a rope round his waist, or by long-range rifle fire from the train. He could then wait until the youth returned with the reply. But the hijackers feared that the police might attempt to rescue him, in which case they would have to shoot. That would almost certainly mean killing him, which was something, they said, that they wouldn't like. So the idea of someone accompanying the Chinese cook was dismissed.

Prins persisted in his attempts to get the deadline deleted; by committing themselves, he argued, the hijackers might involve themselves in another senseless killing. They must give the government more time. They started arguing amongst themselves, and he could see he had confused them. He was not surprised when they turned their wrath on him. "If there are more killings, you will be the first." Their attitude toward him shifted unpleasantly, and they did not amend the note.

Before the cook left the train, he too was threatened, by word and by gesture. "If you don't come back, we'll shoot one of the hostages." But Paul intervened. "We don't want diplomatic troubles. He has nothing to do with all this. He can stay there." Clutching the letters, the young man set off across the fields for Farmhouse Anton, arriving there at 10:30. This meant that the deadline would be 11:30.

During the morning, Manusama called at the offices of the Ministry of Justice in The Hague as requested, to be told by van Agt that he must stop the action at Wijster immediately or force would be met with force. Manusama interpreted this as an order and a threat, and he responded firmly. "It's not necessary to order me. If you heard me on TV last night, you'll know that I want to stop it. All I want is permission to go to the train. But I won't go there on your orders. And I reject the use of force."

Van Agt retreated gracefully. "I regret that I appeared to order you to go. Of course, if you are willing, you have my permission. But we can't rule out the use of force." He ordered a helicopter to take Manusama to Beilen.

The government's reaction to the latest communications from the train was predictable enough. The letter from the hostages was assumed to have been written under duress; van Agt was not going to change his policy for that. The provision of food, water, blankets, medicines, and megaphones raised no problems, and delivery of these was offered in a reply taken to the train by another police sergeant shortly before the ultimatum expired. Finding a driver, it was said, was proving difficult due to the murder of Braam the previous day. (This was a calculated piece of procrastination; there had been plenty of volunteers to drive the train.) Mention of bus, handcuffs, and radios was avoided, and the ultimatum, too, was studiously ignored.

This question-begging reply found the hijackers in an irresolute mood. The story about the train driver sounded plausible, and it offered a breathing space. Emotionally drained by their actions of the previous day, they needed time to recover. Their initial frustration at being unexpectedly stranded on the train was wearing off, and they signified that a delivery of food and medical supplies for the hostages would be acceptable. They still seem to have assumed that a bus was on the way. They did not mention the radios, and their only complaint was about the bullhorns, which they found unsatisfactory as a means of communication. This gave the government the opportunity to offer a field telephone link between the train and the command post, which the hijackers accepted. Meanwhile they allowed the 11:30 ultimatum to expire.

The government's tactics, it seemed, were succeeding, and under van Agt's direction the policy continued to be to condition the hijackers to the strongest possible feeling of dependence and to a slower tempo. It was not until 3:42 PM that lunch boxes, prepared in a Beilen restaurant, were taken to the train by the Red Cross. (They were piled on stretchers, in the hope of retrieving the bodies afterwards, but the hijackers rejected this and refused any sort of parley.) In the same way, the field telephone was not installed and operational until 4:01 PM. Meanwhile Manusama had reached Beilen by helicopter, landing on a grass square adjacent to the town hall, and his arrival at the command post at Farmhouse Anton was announced to the hijackers at 4:05. They made no comment, and he walked alone along the track to the train. But to the hijackers Manusama was a member of the Establishment, too respectful of Dutch institutions and of law and order for their liking, whose purpose could only be to try to persuade them to surrender. His intervention at this stage was unwelcome.

"Don't come another step or we shoot."

"I only want to talk to you."

"You're a courier of the Dutch Government. Go away."

"I'm not a courier—I had to ask permission to come, but I came of my own free will. I feel it necessary to talk to you. You're only harming our cause."

"Where's the bus? We demand a bus."

"A bus is out of the question." Although van Agt had told Manusama that the hijackers would not be allowed out of the country, he had not yet dared to risk an outright refusal of a bus for fear of the consequences. Manusama's remark was made on his own initiative.

"Send someone else. Not the president. We won't talk to the president."

"All right. I'll try to send someone else."

He turned away and began walking back to the command post, a slight, pathetic, yet dignified figure. Two of the hijackers chased after him. In a brief but more friendly conversation, they told him his efforts were appreciated but that they were going to stick to their plan. As mediators they asked for Reverend Samuel Metiary, a fifty-eight-year-old South Moluccan priest who lived in Assen, and his son-in-law Zeth Pessireron. They would accept no one else.

Samuel Metiary was chairman of the Badan Persatuan, and it was he who had ordered Manuputty and Tahapary to try to find out who the boys in the train were and what they wanted. Seven years earlier, alarmed at the fragmentation of his fellow exiles as an ethnic group, following the dispersal of the camps, Metiary had taken the initiative in forming the Badan Persatuan, an organization designed to preserve a sense of community among South Moluccans in Holland. Politically, too, the South Moluccans were divided, and the Badan Persatuan, in providing a focus for social unity, became a focal point for political unification as well. Through his work as a priest and preacher, Metiary was in constant touch with the young and the disaffected, and, from the central office of the Badan Persatuan in The Hague, he dispensed an influence that challenged even that of Manusama, to whom, however, he remained loyal. It had been an axiom of Martin Luther King that, if anything was to be done for the blacks in America, it would have to be through the church, and the history of other revolutionary movements supported this thesis. Whereas Manusama had promptly condemned the hijacking, Metiary had not, and the Dutch Government suspected that he sympathized with the hijackers and might be prepared to help them achieve their aims. Nevertheless he was a major figure in South Moluccan affairs, and his influence for moderation was needed.

Zeth Pessireron, thirty-eight, married to Metiary's daughter, was a second mate in the Dutch merchant marine. He was also a foreman in the Pemuda Masjarakat, the Free South Moluccan Youth movement, and as such was well-known to members of the hijack group. The incident was the sole topic of conversation in Bovensmilde, where he lived, and he decided it was his duty to accept.

Continually being posed in the train was the question, was there a bus coming or not? By the time Manusama left, taking with him the request for Metiary and Pessireron, it was almost dark, and the chance of a bus, for that day at least, seemed to have gone. The dejection of the hostages, faced with another night in the train, was extreme. Irma Martens, still worrying about missing her school test, was weeping. "Why doesn't den Uyl send the bus? Why doesn't he?"

Prins heard the hijackers talking at some length on the telephone, which had been installed at the rear of the first train-set. They too were asking about the bus. He asked them if they had received a satisfactory reply. "We haven't had *any* reply."

Prins had a suggestion to make. Believing that to transport a large number of hostages by bus to Schiphol and thence by plane to some unknown destination was unwieldy and potentially dangerous, he had canvassed the idea amongst the passengers that six of them should volunteer to go with the hijackers and provide the protection they needed. From those who volunteered, six were chosen, four men and two women, and now Prins put the proposition to Eli, who agreed.

"Let me use the telephone. I want to ask the people on the other end what they're intending to do." Rather to his surprise, Eli told him to go ahead.

Prins recognized at once what the difficulty was. After identifying himself, he found he was talking to a police sergeant who would not at first give his name. The policeman's replies were dominated by such phrases as, "The Hague says we can't do that," or, "I must contact my superiors." In charge of the command post were a police captain and a lieutenant, but contact was being deliberately kept at a low level, and Prins could get no further up the ladder of command than the sergeant.

"Where's the bus? We understand you promised a bus."

"Yes—there is a bus being prepared. But the seats are being taken out at the moment. It takes time."

"You've already had more than thirty hours. Please meet the hijackers' demands as soon as possible. The delay is extremely dangerous for the hostages. Please send the bus at once. It didn't take all this time when the Japanese hijackers asked for a bus last year."

Again the policeman's reply was buttressed by corroborative detail. "The Japanese only had to get from The Hague to Schiphol. We have to clear a two-hundred-kilometer route between here and Amsterdam and brief all the municipal police forces whose territories the bus will pass through."

"Please hurry. What about the train driver?"

"He has to come from Maastricht."

Maastricht was at the farthest extreme of the country, 250 kilometers to the south. The government was making as many difficulties as possible, and Prins put the phone down in near despair. He had wanted to speak to someone in authority, and he had failed. Presently he asked if he could speak on the telephone again. This time, after identifying himself, he asked for a direct line to the government in The Hague.

"That's not possible."

In an era when presidents could talk to astronauts on the moon, thought Prins, it was ridiculous to pretend that direct contact could not be established between a train in northern Holland and someone in authority in The Hague. "This is urgent. Lives of hostages are at stake." Quietly spoken and unassertive by nature, Prins found himself shouting into the mouthpiece. "Hold the field telephone and the ordinary phone together, and somebody at The Hague must be able to hear me."

At Beilen and at the crisis center in The Hague, this idea ran counter to their whole strategy. Any such confrontation was to be avoided at all costs. In addition to the danger of a hostage pleading for his life under the threat of having his head blown off, direct contact left no margin for the delaying, attritional policy that the government had elected to pursue. Thus Prins's suggestion was again turned down, on the pretext that it was not possible.

In the next half hour, the hijackers twice repeated their request for a bus. Eventually, through the policeman manning the phone at the command post, they got a temporizing reply. The bus was not coming, but, to soften the blow, it was stated that Manusama had gone to The Hague to report to van Agt. After consultations had taken place, a reply would follow.

Early that evening Metiary arrived at Beilen at the request of the government, and he was asked if he would talk to the hijackers from the command post. "It's far too dangerous," said van Binsbergen, "to go to the train." For Metiary, the exchange that followed proved an emotional ordeal. His sympathies lay with the hijackers' cause, but he knew in his heart that, once they had killed, they were lost. All he could do, he felt, was try to soothe them, in the hope of preventing further bloodshed. "I know it's important that you get the bus," he told them, "but the first thing you must do is allow the bodies to be removed. You can't let them lie there like that any longer."

"We didn't have the intention to kill." Metiary could only guess who was speaking, but he thought he recognized the voice of Joop Metekohy. Then the voice faltered, and he could hear crying and shouting. The boys were hysterical, and he himself was in tears. He knew these boys; they had been brought up as Christians, and he knew that fundamentally they weren't bad. He saw it as his task not to urge them to surrender, as the management center had requested, but to calm them down and rally their strength. Any other approach, he thought, would be counterproductive. "Look," he said, "what's happened has happened. You can't undo it, so let them collect the bodies. You have stated your demands, and now you must await the answers. Stay cool and calm, and use your brains. Treat your hostages humanely. And no more killings."

Then it was Pessireron's turn. "What do you want from me?"

"Come here and talk."

At the train, Pessireron saw Eli, Paul, and Kobus, all of whom he knew. "What are your plans?" he asked. "Why do you send for me? I can't help you politically." They had asked for him, they said, because they had talked to him about their problems in the past and they trusted him. But they did not trust the Dutch. "Try to understand what the Dutch Government can do and what they can't do," said Pessireron. "Don't do any more shooting, and try to be reasonable." But his pleas for moderation, and those of Metiary, were unavailing, and he was presented with fresh demands, including a new ultimatum.

1. The train driver and the bus must arrive before 10:00 AM.
2. If this is refused, a hostage will be killed at ten o'clock. If this does not have the desired effect, there will be a further killing at 11:30.

So much, it seemed, for their "plea in mitigation" that they had had no intention to kill. But even that contention could be justified. They had had no intention to kill provided the government gave way. Pessireron had no choice but to agree to deliver the ultimatum and to promise to make himself available for further talks next morning if required.

Back at the management center, Pessireron was questioned by van Binsbergen. "How do the boys look? Can you give me any names? What weapons do they have? Did you see any explosives? Are there any children on board?" To all these questions except the last, Pessireron stubbornly refused an answer. He simply assured van Binsbergen that all the children had been released at the time of the hijacking. Since the terrorists had asked for Metiary and Pessireron, the government inevitably harbored suspicions of them. "If you don't trust me," said Pessireron at length, "then I quit. I only went to the train to help save human lives. I know nothing about politics." Pessireron was one of those fortunate men whose honesty shows, and his sincerity now went some way to convincing van Binsbergen. Asked to hold himself in readiness, he agreed.

Manusama, on his way back to his high-rise flat at Capelle aan den Ijssel, near Rotterdam, called in at the crisis center at The Hague to report to van Agt as arranged. After he had described his abortive visit, he was asked, "Have you any other idea or proposal?" Manusama mentioned

Mrs. Josina Soumokil. She and her twelve-year-old son had fled to the Netherlands after the execution of her husband, and she held a special place in the hearts of South Moluccans as a symbol of their struggle for independent nationhood. "Would you accompany her?" asked van Agt. "Yes, if she is willing." So after getting Mrs. Soumokil's agreement, Manusama prepared to return to Beilen next day.

The hostages knew nothing of these developments. But they were aware from the hijackers' movements about the train that some sort of negotiations might be in progress. And the renewed threat was implicit in the hijackers' demeanor. During the day, the tension had eased, but now the atmosphere became more and more oppressive.

In his talks with the command post, Prins had been told of the impediments to producing a bus and a train driver quickly, but from these very impediments it had seemed implicit that the government was preparing to provide both. This was the impression he had been given, and he naturally passed it on to the other hostages. They still believed a bus was coming. Some of them, peeping through holes in the papered windows, even thought they saw it, parked outside the command post.

The news about the train driver was depressing, but Prins thought it ought to be possible for one of the hostages with engineering knowledge to move the train the 400 meters down to the level crossing. Brinker, keeping as low a profile as possible, was now sitting in the compartment, and Prins asked him what he thought.

"Do you think you could move it yourself?"

"Yes."

Brinker might have answered differently had he known that Prins would at once tell the hijackers. They reacted angrily. "So you can move the train after all? Well, you fooled us." One of them drew a revolver and stabbed it spitefully at Brinker's temple.

"I don't *know* that I can move it. I've seen it done and I know more or less how it works, but you pulled the emergency handle and that locks the brakes. I don't know how to free them. I can try." But the South Moluccans had changed their minds. The time to move the train was when the bus came. They now had efficient means of communication, and for the hours of darkness, at least, they felt safer where they were.

Those who felt anything but safe were the hostages acting as bullet-catchers, a duty that was kept up day and night. One of the first to be called that day was Cor Ter Veer. "Have you been out there?" asked Paul.

"No."

"Well, it's your turn."

It sounded innocent enough, but with threats and ultimatums still in the air, no one could tell what would happen to those picked out. When Ter Veer got to the passageway, however, the youthful Cornelis greeted him with a grin. The little South Moluccan tied the ropes round him so gently, smiling all the time, that Ter Veer was sure the boy recognized him from the platform incident at Assen. This seemed to be confirmed when, after standing for less than three hours, he was replaced.

The night hours were the worst for the bullet-catchers. This was the time when the marines would attack if they were coming. There were sixteen hours of darkness, and to be riddled with bullets from one's own side while immobilized in this way was an appalling thought, quite sufficient to keep the victim apprehensively awake, listening for every sound.

Called for a second tour of duty that evening was Louis Laurier. In the first twenty-four hours in the train, he had kept strictly to himself, withdrawing into his shell. But a lifelong habit of involvement with his fellows had eventually triumphed. Square, solid, and dependable, his iron-gray hair still luxuriant in middle age, he had answered the call for volunteers to go with the hijackers. Normally a pillar of common sense, he found as he stood hour after hour in the passage that his imagination played all kinds of tricks with his hearing. Several times he was sure he could hear someone scrabbling about under the train.

Most vulnerable of all, perhaps, was Brinker. The hostility of the hijackers toward him had been unmistakable. By smothering himself in a blanket in a corner seat among the passengers, he hoped to escape attention for the night. Two of the hijackers were sitting somewhere behind him, however, and he could hear them talking, mostly in Malay. Occasionally they lapsed into Dutch, and he heard them talking about shooting two hostages. He did not know it, but they were discussing the ultimatum they had recently sent. Another word that kept cropping up was "conductor." Then a phrase in Dutch reached him that filled him with fear. After their earlier bungling they were going to make a job of it. "We'll shoot him behind the ear."

He heard them get up and begin to move down the carriage, apparently looking for someone. They were pulling back blankets and shining flashlights in people's faces. First they checked along the opposite side, then they came back toward where Brinker was lying. He kept his face hidden, but inevitably they discovered him. "You. Come with us."

They took him through to the back of the train-set and sat him in the driver's seat at that end, tying his hands behind his back. His wrists were still swollen and raw from his previous vigil, and he asked if the rope could be eased a little. "That's none of our business," said one. But the other one fractionally loosened the rope.

He heard them loading a gun. Next they pointed it at him. "We're going away now to talk about what we're going to do to you."

By tomorrow, he thought, I'll be dead. I'll have to do something. With all the exit doors near him chained and padlocked and mined with explosive, the only possible means of egress was the driver's emergency hatch. This was released by a special catch that he happened to know how to operate; it had escaped the hijackers' notice. The easing of the ropes enabled him to work his hands free, and he stood up and began reaching toward the hatch.

He had forgotten he was sitting in a tip-up seat. As he took his weight off it, it flipped up behind him and hit the backrest with a metallic click.

He stood stock still. He must have been heard. But no one came to investigate, and, within another second or two, he had the hatch open. This too made a hollow click, but he wriggled through it feet first, then leapt out and ran off down the track. He struck across the fields, fell into a small canal, clambered out, and threw his waterlogged jacket off. He regretted this instantly as he saw his white shirt glowing phosphorescent in the glare of the searchlights that the police had now brought up. But if there were shots he didn't hear them, and no one followed. Eventually he reached the command post and was taken to Beilen.

The idea of escape was in the minds of many others, but only in the rear train-set was it practicable. There the passengers had been continually warned on the intercommunication system that they would be shot if they attempted to escape. But the example of the five who had slipped away the previous night without being fired at encouraged them, and the lack of surveillance on the second day fortified their nerve. That night they made up their minds to go. Another young Chinese cook, twenty-one-year-old King Seng Worker, acted as leader, and a Dutchman with military experience showed them how to stalk like tigers, keeping low and being ready to crawl on hands and knees if they were shot at. A romantic touch was added by the friendship that had developed between the cook and a twenty-one-year-old Chinese waitress named Chiang Ling. "He used to know her before," said one report, "but now he got to know her better."

All eighteen passengers remaining in the rear train-set reached Farmhouse Etten safely, and the happy ending for this group was cemented when the cook took the waitress off to her home in Martinistad.

For the thirty-one hostages in the forward train-set, there was no such relief. The hijackers, fearing that their latest ultimatum might precipitate an attack from outside, were continually on edge. They were conscious, too, that during the night hours, when they took turns to sleep, their numbers were depleted and an attempt by the hostages to overpower them might succeed. Symptomatic of their apprehensions was their treatment of the octogenarian Barger. When he asked to go to the toilet they refused; it meant that one of them had to go with him, further depleting the guard in the compartment, and they suspected a trick.

Barger was a highly literate man who in his day had been an inspiring preacher. He spoke Dutch as it should be spoken, with a mellifluous tone and quality that enchanted the Ter Veers, who were sitting nearby. "Grandpa" and "Grandma" the pair had been dubbed by the other hostages, and the hijackers, although addressing them in the same terms, had treated them with deference. Protected by their age from the hijackers' excesses, they were totally unaware of the killings and imagined that their captors were behaving "correctly." But Barger was not accustomed to having his wishes defied, and the effect was to disorient him completely. He thought he was setting out again on the journey for the christening of his granddaughter. Imagining that the train had arrived at Haren, he got up to go.

"Sit down, Grandpa," ordered Djerrit, not unkindly.

"No, no—we've got to get out. We're visiting my daughter Mia, you see. For the christening. Come on, Bé."

Pushed back into his seat, Barger now imagined he had actually arrived at his daughter's home in Haren. He began holding an animated conversation with her, even to the extent of trying to stroke her dog. Then suddenly he was back in the train again. "It's a good thing Mia brought us to the train, otherwise she'd think the car had broken down and we were stranded." The commotion unsettled the other passengers and infuriated the hijackers, who were more than ever afraid it was a deliberate diversion. They converged menacingly on the place where the Bargers were sitting. Prins was doing his best to pacify the old man, but Eli was brandishing a gun. "If *you* can't keep the old man quiet, *I* can."

The scene of Barger's hallucinations had changed again, and he was now held up at the Swiss frontier. As Eli moved forward as though to carry out his threat, Prins learned from Mrs. Barger that they had often traveled to Switzerland. Seizing on this, Prins humored the old man by pretending that they were indeed delayed at the border. At this, Barger accepted a Valium tablet, but he was still in a highly emotional state, excited and apathetic in turn.

"Let him go to the toilet," said one of the hijackers resignedly, and Barger immediately recovered his poise. "That's where it all started," he remembered triumphantly. "They refused to let me go to the toilet." A sequence that might have been hilarious had been transformed into an ugly drama by the fears of the hijackers.

By filling the space between the bench seats with suitcases, a tolerable bed was made up for the Bargers, and it was ready when the old man came back from the toilet. But he was still disoriented. "This is a funny sort of bed you've bought, Bé," he said. "The middle bit's missing." Then the tranquilizer began to work and he fell asleep.

For the next hour the carriage lapsed into an uneasy silence, through which the hostages, twisting and turning and continually pulling their blankets around them, slept fitfully. One who slept better than most was Wientje Kruyswijk, whose attitude toward the South Moluccans had been sympathetic and indeed almost motherly. Even the killings, so shocking in their unexpectedness and brutality, had not extinguished every glimmer of understanding. Two of the hijackers were sleeping on the seats behind her, another was lying between them on the floor, and she could hear their restless breathing. Once she heard one of them sobbing; then she detected a muttered prayer. They were about the same age as her own sons, and she thought of them as boys—almost, because of her memories of that half-forgotten sea voyage, *her* boys. Boys who had been naughty, and who must be punished, but who were not basically wicked or cruel.

The wan light that filtered through the papered windows from the searchlights threw eerie, grotesque shadows, and, with the boys who were on guard flitting about stealthily in their balaclavas, Wientje was conscious of a Kafkaesque quality in her environment. But now, as she stirred uncomfortably, her handbag fell to the floor, after which a blanket fell on top of it, hiding it from view. One of the South Moluccans, creeping along the aisle, stumbled over the draped handbag, and in his jumpy state he thought she had tripped him deliberately. Seizing the handbag, he drew his gun and prodded her in the stomach.

"Don't think it will save you that you're a woman."

"Don't be silly. I'm not so stupid as to make you fall. Your gun might go off and hurt somebody." And when the pressure on her stomach increased: "Don't be so childish. I tied diapers on you. Please give me back my bag."

For a moment she thought he would shoot her, and she longed to push the gun away, but daren't attempt it in case it went off. She had enraged him, but the authority with which she had spoken had been so genuinely without arrogance or animosity that he relented. The pressure on her stomach relaxed, and he returned her handbag.

"Be careful. It makes no difference that you're a woman." Yet she knew it *had* made a difference and would continue to do so.

The next passenger to be disturbed was Gerry Vaders. He was asleep when Eli came and tapped him on the shoulder. Automatically he looked at his watch. It was one o'clock. Eli was motioning him to get up. It looked like another spell of bullet-catching.

"Up front?"

"No. Halfway." That meant the zigzag passage again. This time he was tied up facing the rear of the train, staring across the entrance hall into the carriage, and a suitcase was stood on its side so he could sit down. His wrists, still red and raw from his previous bondage, were protected this time by handkerchiefs for padding, and this was a relief. But the suitcase concertinaed under his weight, and an old injury to the base of his spine made sitting worse than standing. Soon the pain was more than he could bear, and he had to stand up. Every time he did so, he was told to sit down again.

The Moluccans could hardly wait for daylight. They talked animatedly amongst themselves in Malay, then fidgeted with the ropes that bound him, their minds on their latest ultimatum. Their checks were so cursory that Vaders was able to loosen the ropes around one of his wrists without discovery. Most disconcerting was the way Eli sometimes stood in front of him, staring quizzically, saying nothing. It was as though he was trying to make a decision.

Vaders had been standing there for three hours when Eli brought him a glass of milk. It seemed like a gesture of humanity, but the remark that accompanied it held different implications. "Now is the time for prayer."

Why should Eli suggest that he pray? There was only one explanation. He was to be the next victim. That would account for Eli's peculiar behavior. He had been making up his mind.

Like Brinker earlier that evening, Vaders scoured his mind for some clue to possible escape. The chances seemed so remote as to be infinitesimal. Allowing that they had tied him up less rigorously this time and that he would be able to work his left hand free, he would then have to work on his right. When his hands were free he would have to untie his ankles. All this would have to be accomplished between the regular checks the hijackers were still making. The door behind him, through which he would have to withdraw, was secured with rope, while the outside doors beyond it were chained and booby-trapped. He had seen the cigar-shaped explosives attached to them. The only chance was to get forward to the baggage area and hope that the doors there were not locked. If he didn't get clean away, they would certainly gun him down.

They kept him standing in the passageway until eight o'clock next morning—seven hours. Throughout that time, they made such frequent checks that he never really had a chance to work himself free. Eventually fatigue overwhelmed him, and he kept lapsing into an unconsciousness that lasted no more than seconds as his legs collapsed and he fell against the walls of the passage. Then he would start calculating his chances of escape again, or preparing for death, until the next surge of sleep swept over him.

When at length they untied him, he felt unnaturally calm. The Moluccans were encircling him, but because he believed they had chosen him for execution he no longer feared them. As he moved down the carriage, they pushed him into an empty seat, but he got up again. "I want to speak to the doctor."

"No."

He continued to push forward in Prins's direction, ignoring them. When they saw he was determined to disobey them and nothing but a bullet would stop him, they fetched Prins and sat the two men down together.

"Hans, they're going to shoot me."

The hijackers did not contradict him. One of them, the tall Kobus, asked, "Don't you understand why?"

"No, I *don't* understand."

"These people outside still think we're not serious."

As Vaders leaned across to whisper to Prins, the hijackers pressed in closer. They weren't going to have some plot hatched under their noses.

"Let me talk to the doctor in private."

"No. We will listen."

Vaders lowered his voice. "If you get out of this alive, Hans, try to see my wife, will you?"

"Of course."

"We have two daughters of our own and a stepdaughter. Her father and mother—my sister—died within days of each other when she was twelve. She's become one of the family. Now she'll be fatherless again. I think that troubles me more than anything. My wife will be left alone to face the problems we faced together. My hope is that she'll get a new purpose in life through concentrating on that child."

There were other things, too, of which Vaders spoke, intensely personal things, mistakes in human relations, admissions of failure. Resigned to death, he was no longer afraid to expose his human flaws. And, as he spoke, the mood of the hijackers changed from impatience to embarrassment, and one by one they turned away.

"Look, forget it." They motioned the two men back to their original seats. Then they remembered that they still had to find a victim. As Vaders stood up, one of the Moluccans said quietly, "There's someone else who comes before you. Isn't that so, doctor?"

In that moment of heart-searching, Vaders had changed in the hijackers' eyes from an object to a human being. Yet the thought that he might escape at the expense of Hans Prins sickened him. He wanted to say no, let me go in his place, but the words wouldn't come.

Having already been told that he would be the first, Prins too had had time to think about it. If I'm called out, and I think I'm going to be shot, he resolved, I'll kick at one of the outside doors and detonate the explosive as I go. He reckoned it would cost him a leg or a foot, but he'd blow up one or more of the hijackers too.

CHAPTER 7

"We'll Get Through This Together"

ALTHOUGH THE HIJACKERS had seen their stay in the train as merely transitional and lacking the glamor of a skyjack, the actuality was different. The seizure of the train was having a worldwide impact, not only because of its novelty. South Moluccans in Holland? Who were they, and what were they doing there? Why had they hijacked a train?

The yellow train, standing idle under its overhead cables, arrested in a flat, mist-laden landscape, with no one daring to approach it, had caught the imagination of newspaper readers and fascinated millions by its twice-nightly appearances on TV. The inanimate train, favorite setting for so many stories of murder, espionage, and intrigue, stood firmly anchored in Holland's backyard, visible but untouchable, infinitely more atmospheric than any hijacked plane.

The first move of the hijackers on that Thursday morning was to ask for another talk with Pessireron, and although travel arrangements had already been made for Manusama and Mrs. Soumokil, the request was granted. Meanwhile they mooched to and fro, guns at the ready. The hostages, cold, hungry, dirty, and afraid, sensed that this might be the decisive day. At the management and crisis centers, delivery of the fresh ultimatum the previous evening had kept the tension proportionately high. They had also had to contend with telephoned warnings of terrorist action against government establishments and property, and, wherever possible, reinforcements of security forces had been drafted in.

Mrs. Soumokil had invited two other prominent South Moluccans to accompany her in addition to Manusama—Mr. Theodoor Kuhuwael and Dr. J.J. de Lima. Theodoor Kuhuwael was a civil servant in the Ministry of Education who also held the appointment of minister of education in

Manusama's cabinet. He was a campaigner for bicultural education for all South Moluccan children, and most of the hijackers had once been his pupils in the school at Westerbork camp. Dr. de Lima, formerly the medical officer in charge of one of the camps, was now a medical adviser and psychiatrist in the South Moluccan section of the Department of Culture, Recreation, and Social Work. When they got to the command post that morning, however, they learned that the hijackers were refusing to have any contact with them. If they approached the train, another hostage would be killed. It was Pessireron they wanted. Still hoping to influence events in some way, the party remained at the farmhouse with the idea of trying again later.

Before going to the train, Pessireron was called to the management center for a briefing by the attorney general. He was asked to limit the discussion as far as possible to the problem of ending the hijacking, and to call for restraint in the meantime. "Ask them to end their action and surrender like soldiers," urged van Binsbergen. "I'll do my best," said Pessireron. He boarded the train at 9:25 AM and stayed for fifty minutes, during which the ten o'clock ultimatum expired.

Far from being able to limit the discussion, Pessireron was presented with yet another ultimatum and an open letter to the Dutch people, one of the documents the hijackers had intended to issue from the plane.

APPEAL TO THE DUTCH PEOPLE

People of the Netherlands, we hope this letter will make you wake up and face the injustice that your government has so far done to us, South Moluccans.

This act, committed by us, must not be regarded as an act of revenge, but as one crying for justice. The reason why we hold ordinary citizens to ransom is because they have failed to oppose their government which, since twenty-five years ago, has wronged us.

Also to show that what happens here can happen every day in the South Moluccan Islands, to our people when they voice their protest to the Indonesian Government. And also because the Dutch people remained silent when on 25 November 1975, Queen Juliana said that every nation has a right to independence, which we have been striving for, for a quarter of a century.

For twenty-five years we have fought a nonviolent battle for our independence, but to no avail. The blame lies with the imperialistic Indonesian Government and also with the Netherlands Government, who have deliberately blocked all roads to a peaceful settlement. In other words: the Indonesian and Dutch Governments have forced us to this act by their unjust policies.

Your government has given many promises during the past twenty-five years, but has never stood by them. The South Moluccan Republic was proclaimed on 25 April 1950. This was the will of the people, carried out lawfully. The South Moluccan Islands have some 3.5 million inhabitants; our people live there in miserable conditions. To give an example: many of our people are thrown into prison or concentration camps without any form of trial, and are then labeled communists. We know from reliable sources that they are being tortured.

We do not understand why you, who organize protest marches when there is injustice somewhere else, do nothing for us who have been wronged by your own government and the Indonesian Government over the past twenty-five years.

If you are unaware of your government's wrongdoing, it is because they have failed to inform you and have constantly put our fight for freedom in a false light. You will understand us better after the television broadcast in which our leaders will elaborate on these matters.

People of the Netherlands, we hope that you will make your government repent, so that justice may prevail. People of the Netherlands, we are not murderers; but in order to fight for the future of our people and the independence of our country we are willing to kill again, and also to die.

> Free Young South Moluccans
> *Mena Muria*

This open letter, in the form of a prepared stencil, was to be relayed immediately to the media, for publication by 11:45 that morning, and the hope was expressed that the Dutch people, on seeing the letter, would bring immediate pressure to bear on the government.

Other demands made by the hijackers were:

1. The bus, and a train driver, must be made available simultaneously with the publication of the appeal.
2. Pessireron must report back on their demands by 11:45 AM.
3. Expiry of the ultimatum would be postponed until 12:00 noon.

Pessireron left the train at 10:15 AM.

The tension in the train became almost palpable as news of the latest ultimatum and of the refusal to negotiate with Manusama filtered through. The nerves of the hijackers tautened still further as the minutes passed, and the only relief came from the occasional sick joke essayed by the hostages. "Do you mind if I keep the same shirt on today?" "Shall we take the decorations down?" There was a stream of jokes about Netherlands Railways. "The timetable's all wrong. I shall lodge a complaint." When one of them spilt milk on his trousers he told the others it didn't matter. "This will come out at the cleaners. You're all right as long as they're not blood stains."

Most of the hostages believed that at least four of their number had been murdered—the driver, de Groot, Bulter, and now Brinker, who had mysteriously disappeared in the night. The hijackers felt it was to their advantage not to disabuse them, and indeed Djerrit, questioned by Timmer, confirmed it.

Timmer was sitting at one end of the carriage with two of the older women passengers, Mrs. Jansen, the long suffering asthmatic who was known to the hostages as "Aunt Jo," and the complaining Mrs. Bakker. That morning Mrs. Jansen had a distressing attack, and Timmer called Prins over to examine her. Prins told the hijackers that they must let her go. "You'd better send for a stretcher for her. You must get her off the train quickly, or she will die."

Despite their changed attitude toward him, underlined when they refused to allow him to send for a first-aid kit, Prins was still the closest of the hostages to the hijackers in that he knew most about their plans. When they accepted his diagnosis and called the command post for a stretcher, he wondered if their resolve to kill again at midday might weaken. Would there be another postponement? Last evening and again this morning, they had threatened to kill but had not done so. He soon had his answer.

"You, doctor." It was Eli addressing him. "If our demands are not met, you will be the next victim."

Prins felt his heartbeat quicken and the blood rush to his head. They had told him before that he was next on the list. Now he knew, from Eli's expression, that they had meant what they said.

The stand Prins had taken in the train so far would have surprised his friends. They had not seen him as a man of dominant personality, capable of controlling events. Yet that was what he had consciously set out to do. His influence had been all the stronger because of his quiet, reticent manner, and it was an influence the hijackers feared and resented. Now Prins felt his pores itch with the sweat of fear. Earlier that morning he had seen Timmer praying, and he sought him out.

Throughout the hijacking so far, Timmer had preserved an outward calm, helped, Prins assumed, by his religious beliefs. These beliefs, Prins hoped, might give Timmer some sort of status with the hijackers. Timmer's whole training and his experience of psychological traumas in others had in fact contributed to his composure at least as much as his religious beliefs. But he had been one of the six volunteers chosen to accompany the hijackers, and Prins sensed he would be ready to help again.

"I've heard from Eli that I am to be the fifth victim."

"I don't believe they will shoot *you.* You're the one person who can help everyone, them as well as us."

"No, they mean it. You are a man of faith, Walter, and the South Moluccans are religious too. You must speak to them. Otherwise at twelve o'clock they will shoot me."

Living in Assen and immersed in social work, Timmer knew something of the political background. He had made friends among the South Moluccans at school, and he had a smattering of their language. But the approach he now made to Eli was repulsed.

"Let me use the telephone. Let me speak to them." At length Eli nodded, and Timmer began, "This is one of the hostages, Walter Timmer. The situation here is explosive. We must have the bus soon. Otherwise one of us will be shot. And we must have the handcuffs. Please grant the hijackers demands now."

The voice at the other end was sceptical, the owner suspecting that this was another ruse of the hijackers. "I don't believe that. Who are you?"

"This is Walter Timmer, of Assen. One of the hostages."

"Mr. Timmer, you must be patient. You must wait calmly. I can't help you."

No one had waited more calmly than Timmer, but now he flared up. "What kind of man are you?"

"I'm a policeman."

"Oh, a policeman. . . ." There was despair in Timmer's voice as he realized for the first time that he was not speaking to someone in authority. "As far as I'm concerned you're not human. In one or two hours, another person will be shot. The hijackers are furious at the vague treatment of their request for a bus. What is the delay? We *must* have the bus."

The hopelessness of trying to negotiate at this level led Timmer to suggest two possible mediators, both Dutchmen, men who he felt would consider the plight of the hostages sympathetically, men on whose judgement he knew he could rely. One was a member of parliament, the other an Assen priest. The policeman took their names and promised to refer them to the management center, and despite Timmer's misgivings the request was immediately passed to The Hague. At 10:58 AM, the command post asked the hijackers if they wished to contact the men Timmer had named. At 11:03, they gave their answer: we stick to our demands as given to Pessireron.

Meanwhile Pessireron, who had left the train at 10:15, was being treated with rather less dispatch. He was kept waiting for three-quarters of an hour at Beilen town hall while Timmer's suggestion was being investigated. When delivery of the appeal and the latest ultimatum was eventually accepted, both documents were referred to The Hague.

Van Agt's method, at the daily ministerial conferences that were taking place at the crisis center, was to begin by giving a general survey of events, so as to bring everyone up to date, then ask the assembled ministers for their contributions one by one, ending with the prime minister. He never started with a statement of his own opinion. He then summed up what had been said, a process for which he had a gift, added his own comments, and proposed a course of action. This personal contact between ministers, it was found, was infinitely better than individual soundings by telephone. Van Agt was a good listener, and, under his astute chairmanship, meetings invariably reached a unanimous decision. But full ministerial conferences generally took place in the afternoon, and much therefore depended on the personal relationship of the two ministers principally concerned, Minister for Internal Affairs de Gaay Fortman and van Agt himself. Fortunately these two, although of different religious convictions, had much in common academically and liked and respected each other. One or the other of them was generally present at the crisis center. In the absence of van Agt, the State Secretary for Justice, a tall, well-built civil servant with an air of imperturbability named Henk Zeevalking acted as deputy.

Soon after reaching his office on that Thursday morning, van Agt was confronted by news of the hijackers' appeal and of the postponed ultimatum. This was the third such postponement, throwing serious doubt on the resolve of the terrorists to carry out their threats. On the first day there were to have been further killings at 5:00 PM, but the deadline had been allowed to pass. On the second day, when they released the Chinese cook, they had sent a fresh ultimatum for 11:30 AM. If their demands were not met by that time, they said, another hostage would be shot. That ultimatum, too, had expired peacefully. The third deadline, delivered to the management center by Pessireron on the second evening, had been for ten o'clock this morning, and they had now extended it until noon.

The open letter to the Dutch people represented a marked change of approach by the hijackers, more reasoned, less hysterical. Van Agt's policy, once the initial heat of the action had cooled, was to grant requests from the train only on the basis of some sort of quid pro quo. He had no great objection to publishing the appeal, provided he could extract something worthwhile in exchange. And if a deal could be done over the appeal, demands for a bus and a plane might dissolve, threats of further killings might cease, and the way might be open for Manusama and his group to work toward a surrender.

This was the view from a distance. But at Beilen, where they were faced by an anxious, entreating Pessireron, they were not so sanguine. "I'm sure if you don't react now," said Pessireron, "they will kill someone else. They mean it this time." A suggestion put forward from Beilen that the attorney general talk on the field telephone to one of the hostages in an effort to establish the true position was rejected at the crisis center, where van Agt was convinced that the pressures on the hostages must be such that they would not be free to speak their minds and would have to toe the hijackers' line. "Go back to the train," was the message that eventually reached Pessireron, "and tell them, first, that there will be no bus, and, second, that we are not going to publish their statement until the bodies are allowed to be removed and the old and the sick and the children have been released." This was the quid pro quo sought by van Agt.

"There are no children," said Pessireron.

"Very well, then. The aged and the sick."

At 11:37 the hijackers were told that Pessireron was on his way back to the command post with the government's reply. The news only heightened the tension. Hijackers and hostages alike had become more and more pessimistic about the outcome, and the atmosphere was leaden with fear.

The hijackers were pulling on their balaclavas again. They were hiding their individual indentity—not only, Vaders guessed, from the hostages but also from each other and even, if it were possible, from themselves. In their hideous anonymity, they looked skull-like and cadaverous. The disguise, as the hostages recognized, must presage some terrible act. Something had to be done to divert them from their purpose, and Timmer decided to try reading a passage of scripture. Borrowing a Bible from Cor, he turned to St. Paul's First Epistle to the Corinthians, Chapter 13:

> Though I speak with the tongues of men and of angels, and have not charity, I am become as sounding brass, or a tinkling cymbal.
>
> And though I have the gift of prophecy, and understand all mysteries, and all knowledge; and though I have all faith, so that I could remove mountains, and have not charity, I am nothing. . . .

Charity suffereth long, and is kind; charity envieth not; charity vaunteth not itself, is not puffed up.

Doth not behave itself unseemly, seeketh not her own, is not easily provoked, thinketh no evil;

Rejoiceth not in iniquity, but rejoiceth in the truth;

Beareth all things, believeth all things, hopeth all things, endureth all things. . . .

The bespectacled Timmer, powerfully built and standing over six feet in height, caressed the words with a gentleness that moved some of his listeners to tears.

When I was a child, I spake as a child, I understood as a child, I thought as a child; but when I became a man, I put away childish things.

For now we see through a glass, darkly; but then face to face: now I know in part; but then I shall know even as also I am known.

And now abideth faith, hope, charity, these three; but the greatest of these is charity.

When he had finished, Eli said, "You, priest, pray for a good solution."

Timmer had found a role. Just as the hijackers had taken Prins for a doctor, so they now took Timmer for a priest. Timmer, too, decided against disabusing them. The presence of someone who they thought was a priest must surely have a moderating influence. "Lord," he intoned, "we are all sinners. None of us deserves grace. Let us pray that He will bring us all home safely, passengers and hijackers alike."

Timmer had barely finished when a call came through from the command post. Pessireron had returned from Beilen with the government's reply. He was not invited to the train. "There is no bus," he told them, "and I can't broadcast the appeal until the dead bodies have been removed and the aged and sick passengers have been released." The hijackers said they would ring back. The time was 11:52—eight minutes short of the deadline. Exhausted by his own impatience at being kept waiting and his anxiety to be back in time, Pessireron knew that the crisis had come.

Once again the ultimatum was allowed to expire without violence. But when, after an agonizing lapse of twenty minutes, a reply came from the train, it was uncompromising. The request for a bus and a train driver and for the publication of the appeal, without strings, stood. Failing immediate agreement to these demands, another hostage would be executed.

"Try to be reasonable," urged Pessireron. "Previous killings have achieved nothing. Further killings are pointless." But the hijackers sensed that their credibility would be destroyed if they failed to act this time, and they insisted that they would kill another hostage as threatened. "We won't—we can't—give up now." Finally Pessireron pleaded with them. "Relent your ultimatum. Postpone it until five o'clock, to give the government time to reconsider."

"No. They don't want to listen, so we must kill one more." Then, before he could pass this intelligence back to Beilen, they hung up on him. All his efforts, like the prayers of Walter Timmer, threatened to prove in vain.

The time had come for selecting a victim. After further discussions amongst themselves, the hijackers moved down the gangway and stopped at Hans Prins. They had not come to seize him. They were enlisting his help. They had thought of a solution. They were going to take the seventy-two-year-old Joanna Jansen, "Aunt Jo," the woman who had had the asthma attack. Prins had said she would die if they didn't get her off the train, and a stretcher had been delivered for her. But, very probably, she was going to die anyway. Surely no great harm would be done by precipitating her end. Paul even thought she might die of her own accord. "Then we can pretend we executed her."

It was another example of the muddled humanity that kept breaking through the hijackers' posture as terrorists. First, having shot Hans Braam unintentionally, they had used his body to avoid a second shooting. Then, although they thought they had killed de Groot, they had deliberately given him a sporting chance. There had followed the ghastly bungling of the shooting of Bulter, where again the cause may have been a latent instinct of decency, upsetting them sufficiently to spoil their aim. Now they had chosen someone who they thought was going to die anyway.

"We'll take *her,*" Paul was saying, pointing forward. "We'll free her from her suffering." His tone was in no way cynical. "Will you come and help us persuade her?"

As they moved away from him, Prins followed. The idea was monstrous. Yet it had a certain horrifying logic, offering a cowardly solution to them all. He for one couldn't stomach it. "You couldn't do that, Paul, could you?" And there were other voices raised in protest, Timmer's among them. "You can't do that. An elderly lady. . . ."

Those who protested were well aware of the possible consequences. A reprieve for Aunt Jo might mean death for them.

Unaware of her danger, Mrs. Jansen went with the hijackers willingly enough. "Thank you for letting me out," she said. She thought an ambulance had come for her. But when she reached the front of the train, the hijackers asked her if she would agree to have them help her out of her pain. Her reaction was predictably vehement. Whatever her afflictions, her strength was immediately restored.

Not all the hijackers had agreed to this third shooting. Joop Metekohy had refused to have any part in it, and Kobus Tuny had said, "No women." The other Moluccans eventually found they had no stomach for shooting a frail and frightened old lady, and, after soothing her by pretending that the expected ambulance hadn't arrived, they led her back to her seat.

Eli's determination to carry out their threat, however, remained unshaken. After settling Mrs. Jansen back in her seat, the Moluccans passed on down the carriage almost to the end, scanning the passengers' faces as they went. Everyone averted their gaze. When they finally stopped they were opposite the Ter Veers and the soldier Thys Stevens on one side, and Laurier, Wientje Kruyswijk, and Piet Gruppelaar, a 37-year-old administrator from Oude-Pekela, twenty miles east-south-east of Groningen on the other. The man they selected, quite arbitrarily it seemed, was Louis Laurier. "You. Come with us."

Sitting toward the rear of the compartment, Laurier had been unaware of the incident with Mrs. Jansen, and he thought at first he was due for another spell of bullet-catching. He soon realized otherwise. The balaclavas so aptly fitted the role of executioner. "I have lived for fifty-three years," he thought, "but this is the end." As he stood up to accompany them, one of them intervened. "No. You must not have *him.*" Laurier had no idea to what he owed his salvation.

They returned toward the front of the compartment, stopping eventually beside Vaders. Prins was elsewhere, consoling Mrs. Jansen, and it seemed that Vaders was to be chosen after all. Then one of them pointed. "You. Come with us."

"*Me?*"

Shock, astonishment, incredulity—all these emotions and many more were written on the face of the man thus addressed. He stabbed his chest with his index finger, not once but twice. "Me?"

Vaders, the man so recently under threat, was sitting on the opposite seat. But the finger was not pointing at *him.* There could be no mistake. It was the thirty-three-year-old economist, Bert Bierling.

Bierling had revealed himself as a gentle, understanding person, exceptionally calm and indeed almost aloof, in no way aggressive, and presenting no danger to the hijackers. But he had decided at an early stage not to be intimidated, and this gave him, in the eyes of the hijackers, a slightly unconcerned, even offhand demeanor, suggesting that he was hardly taking them seriously. This may have annoyed them. Yet in the context of the repeated threats to Vaders and Prins, his selection now was stupefying.

Other than this, the hijackers had nothing whatever against Bierling. In that moment, as they went through the carriage, he had been the one person who had refused to adopt a submissive posture. Like de Groot before him, he had looked at them, daring to meet their gaze, and for that he had been chosen to die.

Pale and shaken, but without complaint or appeal, Bierling got to his feet. He knew what was coming, and he was visibly afraid. But he scorned to acknowledge it to the hijackers.

There was still just a chance that they were bluffing, that they only intended to frighten him, that he was in for a spell as a shield. That would mean he would be standing for the next four hours. "May I go to the toilet?"

They took him to the lavatory under guard, and when he came back, they bound his wrists with rope. Then they led him forward. As they went, one of the hijackers was crying and wringing his hands. *"What are we doing?"*

At the forward luggage compartment, Bierling was ordered to kneel in the doorway. Before doing so, he asked the hijackers to take off his wedding ring. "Please give this to my wife."

Djerrit took the ring off Bierling's finger and went back into the carriage with thoughtless alacrity, giving the ring to Riet Overtoom, whom he imagined was Bierling's wife. At a distance of 800 meters, at Farmhouse Staal east of the train, police, military, and an opportunist photographer saw the door open and a figure appear in the gap.

The hijacker with the gun drew back. It was Paul. "I can't do it. I can't do it."

"You must. It's the only way to convince them. What else can we do?"

When the shot came, it was paralyzing in its abruptness. It was Eli who fired it. Felt vicariously by every hostage, it was a hundred times louder than they anticipated. Yet in their horror and panic, their thoughts even now were introverted. Who would be next? If Bert Bierling could be taken, no one was safe.

In that final moment, Bierling had been more fortunate than the soldier Leo Bulter had been. He died instantly, falling forward onto the northbound track.

The doors of the luggage compartment slammed shut, and as the hijackers returned, one by one, to the compartment, the hostages dared not look up. There was one exception, Riet Overtoom, and her face, tilted upwards, was overflowing with grief. Deathly pale, she was weeping, and Vaders, trying to soothe her, was holding her hand. Then Prins took her in his arms. "Try not to think about it," he said. One of the hijackers asked, with unbearable gentleness, "Was he your husband?" Vaders, seeing that she was incapable of speech, answered for her. "No. They were just good friends." She had only known Bierling for two days, but, in that short but crowded period, they had become attached to each other. It was an attachment of extraordinary depth, quite outside the normal range of human contact, one she would never forget.

Aware that many of the hostages were still closing their minds to what had happened, Vaders decided that they must face up to the killings. Staying silent would only make it easier for them to be picked off one by one.

"Let us have a moment of silence for those who have fallen," he said. "The train driver. The soldier, Leo Bulter. Mr. de Groot. And Bert Bierling." For some, this simple statement was the first time the full truth had penetrated.

Paul came back into the compartment in obvious distress and sought out Wientje Kruyswijk. "I couldn't do it," he told her, "I just couldn't, but then I thought, dammit, I've got to." He caught Riet Overtoom's reproachful glance. "You look like you hate us." It was some time before she could answer. "I just feel very sad." Paul, it seemed, would have liked to console her, but he could not find the words to do it. Instead he stroked her hair. It was Vaders who spoke. "That was pointless. If den Uyl won't give in for three or four deaths, he won't give in for six or nine." Paul shrugged his shoulders. "Whose fault is that?"

Eli was talking on the telephone in Malaysian, telling Pessireron of the killing. Would the government, perhaps, believe now that they weren't bluffing? He repeated the demands for a bus and an aircraft, and for publication of the appeal. He also registered some additional demands, chief of which was a request for food, to be delivered to the train by 3:00 PM. Finally, Pessireron must come to the train at 5:00 PM to hear their further demands.

In the farmhouse, Pessireron went to the lavatory and was sick. Then he asked to be driven back to the town hall. "Is that what you wanted?" he demanded of van Binsbergen. "Now someone else has been killed. If you'd let me read the appeal, it wouldn't have happened." His outburst was understood and forgiven. No one was more dismayed at the outcome than the hierarchy at the management center.

Prins, conscious of a personal reprieve, felt that there had been a subtle change in the balance of power in the train. Not all the hijackers, he believed, had been convinced of the necessity for the latest killing, whereas the hostages were drawing together. If they presented a united front they might achieve a moral ascendancy. Earlier he had led the way in supporting the hijackers' demands. Now he put them at the receiving end of an ultimatum. "If you shoot down anyone else, then the promises we have made to support your claims are no longer valid."

Just as the hostages, in self-defense, had needed to seek an affiliation with the hijackers and to gain their good opinion, so the hijackers, in their isolation, now needed the understanding of the hostages. Eli asked Timmer: "Who is guilty of the death of Mr. Bierling?"

"That's a difficult question. I don't know the answer. I believe that our side cannot understand you, but you cannot understand us." This acknowledgement of shared guilt satisfied Eli, the only one of the hijackers who had been able to fire at Bierling. He asked Timmer to read again from the Bible. "Will you ask for forgiveness for us all?" And when Timmer nodded, he said, "Psalm 25. Read it aloud to all the people."

As Timmer began reading, the South Moluccans joined in, fervently accentuating the verses that seemed relevant to them.

Unto thee, O Lord, do I lift up my soul.
O my God, I trust in thee,
Let me not be shamed;
Let not mine enemies triumph over me. . . .
For thy name's sake, O Lord,
Pardon mine iniquity, for it is great. . . .
Turn thee unto me, and have mercy upon me;
For I am desolate and afflicted.
The troubles of my heart are enlarged:
Oh bring thou me out of my distresses.
Look upon mine affliction and my pain;
And forgive all my sins.
Consider mine enemies, for they are many;
And they hate me with cruel hatred.
O keep my soul, and deliver me:
Let me not be shamed; for I put my trust in thee.
Let integrity and uprightness preserve me;
For I wait on thee.
Redeem Israel, O God,
Out of all his troubles.

During the reading, some of the South Moluccans fell to their knees. Paul remained standing at first, but Prins gently pushed him down. By the time Timmer reached the last few verses, all but one of the hijackers were crying. With soft but ardent voices, they joined in the final supplication.

Paul was so affected that he sat down next to Prins to be comforted, then climbed on his lap. Prins nursed him as he would a child. "We'll get through this together."

Kobus and Djerrit were talking of suicide and of giving God an account of their stewardship. They were actually knotting ropes with which to hang themselves. Timmer talked to them as he would to his own sons. "You mustn't throw away your lives. Please don't do it."

Fears of the "antiterror brigade," which the hijackers repeatedly referred to, now became an obsession. But the attitude toward the passengers had changed. Paul, who still saw martyrdom as a consummation, told them, "If we have to, we will fight to the death in this train. The victory will be ours. But if we can, we will go outside the train to meet them. We don't want the passengers to be killed in the struggle. There will be no more sentry duty. If shooting starts, lie down on the floor and keep out of the line of fire." This was a complete reversal of the orders issued so far. "We may have to carry out more executions, but we ask for your understanding."

This last sentence, astonishingly, provoked no dissent. The hostages simply avoided thinking about it, as they had avoided thinking about the previous executions. Hijackers and hostages were now united by a common fear of death. Destinies were interwoven, the sense of abandonment shared.

The shooting of Bierling had precipitated an emotional peak. Trapped together in time and space, murderer and potential victim moved closer to each other in mutual self-preservation. Prins's remark, "We'll get through this together," spoke for them all.

Another thing that united the two groups was a cynical suspicion of the good faith of the government, which seemed as indifferent to the plight of the hostages as to the indignation of the hijackers. Men like Vaders were in no doubt of the liberal, compassionate stance of the government toward oppressed peoples in other countries; their inhumanity, it seemed, was reserved for the less fortunate in their own.

The hostages felt they were standing proxy for the whole Dutch nation. It was not feasible to hijack a state, so they had been hijacked as representatives of it. Yet the government was playing a kind of Russian roulette with their lives. Captor and captive cursed the government in unison.

This reaction was not entirely unwelcome to the government, nor was it unexpected. Their psychiatric advisers had predicted it. The policy remained to condition the hijackers to a growing dependence on the authorities. When they asked for something, an excuse for delay, the breakdown of transport or equipment, could always be found. When deliveries were eventually made, they were often restricted to half what was requested. Kept just above subsistence level, they were denied any chance of making themselves comfortable. All the time the appearance of cooperation was maintained, since the sins of the government were apt to be visited on the hostages. It was a precarious process, but as long as the right balance was achieved, the effect was to isolate both groups and drive them together.

Responsibility for the death of Bierling was laid firmly at the door of the government by both hostages and hijackers. The tactics of the crisis center in making counterdemands that morning, pushing the hijackers into a corner, were seen by the hostages as tragically misguided. Had they agreed to publish the appeal without delay, Bierling's life would almost certainly have been saved.

Solidarity between the groups was further demonstrated at 1:06 PM, twenty-one minutes after the death of Bierling, when Laurier was allowed to use the field telephone. Addressing himself through the command post to a leading trade unionist and a well-known press agency, he pleaded for pressure to be put on the government by all trade unionists to have the hijackers' demands met. Because this would have conflicted with official strategy, his plea was suppressed by van Agt; but the food that had been requested was deposited near the train during the afternoon.

It was some time before the hijackers satisfied themselves that the delivery of food was not a trap. Their fears that the killing of Bierling might precipitate an attack made them doubly cautious, and indeed these fears were justified. In standing firm that morning, refusing to be panicked and insisting on making counterdemands, van Agt had miscalculated. But he had had the support of his colleagues. The killing of Bierling was a tragic setback, forcing him to rethink his policy, yet to weaken over the bus and the plane would be to invite a succession of similar outrages, each one demanding more than the last. Storming the train seemed to be the only solution.

In their ultimatum, the hijackers had threatened a further killing if the latest one did not have the desired effect. Warned by his military advisers that even the most carefully selective attack might cause up to 30 percent casualties among the hostages, van Agt decided to give the resolve of the hijackers one more test. Meanwhile, plans for the exercising of the military option would be finalized. From their methods of surveillence, the government had evidence that the hijackers were as shocked as anyone by what they had done, but it was agreed that, if there was one more killing, an assault would have to be mounted on the train.

In the face of Bierling's killing, van Agt agreed to one concession: the release without conditions of the hijackers' appeal to the Dutch people. Publication was announced to the train by Zeth Pessireron in a telephone call from the farmhouse at the agreed time of 5:00 PM. "I want to come and see you," he told them, and they agreed.

His arrival at the train set off an emotional scene. At least one of the hijackers was crying, and he was crying himself. "We did it together," they protested, in answer to his unspoken question. "Before we killed Mr. Bierling, we prayed. But there was no other way."

"If you don't get what you're asking for, do you intend to kill again?"

"It depends."

"You can't pull the trigger any more," said Pessireron. "If they don't agree, you'll finish up by killing everyone in the train. If you're going to pull the trigger again, pull it now, on me."

While two of the hijackers stood guard on the hostages, one at either end of the carriage, the remainder discussed the situation with Pessireron, and this time he stayed for over an hour. The hostages had learned to recognize the signs that negotiations were in progress, although they could see nothing of them, and this gave them hope. When Pessireron finally left the train, he took with him a long and involved memorandum of explanation of the hijackers' conduct, together with the most elaborate demands issued so far.

DEMANDS

1. The Dutch Government must admit on television that it has done great injustice to the South Moluccan people and that they have neglected the agreements they made at the Round Table Conference and that it has trampled on what was agreed.
2. The Dutch Government must admit or allow direct television broadcasts by the chairman of the Badan Persatuan and/or the council of the Pemuda Masjarakat (Free South Moluccan Youth).
3. The Dutch Government must allow a press conference for the Badan Persatuan and/or the Pemuda Masjarakat.
4. The Dutch Government must organize a confrontation between the Badan Persatuan and the Indonesian Government under the mediation

of a United Nations Commission. There must also be a delegate of the Dutch Government present.

5. The Dutch Government must take measures to ensure that our rightful RMS cause is brought forward in the United Nations, and, in case there are any obligations ensuing for the Dutch Government, they must adhere to these.

6. The Dutch Government must make our demands and motivations known to the Dutch population and also pass a message to them printed in all the dailies and weeklies, without leaving out any words or sentences and be reported verbatim in the newspapers.

7. We request police and/or the so-called antiterror brigade to keep out of our field of view. It could be fatal for our hostages if they fail to do so.

> Free South Moluccan Youth,
> *Mena Muria.*

A separate demand note called for an immediate amnesty for all South Moluccans sentenced in previous years for various acts of violence, arson, armed robbery, assault, smuggling of firearms, and attempts at hijacking, the motivation in all cases, it was emphasized, having been the fight for independence forced upon them by the negative attitude of the Dutch and Indonesian Governments. The memorandum of explanation sought to justify the hijacking of the train and the taking of hostages. "We are sad and regret that the Netherlands Government by acting negatively toward our cause has left us nothing else but this form of protest." "Taking hostages . . . is permitted according to the rights of peoples if it serves the purpose of preventing acts of injustice." "If any blood of the hostages flows then the Indonesian and also the Dutch Governments are responsible."[8]

The change of emphasis, in which provision of a bus and a plane took second place to self-justification and the extraction of political concessions, seemed more hopeful and appeared to offer a breathing space, especially as no timed ultimatum was stated. But since political concessions were an issue on which the government had decided there was no room for maneuver, the situation of the hostages looked no less precarious. Pessireron, however, believed that his protests to the boys had hit home. Back at Beilen town hall, he was asked by the 100 or more reporters gathered there from all over the world, and by relatives of the hostages, who had concentrated in the local Prakken Hotel, what the next move was likely to be. "In my

---

[8]*Motives of the South Moluccan Fighters* (See Appendix C).

opinion," he told them, "there will be no more killings."

If the atmosphere in the train seemed less tense, it was partly through emotional exhaustion. The hostages found that, for peace of mind, it was still best to try to shield themselves from reality. Even thinking about home, husbands, wives, children, or sweethearts was emotionally weakening. Many of the hostages had traveled with serious domestic and business problems on their minds, but they had long since put them aside, even forgotten them. They lived for the present, and, when they weren't thinking about themselves and their own personal survival, they were trying to encourage each other.

Most fortunate were those who had discovered a role. Prins as doctor, Timmer as priest, Vaders as chronicler (no longer harassed in his note-taking by the hijackers), Laurier as representative of the trade union movement, Wientje Kruyswijk as substitute mother—all had a part to play, and all felt more secure for it. Some of the younger hostages too were gaining confidence, sixteen-year-old Frits Santing blossoming as a humorist. He too had found a role. He had with him a faulty transistor radio, which he had been taking to workshops for repair. With the general hunger for news from the outside world, his efforts to make it work were watched with eager anticipation.

To Vaders and Prins, the shooting of Bierling had appeared to be an act of desperation—but was it a final one? If it failed to produce results, would further acts of desperation follow? The hijackers still seemed unanimous on one point: they could not turn back. Had they become brutalized by what they had done?

There was one more attempt at mediation that evening, Manusama and his party arriving at the command post at 7:25 PM. The first to speak on the telephone was Josina Soumokil. "What you do is wrong," she told the hijackers. "My husband, who gave his life for the same cause, would never agree with this action." She broke down and wept. "Don't weep," said one of the hijackers. "You are making us weak, and we are determined to continue our action. We have no choice."

Manusama spoke next. "I came here yesterday. It seems you are still not ready to receive me. I only ask one thing now: give permission for the dead bodies to be taken away."

"All right. Tomorrow morning, let them come for the bodies then."

"One more thing. If you want to meet us, we are always willing to come."

Hijackers of the 1975 train at Wijster: Left to right (top)—Paul Saimima, Jacobus "Kobus" Tuny, Joop Metekohy. (Bottom)—Cornelis "Cor" Thenu, Albert "Abbé" Sahetepy, Cornelis "Djerrit" Hetharia. (Inset)—Eli Hahury.
Rob Brijker Press

Hans Prins. *ANEFO*　　　　　　　　Gerhard Vaders. *Private Collection*

The hijacked train at Wijster, showing the body of Hans Braam (the driver) lying beside the track. *Air Division of the Rijkspolitie*

Robert de Groot approaching Farmhouse
Etten after his escape. *ANP*

Herman Brinker shortly after his
escape. *Private Collection*

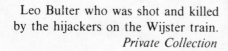

Leo Bulter who was shot and killed
by the hijackers on the Wijster train.
Private Collection

Hassan Tisna sheltering in a doorway after being shot in the stomach. *ANP*

Abedy jumps from the second-floor window overlooking Valerius Street after chalking "Dekken!" (Cover me!) on the wall. *ANEFO*

A plainclothes policeman, covered by a colleague (left), drags Abedy clear.

Bert Bierling falls from the door of the Wijster train after being shot by a hijacker. *Liaison Agency*

Saka Datuk being paraded blindfolded on the balcony of the Indonesian Consulate in Amsterdam. Note gunbarrel and megaphone. *ANEFO*

105

Dr. Dick Mulder, district psychiatrist
for The Hague. *ANEFO*

Manusama and Metiary arriving at the
Indonesian Consulate. *ANP*

Prime Minister Joop den Uyl and Justice Minister Andreas van Agt face a
barrage of questions from the press. *ANEFO*

Wientje Kruyswijk, Hans Prins and Jan Bies leaving the Wijster train after the hijackers surrendered. *ANEFO*

Vera Matron leans over to pick up a food delivery outside the Indonesian Consulate while a Moluccan terrorist stands guard. *Liaison Agency*

CHAPTER 8

Amsterdam: The Indonesian Consulate

B ETWEEN 11:30 AND NOON on that Thursday December 4, when the ultimatum that was to lead to the death of Bert Bierling was about to expire, a second group of young South Moluccans, again seven in number, was converging on Amsterdam Central Station by various routes to keep a secret rendezvous. Some had traveled south by train, others had hitch-hiked. All were members of the same community in Bovensmilde as the seven who had hijacked the train. One of them, Henkie Metekohy, even had a younger brother—Joop, a student teacher like himself—in the train, but none of them had played any part in that action. All were the same age within a few months, twenty-two or twenty-three. Six of them lived in the same street. The seventh, Jacob Ririmasse, known as Jopie, had been working as an impresario in Amsterdam, where he was lodging with a cousin, arranging bookings for foreign pop groups. He had worked with Paul Saimima for a time, so like Henkie Metekohy he had a special interest in the action at Wijster. On December 2, the day of the train hijacking, Jopie had traveled north with his cousin to Bovensmilde to visit their respective parents. During the evening, when he met the other six, the burning topic of conversation had inevitably been the hijacking. South Moluccans love to talk, and the arguments had gone on until late. When they finally parted, they arranged to meet again next day.

By that time, many more details of the hijacking were known, and it was clear that the Dutch Government was not going to give in easily. To Jopie and his friends it seemed that support for the group in the train was needed, to convince the Dutch people of the wrongs that had been done in their name. Petitions and protests achieved nothing, and whatever alarm and disruption a second hijacking might cause, it would be nothing

108

compared to the sufferings of South Moluccans in Indonesia and in Holland over the years. Above all, the group wanted to involve the Indonesian Government, which they saw as their ultimate enemy, fundamentally responsible for the plight of the South Moluccan people. It was Jopie, with his flair for organizing dramatic events, who suggested when they resumed their discussion that their objects would best be served by choosing as a siege target the offices of the Indonesian Consulate General in Amsterdam.

Thus it was that, on the morning of December 4, they set out from Bovensmilde. Although there was no appointed leader, individuals emerged on the strength of their talents and assumed certain responsibilities as the day unfolded. The actual siege was to be stage-managed by Jopie. The diminutive, clean-shaven Josef Huly, known as Otjek, son of a council official in Bovensmilde, carried a Uzi (stolen from a Dutch military armory) and a Bible. Bob Solissa, a clerk, bearded and bespectacled, was the brother of the better-known Noes Solissa, spokesman for the Free South Moluccan Youth of Assen. Johannes Sihasale, a student teacher known as Anies, was utterly dedicated to the RMS cause; a fatalist, he did not expect to survive the action. Jan Lumalessil, known as Ottek, was an electrician; Chris Kaihatu, known as Pablo, was unemployed. Completing the group was Henkie Metekohy, Joop's brother. Each was to bring his own weapon, and, in addition to the Uzi, they had three rifles and two revolvers. The only one who did not possess a gun was Jopie, and he carried a knife. They also carried a selection of literature inspired by the Free South Moluccan Youth movement, to which they all belonged.

Following public revulsion against the killings on the train, they were not intending to shoot hostages, but they were prepared to do so if attacked from outside. They were equally ready to give their own lives for the cause.

The spontaneity of their action, as compared with that of the seven who hijacked the train, meant that they were undertaking it without detailed planning. They had little first-hand information about the layout of the interior of the consulate. Indeed, few of them even knew its location. When some of them missed the rendezvous that morning at the railway station, they had to go to the Dutch Tourist Office to ask where the consulate was. Boarding a taxi, they overtook the others, who were traveling more sedately by tram.

The building that housed the consulate was an undistinguished four-storey block in Old Amsterdam South, a square, dun-colored, brick-faced structure with a frontage facing east dominating the short connecting street of Brachthuyzerstraat, which linked Koninginneweg to the north with Valerius Straat to the south. The south side of the building faced on Valerius Straat. Eight large rectangular windows about eight feet high looked out from each of the first three floors on to Brachthuyzerstraat, and two on each floor looked out on Valerius Straat. The penthouse on the fourth floor housed a kitchen and canteen. The only relief in the sheer vertical eastern facade was a narrow balcony jutting out from a room in the middle of the building on the second floor. There was no access from Valerius Straat, and access was easily blocked from the rear, so a security check at the single entrance in Brachthuyzerstraat would not have been difficult. But despite the news of the train hijacking and the obvious vulnerability of the Indonesian Consulate as a target, no guard of any kind had been posted, although the receptionist, an Indonesian, had a gun.

The building was too big for the consulate offices alone, and accommodation had been rented to two Indonesian travel bureaus. One, Intras, was on the ground floor, and the other, Nitour, was on the third. It was through visits to these travel agencies and to the passport office on the ground floor that such information as the group had of the layout of the building had been gleaned.

Also within the building was a school for Indonesian children, with classrooms on the first floor and in the cellar. There were four staff, all Indonesian, two male, two female, and an average attendance of twenty pupils.

Splitting up into two parties, three as the downstairs spearhead and four to take control of the upper floors, the Moluccans began their siege. Of the leading party, Jopie went to the Intras Travel Bureau on the right of the entrance hall. The other two made for the L-shaped desk of the receptionist left of centre.

"Lie down on the floor and keep quiet, or I'll shoot."

Nineteen-year-old Anita Hoeboer, the Dutch girl thus addressed, screamed at the sight of the masked gunman confronting her. Then, sensibly enough, she did as she was told.

"Put that telephone down!"

Behind Anita was the Intras deputy manager, Wim Simon, a Dutch Indonesian. He was in the middle of making a travel booking. As he looked up, he saw a masked intruder vault over the counter towards him, brandishing a knife. With the knife held an inch from his throat, he replaced the receiver.

In the back office, thirty-six-year-old Vera Martron, a part-time Intras employee, blonde and vivacious, was making sandwiches for herself and her colleagues. She had only just returned from the shops. With three children to get off to school and to care for when they got back, she worked mornings only and would soon be finishing for the day. As it happened, today was something of an occasion for her, though not one she altogether relished: her divorce had been made final. But she was not to enjoy her newfound freedom for long. She heard Anita's screams, and looking round she saw someone holding a knife to Wim Simon's throat. The manageress of the agency ran past her into the street, and she started to follow. Someone shouted, "Stop, or I shoot!" The manageress was through the front door by then, but she was too late. She was pushed down beside Anita on the floor, where she did her best to comfort the younger girl.

Meanwhile, the two Moluccans who had gone to the reception desk had grabbed the receptionist, relieved him of his gun, and were using him as a shield to mount the spiral wooden staircase at the back of the hall. A girl in the passport office on the far left saw what was happening, jumped out of the window, and escaped to raise the alarm. But for everyone else, exit from the building was sealed.

Fifty-three-year-old Raden Suhirman, head of Nitour, was in his third-floor office with a visiting Dutch travel agent, Wessel van Pijlen from Amersfoort. Suhirman sent his secretary to find out what all the noise was about, then saw two gunmen approaching, with the receptionist staggering in front of them. He tried to lock the door of his office but was too late. Together with his deputy, Arthur van Asdonck—another Dutch Indonesian—his secretary, and his visitor, he was ordered down to the second floor.

A senior member of the consulate's economic department, a man named Harsoyo, was in the middle of a long-distance call. The pandemonium downstairs disturbed him, and he sent a colleague named Musni to investigate. He thought, not without amusement, since he had a keen sense of humor, that a heated quarrel was in progress. But instead of his colleague returning with an explanation, he was confronted by two South Moluccans with guns.

At first the travel agency employees on the ground floor were taken to the cellar and locked in a tiny room with ten small children from the kindergarten section of the school. But soon everyone was herded upstairs to Room 25, the office of the consul general, in the center of the main facade on the second floor. This was the room with the narrow balcony overlooking Brachthuyzerstraat. Into this medium-sized room, ten meters by four, were crowded twenty-two Indonesians and Dutch Indonesians (nine women and thirteen men), three white Dutch (two women and one man), and sixteen Indonesian children, with some of the hijackers. All the furniture except a desk had to be removed to accommodate them, and even then, once the atmosphere had cooled a little, there was barely room for them to take the opportunity offered by the hijackers of sitting on the floor.

As with the hostages in the train, there were a number of people whose presence in the consulate was unusual. Unluckiest of all, perhaps, was the twenty-eight-year-old travel agent Wessel van Pijlen. Tall and slim, with close-cropped fair hair, he bore a striking resemblance to actor Steve McQueen, a likeness that was even more pronounced when he said something under his breath to Suhirman in English and revealed an American accent. He had returned from a business trip to Hawaii only the day before, and somehow he had gotten separated from his luggage. It was a problem that he often had had to unravel for customers, but never before for himself. In his suitcase was his raincoat—he never wore a winter coat —and that morning, after first visiting the airline responsible for misplacing his luggage, he called at the offices of another airline and then at the American Consulate, walking from office to office. But his next call, in Brachthuyzerstraat, was a mile or more from the American Consulate, and, although normally he would have enjoyed the walk, his lack of protection against the chill December air following a sojourn in a hot climate persuaded him to take a taxi. Had he walked he would have been too late to be hijacked.

Three Indonesian visitors who had committed no indiscretion other than to call at the passport office had also had the misfortune to be caught up in the siege. Another man who felt the fates had been unkind to him was Dr. Ben Fanggiday, whose wife worked for Intras. He had called to say that she was ill and would not be in that day. A Dutchman of Indonesian descent, Ben Fanggiday worked for the Society of Amsterdam Sick Fund and was a qualified medical doctor.

"Which of you is the consul?" The hijackers wanted first of all to identify the consul. He would be their most important hostage, their major prize.

"He's not here."

The hijackers, taken aback for a moment, reacted with suspicion. "Not here? What do you mean, not here? Where is he? If you try to hide him there'll be trouble."

Ironically, the consul was attending a meeting at the Indonesian Embassy at The Hague at which one of the subjects on the agenda was the train hijack.

"Where's the vice-consul?"

"He's not here either."

"Who's the senior political officer? What's *your* appointment?"

"I'm just an administrator."

"You'd better tell the truth. There's thirty-two bullets in this Uzi, and that's enough for all of you."

"We understand that."

Chief target of their questions was Harsoyo. His cool, phlegmatic personality was proof against all the threats they hurled at him. "I'm sorry," he insisted pleasantly, "I can't help you."

As the hijackers moved away to discuss what they were going to do, those hostages who tried to converse were ordered to be silent. "Don't try to escape," they were warned, "because we'll shoot you down, plus one other. For every one who escapes, we'll shoot two."

What, wondered the hostages, were they supposed to do? There was no book of rules to follow, no instruction manual. Of the consulate staff, some were on posting from Indonesia; others, like Harsoyo, were locally recruited. Most had served at some time in the Indonesian Army, and they brooded over their inability to fight back, but they took their cue from Harsoyo and reacted coolly. The best thing to do was to shut up and do as they were told. Escape looked impossible, and to attempt it, it seemed, was to court disaster, for others as well as themselves. Their only thought, for the moment, was to placate their captors and avoid a general panic.

The employees of the travel agencies, caught up in something that they felt they were not a part of, reacted more emotionally. "What is this? We've got nothing to do with all this." It was the Indonesians who calmed them down. "They've got guns. We can do nothing. Relax."

The Indonesians were no less afraid of the hijackers than the Dutch. Indeed they had reason to be more so. But their stolid exterior, which the Dutch took for apathy, was their carapace. They were simply better than the Dutch at hiding their fears.

Raden Suhirman made a brave attempt to achieve the release of his friend Wessel van Pijlen. "He has nothing to do with this building at all. He is a visitor. I'm a travel agent, and he's a travel agent. It doesn't make sense to keep him here." But the Moluccans were adamant. "No. Everyone must stay."

When Vera Martron recovered from the initial shock, she asked how long the affair might last. "Is it just for the day? I have to look after my children." The answer she got made her wish she hadn't asked. "We could be here till Christmas."

"Can I call my mother? My children will be alone, and nobody will know I'm here. I have to get someone to look after my children."

"O.K., go ahead, you can call your mother. But don't mention where you are."

She went upstairs to the Nitour offices under close guard, with a pistol inches away from her head, but the concession suggested an encouraging spark of humanity. First she phoned her mother-in-law, because she knew her mother was unwell, but on getting no reply she phoned her mother. "Will you go to my place? It's important." "You'll have to go yourself," replied her mother. "I'm not well." "Please, please go, because I've got trouble. . . ." She suddenly felt the pistol cold against her temple. "Put that phone down." She could only hope there would be something on the one o'clock news to alert her mother.

The hijackers telephoned the Indonesian Embassy and announced themselves as members of the Free Young South Moluccans. In this first contact with the outside world, they proclaimed that they were integrating their action and demands with those of the hijackers in the train. The Indonesian Government must put pressure on the Dutch Government to give in to the demands of the train hijackers, and if these demands were still refused, action would be taken against the hostages at the consulate. Van Agt, informed of the siege at 12:50, had only just learned of the shooting of Bierling. He was facing a two-pronged attack.

The hostages soon recognized Jopie as one of the leaders, if not actually the leader. An apparently serious young man, calm and quietly spoken, he was listened to with respect by the others, who generally did what he said. He had the greater sophistication of the town dweller, he wore his hair at a more conservative length, sported a contemporary-style moustache, and spoke better Dutch. His outlook too was less narrow. Typical of the introversion of most of the others was that of Otjek, who gave the impression of being Jopie's equal, even perhaps his superior. "You know what *this* means, don't you?" he asked Vera Martron, indicating the letters RMS on his belt. It was more an assumption than a question. She thought they must be his initials. "You never heard of it? Didn't you go to school? Don't you read the papers?" Obviously an intelligent youth, he was agape with astonishment at such ignorance.

At one o'clock, the hijackers phoned Amsterdam police headquarters with several specific requests. The police, who had already thrown a cordon round the building, must keep their distance. There must be no shooting, otherwise the hostages would suffer. The occupied part of the building, they warned, was mined with explosives. They asked for radio and television sets, a megaphone, and a bus to Schiphol, to be made available immediately. The request for the bus was ignored, but the police superintendent on the spot negotiated the release of the five youngest children in exchange for a megaphone and radio and television sets before the crisis center could intervene. Meanwhile, he set up a command post around the corner on Koninginneweg, in a building out of sight of the consulate. The formation of a management center took longer, but the chief commissioner's room in police headquarters in Elandsgracht in the city center was hurriedly cleared for the purpose, with the same sort of hierarchy, drawn from the district, as at Beilen.

In the consulate, the hijackers showed a further glimpse of their humanity when they asked the children if there was anything they wanted. There was a momentary easing of tension when the children replied, in a unanimous chorus, "I want to go home." But with police activity growing in the streets outside, the temperature was not lowered for long.

"Are you strong?" Vera Martron was asked. She was not tall, but was well built, and she answered that she was. Thus she was given the task of receiving the goods requested at the street door. Later she was sent out onto the balcony with the megaphone to order the police to keep clear. Van Pijlen, too, was pushed out on to the balcony, to find out where the police were located, and he caught a glimpse of sharpshooters in the buildings across the street, but he affected not to be able to see them.

Unknown to the terrorists, six of the consulate staff had evaded capture. Four of them, the chief and three members of the chancellery, had locked themselves in a second-floor room in the right wing of the building overlooking Valerius Straat; the other two were in hiding on an upper floor. The four who had locked themselves in had also barricaded the doors with heavy office furniture and worked out a plan of escape.

The room they were in was the office of a man named Abedy, fifty-two, married with two children. A quiet, kind, friendly character, and a man of wide interests, he was one of the Indonesians whom Vera Martron most admired. A talented artist, he had designed a highly effective poster for Intras; he was also a member of a rifle club and a first-class shot. One of his colleagues, Heru Dharma, the cashier, believed he kept a gun in his office.

Abedy's room had a connecting door to the chief of chancellery's room —the front room at the extreme right on the second floor. Any attempt at escape from a front window would be seen by the hijackers, but the windows at the side of the building looking down on Valerius Straat were hidden from their view. Thus the chief, Hasan Wirasastra, had joined the group in Abedy's room, and the connecting door and the door into the corridor had been heavily barricaded. Completing the group were two more consular officials, another Hasan—Hasan Tisna—and a man named Bustomi.

It was in Abedy's room that the diplomatic mail was packed and bagged, and there was a plentiful supply of rope. By securing a length of rope to a strong point and passing it through the window, all four men hoped to let themselves down safely into Valerius Straat. Having had no contact with the terrorists, they knew nothing of the threat to kill two for every one who escaped.

Meanwhile, in Room 25, the children were getting fretful and asking for food and drink. The drink supply, alcoholic and nonalcoholic, had just been replenished in readiness for a St. Nicholas celebration, but the key to the store was in Abedy's office. Heru, the cashier, was ordered to accompany the hijackers to get the key, and his natural nervousness was greatly magnified by his belief that Abedy carried a gun.

When they got to Abedy's room and found the door locked from the inside, the hijackers banged on it impatiently but got no reply. Somehow they had missed this room in their search of the building. They then tried to force the connecting door, and after charging at it unsuccessfully they fired several shots into the lock, which shattered. But the door itself remained barricaded, and the hijackers couldn't break through.

Spurred on by the commotion outside, the four Indonesians started to put their escape plan into practice. The rope was tied to a radiator under the window, and the first man to go, Bustomi, was able to slow his descent with its help, although he landed awkwardly and hurt his ankle. Hasan Wirasastra followed, and he too fell clumsily, breaking a rib; but plainclothes police were on hand to help the two men to safety.

By the time the third man, Hasan Tisna, started down the rope, the barricade was tottering and the Moluccans were only held back by covering fire from police outside the building. Shouting to their compatriots on the ground floor to stop the escape, two of them raced along the corridor and down the staircase to see what they could do from below.

Tisna was halfway down the rope when the first shots were fired at him. To do the terrorists justice, they appear to have aimed at his legs, but as Tisna slithered down the rope he was hit in the stomach. Losing his grip on the rope, he fell heavily and broke a leg. He dragged himself into a doorway, where he was rescued by a policeman named Dietz. He was taken to a hospital in critical condition.

Abedy, as the last man to go, was the most vulnerable. But if he failed to get away, the hijackers would surely vent their anger at the escape of the others on him. After the shooting of Tisna it was clear that he would have to devise a fresh plan. To descend on the rope as the others had done looked impracticable; the hijackers had that escape route covered. Abandoning the rope, which was suspended from the rear of the two side windows, he selected a piece of chalk and climbed out of the forward window. Squatting on the sill and holding onto the brickwork with his left hand, he wrote *"Dekken!"* ("Cover me") on the dun-colored wall with his right. He then drew an arrow to indicate to the police the direction in which he intended to jump, away from the rope. A mattress that had been produced by a neighbor was then pushed into position to break his fall.

While plainclothes police prepared to give him covering fire from the street below, Abedy made ready to jump. But it was difficult for him, crouching on the sill, to get the impetus into his spring that had been estimated. He fell short of the mattress and landed on his seat on the flagged pavement, badly injuring his spine.

In the exposed position in which he was lying, Abedy was still in danger. Covered by his colleagues, but at considerable personal risk, the policeman Dietz passed a rope under Abedy's armpits and dragged him clear.

While all this was going on, the two Indonesians in hiding on the third floor remained undiscovered. The hijackers, preoccupied with consolidating their position and opening negotiations, made no more searches that day. Instead they telephoned fresh demands to police headquarters, asking for contact with Metiary and Pessireron, and for food. The first request was ignored, but the food was delivered by a police official soon after dark. Detailed to collect it, with the point of a rifle pressing between her shoulder blades, was Vera Martron. "Why are you treating me like this?" she demanded. "Because otherwise you'll run away." "Why should I? You'd only shoot someone upstairs." Nevertheless, when she looked outside and saw her car parked in front of the building, almost within reach, the temptation was real.

At the crisis center in The Hague, news of the second hijacking could not have arrived at a more inopportune moment. The decision that another killing in the train would be the signal for an attack had barely been made, and the timing of the consulate siege was assumed to have been premeditated. The terrorists had got it just right. When it was learned that the consulate group had been given radio and television, the implications for the hostages in the consulate of an attack on the train became embarrassingly clear. It would be virtually impossible to keep such an attack secret. Even if the Dutch media cooperated, foreign correspondents, to whose broadcast reports the consulate group would have access, could not be silenced. This meant a simultaneous attack on train and consulate, something that, if only because of the vastly different problems the two targets presented, would greatly magnify the risks.

Van Agt hoped to base his handling of the consulate siege on the same principles as for the train hijack; but there were several factors militating against such a course. First, as in the French Embassy incident the previous year, there was the government's responsibility for foreign nationals of the diplomatic service. The Indonesian ambassador was quick to stress to the Dutch minister of foreign affairs that his government would hold the Dutch responsible for their safety. Second was the overriding priority that the government felt bound to give to the release of the children.

The uncomfortable truth was that the second hijacking severely restricted the government's freedom of action. If the group in the train could not exactly kill now with impunity, it was going to be doubly difficult to apply the ultimate constraint.

Under these pressures and bearing in mind the experience with the train and in previous incidents, van Agt decided on a change of tactics. Communication with the hijackers through two intermediate stages—management center and command post—was a safety measure that had perhaps been overdone. To this extent, he appeared to concede that there was some substance in the complaints of Hans Prins and Walter Timmer. Closer contact might be worth trying, and he decided not to interrupt the direct line that had already been established between consulate and police headquarters. To man this line, as soon as the management center was ready to function, he appointed a specialist, someone who would conduct all conversations with the hijackers other than the purely routine.

The man he selected was Dr. Dick Mulder, the Ministry of Justice's district psychiatrist for The Hague. Although Amsterdam was outside his parish, he was an obvious choice. His experience in handling difficult and deviant individuals gained through his in-prison therapy work in the rehabilitation of prisoners (he was the government's top prison psychiatrist) was unrivaled. And, however stable the personalities of the hijackers might normally be, their action suggested an ideological egocentricity that bordered on the obsessional. To this would be added the almost intolerable mental strains to which their action would subject them.

Twice before Mulder had been called in to negotiate with terrorists, the first time during the siege of the French Embassy at The Hague in September, 1974, the second when mutineering prisoners at Scheveningen Jail near The Hague took a visiting choir hostage a month later. His handling of these two incidents had gone some way to establishing his reputation.

Dick Mulder was an affable, responsive man in his early fifties whose boyish good humor was never far from the surface. A full crop of brown hair, scarcely flecked with gray, eyes that glinted mischievously behind gold-rimmed bifocals, and a face that was totally unlined, completed the impression of buoyant verve and enthusiasm. Yet the soothing, persuasive voice of almost hypnotic timbre was evidence of a riper, less-fathomable resilience. Qualities of flexibility tempered by a basic tenacity made him a formidable member of any negotiating team.

To what extent would he or anyone else be empowered to negotiate? Would he be allowed more than a pacifying, placatory role? Van Agt remained determined not to give way, and even the prime minister, Joop den Uyl, who exercised a coordinating responsibility, was pessimistic of the government's chances of resolving the impasse without recourse to violence—although he regarded the military option as a last resort. Mulder, too, believed that armed intervention must always be a possibility, partly for psychological reasons, and indeed it was on his advice that such intervention had been decided upon at Scheveningen, but he too saw such intervention as a last resort. Indeed, until a crisis was reached, he believed that demonstrations of superior strength were more likely to precipitate the violence it was hoped to avoid.

Mulder's immediate function in Amsterdam was to act as a catalyst, oiling the contact between terrorists and authorities, reducing anxiety states and the danger of violence, gleaning information, encouraging cooperation in routine matters between hostage and terrorist, and introducing rhythm into an unfamiliar life situation to bring both groups back to reality.

Why had Dr. Mulder's unique experience and expertise not been used in the train situation at Wijster? The answer is that the situation there developed too quickly, and that once a channel of communication had been established, it seemed wiser not to disturb it. (Its limitations were not immediately apparent.) Psychiatrists and psychologists were present in the management center at Beilen and in the command post throughout, but their role was entirely different from that given to Mulder. They were there to guide, advise, comfort, and observe the police and the military.

In this initial phase, with power apparently vested in the terrorists, it was Mulder's policy to recognize their *de facto* authority, thus underlining their responsibility; no use to attempt to cajole or coerce them at this stage. Although he liked to be kept aware of government policy, he did not see himself purely as an instrument of it. Such an approach, he felt, would have been inconsistent with the ethics of his profession. True impartiality was impossible, but he had to be more than just another voice from the government side.

The harsh exterior displayed by the hijackers, the threats they uttered, and above all their own pathological nervousness kept the hostages in Room 25 in a state of constant anxiety for the whole of that first day, and there was nothing Dr. Mulder or anyone else could do about it. "Are you going to kill us all?" someone asked, and the abrupt negative reassured no one. The killings in the train remained too stark in their minds. All the adult hostages were fully aware of the knife-edge precariousness of their position, poised in a sort of limbo, halfway between life and death. As in the train, home and family were forgotten, and every alternate thought was the selfish one of personal survival.

The unpredictability of the hijackers was another unsettling factor. At one moment it was easy to believe them capable of almost any brutality, at another they continued to reveal an encouraging humanity. Early that evening Wessel van Pijlen asked if he could telephone his parents; it was their wedding anniversary, and he had promised to join them for dinner. At first the terrorists said no, but when he explained that his parents could not possibly know where he was and would be greatly distressed as a result, ruining their anniversary, the hijackers relented. He was able not only to wish them a happy anniversary, but also to explain that he was being held hostage in the consulate. Yet, later that evening, when Vera Martron, suffering from a crippling headache, asked to be allowed to fetch a sleeping pill from her handbag, which she had left downstairs in the Intras offices, she was refused. It was as though the hijackers feared that too many concessions would weaken the image they needed to create.

The hostages in the consulate had one great advantage over their counterparts on the train: warmth. But at ten o'clock that night, when the hijackers turned off the lights, the struggle for sleep was no less of an ordeal. Men, women, and children, mixed up together higgledy-piggledy on the floor, didn't know where to put their bodies and limbs. It was especially painful for those like Anita Hoeboer who carried no surplus flesh. But with the carpet for a mattress, cushions from the chairs for pillows, and tablecloths from the store for bedding, they somehow contrived to settle down for the night.

CHAPTER 9

An Accidental Shooting

"S ANTA CLAUS DAY—a day for surprises!" That was how Frits Santing greeted the daylight on Friday, December 5. After a cold night
in the train and sixteen hours of darkness, another clear, crisp winter's day
seemed in prospect.

For once it was impossible not to think of family and home—what they
would be doing, what the children would be doing, what they themselves
would have been doing but for their captivity. The filtered morning sunshine accentuated the atmosphere of wistful sadness as the hostages
wished each other the most precious of all St. Nicholas gifts, the only one
anyone was interested in—the gift of freedom.

In this case, the trouble with surprises was that they were apt to be
unpleasant. Would the hijackers keep their word? Would the government
intercede? Would they have to endure another night in the train? The
hostages played back the hijackers' promises in their minds and tried hard
to believe them.

Willem Albracht felt that the longer they were held captive the less
danger there might be, but he saw the situation as having an "X" factor,
an unknown quantity from which disaster could always spring. There was
nothing one could relate it to, no precedent to indicate how things would
go, other than the likelihood of eventual attack from outside. As for the
hijackers, he still felt he could not make friends with them, as some seemed
able to do, but he was careful not to make enemies of them either. He had
no confidence in their promises, but he knew he needed their good-will to
survive.

Typical of the many paradoxes was his acceptance, in exchange for the

121

light raincoat he had been wearing, of a warm topcoat offered him by the hijackers. It had belonged to Bert Bierling.

Peeping through a crack in the covering of the windows, he got the impression that the dead bodies were still there. In his mind's eye and in his nightmares, he had continually seen his own body lying in a watery ditch alongside the train. The image was so vivid that he could not dispel it. If I have to go, he thought, I have things I want to say to my wife, my children, and my grandchildren, and I must write them down. They will be my last will and testament. Taking out his diary, he wrote for more than an hour in the space remaining to the end of the year.

Opposite him, agricultural engineer van der Boon did the same. His nightmares and imaginings had been similar to Albracht's. "We must keep what we have written dry," he told Albracht. "If we are lying outside the train and it rains, our writings will get wet and be impossible to read." Each man wrapped his diary in plastic packing from the previous day's lunch boxes and put it in an inside pocket.

Sitting next to Albracht and aware of what they were doing was the octogenarian Smit. "I don't care about dying," he told them, "so long as I don't suffer." He and Albracht had sat close together and wrapped blankets round each other during the night to retain body heat, and Smit had pulled his hat down over his eyes and tied a scarf round his face. Troubled by gnawing pains from his stomach ulcer and hard of hearing so that he missed much of what was going on, he asked no favors and made no complaint.

On this fourth day in the train, the unkempt and unshaven appearance of the passengers and the inability to wash or to clean the teeth were beginning to pass unnoticed. They had become accustomed to it. The main problem now, with the tension marginally reduced, was to keep themselves occupied. Movement about the train was still restricted, passengers always having to ask to go to the lavatory, and no other excuse was tolerated. Stiffness in limbs and joints and sore buttocks were a common complaint, and Prins organized them to exercise where they sat.

Few people were able to concentrate sufficiently to read books or magazines, but guessing and general knowledge games were popular. Albracht put his manual dexterity to practical use by making playing cards from technical books provided by van der Boon, and he also made a set of dominoes, after first compiling a graph to see how many pieces there ought to be. Smit then explained the rules of the game. Thys Stevens, the soldier from Nieuw Buinen, collected ten-cent pieces for use on an improvised checkerboard.

The apparent indifference of the government remained the chief complaint amongst hijackers and hostages alike. They knew nothing of the daily ministerial debates at the crisis center in The Hague, nor were they aware of the siege of the Indonesian Consulate and its inhibiting effect on government strategy. Even the prime minister, regarded by many as a dove amongst hawks, had pointed to a distinction between the killings of the first day, which could have occurred in the heat of the action, and the cold-blooded murder of Bierling, and arguments were still being put forward at the crisis center for an armed assault on the train. These arguments always foundered on the restraining fear that action at one incident would have fatal repercussions at the other, while the risks of simultaneous assaults were not yet thought to be justified. Plans for such enterprises, however, were constantly being cast and recast. One positive decision taken by van Agt was that, now that contact of a kind had been established between the train and the group of four mediators led by Manusama, other intermediaries would not be admitted.

Outside the train, the whole perimeter resembled an army camp, with steel-helmeted troops in battle dress and carrying submachine guns blocking all approaches. One unit alone, the Forty-third Infantry Battalion, had assembled 500 troops to guard the outer ring and worked in three shifts of eight hours each, supported by forty tracked vehicles. The inner ring, on a much smaller perimeter, was even more closely guarded, but none of the troops ventured within 300 yards of the train. It was into this no-man's-land, just before midday on December 5, that three Red Cross volunteers, flimsily clad at the behest of the hijackers, made their way across the bleak, fallow fields toward the train. Covered by the hijackers' guns, they lifted the bodies onto a stretcher one at a time, returning twice to retrieve all three victims. This macabre ritual was watched in silent anger by the majority of the Dutch nation on that night's TV.

When Cor Ter Veer heard that the bodies had been taken away, he reflected that the hijackers had at least kept one of their promises. It gave him a little more hope for the outcome. "We have a much better chance," he told his wife, "now we know we can count on their word."

Others still saw the chief characteristic of the hijackers as unpredictability. That they had kept one promise was no guarantee they would keep another.

Early that Friday evening, the hostages got their first hot meal since before the hijacking, delivered in insulated canisters by the Red Cross. It was a typical Dutch stew, thicker and firmer than an Irish stew, and made not from meat and potatoes but from sausage and curly kale. But because of a misunderstanding between the Red Cross and the police, all forms of cutlery were omitted. The hostages took this as either stupidity or indifference on the part of the authorities. Even if they thought the knives and forks might be rejected by the hijackers as potential weapons, they must surely have heard of plastic cutlery. The viscosity of the stew was such that neither eating with the fingers nor drinking from a cup proved practicable, but empty stomachs soon brought improvisation. Cor Ter Veer produced a pair of scissors that he always carried for professional reasons and cut plastic glasses into the shape of spoons. Some stamped the glasses into makeshift plates and gobbled the food off them like dogs or cats. Others used them as they were, filling them with food and then squeezing from the bottom. Grandpa Smit used a pocketknife, Irma Martens a plastic clip from her diary. Prins, afraid of stomach upsets, advised them all not to eat too much, and to avoid the greasy top layer.

The hijackers ate with a shrug of the shoulders. "There's your government for you."

The effect of the hot meal, with coffee to follow, was to induce a sense of well-being. The Red Cross had sent in a supply of cigarettes, and the air was thick with smoke and the hubbub of after-dinner conversation. It was, after all, St. Nicholas night. As tongues were loosened, tolerance and good humor returned, and the mistake over the cutlery was exploited as the joke of the day. Vaders, having run out of cigars, changed to cigarettes. "From now on, you'll always find me smoking," he told Riet Overtoom. "Go ahead," she said, "I'll move to a nonsmoker."

Had it not been for a South Moluccan guard at either end of the carriage, pointing a gun perpetually in their direction, they might have been tourists on some excursion in a primitive country. But the playful attitude toward firearms of the hijackers, some of whom treated them like toys, was a continual source of disquiet. Now Djerrit, standing behind Wientje Kruyswijk and Bette van Overeem at one end of the carriage and resting the barrel of his Sten gun over the back of the seat, kept letting it fall forward, to the intense vexation of the four passengers in that compartment—the soldier Jan Bies, Mrs. C. van Hille from Amsterdam, Wientje Kruyswijk, and Bette van Overeem. Djerrit had always been one of the worst offenders, and now, bored perhaps with his guard duty and tired of holding the barrel at the horizontal, he asked Wientje, "May I rest it on your head?"

It was an extraordinary request, and Wientje, with her compassion for her "boys," was probably the only one who would have countenanced it.

But she regarded it as an improvement on what they had been subjected to before, and she agreed.

"You don't complain?"

"No. But please don't play with it."

The passengers went back to their homemade games, and the air of relaxation and contentment was restored. But within a minute there was a flash of flame and a shattering explosion, reverberating round the carriage like a richochet in a Western movie. So deafening was the noise that everyone thought a hand grenade or one of the sticks of explosive had been detonated. In fact, the exhausted Djerrit had allowed the Sten gun to slip from his grasp. Fortunately it had not been set to repeat. But the single bullet that was fired hit a metal coat hook below the luggage rack and splintered it, spattering fragments of metal through the carriage like shrapnel.

In that soporific atmosphere, the shock was so totally unexpected as to be paralyzing. Everyone winced at the assault on their eardrums, and Wientje's hearing was completely benumbed. Someone—she thought it was a South Moluccan—fell heavily in the aisle beside her, and she reached down and felt blood and thought he must be dead. Then she heard him crying. One of the hostages struck a match, and she saw that it was Paul.

In the semidarkness, few could tell where the screams of the wounded were coming from. To add to the confusion, bullets were rolling around the floor like marbles.

Paul had been walking down the aisle to the rear of the carriage and had been sprayed in the face by metal splinters. One splinter had pierced his eye. Cor Ter Veer had also been hit in the eye, or in the eyebrow, he wasn't sure which. Blood was streaming from the wound and he could see nothing. Several other passengers were hit by flying fragments, but the bullet itself landed innocuously in Oosting's lap.

Eli burst into the carriage from somewhere up front, and his attempts to reimpose order compounded the chaos. "Stay in your places. Stay seated. Don't move around." He feared a surprise attack by the hostages. Above the moans of the wounded could be heard the sound of guns being loaded. As one by one the hostages moved to each other's aid, more warnings were shouted and more guns cocked. "It was one of us!" shouted one of the hijackers, and Vaders and Timmer appealed for calm. Ignoring the warnings, Prins went to the rear of the carriage, where he found Paul slumped on the floor, bleeding profusely from the head.

In the dim, sepulchral light Prins couldn't see how serious Paul's wounds might be. There was so much blood on his face that he had to run his fingers over the South Moluccan's head to locate the source. When he found it, he realized that the wound was deep. Pushing a handkerchief into it to staunch the flow, he called for something to use as a bandage. Eli's refusal to allow him to send for a first-aid kit now rebounded on the hijackers themselves.

Paul, convinced he was dying, struggled to his knees and began praying in Malaysian. "Our father . . ." Timmer, despite splinters in his face and leg, went back to help Paul with his prayers. Meanwhile Prins tore up a proffered shirt and bandaged the wound. Then he went to help Ter Veer.

Ter Veer was appalled at the amount of blood he was losing, and he too feared that without swift and expert treatment his injury would be fatal. In his dazed state, he was conscious of Prins bending over him, bandaging his injured eye. Shocked and weakened as he was, he was also aware that his wife was in a state of collapse. Throughout the hijacking she had sustained him, but now she was crying and wringing her hands in torment. "I must go to him! A wife belongs with her husband at a time like this!" Clinging to Vaders in a frenzy of distraction, she appealed to him to help. Eli told her to sit down and keep out of the way.

Prins, too, was importuning Eli. "Paul has to go to a hospital. We have to get him off the train. Otherwise he will die." But Eli showed no more sympathy for Paul than for the Ter Veers. "He has fallen for his country. We shall let him stay here."

All the hijackers had said many times that they would gladly die for their country. But, resigned to their fate though they might be, the accident had shaken them severely, and they were not all impervious to suffering. When Prins followed up his request with an appeal on behalf of Ter Veer, he sensed that Eli hesitated. "All right," he said eventually, "the two wounded can go."

With this surrender of initiative on the part of the hijackers, a handful of the hostages took control of the train. While Prins began getting Paul onto the stretcher brought the previous day for Jo Jansen, Timmer grabbed the telephone. "There's been an accident. We are going to open the train and bring out two wounded. We will carry them a hundred meters down the track and leave them for you to collect. Please be ready, and please have an ambulance waiting."

"What's happened? Are they blacks?"

Timmer, superficially wounded himself, reacted angrily. What did it matter whether they were black or white? "It's an accident. People are wounded." Then he looked beneath the surface of the question. "If you try to attack the train, you should realize there will be many dead. Please don't use the situation to try anything. We simply want to get the wounded to a hospital."

With the help of the South Moluccans, Prins got Paul onto the stretcher, but they couldn't get it through the door onto the entrance platform without tipping the stretcher so steeply that Paul would have fallen off. They had to lift him off the stretcher, take it through the door, then put him on it again. The next problem was the height of the entrance platform above the ground, requiring the stretcher to be tipped forward as it was lowered. Prins called for neckties and belts from the passengers. When they were brought, he tied Paul securely to the stretcher. The tall Kobus stepped down from the train and took the weight, while Prins passed the stretcher through the double door.

There was no stretcher for Ter Veer, so they would have to improvise one. The solution reached was to take the toilet door off its hinges and strap Ter Veer to it. Then he too was carried out of the train.

Inside the train, Dinie Ter Veer had to be physically restrained from joining her husband. "My husband is dying, and I'm not allowed to be with him!" Vaders comforted her as best he could, at the same time appealing to Eli. "Let her go!" The commotion reached the ears of Prins, who was now outside the train, and he added his support. "She's in a state of deep shock! I say she must go!" "And I say, no!" shouted Eli.

With a hysterical woman to pacify, Vaders kept up the pressure on Eli. "I can't cope with her. You'll have to let her go. It's inhuman to let her husband go and keep her here." Cornered, Eli looked for a face-saving formula. "She has to identify herself!" Helped by Vaders, Dinie Ter Veer produced her driver's licence, and a few moments later, to Prins's relief, she appeared in the entrance door, and he helped her down. Calmed by the hijackers' acquiescence, she spoke softly to her husband. "They also let me go." Her release was another indication of whose authority for the moment held sway.

Fearing a surprise attack now from outside, Eli refused to spare more than one of his team for stretcher-bearing. So, in the shadows thrown by the searchlights, Prins and Kobus carried Paul along the track to a point 100 meters in front of the train. Then they returned for Ter Veer. His wife had remained with him, and she followed them with difficulty along the stony track in her stockinged feet. In her shock and confusion, she had left her shoes on the train.

When Prins and Kobus started off along the track with Paul, Timmer alerted the command post. But even after the second and more difficult lift with Ter Veer on the toilet door, no one came into view. The authorities were playing it safe.

"We've got wounded here," shouted Prins into the glare of the searchlights.

"Leave them there. We'll collect them when you've gone back."

Equally apprehensive was Kobus; he feared he might be picked off by a sharpshooter. As soon as Ter Veer had been placed alongside Paul he hurried back to the train.

Prins, feeling a duty to hand over his patient, lingered. Paul, who still thought he was dying, asked him to perform a service for him.

"Would you take the chain from my neck and give it to my girl, when this is over?"

"I will, if I survive."

Prins knelt down and fumbled with the chain. His fingers and hands were clumsy with cold and with the strain of carrying the door, and it was some time before he got the chain free.

Kobus had covered the distance back to the train in quick time, and Prins found himself standing alone in the darkness. Why go back to the train? It was no more than a few steps to freedom. But his legs were anchored as in a nightmare. They were steps of the mind, steps he could not take.

Several times the hijackers had threatened him with death. They had promised him he would be the next to die. Since then they had had a change of heart, but there was no saying how long that would last. Someone else might suffer if he escaped, and if that were so it would be a decisive factor. But they had let him go and left him unguarded, making no conditions. Wasn't it beyond all reason to expect him to return?

As he mulled these thoughts over, he realized that none of them counted for much. What dominated his mind was the feeling, hardly more than subconscious, that he was inextricably bound up with the fate of that motley community, that they couldn't do without him, and that in an odd sort of way he couldn't do without them. He would have to go back, to see the thing through. "They'll be along to pick you up soon," he told Paul and the Ter Veers. He turned and clumped back to the train.

When he got there, he found that the entrance doors had been closed. He had to bang on the door to attract attention, and shout, "May I come in?"

He found the South Moluccans still in a state of shock. "Put your guns down for a while," he told them. "You're too jumpy, and you've seen what the result can be. I'm going to take some water round. Everyone must drink some water."

It was his way of signaling his return, of marking his reassumption of the authority he had wielded as the doctor. He called the command post on the telephone and explained how the accident had happened, then sat down opposite Vaders, naked to the waist because he had pulled off his blood-soaked shorts and undershirt. Despite the cold, he was sweating. "Have a cigarette," said Vaders. Although he was a nonsmoker, he took one.

At 300 yards distance, it was impossible to recognize that the last man to return to the train was one of the hostages. Safety first remained the rule, and nobody came to collect the casualties until the last of the stretcher-bearers was back on the train.

As the two injured men lay beside the track, a twenty-five-year-old hijacker and a forty-nine-year-old hostage, it was the hijacker who broke the silence. "I am still your brother." Ter Veer tried to accept this, but for the moment he couldn't. All he could find to say was, "This is not the way to realize your ideals." Yet, in his heart, he understood. From their elders, from their environment, from their religion, these young men had been given a focus for their ideals, an identity, a love of country, a vision. It was a vision of something that did not exist and perhaps could not exist. Yet those who would deprive them of it, after a lifetime's indoctrination, needed to act with compassion.

The two men were taken to the same hospital, the Bethesda Hospital in Hoogeveen. For a short time, while Paul's injuries were too serious for him to be interrogated, they remained equal. Then, as they began to recover, Ter Veer was the hero and Paul the criminal. "I did all the killings," he claimed.

For all the intense happiness of reunion with his family, Ter Veer was left with a sense of guilt. He felt he had abandoned his friends. By escaping their fate, he had let them down. The emotions generated in captivity proved more tenacious than those of release. Like Prins, he felt spiritually locked in the train.

It was some minutes after Prins's return to the train before the hijackers recovered their composure. But with the situation restored, Eli reasserted control. "Go back to your places. I am the captain now."

The hostages were aware that Paul had been a restraining influence on the hardliner Eli, and they feared that this signaled a return to threats, ultimatums, and killings. A deterioration seemed all the more likely when Kuhuwael and de Lima, who had been at the command post at the time of the accident, called upon the hijackers to surrender—after pressure had been applied by van Agt—and received a blunt rejoinder: if they persisted with this request, they would no longer be acceptable as intermediaries. And if the police or army tried to take advantage of the recent emergency to storm the train, "All hell will break loose."

This was for outside consumption. Inside the train, the relationship between captor and captive had undergone another subtle change. It had not gone unnoticed that, in the crisis of the accident, the hostages had acted with complete impartiality, as quick to attend to Paul's injuries— and to beg for his release—as to Ter Veer's. These people, the hijackers said to themselves, helped us when we were in trouble. What are we doing to them? They are not the government. They are innocent people, ready to understand us.

It was Eli himself who translated these thoughts into words. "There will be no more killings. No more harm will be done to any one of you." They did not doubt for one moment that he was sincere.

CHAPTER 10

Amsterdam: The Balcony Scene

A T TEN O'CLOCK on that Friday morning, December 5, the Moluccans in the consulate followed the example of their compatriots at Wijster by issuing an ultimatum, to which was attached a threat to the life of a hostage. However, they selected the victim at the outset, and, under Jopie's direction, they exploited the theatrical possibilities to the full, displaying him on the narrow balcony of Room 25 for the world to see. Blindfolded and at gun point, barefoot and clad in little more than his underwear, the unfortunate victim was forced to stand only inches back from the waist-high balcony rail, staring sightlessly ahead, yet imaginatively aware of the menace of violence behind him and of the sheer drop below. A length of rope looped into a noose around his neck, fixed to a strong point inside the room, and tightened puppet-like at the whim of a hooded gunman (who would have remained invisible but for the telescopic lenses of press cameras), compounded the torture. With a robotlike voice bellowing threats in his ear through a megaphone and the long barrel of a rifle digging into the small of his back, he somehow stood with an appearance of calm, arms folded, the focus of a situation of scarcely conceivable terror.

The man selected for this ordeal was the thirty-year-old headmaster of the kindergarten, a man called Saka Datuk, to whom the kidnappers had taken a dislike. Of sensitive features and temperament and an elegant dresser, he appeared precious and effeminate to the hijackers, who picked on him for no better reason than that. He would be executed, they promised, if the demand for the introduction of Metiary as mediator, first made the previous afternoon, was not met. On the other hand, if it were

131

complied with, they would release three of the children as a gesture of good-will.

After consultation with the crisis center at The Hague, the management center in Amsterdam contacted Metiary and proposed to him that he and Pessireron mediate with the hijackers, on the understanding that they release all the children. Van Agt was making this release his top priority, even before that of the hostages on the train. Metiary agreed to journey from Assen, but the weather ruled out travel by helicopter, and a car was sent for him. Another influential South Moluccan, thirty-six-year-old Etty Aponno, son of the sergeant major in the KNIL who had led the military delegation to Holland in 1951, entered the mediation field by declaring, in a radio interview, that he thought he could bring the siege to an end. Chairman of the Free South Moluccan Youth movement and one of its leading intellectuals, he too was invited to talk to the kidnappers.

Meanwhile the young schoolmaster Saka Datuk remained on the balcony, sickened by vertigo and shivering with cold. Two other hostages, Harsoyo and an engineer named Mizar, one of the visitors from Jakarta, were roped to him, and a gunman repeatedly jerked the leash and shouted the demand for Metiary. Above them on the third floor Henkie Metekohy, placed in charge of the telephone, called the management center. "Do you agree to our demands? If not, we will shoot these men in two minutes." Also linked to the threat of executions was a request that police, firemen, ambulancemen, press, and cameramen retreat to a distance of not less than 200 meters from the building. "We'll shoot them if the police don't go back."

One of the recurring problems in dealing with terrorists was that the language used by governments tended to be formalistic, while the language used by terrorists was emotive. The effect was of two rough surfaces rubbing against each other. In a situation that was clearly one of great menace, it was Dr. Mulder's task to reduce this abrasive effect. Starting out with the assumption that he was dealing not with terrorists but with human beings, he accorded the hijackers respect and hoped to be treated with respect in return. He offered no moral judgements and neither approved nor disapproved, relying on a realistic approach. He met the Moluccans' threats equably, taking them seriously, but adopting a tone of sweet reasonableness. He conceded that they were in charge. They had the power, they held the whip hand, they must do as their consciences bid them. But since Metiary was already on his way to Amsterdam, they would naturally consider whether violence at this stage would advance their cause.

The tension created by the proximity of the police, Mulder felt, could be substantially reduced without hampering efficiency, and the police agreed. A number of sharpshooters, keeping out of sight in nearby buildings, remained in position, but the area that could be seen from the consulate was summarily cleared. Eventually, after two exposures on the balcony in the course of the morning, Saka Datuk was withdrawn.

At three o'clock that afternoon, when there was still no sign of Metiary, the whole process was repeated. And whereas, in the morning, Datuk had spent no more than half an hour at a time on the balcony, this time the unfortunate schoolmaster, tethered as before to Harsoyo and Mizar, was left to endure the extreme cold indefinitely, while the threat to his life was reiterated. Mulder kept the talking going, but the terrorists were approaching a crisis of their own making. Were they to believe what Mulder was telling them, or was he just a government stooge, trying to borrow time? What of their own credibility? If Metiary didn't arrive soon, they would be faced with the choice of killing Datuk or climbing down.

Were they capable of killing? Soon they would have to ask themselves that question. They scarcely knew the answer. But most of the hostages, suspecting that they were dealing with creatures of impulse rather than reason, feared that they were.

Metiary and Pessireron arrived in Amsterdam in midafternoon and were taken to the management center, where their proposed mission was defined for them by the chief commissioner of police, Mr. T.J.C. Sanders, and by Dr. Mulder. They were to secure the release of the children and put pressure on the hijackers to surrender. "Manage it how you like," they were told. Metiary had no reservations on the first point, but he was cautiously noncommittal on the second. "I'll talk to the boys," he said, "and see if they want to surrender." He had no intention of attempting to persuade them to do so. After speaking on the telephone to the hijackers, he and Pessireron were taken to the command post, from where they walked across the street to the consulate. On their arrival, the question of whether or not the terrorists would have killed Datuk became academic, but it seemed to the hostages that Metiary had arrived just in time. Datuk was brought in blue with cold and was treated by Dr. Fanggiday for heartbeat irregularities and hypothermia.

The two mediators were admitted to the consulate by Vera Martron at 4:30 PM, and it was obvious to her that the hijackers were well known to them. Indeed Metiary made no secret of it. They were *his* boys, and fine boys at that. Yet he had never imagined that they would take such a responsibility as this on their shoulders.

The hijackers who greeted the mediators were Josef Huly (Otjek) and

Henkie Metekohy, and it was Otjek who did most of the talking. The release of the children, he said, must be linked to government concessions, a proposition that Metiary did not disagree with. The chief demands of the group were: 1. a meeting between Manusama and Suharto in Geneva; and 2. the transfer of the train group to the consulate in Amsterdam, from where both groups would leave by bus and plane. Metiary's advice that a Manusama-Suharto meeting was impracticable did not convince them, and they insisted on delivery of their demands to the government—it was up to the government to solve the problem. As for the children, they offered to release three of them if Pessireron would take their demands at once to the management center.

Soon afterwards Pessireron emerged from the consulate entrance with three small Indonesian children, all girls. One of them, with long black hair and a bright yellow pullover, showed a precocious awareness of the television cameras by smiling and waving to ambulancemen lined up in Valerius Straat.

To Metiary, the saddest thing was that the boys seemed to have no strategy, no clear idea of where their action was taking them. They were young Christian people, and they assured him that they had no intention to kill. But their leaders, they said, were not respected, no attention was paid to their case, and rumors of persecution in the South Moluccan islands had exerted an intolerable pressure. "Reverend, we had to do something," they said. Eventually Metiary succeeded in getting them to downgrade their demands to a TV confrontation between the Indonesian ambassador and himself, a demand he would pass on to the government. The boys would telephone the request to the Indonesian Embassy. If the ambassador agreed, the rest of the children would be freed. This was not quite Metiary's brief. All the children were supposed to have been released in exchange for his visit, but the hijackers had never promised this, and the management center was pleased enough to get a dialogue going. Their suspicions of Metiary's impartiality, however, were not allayed by his willingness to involve himself in the hijackers' demands. Metiary, of course, was not impartial and did not pretend to be.

After gathering the group together, Metiary led them in prayer, praying for their spiritual strength. He urged restraint, appealed to them to avoid ultimatums, and stressed the dangers of the careless use of firearms and explosives; evidence of the latter was noticeable at strategic points. Surrender was not mentioned. At his own request, he was allowed to go into Room 25 and reassure the hostages. "Keep calm, and no harm will come to you."

To demonstrate their good faith, the hijackers released two more children, boys this time, when Metiary left. By that time it was completely dark, and the boys were so dazed by police floodlights, TV spotlights and photographers' flash bulbs that a doctor in an ambulance shouted at the cameramen to desist. With the five children released the previous day, ten of the sixteen were now free.

Mistrust of Metiary was evinced by his reception back at the management center, where he was told that he would have to be searched, "according to Dutch law." "If you search me now," he told them, "be ready with the car. I shan't talk to the boys any more. I'll go home." The threat was enough to cause the search to be abandoned, but the mistrust remained.

Metiary then delivered the kidnappers' revised request, and soon afterwards the Indonesian ambassador, General Sutopo Yuwono, was called to the Dutch foreign ministry by the minister, Max van der Stoel. But the ambassador would not agree to a meeting with Metiary or anyone else. It was up to the Dutch, he said, to solve the problem created by the terrorists. Later, under pressure from the parents of the children still in the consulate, he suggested a possible compromise: the head of his political department, Mr Soerjadi, could take part in private and informal talks with Metiary on a "strictly personal" basis. The suggestion was rejected by the kidnappers.

At a press conference that evening, prime minister den Uyl announced that his government was standing firm on both sieges. They would not bow to demands from the train or the consulate, and there was no question of allowing either group to leave Holland. There would be no deals, and the use of force was still not ruled out. But toward minor requests the crisis center was anxious to be conciliatory. A delivery of hot food was prepared, and at seven o'clock the claims of Etty Aponno were put to the test. He succeeded in getting the kidnappers to release two more of the children, leaving only four still in custody, but no progress was made toward a surrender.

In a broadcast addressed to the hijackers that evening, Aponno appealed to them to lay down their arms, assuring them that their objective of worldwide publicity had been achieved. But the gunmen in the consulate were in no mood to give up until they had won some major concession, and the gunmen in the train had no radio.

Asked by van Agt to mediate with his followers in the consulate, Etty Aponno demurred. "I am in a delicate position." A sincere advocate of nonviolent action—in trying to calm his followers during a demonstration, he had sustained head injuries which had resulted in partial paralysis —he nevertheless spoke of the Dutch as "our enemy" and once again had been unable to control elements in the movement he had helped to create.

In another radio broadcast, recorded from a call to a journalist from the consulate on a forgotten telephone link, one of the gunmen recalled the South Moluccan demand to be allowed to return to their native islands independent of Indonesian influence, and he repeated the request for talks between Metiary and the Indonesian ambassador. "We do not fight against children," he declared, "and we are not murderers. The Dutch have made murderers of us." This use of a nationwide radio service to disseminate terrorist propaganda embarrassed and irritated the government, who were already being criticized for employing too liberal an approach. How many more innocent people did the terrorists have to murder and humiliate before the government acted? "We need a dictator now," was a popular theme.

Soon after this broadcast, the loophole of the forgotten telephone link was closed. Police then brought crates of hot Indonesian food to the consulate, and a lone hostage in white shirt and tie walked slowly from the entrance in the glare of the floodlights to collect them. Covered by a hooded gunman and silhouetted against background shadows, he walked with hands held high, then stooped to carry the crates one by one into the consulate.

The promise volunteered by Eli to the train hostages that same evening, Friday, December 5, coupled with the establishment of something approaching a daily routine, brought a palpable easing of tension in the second-class smoker on Saturday, the fifth day on the train. The day began in a mood of restrained optimism, fertilized by a rumor that Robert de Groot, the first man to be taken out for execution, was not dead but wounded. The hijackers seemed ready to talk through mediators, and the hostages believed that the psychological moment for concessions had come. What was the government doing about it? The impatience of the hostages was summed up by Albert Oosting, hitherto one of the most relaxed, who suddenly exploded. "When we're free, we're going straight to The Hague, to hold den Uyl and the rest of his gang hostage."

Helping to improve the atmosphere in the train was the greater freedom of movement given to the hostages, and Prins was able to organize a program of exercise at the rear of the carriage. Full advantage of this was taken by all, from the young to the very old. Even Grandpa Smit took part, while Albracht was one of those who lay with his back supported by the wall of the train and pedalled an imaginary bicycle.

In talks that morning with Kuhuwael and de Lima, the train hijackers harked back to their sevenfold political demands of December 4, and they asked for discussions with Manusama. Taking much the same line as the group in the consulate, they insisted that there could be no question of surrender until their demands were fully considered and worthwhile concessions were made. When the two mediators reported this back to the government, a further meeting was authorized, this time with the approved group of four. But in briefing Manusama, van Agt insisted that surrender must come first. There could be no discussion of demands before then. This had all the ingredients of stalemate, and, despite protracted talks that afternoon, deadlock was duly reached. The only promise offered to the hijackers was that they would not be fired at during surrender. The only comfort Manusama could extract from the hijackers was a request for a break until 2:00 PM the next day, Sunday, to talk things over amongst themselves.

In fact, in a mood of determined realism, the hijackers made up their minds that evening. Despite the killing of hostages, they had failed to get the concessions they sought, and they recognized this as a defeat. But if self-conceit was diminishing, and they no longer saw themselves as masters of the situation, they had two attributes to fall back on: an unshakable belief in the justice of their cause, and courage. Right from the beginning, they had been prepared to die. They would continue their action to the bitter end.

The hijackers took their decision openly, and the hostages were aware of it. After the hopes engendered of a speedy solution, expectations plummeted.

The resolution of the South Moluccans in the train would have been greatly fortified had they known of the support they were getting in Amsterdam, but they remained totally ignorant of this parallel action, and the government, still not certain that the train group had no radio, wanted to maintain this situation as long as possible. A complete embargo on news was impractical, but agreement was reached with the media that they would refrain from live coverage of either siege and avoid mention of the position and movements of police and military units. All journalists were accordingly banned from Wijster, and the growing army of reporters of various nationalities was herded into a large tent at Beilen, where an official spokesman gave the latest news at intervals. This arrangement, although necessary for security, subtracted from the immediacy of press coverage and removed the horror of the train to a distance.

In contrast, the terrorists in Amsterdam were comparatively well-informed. And in the heart of the capital city, they were bound to remain in the public eye. Some progress in meeting their demands was made in the next forty-eight hours. Told by Dr. Mulder on that Saturday morning that, while the Indonesian ambassador still refused to see Metiary, the Soerjadi offer stood, the kidnappers notified their acceptance to Metiary when he called at the consulate that afternoon. Conditions for the meeting, incorporating terms laid down by the Indonesians, were then drafted at the crisis center. The discussion must be on a personal level, and Metiary must first go to the consulate and bring back the four remaining children. The meeting could then take place at the management center. After the meeting, the kidnappers must release two sick hostages, Saka Datuk, suffering from the effects of exposure on the balcony, and a sixty-two-year-old consulate official with a heart complaint, J.P. Pardede. A statement of the attackers' wishes could be made public provided it was worded as a request, without any appearance of government endorsement, and the talk between Metiary and Soerjadi would be completely self-contained and would not lead to further talks of any kind.

All this was explained to the hijackers by Mulder on the telephone and during visits by Metiary on Sunday, Monday, and Tuesday, December 7, 8, and 9. Prior to these meetings, Metiary was continually urged to advise the hijackers to surrender, and at debriefing, he was reproached for not doing so. But he would not change his attitude. "What message can I give them, so that I can tell them to surrender?" To the Dutch, he seemed quite prepared to use the hijackings to extract concessions, putting him, in their eyes, on a par with the hijackers. Possibly his difficulties were not fully appreciated: to demand surrender without concessions would be to forfeit the confidence of the boys. Kuhuwael and de Lima had met outright rejection when they proposed surrender to the group in the train.

To Metiary, the hijackers merely reiterated their demands. They still wanted, some time in the future, a meeting between Manusama and Suharto. They wanted freedom for imprisoned South Moluccans in Indonesia and Holland, and they demanded a dialogue between their political leaders and the Dutch Government. "I tried to explain to them," Metiary told the press, "that these demands were not possible, but they didn't want to listen to me and threatened violence if their demands were not met."

The meeting between Metiary and Soerjadi was arranged for 2:00 PM on Tuesday, December 9. On the evening of the eighth, in advance of this meeting, the last four children were led from the building by Metiary, leaving twenty-four adults remaining inside. In a broadcast, recorded before the children were released, Manusama told the terrorists, "You boys in the Indonesian Consulate in Amsterdam have asked for Reverend Metiary, and he has come to help you. Listen to him, and to God's voice in your hearts. Our struggle is a just one. Isn't it shameful that you hold children hostage for a cause like ours? I ask you, I beg you, I pray you to put an end to it. Boys, I pray for you." Only Manusama, perhaps, had the prestige to issue this kind of appeal.

During this period, the hostages reflected the mood of their captors, as did those on the train. The guards kept their firearms constantly at the ready, and almost every movement from the hostages attracted a threatening gesture. Metiary's advice that, if they remained calm, no harm would come to them was not so easy to act on when the Moluccans were screaming orders and pointing their guns. Anita Hoeboer, for instance, had a pistol pointed at her head by Otjek. As the gun neared her temple, she began to pray. She hardly knew to whom she was praying, but, with tears streaming down her cheeks, she prayed with mounting fervor. Suddenly Otjek laughed and put the pistol away. It was only a joke, he said. But after the killings at Wijster, no one could be sure.

As the two opposing groups sized each other up, probing for signs of weakness, compassion, or aggression, each wondered to what extremes the other might go. Worst of all for the hostages, as with those on the train, was the uncertainty, together with the complete absence of contact with the outside world. The suppression of radio bulletins, which were always turned down so low that not a word penetrated, was especially tantalizing. The smallest morsel, an odd word overheard in a telephone call or a radio announcement, was enough to set them talking and speculating, to raise or lower morale.

The sight of twenty-four people laid out in attitudes of unease and discomfort made a grotesque start to each day. Cautiously, and with many a stifled groan, they dragged their stiffened bones together and rose from the floor. Then one by one they were allowed to go to the lavatory. Tea was brought by the sisters Nies and Nus Sumarno, daughters of an ex-minister of finance in Indonesia. They took on many of the chores and handled the terrorists better than any of the men. One had been working in the consulate and the other in one of the travel agencies. This first hot drink of the day was accompanied by such an orgy of inhaling and belching of tobacco smoke that the fetid atmosphere of sleep and sweat, in a smallish room in which the blinds were always kept drawn, thickened until the coughing became epidemic. Then, while the majority were herded elsewhere, the room was aired and cleaned by two or three female hostages. Thus each day began with individual hostages keeping to themselves the fear that it might be their last.

The impression of unreality and hallucination was heightened for those hostages detailed to collect deliveries of food. Adjacent buildings had been cleared of occupants, the streets, unnaturally silent, were devoid of traffic, and only an occasional telephoto lens peeped obliquely from a distant upstairs window. All evidence of the buildup of armored vehicles and commando-type troops was kept out of sight, and the sense of isolation at these times was doubly acute.

Questions were continually being hurled at the consulate staff. "What is your position here? Who is your superior? What are his policies? Is he against us? Are you for or against our ideology?" Failure to answer meant further threats and intimidation. Safes were plundered, documents turned out of cupboards, desks rifled. The staff were on tenterhooks that something might be discovered to incriminate them personally. When the terrorists got hold of a staff list, they suspected that some members were unaccounted for and began a renewed search of the building.

The revelations that followed were not without their humor. One man from the accounts department was discovered in hiding on the third floor. He had found refuge under a table, where he had remained, except for occasional visits to a wash basin. He would probably have been discovered anyway, but at the time of the search his legs were sticking out. Another man was in one of a number of locked offices that the terrorists had thought were unoccupied, and he was only discovered when he fell asleep and began to snore. When the terrorists divined where the sound was coming from, they forced their way in. He too had existed for three days on water alone.

This second man, Pandji Asaari, quiet and uncommunicative, worked for the political department. That and his apparently furtive behavior were enough for the Moluccans to suspect him of being a spy. They screamed the accusation at him, then blindfolded him and announced their intention of executing him. Before facing the firing squad, he was allowed to leave a final message for his family. Then he was ordered to stand against a wall. The terrorists fired at the space between his ankles and were highly amused when Pandji, thinking he had been shot, fell to the floor as though dead.

The baiting of Pandji, like the enactment of the balcony drama on the Friday, proved to be no more than a sick and macabre charade. It was no less traumatic for Pandji on that account. Equally disturbing were the threats, frequently repeated, that if the antiterror brigade attacked, the building would be blown up. Such a conclusion seemed more and more probable as the days passed.

For the Dutch Government, the hope remained that the release of the children, followed by a meeting between Metiary and Soerjadi, presaged an early end to both sieges. The alternatives seemed uniformly unpleasant: grave risk to the lives of the hostages if they took military action, and mounting public revulsion and even racial clashes if they did not.

Dutch sentiment, normally liberal and progressive, was suddenly ranged on the side of the advocates of capital punishment for terrorists. Hundreds of people queued to sign petitions for harsher penalties, and many wrote letters demanding the liquidation of the terrorists and suggesting how it might be achieved. "Shoot the bastards!" was the prevailing attitude. The impotence of the government in the face of the terrorist challenge was frustrating to the average citizen, and there were isolated cases where members of the public took the law into their own hands. Railwaymen refused to carry South Moluccans on trains; angry passengers turned them off when they attempted to travel. In trying to achieve perspective, one former government minister made a distinction between ordinary crime and terrorism, arguing that terrorism involved not criminals but people who felt they had been cheated and who in any case were unable to grasp reality. The sister of the one of the train hijackers, interviewed on TV, said it was a pity that Dutch people had to die, "but before this no one in Holland, let alone the world, had cared about the South Moluccan cause." These were not arguments likely to mollify a people who believed they had given shelter and a home to refugee South Moluccans and who had seen the tragic results of their hospitality on TV.

On the morning of Tuesday, December 9, the consulate siege claimed its first victim. Abedy, the last man to jump from the second-floor window five days earlier, died from his injuries. Tisna was recovering, but the news of Abedy alarmed the terrorists, and later that morning, on the strong recommendation of Dr. Fanggiday, they released Saka Datuk, who had contracted pneumonia. "If you don't release him," warned the doctor, "he will die, and his death will be on your charge." After his release, the hijackers prayed for his recovery. That afternoon came the scheduled meeting between Metiary and Soerjadi.

It was a strange affair, a one-sided dialogue in which Metiary did the talking and Soerjadi kept silent—he had only agreed to "listen." To emphasize the informal nature of the meeting, Soerjadi, a cheerful character at any time, turned up in a battered trilby hat and with his face wreathed in smiles. The monologue was delivered in the presence of Mr. Sanders, the chief commissioner of police (impeccably uniformed), and all documents given to Soerjadi were handed straight over to Sanders. "Why is there no way to talk except when we have a hijacking?" asked Metiary. "The door is always open for conversations between us," replied Soerjadi, "to look for ways of understanding." At six o'clock that evening, the management center issued a press handout repeating the terrorists' demands—much the same demands as those sent three days earlier to the Indonesian ambassador and rejected as unrealistic by Metiary:

DEMANDS

1. Release of all South Moluccan political prisoners in the South Moluccan Islands and in Indonesia, under supervision of Amnesty International.
2. Freedom of speech for the South Moluccan people in the mother country on the subject of RMS.
3. Moves to initiate talks between Suharto and Manusama in Geneva.

We, Young South Moluccans, strongly demand from the Dutch Government, the Dutch Parliament, the Dutch people, and all Christian churches in the Netherlands the steadfast support of our claims, for the sake of the peace and well-being of the oppressed South Moluccan people and for peace in the world.

Signed with the blood of thousands of South Moluccans who lost their lives at the hands of the Japanese and Javanese oppressors during the Second World War, during the Red White movement of Indonesia, in loyalty to the Kingdom of the Netherlands and the Crown. Actions undertaken by South Moluccans are unavoidable since the Netherlands, responsible for this matter, have stood aside for twenty-five years. Who can now prevent South Moluccan people from dying for their own country and flag, when legal punishment and/or death cannot put the strength of the South Moluccan soul in irons?

Finally: Thousands of South Moluccans have given their lives for the Dutch cause; only a few Dutch have lost their lives for us, and, incidentally, that was never meant to happen.

On behalf of the Free Young South Moluccans

In a footnote appended to this declaration, the management center dissociated itself from it by pointing out that publication had been a condition of the release of a number of hostages (the heart patient Pardede was released immediately after the Metiary/Soerjadi meeting). But van

Agt's view was that a worthwhile concession of material value to the cause the terrorists were espousing had been made, and that the group in the consulate could now be expected to release the rest of their hostages and give themselves up.

The attitude of the Indonesian Government to this and other South Moluccan claims and demands, overtly at least, was one of benevolent tolerance. In the last twenty-five years, Indonesia had become a nation, there was no enthusiasm for independence in the South Moluccas, and the idea of RMS was as ridiculous as it was obsolete: so declared the Indonesian foreign minister, Adam Malik, in Jakarta. He also expressed the fear that the occupation of the consulate might have unfortunate repercussions for the many thousands of South Moluccans living in Indonesia.

CHAPTER 11

"We Are Not Alone!"

O N THAT SATURDAY NIGHT in the train, after the Moluccans had resolved to go on to the bitter end, Louis Laurier was again disturbed by scraping and scratching noises under the train. Knowing that the hijackers had mentally prepared themselves for death, he feared that they were planting explosives under as well as inside the train, and he racked his brains to think of a way of escape. The window at his side had been pierced by a fragment of bullet or metal, and he decided that his best chance was to hurl a suitcase through the weakened window and jump after it in the general confusion.

The heating, which was always switched off during the night, was now giving trouble during the day, and the Moluccans were trying to repair it. But if there were noises from under the train, they may not have come from the hijackers. Dutch military circles were indicating to the foreign press that marines had succeeded in planting listening devices under the train to monitor the conversations and assess the attitudes and morale of the gunmen.

To Laurier, the paradox of the hijackers' personalities became daily more puzzling. Most of them seemed decent enough boys; they were not the unintelligent semicriminal types he had expected. If anyone showed distress, they would come round with a glass of milk or water, and they were quick to offer their own scarves or coats to passengers who complained of the cold. When emotions ran high, they comforted the hysterical, especially the old. "Don't worry, Granny," he heard one of them say to Mrs. Barger late one evening, "nothing's going to happen tonight." Yet, driven by a distorted sense of justice and patriotism, they were capable of cold-blooded murder. He could not forget that. He was relieved when

Sunday morning came. He believed that because of their religion they were unlikely to do anything violent on a Sunday.

Breakfast that morning consisted of ham and cheese with crackers, taken round by Prins on a drawing board belonging to Luuk Verver that served as a tray. Still pinned to one side of the board was the blueprint of the proposed hotel development. What had once seemed an exciting business transaction now seemed less than insignificant to Verver compared with his anxiety for the fate of his son-in-law. "What do you think of the rumor that Rob survived the execution?" he asked Vaders. "He was in the army, you know. He does know about that sort of thing." Vaders related how he had heard one of the Moluccans say "not dead," and Verver went back to his seat reassured.

Timmer sensed that the problem now, as day succeeded day without apparently bringing a solution nearer, would be to sustain morale, not only of the hostages but also and even more importantly of the hijackers, whose desperation might lead them all to disaster. At 10:20 that morning he held a makeshift religious service, in which the Moluccans joined. By way of justifying themselves, Kobus asked him to read from Ecclesiastes, Chapter 3, and he did so:

> To every thing there is a season, and a time to every purpose under heaven: a time to be born, and a time to die. . . . a time to kill, and a time to heal; a time to break down, and a time to build up; . . . a time to love, and a time to hate; a time for war, and a time for peace.

He could see that these lines held great comfort for the Moluccans, and in a short address he tried to emphasize the positive side. Surely now was the time to heal, the time to build up, the time for peace. His fear was that they were in the grip of a death wish, that they had lost the will to live. His task was to help them regain it. Respect for their own lives would mean respect for the lives of others.

He read St. Matthew, Chapter 14, to them, where Peter attempts to walk on the water but loses faith and sinks, and Jesus saves him. They must hold on to their faith, he told them, or they were lost. There were times in life when one group of people failed to understand another. But God understood, and He would listen.

Whenever Manusama traveled north from Rotterdam to Beilen, he called in at the crisis center at The Hague, a call that was usually repeated on the way back. Protocol decreed, because of his self-styled presidency of a nonrecognized republic, that he be kept apart from den Uyl. But he was always met by Zeevalking, with whom he had an acquaintance socially, and he was taken in to see van Agt. His outspoken denunciation of the train hijacking at the outset showed him to be a man of integrity and moral courage, but he stood up to van Agt when he thought it was necessary, and he soon earned the latter's confidence and trust. The resolve of the hijackers to continue to the bitter end was not yet known outside the train, where it was thought they were still "thinking things over," and van Agt's hopes were centered on the talks with Manusama and his contact group that were due to be resumed that afternoon. Action on a long list of requirements issued from the train—food, drink, medicines, underclothes, cutlery, tobacco—was postponed until the talks had taken place.

The contact group reached the train at 2:30 PM, and the subdued atmosphere and disappearance of all but two of the hijackers to the forward carriage confirmed to the hostages that negotiations were in progress. But Manusama brought no news of any relaxation of government policy, and he found the hijackers equally unyielding. They had thought things over, they told him, and they were as determined as ever to carry on, at least until concessions were made.

"We have already killed three people. We have no alternative but to fight to the death."

"And the innocent passengers?"

"They may be killed too. But that can't be helped."

"All I can do is tell you the truth—that the Dutch Government will never yield to your claims."

Hoping to delay the moment when the government would feel obliged to meet force with force, Manusama pressed for the release of the sick and the elderly, and the hijackers agreed to make a gesture. At 4:05 PM, Eli appeared briefly in the second-class smoker and said that Grandpa and Grandma Barger would be released shortly, would Prins help to get them ready. The reaction of the two octogenarians brought a wave of admiration. "Is it fair? Is it fair to the other passengers to leave?"

Conditional upon the release of the Bargers was the dissemination to the press of a further short statement from the train:

> We, Free Young South Moluccans, have decided to release a few people to show the world we are not inhuman. We have realized that the Netherlands Government does not value the lives of its own people, but allows them to be killed rather than admit they have wronged the South Moluccans. This does not mean that we shall end our action.

There was consolation in the release of the Bargers, and also in their physical condition, which proved to be fair, but the gesture could not obscure the fact that the talks in which the government's hopes were vested had broken down. The fact that the talks had lasted throughout the afternoon made the severance all the more final. By the time the food and other supplies were delivered, it was already dark, and the hijackers, again fearing a trap, refused to collect them. Additional searchlights brought up by police and army only fanned their suspicions, and the result was that, on a day when the temperature hovered around the freezing mark, the hostages went hungry, and there was nothing to drink, not even water. Once again, ignorant of the circumstances, they railed at the government's carelessness of their plight.

Van Agt's growing disillusionment was clear to Manusama when he reported back to the crisis center. "You've been four times to the train without result. We shall have to take action."

"That's up to you, but I advise you not to do so."

"Isn't it useless to go to the train again? Do you think they will give up?"

"Yes, in the end, I think they will."

"Conditions are getting very bad for the passengers."

"I know that. But they will be worse if you attack."

Manusama had touched on a sore point. During the day, a Dutch marine commando group—the so-called antiterror brigade—had made a series of feint attacks on an empty, stationary four-carriage train not far from Beilen. Among the objects had been to test the effectiveness of such an attack and the vulnerability of passengers held captive inside. The exercise had not materially altered the estimates van Agt had been receiving from the start, that such an attack might result in as many as fifteen or twenty dead.

That night Manusama cabled the United Nations general secretary, Dr. Kurt Waldheim, reminding him of the South Moluccan claim to independence and asking for his personal intervention. But he had little hope that any more interest would be shown than on previous occasions. He also issued an appeal for help to the International Red Cross.

While South Moluccans as a whole condemned the killings, they would not denounce the young men responsible, whom they saw as potential martyrs acting selflessly in sacrificing their future for the RMS cause. This equivocal attitude angered the Dutch. As a gesture of reconciliation, the South Moluccan residents in Assen requested—and were granted—an ecumenical service in a Roman Catholic church at which prayers were offered for the hostages, the gunmen, and the victims. But, that same day, a young South Moluccan was roughly handled by a crowd of angry Dutchmen in Amsterdam.

Each day of the second week in the train began with the hope that it might be the last of the ordeal, each evening brought disappointment and another seemingly endless night of cold and discomfort, full of horrific visions and nightmares. Although to some extent mentally resigned and acclimatized, all the passengers were suffering from the lack of personal hygiene. Either through their experiences or because it was their time, several more of the women had started menstruating, and Prins's appeal for remedies brought outsize sanitary napkins that few could wear and paper underslips so small that only one girl could get them on. Men had to stay in the same underwear, with little chance to wash, and when water was sent in it was so cold that it had little soothing or cleansing properties. Inside and outside the train lay the litter of empty cartons and wrappings, and symbolic of the general stagnation was the rust that already obscured the polished surface of the northbound rails. Worst of all was the choked, stinking toilet, yet when Prins asked the command post for liquid antiseptic, explaining that it could be bought at any shop stocking camping equipment, all he got was a supply of air fresheners, the sort that hang from lavatory seats. "When you pull the chain," said the inscription on the box, "it will produce a fresh scent." But with no water to flush the system, such advice made the authorities a laughing stock. These and other disappointments all helped to throw the two groups together.

Another example was the shortage of tobacco. Vaders had no cigarettes, no cigars, and until Djerrit gave him a hand-rolled cigarette, he drew optimistically on an empty pipe.

Prins asked for a supply of woolen socks, since everyone complained that their feet were like lumps of ice. Because of the risk that such material might collect moisture in the daytime and then freeze in the night, causing frostbite, his request was refused. Had he known the reason, he would have insisted that approximately thirty people in one compartment would always keep the inside temperature above freezing.

After going hungry on the Sunday, they all enjoyed a hot pot on the Monday, and on Tuesday a cold meal was prefaced by a delicious hot soup. They had become less and less fastidious over their food and utensils, but in one case at least they took special care. Small pots of baby food were sent in for Grandpa Smit that were supposed to have been heated first, but they were cold, and Albracht and others, surviving the initial shock, warmed them on their stomachs.

Following the stalemate in negotiations, a request by the hijackers for alternative mediators was ignored. But the complete breakdown of the train's heating system, which occurred that week, convinced van Agt that a long-term siege was no longer tenable. "What we want," said one member of the ministerial council, "is a few more freezing cold nights to flush them out." But the considered view was that the stamina of the hostages must not be tested to destruction. The crisis center was less well informed about conditions in the train than many of their critics imagined, and they had learned little from the release of the Bargers, cushioned as this pair had been because of their age from the full impact of the experience. For the moment van Agt decided to await some initiative from the hijackers, but his concern for the hostages was mounting.

Morale in the train remained remarkably high, although many of the hostages were ailing. Sixty-one-year-old Mrs. van der Giessen, one of those who had boarded the train at Assen, had developed badly swollen ankles and could hardly walk, and Grandpa Smit, when finally persuaded to lie down, looked like a corpse. Yet when Albracht and van der Boon made paper playing cards, Smit and Mrs. Giessen joined cheerfully in a game of pontoon. "If the hijackers are going to fight to the death," said old Smit, "we'll play our games to the end."

Plans concocted by the hostages did not get beyond the suggestion of a protective cordon for the hijackers if they surrendered, and getting the train moving so they could escape. "But they'll have to move the explosives first," said Prins. "Otherwise we could push the wrong button, open the doors and blow ourselves up." The protective cordon still seemed the best bet.

The most significant event in the early part of that week was the revelation that Frits Santing had at last managed to make his radio work. When the next news bulletin was broadcast, hijackers and hostages alike learned for the first time of the occupation of the Indonesian Consulate. "It's great news! Another group! We are not alone!" The hijackers' reaction of amazed delight was convincing proof that they had known nothing of any such plan beforehand. Was it good news or bad, wondered the hostages? Would it strengthen the hijackers' resolve, which some had believed was faltering? Or would they now think they had done enough?

Opinion at first was divided, but successive news bulletins showed conclusively that the actions of the two Moluccan groups had won worldwide publicity, giving the hostages the chance to argue, as Etty Aponno had done to the consulate group, that the hijackers had achieved their aim. Prins, Timmer, Laurier, and Vaders all set this out in open letters to their captors, and in verbal appeals.

"You've achieved your aim—you've made yourselves known. You're still young. You've got your whole lives before you. Your deaths won't help your cause one jot. You must continue the fight in other ways, through the courts, for instance. That will also get you publicity. The passengers are on your side. They've promised to speak up for you, and to protect you if you surrender. You need the goodwill of the Dutch people. Now that you have allies among them, make the best use of them. We've been imprisoned now for 168 hours, and it's time to bring your action to an end, before there's an attack by the marines."

Eli's answer was brief. "Your proposals cannot be implemented. You may have been hijacked in the train for 168 hours, but we've been hijacked in Holland for twenty-five years. If we stay any longer, we shall lose our identity." But he added a word of comfort that meant much to them. "Your lives are not in danger." While the hostages feared that the climax of their sufferings was still to come, Eli believed—correctly, at that time—that the government had resolved on a policy of attrition. "They're leaving us to stew in our own juice."

The improved relationship between hijackers and hostages, the natural prejudices of the latter, and the extent to which they had been indoctrinated, were accurately reflected in a letter written by Laurier on Tuesday, December 9, addressed to the chairman of his trade union and to the Dutch press:

This is a voluntary letter, which I am writing from the train. I have been having conversations with the hijackers for a week, and I must say with emphasis that this action was started to convince the Netherlands population that the way the government has treated the Moluccans lacks respect for human rights and human dignity. These people have been tortured and murdered in their own country. Their demands were made to get concessions from the government to discuss with third parties a structural framework within which their aims could be put forward, and because of some temporary factors at the beginning of their action, they weren't taken seriously and some of their victims suffered. But there was no reaction to this, nor to my telephone call of December 4. Nobody believed there was a need for positive action. It is now everybody's duty to react positively to their demands. The hijackers will stop their action as soon as they find that they are being taken seriously by the Dutch Government, who should give them assurances for the future, either by telegram, telex, or letter. This letter is meant to allow the hostages who've been here for a week in this cold train under severe conditions the chance to be set free within a short period of time, so that they too can convince the outside world that the hijackers acted with honest, patriotic aims based on a belief in God inspired by the Bible. Please help both hijackers and hostages out of this impasse and give room for their action to be terminated.

Laurier himself realized how subjective his letter was. "Funny that you're prepared to listen to their ideals and think twice when a pistol is pointed at your head. Like most Dutch people, I had taken no notice of the Moluccan question before this."

The letter was given to Eli to read before it was sent out of the train. Vaders hoped to send his diary with it, for publication in his newspaper. "You know I'm a journalist," he reminded them.

"You said you worked for *Nieuwsblad van het Noorden?*"

"Yes. I'm its editor."

"Prove it."

Vaders produced his press card. "I've been writing an account of what's been happening. It's a fair account. If they would give us safe conduct, I could take it to the press center under guard, then come back. It's publicity you want, and this will help." Eli took the manuscript, and Vaders saw him reading it. "It can't go," he said, "it's too detailed."

"Then give it back to me," said Vaders, "it's worth a lot to me." Later Eli did so.

The hijackers had been unable to repair the heating, and they reported their failure over the field telephone and asked for more blankets, which duly arrived. Another arrival that day was a reconnaissance aircraft. "They've started running sightseeing trips," was the comment of Frits Santing. In fact, during the weekend, police and military had turned back thousands of sightseers who had driven out for a glimpse of the train.

The only other significant news that day came in a radio report that Paul had appeared in court and been charged with murder. To the hostages, this seemed encouraging news, and they urged that the hijackers had nothing to fear from surrender but the due processes of law, which Paul should not be left to face alone.

That night the hostages ran a comedy session, in which everyone had to tell a joke. With Christmas only a fortnight away, Hans Prins parodied the most popular of all carols: "While Moluccans watched their hostages by night." But although the guards maintained their brooding vigilance, the other Moluccans were rarely seen carrying arms. When they did, they were as careless as ever. On Wednesday morning a pistol went off in the carriage, though no one was hurt. Djerrit and another hijacker then disappeared up front, and the explosions that followed alarmed the passengers, until they realized that the boys were shooting at gulls.

Such activities reflected the boredom of the hijackers, and at 11:30 that morning the initiative for which van Agt was waiting came when they asked for another intermediary. Anxious to know what was going on inside the consulate, they named Metiary and Pessireron, offering the release of a sick hostage as bait. Prins had advised them to release Grandpa Smit, who in his opinion could not stand much more. The hijackers had been careful not to reveal that they now knew of the consulate siege, but isolation of one group from the other was an essential part of the government's strategy, and the mutual encouragement that a visit from Metiary might offer was the last thing they wanted. Late that afternoon, pursuing his usual policy of keeping the hijackers waiting, van Agt offered another visit from Manusama and his group, to which the hijackers agreed. Manusama's offer to go to the train next morning, Thursday, December 11, was accepted.

As darkness fell, Vaders noted in his diary: "There's probably a good reason why no one has come to negotiate. It's now too late for anyone to come today. Did the Moluccans' request come as a complete surprise? You can certainly put the hijackers under pressure by delaying, but it's a two-edged sword." He had reason to remember this next morning when the hijackers, after confiscating the radio, announced that, if no one came to negotiate by noon, they would start more executions. "They're bluffing," was Vaders' diary comment, but he wondered. The renewed threat was exactly what he had foreseen. And when twelve o'clock came with no further word from the government, he could not forget that the last time the hijackers had felt themselves cornered they had shot Bert Bierling.

By 12:30, the tension in the train was right back to that of seven days earlier. Minds resolutely closed to the horrors of the previous week were suddenly vivid with images, and the aura of death was so strong that many felt physically sick. Then, just before 1:00 PM, Manusama and his party tramped along the foggy embankment to the train. Four of the terrorists withdrew to the front carriage, leaving two guards, and as before the hostages guessed that some fresh attempt at negotiation had begun.

It was on this visit that the contact group discovered that the terrorists knew of the parallel action in Amsterdam; hitherto they had adhered strictly to government policy and kept the train group in ignorance. Manusama was now free to urge that the peak of publicity had been reached and that any further prolongation would be counterproductive. He was also free to stress a development of equal significance, the possible repercussions of the consulate action for South Moluccans in Indonesia. To the objection that this did not apply to the train hijacking, Manusama argued that the consulate group would take their cue from the group in the train. Manusama also had another piece of news that he thought might prey on the hijackers' minds: the previous day, in the court at Assen, Paul Saimima had pleaded guilty to the murder of Bulter and Bierling. This enabled him to argue, with even more force than the hostages had done, that Paul should not be left alone to face the music. The hijackers' reaction was that any one of them would have done the same thing, and they proved as stubborn as ever. In another letter for Manusama to take to the government they wrote:

> We, Free Young South Moluccans, declare to end this action only when the Netherlands Government see that justice is done. We have already mentioned Queen Juliana's message that every nation is entitled to independence. This and this alone is the aim of our people.

Manusama was also given the letter written two days earlier by Laurier.

The terrorists kept their promise to release a sick hostage; indeed they went one better and released two. They returned to the second-class smoker in better humor, or so it seemed, and first announced that Grandpa Smit could go. Smit was playing cards with Albracht, van der Boon, and Mrs. Giessen at the time, and his absorption in the game, coupled with his deafness, meant that he had to be told three times before he grasped that he could go. Tears of joy, gratitude, and of sorrow at parting streamed down his white-bearded face, and he shook hands warmly with his fellow passengers before shuffling forward to leave. They in their turn rejoiced that this brave old man who had suffered so much without complaint was free.

The other hostage to be released was seventy-four-year-old Mrs. Bakker, and if it could not be said that she had never complained—Timmer, who sat with her, had been especially long-suffering—she redeemed herself by asking, in a tremulous voice, "Can I take my friend with me?" She was referring to Mrs. Jansen, and she well knew that by doing so she was risking the hijackers' displeasure, even perhaps her own chance of release. "Get a move on," was the gruff reply. "Don't ask questions. Be glad you're getting out. Timmer will be." As soon as she had gone, Djerrit asked Prins: "Doctor, which of the two ladies had asthma?" When told it was Mrs. Jansen, he laughed ruefully. "Oh. Sorry, we picked the wrong one!"

"Then let Mrs. Jansen go as well."

"No. Two's quite enough for one day."

Stepping out unsteadily into the freezing fog, Smit was so confused that his first act was to look for a taxi to take him home. He was amazed to see Red Cross people near at hand, and the cordon of police and marines in the distance. Both he and Mrs. Bakker insisted on walking along the track unaided, and soon they were being greeted by relatives who had been waiting for them at the Prakken Hotel.

Manusama, on his way back to Rotterdam, delivered the two letters to the crisis center, where he told van Agt that he needed more time. The hijackers were not yet ready to surrender. He recorded his firm belief, however, that eventually they would be persuaded to do so. He had nothing concrete on which to base this conviction, other than the release of two more hostages and the more moderate tone of the hijackers' letter, and van Agt was sceptical. As for Laurier's letter, van Agt decided that, whether or not it was written under duress, publication would only be an embarrassment at the moment and he put it to one side.

Manusama asked for a further meeting at the train next day, to which he proposed to send only two of his party, Mrs. Soumokil and Kuhuwael, the one as a symbol, the other as a man who had known the hijackers from their boyhood. Van Agt agreed.

Smit and Mrs. Bakker described the atmosphere in the train as "cheerful," and first assessments were that conditions were "relatively good." But next morning, confidential medical reports reached the crisis center that indicated a marked deterioration in the health of the hostages and stimulated an urgent review of the feasibility of armed intervention.

Following the meeting in Amsterdam on Tuesday, December 9, between Metiary and Soerjadi, the task of conducting what further talks might be necessary with the group in the consulate was left to the management center, and in particular to Dr. Mulder. Although deferring to the crisis center for important decisions and for supervision, he was relied upon for specialist advice, and to this end he was kept aware of government policy, so as to be in a position to evaluate the terrorists' likely reaction to it. His insight into the mental state of the hijackers through his talks with them remained a vital factor in formulating that policy.

In a sense Mulder was no more than a member of a team, yet in another sense he had to keep aloof from it, seeing events through the terrorists' eyes. He had an independent role, too, within the management center itself, which was potentially charged with conflicting interests and departmental jealousies. It was not only among the hijackers that aggressive and assertive instincts had to be reckoned with and kept under control. But with van Agt sticking to the view that the terrorists in the consulate could now be expected to surrender, the temperature in the management center was lowered, and contact with the terrorists was diminished in a natural process.

A request by the terrorists for a further talk with Metiary could not be granted immediately, as he was not available. He had gone to attend a conference of the Badan Persatuan. At this meeting, with Metiary in the chair, the members called upon the Dutch Government to guarantee a meeting between Manusama and Suharto and to change their policy and state their belief in the justice of the demand for an independent republic of the South Moluccan Islands. On this basis the Badan Persatuan, as the political council representing 90 percent of South Moluccans in the Netherlands, would put its full weight behind a call to end the sieges. This was little more than a précis of the hijackers' demands. A more flexible line was taken by Manusama, who expressed the view that some indication by the Dutch that they were willing to recognize that the South Moluccan fight for independence was a just one would be enough for a successful appeal to be made to the gunmen.

On Friday, December 12, Metiary returned to Amsterdam at the request of the management center for a briefing by the attorney general, J.F. Hartsuiker, and Dr. Mulder. The belief that Metiary was not an impartial negotiator, and that he would do all he reasonably could to help the hijackers achieve their aim, had long since hardened into certainty. But he was the only man the consulate terrorists would deal with, and an effort had to be made to understand the impossible position in which he found himself. This time, to Metiary's resentment, the smooth approach was abandoned, and his reception was blunt: he must order the terrorists to surrender. The alternative would be a military assault.

"They will only surrender," he retorted, "if their demands are met." When he was finally persuaded to talk on the telephone to the consulate, he covered himself by telling the hijackers that he had been ordered to tell them to surrender. He added that he wouldn't visit the consulate again unless they called upon him to do so. Before he left police headquarters, he told Hartsuiker that he wanted no further part in the talks.

Within minutes the consulate group asked to see him, only to learn from

Mulder that he was already on his way back to Assen. This infuriated them. "We are sitting here for our combined purpose, a good purpose," they told Vera Martron, "and now he abandons us." This further clarified the relationship between Metiary and his "boys."

The hijackers told Mulder that they wanted to convey one last demand to Metiary, on the granting of which the release of the hostages depended. But they would not divulge the nature of this demand to Mulder, and Metiary could not be contacted.

It seemed to the consulate hostages that the Moluccans were losing their sense of cohesion, and that the knowledge that they faced prison sentences might predispose them to act rashly. This impression was strengthened when they began wiring up the entire building for destruction. But they made such a show of it that it seemed more like a tactical ploy, to put the government under pressure. Nevertheless notice was taken by the management center, and a bomb disposal squad that had been standing by was alerted.

Meanwhile Vera Martron was asked to help with the typing of the final demand. Sitting in an office that had been wantonly vandalized by the hijackers, and with the Moluccan Anies Sihasale standing in front of her, pointing a rifle at her forehead, she was told to get on with it. "Put that gun down," she told Anies. "Otherwise, I shan't do the typing."

"You have to do what I tell you."

"No I don't. I'm not scared."

The Moluccan's self-confidence was shaken. "You're not scared? Why not?"

Vera Martron had been as frightened as anyone, but now she was tired. The depression of her divorce had caught up with her. If her time had come, so be it. "I don't care what you do any more. I just won't type until you put that thing down."

Anies had been the most aggressive of the hijackers. When Saka Datuk was on the balcony, it was Anies who had prodded him with a gun. He had seemed to take a delight in it. But this woman who was defying him, who was not even afraid of his gun, nonplussed him. He began trying to explain his motives. "Keep your mouth shut and don't argue," he told her when she interrupted. But eventually the gun was put down, and she was allowed to get on with the typing.

This was not the first attempt by the Moluccans to explain their action. Several times the hostages had been coerced into reading passages from books and pamphlets devoted to the injustices the Moluccans had suffered. But they were never forced to cooperate if they resisted. To begin with, the hostages, if they responded at all, were careful to agree with everything that was said. But eventually Wessel van Pijlen, although protesting his ignorance of politics, made it a condition of taking part in discussions that he would be allowed to give his honest opinion, without reprisals, and the condition was accepted. Discussions were limited to what the Dutch had to say, plus one Indonesian—Suhirman—who had been out of Indonesia for twenty years. None of the consular officials joined in. When the terrorists asked afterwards if their motives were understood, they got a deathly silence, but they accepted this philosophically. "I suppose you don't understand a word of it."

Van Asdonck found the discussions stimulating but felt himself in a minority. "What do you expect to achieve by your actions?" asked Vera Martron. She was never able to get a straight answer. "What are *your* ideals?" they countered. "My ideals are my children," she said.

There was a lot of praying, by both Moluccans and Indonesians, and a surprising amount of drinking, sometimes until late at night, though never to excess. Jopie's birthday was celebrated that week, together with the birthday of one of the hostages, and bottles of champagne were brought up from the cellar.

The hijackers began to join in the card and other games with which the hostages sought to relieve their boredom, and the Indonesians came to life on these occasions, playing cards with fanatical enthusiasm. There was an ugly moment when one of the Moluccans, outmaneuvered in a game of chess, turned on his hostage opponent and pinned him to the wall, threatening him with a gun, but he was quickly restrained by his colleagues.

Van Asdonck couldn't learn the card games the Indonesians tried to teach him, but he remembered that Dr. Herrema had passed the time by pretending he was having a normal day at the office, and he imagined that people were coming in to the travel agency to book holidays and cruises, and he was organizing their travel arrangements. To Raden Suhirman, he joked, "I've never done such such good business in my life!"

Suhirman and van Pijlen, too, absorbed themselves in business matters, devising new itineraries, discussing problems they had had with their clients. "We'll never have such an opportunity again," said van Pijlen.

Suhirman was one of the few who felt they understood something of the South Moluccan dream. He thought their spirit was not unlike that of the Indonesians in 1945. Yet what they wanted, he was sure, was unattainable.

Van Pijlen found the hijackers understandably aggressive, yet painfully unsure of themselves. Once, when he had to go to the lavatory during the night, he confided in Henkie, the youngest of the hijackers, that he was afraid. "Yes, I'm afraid too," said Henkie. "Then what are we doing here?" asked van Pijlen. "I said yes when they asked me," said Henkie, "and now I have to finish the job. But if I'd known what it meant, I would never have come." His greatest fear, van Pijlen learned, was that they might shoot one of the hostages.

Misguided though the Moluccans might be, van Pijlen admired their willingness to sacrifice their lives or spend years in prison for an ideal that was unlikely to be fulfilled in their lifetime. Vera Martron saw them as well-brought-up boys, obviously from good homes. As a mother, she was concerned for their parents and what they must be going through. One night she awoke suddenly, and Henkie came over to her. "You must be cold. Shall I get you something?" He spread his coat over her.

The Moluccans showed more and more consideration for their hostages as the days passed. They abandoned the wearing of masks, and they stopped brandishing arms, except when accompanying hostages to the street door to collect food. The plentiful supply of food and drink struck the most bizarre note of all. "What would you like to eat tomorrow?" asked the Moluccans, "Indonesian, European, or Chinese? *Rijstaffel?* Okay, we fix you *rijstaffel.*" When van Pijlen asked for whisky, he was given the choice of Johnny Walker Black Label, Seagram's, or bourbon.

Toward the end of the week, the hostages were allowed an occasional sight of TV, but not if there was anything on about the hijackings. News broadcasts too were always turned down. Thus they knew nothing of how matters were developing on the train.

CHAPTER 12

"See You in Cell 580"

T HAT SECOND FRIDAY in the train was a day of low threatening clouds, banks of mist, and a steady drizzle, bringing a chill dampness that penetrated to the bones. An offer from the command post to send a mechanic to repair the heating was refused by the hijackers, and although the rail authorities sent in another fifty blankets, so that everyone in the train had at least five, the cold was becoming unbearable. Worse still, in the course of the day, the passengers were once more subjected to the ultimate threat.

The hijackers had repeatedly told the hostages that they would never surrender, and when Josina Soumokil and Theo Kuhuwael visited the train that morning and urged them, in the name of the Moluccan community in the Netherlands, to do so, their efforts proved entirely abortive. The hijackers refused to release any more hostages and insisted that it was the government's turn to make concessions. This defiant response, reported to the management center and thence to van Agt, sounded like the final challenge.

That evening, listening to the radio, the hijackers heard a report based on a statement by the public relations consultant to the judiciary, Mrs. Toos Farber, assessing conditions in the train as reasonable apart from the cold and opining that the lives of the hostages were not in immediate danger. This statement, hedged with qualifications in the original, was intended to allay the fears of relatives. But the phrases quoted, taken out of context, infuriated the hijackers, suggesting to them a complacency in government circles that they felt it was in their interests to dispel, since concessions were unlikely to be made except under duress. Bursting into the second-class smoker in their old aggressive style, armed as at the first

159

moments of the hijacking, and talking in a flood of Malay, they bounded threateningly down the aisle. One of them, Djerrit, had a Sten gun in one hand and a *klewang* in the other. In the darkness, the group's antics were reminiscent of some tribal war dance. Stopping at the last compartment but one, they picked out Piet Gruppelaar, the administrator from Oude-Pekela. "You! Come with us!"

"You're not going to shoot me, are you?"

"Don't ask stupid questions."

Gruppelaar feared that they were, but he had no choice but to accompany them to the rear of the train, where they tied his hands behind his back and sat him in the cabin. Next they picked out the soldier Thys Stevens and motioned him to the old bullet-catching position in the connecting passage. He was allowed to put on his coat and gloves before his hands were tied, and this gave him hope.

Were they really planning more executions? Or were they expecting an assault on the train? If the latter and they were using the hostages as a shield, they were going back on their promise that there would be no more sentry duty and that they would face their attackers alone. But Prins suspected a third alternative. "Perhaps they're planning to break out."

With the two hostages tied in position and the tension in the carriage almost tangible, the terrorists stopped and whispered to seventeen-year-old Irma Martens.

"Are you really a girl?"

Despite the unisex hair style, they could hardly have been in much doubt.

"Yes."

"Come with us. You're free."

"What?"

"You're free to go. Go now. Quickly."

"Can I take my bag and books?"

"Hurry up."

The youngest of the female hostages, still not quite sure if she had heard correctly, crawled between the legs of Thys Stevens and out of the train. Soon after she had gone, Gruppelaar and Stevens were released and sent back to their seats. The whole episode had been a charade to persuade the government that conditions in the train were not quite so cozy as the broadcast had suggested. Hence the necessity to release a witness, someone articulate and impressionable, who would record the physical and psychological pressures in the train.

Seeing the state of terror to which the hostages had again been reduced,

Eli chided them. "We promised last Friday that no harm would be done to you. What were you afraid of?" His injured tone actually made them feel ashamed. At moments like these, a glimmer of understanding of the complex and irrational nature of the terrorists shone through the train. They had given their word, and, despite all that had happened, they expected to be trusted. It was this ethical principle, amounting to a religious conviction, that a promise must always be honored and that one's word was one's bond, which the Dutch had instilled into them over the centuries—and which, rightly or wrongly, they believed the Dutch had betrayed.

Most of that evening the hijackers squatted round the small transistor radio and searched for foreign broadcasts to check for news. They had guessed by now that Dutch radio bulletins were heavily censored. They heard that the Dutch cabinet had met in The Hague to discuss their next move, and that den Uyl was pessimistic about a quick end to the siege. "There are no prospects whatever," he was quoted as saying. "Nothing has come out of the mediation attempts so far." Unknown to the hijackers, although strongly suspected by them, armored cars, police, marines, and sharpshooters were active on the perimeter of both siege positions. Revised plans for simultaneous assaults were ready, and although it was thought that conditions in the consulate were still supportable, the need for action at Wijster was driving van Agt toward a decision. Other factors were the disruption of normal duties among police and military and a natural impatience, once plans were finalized, to put them to the test. The imminence of military action was made abundantly clear to Manusama by van Agt on Saturday morning, December 13, but Manusama begged to be allowed one more mediation attempt. It was his belief that the group in the train were much nearer to crumbling than their surface antagonism suggested. All right, conceded Van Agt, but this will be your last chance.

If further justification for the government's stern attitude were needed, it would be forthcoming from Hans Prins, who was in the process of compiling an alarming list of maladies for treatment from a distance by the management center:

One patient, male, eczema, inflammation of the scrotum and groin, spreading. One patient, male, purulent infection of the foreskin. One patient, male, stabbing pains in the back, left, below the ribs, urine dark brown. Physical and psychological condition rapidly deteriorating. One patient, female, age 72, asthmatic bronchitis, general physical and psychological condition quickly deteriorating. Acutely short of breath at times. One patient, female, age 61, serious edema of both feet, barely able to walk. Feet and ankles twice the normal size. One patient, male, age 63, operated at the base of the spine in January 1975. Sitting painful. Most passengers are in danger of becoming infected as a result of continued sitting and no change of underwear for thirteen days.

Prins was not qualified to prescribe for all these illnesses himself, even if he had the medications to do so, and he felt duty bound to refer them to the management center. But he suspected that his list, combined with falling temperatures, might be all the government needed to convince them that they must act.

It was a beautiful morning, bitterly cold but sunny, with only a few scattered clouds on the horizon, and there was a strange atmosphere of expectancy in the train, uneasy but not wholly fearful, that no one could account for. A soothing influence was the temporary return of the radio, on which Vaders and others recognized the familiar cadences of Mozart's Piano Concerto No. 21. They feared it would soon be switched off, but they were allowed to hear it right through. Afterward, Vaders learned that Eli was an ardent listener to classical music and had forbidden the others to change the program.

By day, the Moluccans now went about virtually unarmed, and at night all but two slept. Yet the hostages had no thought of overpowering them. In that small space, even a single shot could be catastrophic, as they had seen, but this was not the real inhibition. After the first shock of the hijacking, the hostages had gone through a prolonged stage of alarm and anxiety before achieving a kind of mental and physical adaptation. They had learned to play a role, if only the passive one of hostage, and their motivation had been survival. To achieve it they had moved closer to their captors, identifying with them and their political aims. At the same time, the terrorists, isolated from their own community and needing approval, had sought contact with them. The two groups had met on a human level, and neither group could now betray the other.

That morning the hijackers hung blankets over the windows, ostensibly to keep out the cold; but the effect was to darken the interior and blur any silhouette that might be visible from outside, making selective attack difficult. This was their only apparent reaction to the entreaties and warnings of the mediators. In the forward carriage, they plastered the windows with plastic rubbish bags, with the same effect—not exactly an indication, as Vaders noted, that they were thinking of surrender. Yet a hint of fatalism had crept into their talk. When a stereotyped Dutch meal of meat, peas, and potatoes arrived at lunchtime, Vaders told Kobus: "Next time we'll ask for *nasi goreng*" (an Indonesian speciality).

"In that case," said Kobus, "I don't think there'll be much left over for the passengers."

"Then we'll come and eat *nasi goreng* at your place."

"Sure," said Joop laconically, "See you in Cell 580."

Did this mean that the hijackers were contemplating surrender? It was against all their solemn declarations, and the hostages did not believe it.

Manusama again chose Josina Soumokil and Theo Kuhuwael for the final meeting. The hijackers agreed to see them, and, at 3:25 PM on that Saturday afternoon, they entered the train. An assault, they promised, was imminent. They would not be coming to the train again, and the hijackers had nothing to look forward to but annihilation. The group responded as stubbornly as on the previous day, but the two mediators persisted, returning to the argument first introduced by Manusama two days earlier—that the consulate siege, mounted in support of their own action, had become a liability. If they were determined to force the government to intervene militarily, members of the Indonesian diplomatic corps would be killed and wounded, and retribution would fall on the very people whose oppression they were trying to relieve.

Surrender was so totally incompatible with South Moluccan tradition that the atmosphere of the talks became strained. But after a short discussion among themselves, the hijackers came up with a proposition that was startling in its moderation. They wanted Manusama to go to Amsterdam without delay and tell the group in the consulate that, if they ended their siege, the train would be surrendered at midday next day, Sunday, December 14. There were two additional conditions, both minor:

1. Mrs. Soumokil and the other three mediators must be allowed to pay occasional visits to them while they were in prison.
2. They would surrender not to the Dutch but to Manusama, who would pass them on to the police.

The hijackers may well have discussed surrender on these terms before the visit of the mediators that afternoon. But the decision, when it came, had all the marks of spontaneity. Surrender might not be so humiliating when the mainspring was not self-preservation. Whether this was a rationalization or not, the hijackers genuinely believed that their fellow countrymen in the Moluccas were enduring persecution and imprisonment without trial. Exaggerating the scope of Dutch influence, they had sought to coerce the government into supporting their campaign. Then a second group had challenged the Indonesians themselves. The two actions, as Manusama had suggested, had become counterproductive, and the consulate siege, which had sustained their morale in such timely fashion when they first heard of it, had proved to be the Achilles heel.

It was the terrorists' turn to suffer anguish, and reconciliation with their sudden decision was not achieved without great torment of mind. When the mediators left at 4:15 PM and the hijackers filtered back into the second-class smoker, some of them could not conceal their distress. "Djerrit must have had bad news," noted Vaders, who, like the other hostages, hardly knew that negotiations had been taking place. "He strikes his forehead and walks up and down the aisle. He sits on the arm of a seat with his head in his hands, crying. It's dead quiet. Two Moluccans begin to sing a duet, an Ambonese song intended to comfort him perhaps. Eventually he lies down. Crying, he takes out his pocket Bible . . . by the light of a flashlight he crosses out something on the flyleaf and then reads. Later on he is unusually gay. Strangely enough, we feel sorry for him, even though he is an accomplice in the murder of three hostages."

Pity for their tormentors was something the hostages had never expected to feel. Yet now, as they saw their wretchedness and suspected the reason, they found it impossible to withhold compassion. Even more than their fellow hostages in the consulate, they saw their captors as young men imbued with a spirit of self-sacrifice. They had started out to do something they had imagined as heroic but had found themselves acting out a situation beyond their control. Now they looked even more forlorn than their victims; it was the helpless and once-despised hostages who were emerging with the greater strength. Everything had been in vain. The Establishment was going to win. They had killed people and marred their own lives for nothing.

Although the stigma of terrorist had rightly been attached to them, they hadn't had it in them to go on killing, and they had finally been brought down by the arguments of their own side. They came from a background with strong military traditions, where in some situations it was dishonorable not to die. This they had felt was such a situation, yet they were surrendering. It was to salve some vestige of their injured pride that they had agreed to surrender only to Manusama.

The hostages were aware that some traumatic decision had been taken, but they still dared not guess at the truth. When Timmer asked if it might be possible to bring in a pastor from outside the train, Eli said: "We must wait. The situation at the moment is very difficult." He promised to explain it to Timmer as soon as he could.

After consultations between the crisis center and the two management centers, it was agreed that Mrs. Soumokil and Kuhuwael, joined by Manusama, should go to Amsterdam that night in the hope of ending the consulate siege. Armed with the news that surrender in the train would automatically follow, they expected to succeed. But when, at ten o'clock that night, Manusama telephoned the consulate from police headquarters in Elandsgracht, the attackers would not be deterred from their demand for Metiary. They refused to see anyone else.

Everything now depended on the reaction of Eli Hahury and his group. The single condition they had imposed could not be fulfilled, and a further stalemate was feared. But once having accustomed themselves to the idea of giving up, the train hijackers were vulnerable to the argument that their surrender would trigger off a similar capitulation in Amsterdam. To the relief of the authorities, they agreed that their surrender need not after all be conditional on surrender at the consulate, although they firmly believed that that would be its effect.

Saturday night was the coldest so far, temperatures falling to six degrees below zero. The train was encrusted with ice, and condensation streamed down the windows of the second-class smoker. As medical teams prepared to accept the released hostages, security precautions were redoubled and cordons reinforced in case the hijackers changed their minds. Indications in the train next morning, however, seemed favorable. The hijackers returned personal effects to their owners, cleaned themselves up, combed their hair, packed their kit, emptied their ammunition magazines, and transferred the RMS stickers from their guns to their bags. Then, at nine o'clock, Eli went to Timmer and told him, as he had promised, what had been decided. "The action will be ended at twelve noon. When the time comes, will you pray with all the people in the train?"

At ten o'clock, Mrs. Soumokil arrived at the management center in Beilen, followed by Manusama, Kuhuwael and de Lima. Soon afterwards they were joined by Metiary. Transport for hijackers and hostages had been made ready and roads cleared, but for security reasons all preparations were kept secret. The press were excluded, and relatives were not informed.

At 11:40 AM Timmer called for attention for prayers, but Eli asked him to wait. "It's an old custom of war," said Vaders, "to cease hostilities in winter. Why don't we strike camp and meet again in the spring?"

Kobus replied enigmatically: "Who knows?"

Djerrit began tearing down the paper at the windows. Then he saw a helicopter circling, and he opened a small window and fired at it with his empty rifle. The firing pin clicked harmlessly. "Where's that ointment for sore hands?" he asked Prins, and Prins gave it to him.

"Can I keep it?"

"Of course."

"This is the 290th hour," said Frits Santing. Then the telephone rang. At 11:45 AM, Manusama and his party boarded the train. After a few minutes' conversation with the hijackers, they entered the second-class smoker. "It's all over," said Manusama.

Eli spoke to Manusama, and Manusama asked Timmer if he would lead them in prayer. "On Your day," began Timmer, "the day of the Lord, we stand before You." He called it the day of reconciliation, and he prayed for God's forgiveness for the situation in which they found themselves, for all the problems and actions that had brought grief to so many. Both sides had had their difficulties. "But we are all made in Your image. We all bear the responsibility. We hope to make that clear when we are freed. And we ask God for strength for both groups, hijackers and hostages, to face the days ahead." Several of the Moluccans were crying as they began reciting with him the Lord's Prayer.

Eli, whose psychopathic streak had made him the most feared of all the hijackers, thanked Timmer for all he had done. "We didn't know the Dutch could be so understanding." Herein lay the germ of the tragedy, in which both sides were implicated. Eli had spent the whole of his twenty-three years in Holland, yet he knew so little about the Dutch.

On Manusama's instructions, Timmer called the command post and told them the hijackers had surrendered and would leave the train in five minutes. He could not keep the jubilation out of his voice. Prins asked Djerrit: "Hadn't you better remove the explosives?"

Djerrit, who had taken the surrender harder than anyone and refused at first to give up his gun, relapsed into near hysterical laughter. "We've made fools of you for thirteen days—they're fakes!" He picked up one of the supposed sticks of dynamite and offered it to Prins. "You can have it as a souvenir!"

Soon afterward, the train doors opened, and the six hijackers, led by Manusama, stepped out one by one. With hundreds of troops and police looking on, they walked south along the rails halfway to the level crossing, where Manusama delivered them into custody. Soon the hostages, too, were being led along the rails to waiting ambulances. All but three of them were able to walk, indeed insisted on walking, bringing the first clash with authority. There were many more clashes to come.

Most of the hostages had only one thought—to get home. They did not want to be hospitalized. They did not want to be psychoanalyzed. All Gerry Vaders's repressed aggression came out when the rescuers tried to put him on a stretcher, then isolate him in a hospital. "The hijacking is over," he told one overzealous official. "Buzz off." Only when he had gotten a message to his wife and his copy to his newspaper did he agree to submit to medical and administrative routine.

CHAPTER 13

Once a Hostage, Always a Hostage

REJOICING AT THE COLLAPSE of the train hijacking was tempered by the knowledge, recalled by van Agt in a broadcast, that three hostages had died in the train and that another group of hostages was still being held in the consulate in Amsterdam. Meanwhile, at the Ministry of Justice at The Hague, Manusama was being given an assurance by the ministerial council that, after the actions were over, discussions with prominent South Moluccans would naturally take place, to avoid repetitions of such actions. This was as much as Manusama felt he could expect at this stage, and the public confirmation of it by van Agt on radio and TV, backed up by a radio interview in which Manusama expressed great faith in the promised exchange of views, encouraged the hope that the group in the consulate would regard it as an acceptable basis for surrender.

Interest in the meantime was inevitably focused on the hostages released from the train, most of whom managed to persuade the doctors to let them go home that night. By that time, however, the attitude of men like Vaders, Prins, and Laurier, as expressed in interviews, had shocked and revolted the Dutch public. Prepared to welcome the hostages as heroes who had survived a vile incarceration, they found them sympathetic with the terrorists who had murdered three of their number and highly critical of the government who had worked day and night for their release.

Of the government's principal critics, Vaders had no quarrel with the policy or priorities in theory, but he felt the government had blundered in practice. He accepted that the duty to protect the judicial framework on which the state stood and the need to discourage future incidents took precedence over the freeing of hostages. But he felt that the government

168

had underrated the ideological motivation of the terrorists and the fanaticism that flowed from it. They had failed, in his view, to face up to the fact of the first two killings, much as the hostages themselves had done. They should not have attached conditions to the publication of the hijackers' appeal. In the end, they had agreed to publish it, but the delay and consequent frustration had contributed directly to the death of Bert Bierling. They had shown lack of imagination over conditions on the train, and there had been too little expertise at local level, so that advantage had not been taken of the unique opportunity offered of direct contact with hostages, who might otherwise have been able to exert a material influence on their situation. In Amsterdam, the government had appointed an experienced psychiatrist as contact man, but no such direct contact had been permitted for the train. This Vaders saw as the greatest blunder of all.

In these criticisms, he was fully supported by Prins, who saw it as a psychological blunder of the first order that the authorities, however unwittingly, should have allowed the impression to be gained in the early stages that the affair was not being taken seriously. And like Vaders, he could not understand why direct contact with the train had been kept at so low a level. Indeed, some of the hostages felt that, since they were placed in the position of standing hostage for the government, members of that government should have been prepared to negotiate directly, if necessary by coming to the train. Such a gesture, they believed, would have ended the siege many days earlier and possibly averted the third murder.

Of all the subjects of controversy, the most persistent was whether or not the terrorists had been promised a bus. The hostages were satisfied that the impression had been given that a bus was coming. The government denied that any such impression ought to have been gained. The principal message in contention was the one signed by the burgomaster of Beilen and delivered to the train on the day of the hijacking:

1. Your demands have been received at Beilen Town Hall at 12:15 PM. You will realize that a decision cannot be made in thirty minutes.
2. Your demands have been passed to the Dutch Government. We will contact you as soon as a reply is received.
3. Meanwhile I have contacted Raterink Travel for the preparation of a bus.
4. In view of the above, we request that you refrain from irresponsible moves, in order not to impair negotiations.

The government could reasonably argue that implementation of item 3 was conditional upon the reaction awaited under item 2. The bus was being prepared in case the government agreed to supply one. But the message, hurriedly prepared, didn't specifically say so. And it seemed implicit in item 4 that worthwhile negotiations were in prospect.

The misunderstanding over the bus was compounded later in conversations with the command post in which implausible excuses were offered for its nonarrival. The first indication the hijackers had that a bus might not be forthcoming seems to have been from Manusama on his own initiative during his first (abortive) visit.

However, one of the first psychological principles enunciated by Dr. Mulder and others was that the contact must start by strengthening the ego of the terrorists for a limited period in order to alleviate the paranoid state. If, in this period, the impression was given that concessions might be granted, that was inevitable, and the government eventually conceded this.

Not every hostage took the same critical attitude as Vaders and Prins. One who sided with the government—as he had all along—was Albracht. Since this was the first-ever train hijacking in which hostages had been taken, there had been no precedent to follow, and it would have been astonishing if mistakes had not been made. The only way to discourage future hijackings was to make quite sure they failed. Yet he found himself out of sympathy with relatives and friends in that he could feel no bitterness toward the hijackers. He recognized that in actions of this kind, as in war, everyone was a victim.

Fellow-feeling with captors and forbearance toward them, coupled with a critical attitude to officialdom, were well-known symptoms in released hostages, but the conclusion that they had been brainwashed was an oversimplification. None of them had taken much interest in the South Moluccan problem before the hijacking, and their outlook had undoubtedly changed. But for the psychiatrists, it was difficult to separate the hostages' natural compassion for the sufferings of fellow human beings from the overidentification with captors which experience had shown was typical of the hostage situation.[9] For relatives, fiercely resentful of the ordeal of loved ones, the attitude they displayed was at first puzzling, then

---

[9] The close personal relationships that can develop between hijackers and hostages had been exemplified in August, 1973, during the siege of Kreditbanken in Stockholm, when four of the bank staff, one man and three women, were held for six days. The phenomenon became known as the Stockholm syndrome.

hurtful, and finally incomprehensible. Indeed, to the Dutch public, the sympathy of the hostages with cold-blooded murderers and enemies of the state, and their disloyalty to the government, appeared treasonable. Thus, to the problems of adjustment after the traumas of the train were added reproaches in the home and hostility outside it. Those most vocal in finding fault with the government and showing understanding for the terrorists were bombarded with threatening letters and telephone calls.

"Don't think that at the moment of liberation the whole thing will be over," warned Professor Dr. Jan Bastiaans, a leading Dutch psychiatrist, Chairman of the Department of Psychiatry at Leiden University. Holland had had considerable experience of what was known as the late sequelae of war stress—psychiatric and psychosomatic reactions in later life—and after examining and treating hundreds of war survivors and former inmates of concentration camps, Bastiaans had concluded that the best form of comparison for what he called the post-concentration-camp syndrome (Konzentrations Lager—KZ syndrome) was a well-known adaptation syndrome consisting in essence of four phases: shock, alarm and arousal, adaptation, and exhaustion.[10] Bastiaans saw the hostage situation as an acute stress situation in which the hostages went through this entire syndrome in microcosm. The initial phases of shock and arousal would be followed within hours or days by adaptation. And, with the necessity to suppress aggressive tendencies in order to survive, the natural consequence of the loss of normal security and safety would be affiliation-seeking behavior and identification with the aggressor. Eventually would come the phase of exhaustion, with the same tendency as in the KZ syndrome to the phenomenon of late sequelae, bringing mental or physical breakdown.

Bastiaans wanted the released hostages to have the opportunity as a group to discuss their experiences in an informal setting, to talk it out of their systems. Once the group broke up, individuals would suffer a second isolation, in which no one would understand what they had been through or why they had reacted in the way they did. But most hostages, as we have seen, wanted to get home and forget the experience as soon as possible. Bastiaan's presumption was that repression only led to neuroses, and that painful memories had to be worked through. They could not be dismissed as belonging to the past until they had been digested.

The obvious danger that, by publicizing these findings and emphasizing the phenomenon of late sequelae, psychiatrists were predisposing the

---

[10]Selye's General Adaptation Syndrome.

hostages toward it, was well understood by the psychiatrists themselves. But based on statistics, they estimated that 70 percent of the hostages would suffer some psychiatric damage.

Most of the hostages maintained their resistance to being treated as patients. They simply wanted to pick up the pieces and get on with living their lives. For many, indeed, the experience had had its positive side, giving them a new perspective, and they felt traumatized as soon as they were referred to a department of psychiatry. If they thought that the experience might leave any mark on them at all, they saw it as more likely to be in the label on the box than in the contents. From heroes they found themselves being transformed into victims, and victims, in the concept of social placement, they did not want to be. Once a criminal, always a criminal; that was the way with society. And once a victim, always a victim. That was what they feared.

The idea that science might be traumatic in itself, and that the patient must be protected from scientific analysis on the ground that it might harm him, was often prevalent at the level of the general practitioner and social worker too. All these reactions complicated the work of the scientists, the validity of whose theories remained to be proved.

The day after the surrender in the train, Metiary rang the management center in Amsterdam at Manusama's request, and a car was sent for him. The suggestion of the center, put to Metiary by the attorney general, the queen's governor, the burgomaster of Amsterdam, and Dr. Mulder, was that he go to the consulate as requested by the attackers to hear their final demand, but that he inform them that after this he would only return "to accompany them out of the consulate." Metiary asked for time to think this over; and that evening he telephoned his agreement to Hartsuiker. When he went to the consulate the following afternoon, he did what the management center had been asking him to do all along. He advised the hijackers to surrender. They in turn asked for time to think it over, and they made no mention of the final demand that they had regarded as so important the previous week.

Mulder sensed that the reaction of the group in the consulate to the train surrender would be an ambivalent one, partly relief, partly a feeling of betrayal. They would not lose face now by giving up, but they might feel let down by the men they had gone into action to support. They might also feel betrayed by their leaders, whose policies they were loyally supporting and publicizing, but who now seemed prepared to allow them to surrender without any assurances for the future, taking whatever punishment the Dutch courts saw fit to exact. The hijackers' reaction to this, he thought, might well precipitate a fresh crisis.

Mulder felt it was a psychological error to assume that, because the group in the train had surrendered, capitulation in the consulate must inevitably follow. This relegated them to a secondary role, which, accurate though it might be, they would resent. To assert their independence, and perhaps to spite their leaders, they might become more aggressive. Rather than risk adding to this kind of pressure or displaying any hint of triumph, Mulder avoided the subject of the train surrender, and it was the Moluccans themselves, after they had had a day or two to think about it, who asked why he hadn't referred to it. "Why should I? I knew you were aware of it, so what was the good? You didn't need to hear it from me." Without actually saying so, Mulder was implying that the hijackers had to make their own decisions, independently of the train and of outside pressures. This way they would be more likely to act responsibly.

The hijackers now demanded a meeting with Metiary and Mulder together, preferably at the consulate. Mulder suggested that such a meeting would have to take place outside the consulate, perhaps in a bus, but any such meeting was promptly vetoed by van Agt on the grounds of security. That evening, Wednesday, December 17, the hijackers, in a telephone call to Mulder, spelled out their final demand:

We want a public undertaking from the Netherlands Government that a discussion will be arranged between the government, Mr. Manusama and our leaders. In this discussion, the political aspects of the RMS must be dealt with, or raised. In other words: it should concern the political problems, not the social ones. Another matter to be brought up is the legality of the Round Table Agreement [of 1949] as a basis from which to approach the political aspects. If this demand is met, the siege will be called off.

The demand seemed more realistic than anything that had preceded it, but that evening Mulder detected a change of attitude on the part of the hijackers that puzzled him. If they were not exactly belligerent, they were surprisingly offhand, and there was a suppressed excitement in their voices. When police on the spot heard shooting inside the building and noticed an unusual degree of movement, fears grew that the hijackers, anticipating rejection of their final demand, were preparing some act of violence. The contingency plan for a military assault on the consulate was reconstituted, and that night a state of special alert was declared.

A report that the hijackers had resolved to hold out at least until

December 27, the anniversary of the granting of independence to the Federal Republic of Indonesia (of which the South Moluccans had been happy to form a part), drew a sharp reaction from van Agt. "We shall decide when the siege ends, not the South Moluccans." The scene was set for the trial of strength whose outcome everyone dreaded.

The night passed quietly, and it seemed possible that the hijackers had merely been letting off steam. At 7:45 AM, Mulder reopened the contact by reporting that the final demand had reached the government and that a speedy reply was expected. At ten o'clock, Mulder called again with the text of the reply. The government, he said, reminded the attackers (the word "terrorists" was always avoided in these exchanges) of several utterances during previous days regarding the dialogue between them and prominent South Moluccans. The aim of these discussions would be to find ways of preventing repetition of recent serious outbreaks of lawlessness such as at Wijster and in Amsterdam. Obviously such discussions would include problems connected with the South Moluccan presence among the Netherlands community. Manusama had stated on the radio on December 15 that he had much faith in an exchange of views between the government and South Moluccan leaders. When both actions were over, the government point of view would again be published through the usual information services. This reply did not satisfy the hijackers, and, complaining that their demand had not been met, they asked for newspaper reports of the statements made and for consultation with Manusama to check on government promises.

At 2:40 PM, Mulder reported back to the hijackers that van Agt would meet Manusama that afternoon. After the meeting, Manusama reaffirmed his confidence that van Agt's statement after the Wijster surrender, since broadcast on TV and radio, would be honored. He then returned to Amsterdam to relay this assurance to the hijackers.

He arrived at the consulate with Metiary at 6:00 PM, and there was a moment of panic when the hijackers discovered they had lost the key to the entrance door. They feared that the authorities would suspect treachery. They were calmed down by Mulder on the telephone, and the key was found. At 6:15, Manusama reported that the hijackers were willing to surrender without further conditions at 2:00 PM next day, Friday, December 19, the sixteenth day of their siege.

Metiary addressed the hostages and told them they would be free on the morrow. As in the train, no one felt any hatred for their jailers, and indeed a similar attraction between the two groups had developed, if not on quite the same emotional level. This applied less to the Indonesians than to the

Dutch. "Not for a moment," said one Dutch hostage, "did I see any of the Indonesians lose their cool."

The collapse of the two sieges was hailed as a spectacular victory for the policy of standing firm and wearing the hijackers down, and the work of Dick Mulder earned special acclaim. But for all Mulder's subtleties, the final clash of wills had lain between the young South Moluccans and their elders, leading to a patching-up of the generation gap by the South Moluccans themselves—a repair that might prove to be no more than temporary.

There were no complaints from the consulate hostages about the government's handling of the siege. The only criticism was of past omissions that had allowed such tensions to develop. But conditions in the consulate were never comparable with those in the train. The fear induced was real enough, fully justifying the epithet of terrorism in those first few days, but no one had actually been murdered, although Abedy had died from his injuries. There was physical discomfort, but nothing so extreme as on the train. They were always warm, and the food was excellent.

There were light-hearted moments on that last evening, the terrorists allowing their hostages to borrow guns and masks and reverse their roles, equally enjoying the joke. "You, sit down there! It's our turn now!" Like the Moluccans on the train, they took great delight in revealing that their homemade bombs were fakes.

Vera Martron was not alone in feeling sorry for them, their whole future in jeopardy. "What do you think we will get?" they asked.

"No victims?" She calculated. "About five years." She asked them what they would do after serving their sentence.

"I'm young enough," said one. "When I'm released I'll make a fresh start."[11]

When the time came for good-byes, there were tears on both sides. "You will be free," said one of the hijackers. "You can meet again with your family. You can celebrate Christmas and the New Year." Despite all the bullying and propaganda they had been subjected to, none of the hostages could find the callousness to say: "It's your own fault."

Otjek wrote a message with a red pen on Anita Hoeboer's T-shirt. "We are like two trees. Fate separates us from each other. Between us is a wide road, but across it our branches meet." In the euphoria of release, she forgot how he had frightened her with the gun, and she told reporters: "He was really nice and kissed everybody on the cheek. They didn't really do

---

[11]The Consulate group was released from prison in December 1979.

anything bad to us. I had tears in my eyes—I do understand them better now."

Despite this happy ending, one man was dead and another severely wounded, while all that the psychiatrists feared about the phenomenon of late sequelae applied equally to the consulate hostages, especially the Indonesians, who had been the particular targets of the terrorists' intimidation and threats. The psychological problem that faced them, although fundamentally the same, was expressed somewhat differently by Saka Datuk. "Anyone who has been in a train or a school or a consulate as a hostage is never going to get out completely. Once you are hijacked, you are always hijacked.

"For the rest of my life, I shall be called Saka of the Balcony, *Datuk Balkon.*"

Part II
1977—THE TRAIN AND THE SCHOOL

CHAPTER 14

The Motivation Changes

T HE PROMISED MEETING between Manusama and the Dutch Government took place on January 17, 1976, four weeks after the end of the
consulate siege. The Dutch delegation was led by Prime Minister Joop den
Uyl, and Manusama was supported by his cabinet. Both sides described
the conversation that took place as realistic, but the only executive decision taken was the appointment of a consultative commission, half-Dutch
and half-Moluccan, with the following terms of reference:

1. To consider the problems created in Holland by the presence of the
   South Moluccans and their political ideals and expectations, which the
   Dutch Government could not share but of which they acknowledged
   the existence and seriousness.
2. To see whether the history of what happened in the past confirmed the
   South Moluccan view of how the problem originated, and to study the
   situation of the South Moluccans at present in Holland and how it could
   be improved, and to make recommendations to that end.

Although this decision was taken in mid-January, it was not until May
25 that the ten-man commission was formed. Headed by A.J.F. Köbben,
a professor of cultural anthropology and sociology, and L. Ch. Mantouw,
a South Moluccan social worker, it met five times in the next six months
and on November 24 produced an interim report on its work. Much time
was spent initially on procedural matters, while the compilation and study
of the extensive historical documentation that was made available to the
commission was also time-consuming. They had not been able to meet as
frequently as they had hoped, but their discussions had been marked by

179

a relaxed and cordial atmosphere, and they planned to meet once every three weeks in future. It was a sincere and hard-working committee, but its early pronouncements revealed little more than a capacity for stating the obvious. One or two immediate problems of a minor nature were successfully dealt with, but at this stage the commission was feeling its way, groping for solutions, unable as yet to point the way forward. Under the burden of twenty-five years of neglect, this was inevitable, but the enthusiasm with which the formation of the commission was greeted gradually faded as nothing of a very positive nature emerged. Indeed, there was disillusionment within the committee itself. "What on earth," asked one of its Dutch members, "can we do?"

Even before the publication of this first interim report, South Moluccan susceptibilities had been further offended by police ruthlessness in operating the government's rehousing policy, which involved the evacuation of barracks in which Moluccans had lived for many years. When the inhabitants of a camp at Vaassen, north of Apeldoorn, resisted the order to move out, more than 500 state and municipal police supported by armored cars evicted them, demolishing a substantial part of the barrack accommodation in the process. The resistance had no doubt been unlawful, but the manner of its liquidation was seen as a disastrous overkill, insensitive and even racially discriminating. The Köbben Commission was denounced by young South Moluccans as a cynical government diversion, and even many Dutchmen suspected that it was too remote and academic to make much impact on the young.

One positive result of the fracas at Vaassen was the formation in Utrecht on November 13, 1976, of a National South Moluccan Action Committee (Landelijk Comité Zuid-Molukken) under the chairmanship of ex-hostage Karel F. Wielenga, one of several of the train hostages who remained sympathetic to the Moluccan cause. Others who served on this committee were H. Baudet, a professor of economic social history at the technical university in Groningen; H.W.J. Droesen and W.G.A. Kousemaker, Dutch lawyers who had concerned themselves in the defense of the hijackers; and South Moluccans Etty Aponno and Franz Tutuhatunewa, a general practitioner from Burum, west of Groningen, who was Minister of General Affairs and Health in Manusama's government-in-exile. The declared aim of this committee was to achieve a better understanding between Dutchmen and young South Moluccans. Unfortunately, this practical attempt to get to the roots of the problem came too late to avert another crisis. Young South Moluccans already felt that, despite the lessons of Wijster and Amsterdam, their struggle for recognition was being ostracized, and their frustration this time was directed against their own leaders in the government-in-exile and in the Badan Persatuan rather than against the Dutch. Another source of discontent was the punishment meted out to the 1975 hijackers. Although most of the group in the train regretted the killings, they insisted on taking equal responsibility for them, and they all received sentences of fourteen years, while even the group in the consulate got seven. In the eyes of the world, they were terrorists, but to the Moluccans, although their methods were by no means universally condoned, they were freedom fighters. The taking of fresh hostages to blackmail governments into releasing previous offenders had become a standard pattern of terrorism, and at the end of 1976, as a New Year resolution, a group of young South Moluccans centered on the village of Bovensmilde, hometown of most of the prisoners, began planning an action of this kind.

Rumors of some such plan had been circulating for many months, and the fact that none of them came to fruition was due more to moderate forces within the South Moluccan community than to Dutch vigilance. Special surveillance of the Moluccan population was rejected by van Agt because he believed it would turn Holland into a police state, so the initiative, as always in a democracy, lay with the aggressor.

The village of Bovensmilde, although unique in some ways, was something of a microcosm of Dutch/South Moluccan social problems and inhibitions. When, in the 1960s, the camps were first broken up and the inhabitants distributed in small communities over various parts of Holland, some 750 from the camp at Westerbork were housed in a new estate in Bovensmilde. Progress toward coexistence and eventual integration was impeded by existing disparities in the Dutch population, which was partly of peasant stock and partly of new suburbia, the latter commuting to and from the urban centers of Assen and Groningen. Social workers were appointed to bring the three groups together and to expand local welfare work, and a genuine effort was made to involve all three groups in the life of the village. But the Moluccan group, resenting the new policy as a move toward integration, which they felt meant assimilation, and with their own social structure already under strain as traditional patterns came under fire from within, proved a tightly knit community, sheltering behind barriers of their own making. Meanwhile the Dutch complained that Moluccan membership in committees and societies always ended in disillusionment as the newcomers either failed to pay their dues or elected to go it alone. Rowdyism and vandalism by young unemployed South Moluccans created bad feeling, as did their apparent dependence on state

welfare sources, and the siting of the Moluccan housing estate as a separate entity, although adjacent to the Dutch, helped the Moluccans to
establish an enclave. They preferred to have their own church, sports and
social clubs, and the only two things the groups had in common became
the supermarket and the primary school.

As in the camps, the Moluccans were allowed to run their own paramilitary internal organization for the preservation of order (the KPK), encouraging a ghetto mentality and making their housing estate a no-go area
for Dutch police. Training in the use of firearms was not as general as
some believed, but it certainly took place, and access to firearms through
black market sources was easy. Warnings of further trouble, although
issued by responsible local politicians, went unheeded, and anyone who
complained was liable to suffer such harassment as minor damage to
property and to be labeled racist. Yet, despite all this, a referendum taken
early in 1977 showed that all three groups wanted better relations, while
at the primary school, sandwiched between the two communities, Moluccan children were joining enthusiastically in sport and other communal
activities, attending the birthday parties of their Dutch school friends, and
doing well at their studies. But the language problem remained a stum-
bling block, much prejudice remained, and, so far as long-term solutions
like those occupying the Köbben Commission were concerned, the opinion of one of the lawyers acting for the Moluccans was that "not much
of what they did would penetrate to Bovensmilde."

Before Wijster, the government had refused to talk to Manusama; after
Wijster they had done so. To that extent, terrorism had succeeded. The
impact on the media, too, had been worldwide. But what had been gained
in 1975 had since been whittled away—that was the verdict of young
South Moluccans. The Dutch still looked for integration, and Manusama
and his cabinet talked in the same passive, complacent platitudes that
young South Moluccans were accustomed to hearing from their parents.
It was essential, they felt, to get a more militant attitude through to
Manusama, to persuade him to relax his autocratic grip on South Moluccan politics and to get more involved with Marxist groups abroad. At the
same time there was the pressing need to act on behalf of their friends and
relatives in jail.

An important lesson learned from 1975 was that the killing of hostages,
so far from precipitating a government surrender, was likely to produce
a stalemate. Once there had been killings, the government would never let
hijackers leave the country, with or without the prisoners they hoped to
release. When the Japanese Red Army group had been given a free depar-

ture in 1974, there had been no killings. For any hijacking, weapons were essential, but merely to carry them, and perhaps to fire one or two warning shots, was enough. Great care would have to be exercised, especially in the initial stages when nerves were taut, to avoid accidents. But, if that could be achieved, success was possible.

This was one of the points discussed at a meeting of four young South Moluccans in Bovensmilde on New Year's Eve, 1976. Two of the group had been concerned in the abortive plan to capture Queen Juliana two years earlier, and the leader, twenty-six-year-old Willem Soplanit, married to a Dutch girl and with two small children, had served a jail sentence for a similar offense. The possibility of seizing a spectacular target, such as the television studios at Hilversum, was canvased, but ignorance of the internal layout was a deterrent.

During the 1975 hijackings, the government had made it clear that their first consideration must be the release of the children. Although the adult hostages in the train had been in greater danger, the children in the consulate had been given priority. From this it was concluded that the capture of a Dutch school would be the bargaining point par excellence, exerting such pressure on the government that they would quickly cave in, allowing hijackers and prisoners to leave the country without hindrance for the sake of the children.

Once the overwhelming advantages of a school had been conceded, what more natural than to choose a school they knew? The primary school at Bovensmilde? There would be no traveling, so the chances of being apprehended with weapons, which was a real danger with any target at a distance, were minimal. The school was sited in open ground, easy to defend. The only adults to confront them would be the six teachers, four men and two women. They expected no trouble in controlling the children, but if any of them managed to escape, they would simply let them go.

The seizure of the school was originally planned for February, 1977, but as the size of the action group grew, the possibility of a second and parallel hijacking, as in 1975, became attractive. Soon afterward the Dutch Government collapsed, and a synchronizing of the action with the election due in May seemed likely to have maximum impact. This made the TV studios a particularly attractive target, but they were eventually dismissed for the same reasons as before. As the shortage of worthwhile and accessible targets became apparent, the choice eventually fell on another train.

It was early May before this choice was made. Twenty-three-year-old Marcus Lumalessil, known as Rudi, a member of the original group and a brother of Jan Lumalessil of the consulate group, was appointed to organize it. After studying the area on foot, he chose a good strategic point nine miles north of Assen and six miles south of Groningen. Here the line ran between swamps and marshy land beside a river in open country, 300 meters from the nearest woodland to the east and 1,000 meters from the main north-south highway to the west. They proposed to board a northbound train at Assen and stop it on a straight section midway between the villages of De Punt and Glimmen, short of a point where the track curved sharply to the right. They would carry a variety of equipment, including papers and tape for covering the windows, padlocks and chains for the doors, and a radio. Each would be responsible for the provision and care of a weapon. Rudi himself, although he had no previous experience with guns, had acquired an Uzi.

There were two other important lessons that the Moluccans had learned from Wijster. One was to be wary of forming personal relationships with hostages. Although this gave the hostages a better understanding of their captors' motives, it led to confusion among the hijackers and a weakening of resolve. Safety in this respect, it was thought, was increased by numbers, and the group planned to take many more hostages this time.

The second lesson was that the employment by the government of professional psychiatrists to advise them and to conduct negotiations put the average South Moluccan at a disadvantage. Much had been written and broadcast since 1975 about the success of the government's tactics in the two sieges and of the contribution made by psychiatrists, particularly Dr. Mulder, and both groups were conscious of their lack of sophistication and their consequent vulnerability. They therefore looked for some mature personality to join them and do the talking for them.

Their choice fell on a twenty-four-year-old civil servant working in the registry of the provincial government in Assen. Max Papilaya was a serious and intelligent young man who was well thought of by his employers and who had been active since Wijster in working to improve relationships with the Dutch. He was known to the Köbben Commission as a gentle, basically decent, and deeply religious person, who played a full part in social work among his people. He was active in the South Moluccan Organization of Christian Youth (the PPKM) and was a respected figure in Moluccan affairs. But his greatest concern was for the welfare of Moluccans in Indonesia. Two years earlier his cousin, Pieter Papilaya, thirty-eight, who had once trained for the Church but was now a social worker in Utrecht, had visited Indonesia to present funds collected in Holland for his village of origin (many Moluccan families contributed to funds of this kind). The impression he brought back, rightly or wrongly, was that the Ambonese people felt themselves oppressed and exploited by the Javanese. On hearing his cousin's description of conditions in the Moluccas, Max asked, "What is the point of us living here while our people over there do no more than exist?" As proof of his sincerity, he abandoned his studies at a teacher-training college at the end of his first year and resolved to dedicate his life to his people.

In the previous year, some of the South Moluccan leaders had made contact, through a Dutch journalist, with a Frenchman named Guy Charpentier who was thought to be in a position to act as a plenipotentiary for Vietnam, and he was apparently willing to open unofficial discussions. The Vietnamese felt no sympathy for noncommunist Suharto, and if the South Moluccans chose the socialist road with real conviction, said Charpentier, they could look forward to support and even recognition from Vietnam. In April, 1976, Mrs. Soumokil went to Paris to meet Charpentier, accompanied by Pieter F. Tuny, editor of a South Moluccan newspaper and a brother of Jacobus Tuny (Kobus), one of the Wijster hijackers. Metiary made a similar visit in July, and in October the Badan Persatuan sent a delegation to Paris under Metiary for further informal talks. In return for reorganizing their political stance on the Asiatic socialist model and for refraining from terrorist acts in Holland, the RMS was to get military and financial support for guerrilla intrusion into the island of Ceram.

Delegations of young South Moluccans made several visits to Manusama to urge him to broaden his outlook and develop this new contact, but Manusama steadfastly refused, on the grounds that it was unreliable. Finally, in December, under mounting pressure, Manusama checked with the Vietnamese Embassy at The Hague and was told that Charpentier was unknown to them. Whatever the truth may have been, Manusama acted on this information by forbidding all further contact with this source.

Subsequently the RMS was declared to have embraced "progressive socialism," which enabled the appearance of unity between Manusama and Metiary to be preserved. But militant young South Moluccans, impatient with Manusama and disappointed in Metiary, looked for some other outlet for their frustrations.

Max himself was not the sort of person who would conceive or inspire a hijacking. But once the project was brought to his notice and he saw that he was being asked to play an essential role, one perhaps that only he could play, his sense of duty was aroused. He was egotistical, so no doubt he was flattered, and he probably foresaw that, if the sieges lasted more than a few hours, he would find himself assuming the role of leader. He was also a born gambler, something that only a few of his acquaintances knew. But he had other, more practical, reasons for joining. As a member of the group, he could exert some control over its aims and behavior. Sensitive to the fanatical mood that had inspired the enterprise, he accepted his part in it on one condition—that there should be no killings. Although this restriction had already been agreed upon by both groups, Max's presence reinforced it.

Another resolve that the recruiting of Max Papilaya greatly reinforced was the determination not to give in until their demands were met. Among the hard core of militant South Moluccans, the collapse of the 1975 hijackings had been regarded as premature. Max was nothing if not tenacious. This time they would see it through to the end. But assuming the government gave way, as they surely must, the hijackers would be looking to Vietnam for asylum and would hope to join up eventually with some guerrilla group in the South Moluccas.

Physically Max was a slight, even tiny person, but a purposeful gait, neither quick nor slow, suggested reserves of moral strength. He had a keen sense of humor, and his expression was almost always suffused by a smile. But the lightly-tinted glasses that he affected could not hide his dominant feature, the expressive brown eyes that so often seemed burdened by sadness. Alert and friendly, he had a light voice that varied little in pitch but was somehow not toneless or monotonous. His habit of seeming to think carefully before he spoke and the fact that his listeners often had to strain their ears to hear him were peculiarly effective, lending authority to what he said.

In happier times, it had not been unusual for Moluccan children to stay with a Dutch family for a part of the holidays, and as a small boy, brought up in Westerbork camp, Max had proved a likeable and rewarding guest. His knowledge and understanding of the Dutch was unusual in a South Moluccan, and he had mastered the language to an extent achieved by few of his countrymen. He dressed neatly, kept his beard trimmed, and wore his hair at half length, and his speech and mannerisms were more those of a Dutchman.

Invited solely for the purpose of waging the psychological warfare that had to be expected, Max soon found his talents being put to other uses. The demands that were to be issued from school and train were typed out by Rudi, but Max helped to draft them. Letters were also addressed to the media, to be posted overnight, warning of the proposed hijackings. Once these letters had been sent, there would be no turning back. Actions against train and school were to begin simultaneously soon after nine o'clock on Monday morning, May 23, 1977, two days before the general election.

The group that assembled in three separate sections on the platform at Assen that morning consisted of eight men and a girl. Rudi Lumalessil, ostensibly the leader, was accompanied by another of his brothers, Ronnie, who was twenty. Both had had a technical education; both presented a somewhat dour, humorless exterior.

Junus Ririmasse, twenty-seven, was an elder brother of Jopie, the leader of the consulate group. An art student, he was athletic as well as aesthetic. Mattheus Tuny, twenty-three, known as Thys, quiet, friendly, and unaggressive, was a younger brother of Kobus of the Wijster group and of Pieter, the man who had accompanied Mrs. Soumokil to Paris to meet Charpentier.

George Matulessy, twenty, was of a more stolid disposition. His shaved head earned him the nickname of Kojak, generally shortened to Jo. Andreas Luhulima, eighteen, a technical student, was a good listener who was intensely interested in his environment.

Domingus Rumamory—at 17, the youngest—was generally known as Mingus. A good-looking boy, he was intelligent, talkative, and musical. Hansina Oktoseja, twenty-one, the only girl in either group, was a dental assistant, and in her normal environment she was a natural, energetic, pleasure-loving girl.

The school group, led by the original prime mover, Willem Soplanit, was depleted by the transfer to the train group of Junus and Ronnie, Junus because of a lack of enthusiasm for kidnapping, Ronnie because he preferred to be with his brother. They thus numbered four only: Soplanit himself, big and inclined to obesity, a difficult man to fathom; Isaac Thenu, twenty-eight, whose brother Cornelis had been the youngest of the Wijster group, and Guustav Tehupuring, twenty-four, both proud of their involvement in the plot to abduct Queen Juliana; and Tommy Polnaya, eighteen, sometimes called "little comrade," raw and immature but thrilled at being part of something as grown-up as a hijacking.

That morning, the members of both groups were extremely nervous and unsure of themselves, but at least one of those on the platform at Assen, Max Papilaya, remained outwardly cool and inwardly optimistic. He had issued a final warning on the care they must take with firearms. "As long as there are no accidents at the beginning, because of panic or some other reason," he assured them, "we will make it."

The girl Hansina had gained admission to the group, despite some opposition, as Rudi's girl friend. But she was a fully committed supporter of the militant cell of the Free South Moluccan Youth. A previous boy friend was one of the prisoners whom they sought to release. Her dedication to the RMS ideal, her religious faith, and her attitude to her parents, were not untypical. This was the letter of explanation she wrote to her parents, posted so as to reach them the next day:

To Papa and Mama, who live constantly in my heart, as do my brothers and sisters.

Papa and Mama, when you find this letter I shall not be at home any more, but with my friends.

I write this letter because I know that you will worry about where I am. But don't be afraid or worried, because I am not acting to create strife or in a bout of madness.

After I have written this letter, you will not know where I am. I am a South Moluccan and a Christian, and I am not afraid to die. I will act from my belief in Jesus Christ.

You knew me at home as a child who was not interested in the battle, but in a short while you will hear via the radio or television why we are acting in this way.

Now I want to be frank with you, Papa and Mama: I am afraid, because I don't know what's going to happen. I am rather a loud-mouthed and self-opinionated girl, but I am also afraid. The weapon I carry, I carry with a belief in myself. Therefore don't be afraid that I will use this weapon lightly. Don't regard me as a child that means to use this weapon to kill people.

I am asking you, Papa and Mama, to forgive me my many faults and the deeds I have done wrong. If I am killed it doesn't matter because it will not be for nothing. It is not a senseless goal.

If I or any of the other boys are killed, our friends will continue. I ask you, Papa and Mama, to pray for us. In spite of all my faults, please don't abandon me. I will end this letter with the words that truly come from my heart.

I know that although our road will be very long and difficult to get our liberty, with the help of God we shall reach it. I also want to say that with God's will, we will see each other again, perhaps not here but in another place.

That is in God's hands.
Hansina.

CHAPTER 15

"You Have to Stay Calm"

G EORGE FLAPPER, twenty-nine-year-old psychology student from Zwolle, was one of many students traveling on intercity Train 747 back to Groningen that morning to resume their studies after a weekend at home. Tousled dark hair, glasses, and a high-pitched voice were his distinctive physical characteristics, and he was a man of forthright opinions who loved to talk. Unashamedly inquisitive about people, he was listening to a conversation on the relative merits of road and rail travel. "In a car you can have an accident," the man opposite was saying. "Yes," said his companion, "and in a train you can get hijacked." Flapper thought it a stupid argument. Eighteen months after Wijster, rail traffic to the north, noticeably slack for a time, had largely recovered. But some people still had misgivings. "This train stops only at Assen and Groningen," announced a railway official before they left Zwolle. "Sometimes," muttered one of the passengers, not quite under his breath, "it also stops at Wijster."

Ton Kroon, small in stature but dapper and neatly proportioned, was a buyer in ladies' clothing. He was twenty-eight. He too boarded the train at Zwolle, taking a seat in the second carriage from the front, the first-class section. It was a two-set, four-carriage train, with access from one carriage to another throughout. Most Monday mornings Kroon took this train to visit his firm's headquarters in Groningen. He saw a group of South Moluccans get into the train at Assen, and, although he had seen their like many times on this line, he was disturbed by it. It was not so much their appearance as the heavy bags they carried. It was even in his mind to operate the emergency brake. But then he thought: no, it's not possible, I shall make myself ridiculous. Just as Hans Prins had thought eighteen months before him.

1977 De Punt Train; Number 747

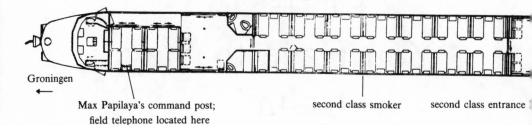

Groningen
←

Max Papilaya's command post;
field telephone located here

second class smoker   second class entrance

One or two of the Moluccans mixed with the passengers and reconnoit-ered the train, but most took up positions on the entrance platforms at the front, center, and rear. Finding themselves alone, they began opening their bags and assembling their guns.

The task of operating the emergency brake had been given to Max, and it was important to time it correctly. It was an unfortunate choice. When the moment came, the diminutive Max didn't have the strength to pull the lever through the stop-valve. While he was tugging at it, the train thun-dered on at rather more than twenty-five meters per second. By the time he had shouted for someone to help him and the brake had begun to operate, the train had run to the end of the straight section where they planned to stop and was entering the curve to the right. This curve was so heavily cambered that, as the train lurched to a halt, hijackers and passengers alike felt themselves tipped to one side.

Berend van der Struik, a forty-eight-year-old painter, sculptor, yachts-man, and man of many parts, was due to lecture that day at the Academy of Art in Groningen. He noticed the neurotic behavior of a South Moluc-can who got on at Assen, but he paid no attention to it. The fellow sat down, got up, meandered around, then sat down somewhere else, repeat-ing the process two or three times. Joke Winkeldermaat, an eighteen-year-old student dietician, noticed him too, but she had an examination that week and was absorbed in study. As soon as the train stopped, the fellow jumped up and shouted, "This is a hijack! Keep quiet and stay in your seats!" Trembling with astonishment at the sound of his own voice and with his revolver aimed considerably at the floor, he looked more startled than the passengers, who took some time to realize what was happening.

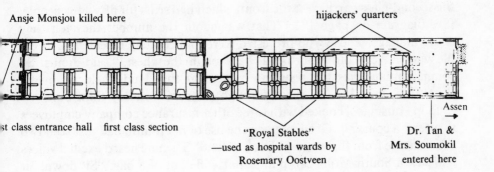

Ansje Monsjou killed here   hijackers' quarters

st class entrance hall   first class section   "Royal Stables"   Assen →   Dr. Tan &
—used as hospital wards by   Mrs. Soumokil
Rosemary Oostveen   entered here

Mini Loman was a young woman who eight years previously had dedicated her life to Christ. An attractive and feminine twenty-nine-year-old, she had fair hair, blue eyes set wide apart, a turned-up nose, and a sensitive mouth. Living and working in Groningen, she had been visiting her friend Michele in Utrecht. The two girls had studied together at the Central Pentecostal School in The Hague. During the weekend they had gone to church, listened to gospel records, and otherwise talked and relaxed. Perhaps they had talked too much and relaxed too little. Anyway they had overslept, so that Mini had missed her train and would be late for work. Late, and a bit washed out—that, thought Mini, was bad Christian witness. But Michele cheered her up. After driving her to the station, she told her, "Jump in one of the two small compartments just behind the driver. They're special ones where people can study. You can be quiet there and have a good sleep."

It was nearly two hours later, at 9:07 AM, when Mini Loman, conscious that the train was stopping, opened her eyes and focused dreamily on a young girl sitting opposite with a pile of school books on her lap. The girl's face was deathly white, and a moment later she dropped her books and screamed. Following her gaze into the corridor, Mini saw a little man with a smiling face, gold-rimmed glasses, and black frizzy hair pointing a gun at her. He put his finger to his lips, and for a moment she thought it was a joke. Then the door slid open. "This is a hijacking," said the man quietly. "Come with me." There was a third girl in the compartment, and the man waved his gun at them in an impatient gesture. "Be quiet, don't do anything silly, and you'll be all right." Mini felt the gun in the arch of her back. "Don't try and run away, or you'll get a bullet."

Elsewhere the passengers were still more stunned and incredulous than afraid. The intention of the hijackers was to drive everyone forward from the rear of the train, through the restaurant and the first-class section into the second-class carriage at the front, which had seats for fifty-four people. (See diagram on page 191.) That was about the number they felt they could manage. Those who protested were immediately threatened. "People who have a big mouth will be shot in the chest," said Junus. So somnambulant was the resulting movement that Rudi, held up in the restaurant, fired his Uzi twice through the roof to hurry things up.

Joop Huismans, booked with three other insurance company employees to attend a course in Groningen on the use of microfilm, had just seen two deer emerge from the woods. "Look at that!" Then he heard excited voices and saw a South Moluccan pull a short rifle out of a bag. "Sit down! Sit down!" Presently the orders changed. "Everyone stand up and go forward." Huismans couldn't believe it. He was passing through the restaurant a few moments later when Rudi fired through the roof, and he dived for the floor.

"What's going on?" asked nineteen-year-old Ansje Monsjou. Her father, half Indonesian, had come to Holland in 1934, married a blonde Dutch girl, and had four blonde children, of whom Ansje was the youngest and some said the prettiest. She was also the most highly-strung. Sitting opposite her was twenty-three-year-old Marc Hustinx, and, as befitted a law student, he replied cautiously, "I think we're being hijacked." The girl began to tremble violently.

Next to Marc Hustinx sat Jan Cuppen, a forty-six-year-old portrait painter and art teacher of unconventional, Bohemian temperament on his way to the Academy of Groningen to assist in an examination in artistic anatomy, which he taught at Tilburg. Perhaps it was this flair for anatomy that made his snap assessments of people so accurate. "It's mostly sabre-rattling," he told Ansje Monsjou. He thought her transparently acute reaction was like that of a highly-bred animal.

Kees Huibregtse-Bimmel, twenty-nine, fair-haired, with a small moustache that he greased and brushed daily, was a geology student who was planning to switch to a course in hotel management; he hoped soon to open his own restaurant. The first thing he noticed after the train stopped was the driver and conductor walking past the window; he imagined they were checking some fault. Not until later did he realize that they were quietly making their escape. Then he heard excited shouts in Ambonese, and some shots. "You've been hijacked! Everyone stays where he is! The first one to move will be shot!" Bimmel had completed a period of military service in the commandos as a draftee, and he was used to seeing and handling weapons. Of cheerful, cool, philosophic temperament, he decided that under this threat he would find little difficulty in keeping still. What amazed him most was the amount of equipment the hijackers carried. Surely suspicions should have been aroused. Then the orders were changed, and he was driven forward.

In the first-class carriage, Ton Kroon was beating his fists on his brow in vexation. He had been forewarned, and he had done nothing about it. One of the hijackers was shouting at him. It was Rudi. "You damned rotten capitalist, get moving!" So much for the advantages of first-class travel. Losing himself in the crowd that was surging round him, he tore off his tie, removed his blazer, and rolled up his sleeves, changing his image as drastically as he could from the dapper buyer of ladies' clothing of half a minute ago.

Also traveling first-class was Victor Nijmeijer, a handsome young fellow over six feet in height on his way back to Eelde Airfield, three miles to the east of the hijacked train, after a weekend with his wife and three-year-old daughter in his Rotterdam home. He could actually see the antenna on the top of the airfield control tower from where he sat. Now twenty-five, he had been flying as a private pilot since he was 17. Recently, after five and a half years in the Rotterdam police force, he had transferred to the state police to train as a police pilot. He was carrying a briefcase crammed with police papers and manuals, and before he was driven forward, he hastily hid it under his seat.

Thirty-six-year-old Wim Fakkert, a priest who had abandoned his ministry for social work, was on his way to attend a course in Groningen. Sitting near him was a lad from Eindhoven of retarded development who was traveling north to visit his parents. Anxious that the lad should not attract the attention of the hijackers, Fakkert shepherded him forward.

Already, as they assembled in the front carriage, the passengers identified Max as the leader, although strictly the distinction was still Rudi's. The other terrorists seemed either nervous and excitable or uncertain and confused. Only Max seemed to know what he was doing. Curiously enough, he gave the passengers confidence. The well-cut clothes, the collar and tie—he was the only hijacker wearing a tie—and the grey raincoat, were symbols of conventional civilization, making the revolver that accompanied them incongruous. His orders were delivered firmly but softly, without histrionics. And he smiled. Yet as more and more passengers crowded into the carriage, there was no mistaking the spreading contagion of fear. What did the terrorists plan? Were they going to kill again, to put pressure on the government to agree to their political demands? So far they had done nothing brutal, but there were few who did not remember Wijster.

"Everyone sit down and keep quiet," said Max. Those who couldn't find seats sat on the floor. Marc Hustinx was pleased to see someone he knew —twenty-three-year-old Rosemary Oostveen, in her fifth year as a medical student at Groningen University Hospital. She was about to sit down in the aisle with her boy friend, but she was wearing a long white dress. "Sit down on the arm of my seat," he told her. The seat itself accommodated two, but Hustinx and the man next to him were slim, and they made room for Rosemary, whose build was more generous, to squeeze in between them.

An outbreak of hysterical crying brought reassurance from Max. "Don't panic. You have to stay calm. Nothing will happen to you if you only keep quiet." It was a warm May morning, the sun was shining through windows that were mostly closed, and perspiration was mingling with the sweat of fear. Partly to relieve the pressure on space, partly for considerations of security, Max began a process of selection of those he wished to release. Old people, mothers with small children, and anyone who showed signs of hysteria or aggression were told they could go.

Max was not above the slightly sick joke that had amused the hijackers of Wijster and Amsterdam. Pressing his pistol against the temple of one male passenger, he waited for the inevitable reaction, then said, "You can go." The man was paralyzed with fright. Forty-eight-year-old Saskia Sein, matronly and bespectacled, but blessed with an effervescent sense of humor, saw the funny side of it and nearly burst out laughing. This lucky devil was free, yet he was too frightened to move.

One woman passenger had done herself a good turn by agreeing to look after a small boy put on the train by his mother, to be met by a relative in Groningen. She walked off the train with him, passing him off as her own.

A South Moluccan girl and her eighteen-year-old Dutch friend, Rolie Brinkman, a chubby fashion-design student, were not so fortunate. "Let my friend come with me," pleaded the colored girl as Max released her, and when Max refused she said, "Then let me stay. We're together." Max shook his head. "Go before there's trouble." "Here, then," said the Moluccan girl to her friend tearfully, "take my sandwiches. You may need them." Then she was hustled out.

One of the first men to be released was given copies of the documents in which the terrorists had drafted their demands, to be delivered to the authorities. He set off at once across the fields to the highway, hoping to get a lift into Groningen.

Max showed himself to be professional in his attention to detail. One of Joop Huisman's insurance colleagues, of powerful physique, was told by Max: "Stand up. Out." He also picked out men with beards, presumably because he thought they looked impressive. Pointing his gun at another man, he told him: "You are not going to see how this action ends." This sounded like the prelude to murder, but in fact it was another sick joke. Perhaps Max had sensed something abrasive in the man's aura, but after he was led in terror to an entrance platform, he was told to go.

One frightened girl had been recognized by van der Struik at the start of the hijacking as one of his pupils, and he beckoned to her. "Come and sit with us." Van der Struik had the typical restless temperament of the angina sufferer. He also had courage. Now it was to Max that he beckoned. "Let this girl out," he said. "She has an examination today." Max's reply was an abrupt negative, but soon afterward he came back and spoke to the girl. He was pointing his gun at her, but his tone was not unkind. "What kind of exam are you taking?" She told him that she was at the Minerva Academy of Art in Groningen. "That's nice. You can create a work of art for the RMS." And he let her go.

Next Max turned to the people sitting on the floor. "Everyone in the aisle, out," he ordered. Marc Hustinx caught Rosemary Oostveen's eye and they exchanged a rueful grin. But for his old-fashioned courtesy, she would have been leaving with her boy friend.

For Rosemary, one way of resigning herself to her misfortune was the expectation that she might have a job to do. "Do you think I should tell them I'm a nearly-qualified doctor?" she asked her companion. Hustinx' advice seemed sound, and she took it. "I don't think so. Let them ask for a doctor first. It'll be much better if you volunteer then."

While the doors were being chained and padlocked, some of the passengers were given newspapers and tape to curtain the windows. Only the small transom windows were left uncovered. One woman, twenty-five-year-old Nelleke Ellenbroek, worked so neatly and methodically that van der Struik eyed her quizzically. She looked pregnant to him. Perhaps that accounted for her stoical calm. He waited for a chance to tell Max. Perhaps he would let her out.

"I hope it's over by this evening," said Nelleke to the man in the neighboring seat. He doubted it, but he kept his thoughts to himself. "I hope so too." She was on her way to keep an appointment at the hospital in Groningen, where she was undergoing intensive treatment concerned with her pregnancy.

How long was it going to last, van der Struik asked himself? The thought that the Wijster hijacking lasted thirteen days appalled him. He believed, or wanted to believe, that the Dutch Government would act long before then. "The marines will have us out by tonight," he told Huismans. "I don't think so," said Huismans.

He began keeping a diary. It helped to relieve his frustration, gave him something to do. He scribbled his entries between the lines of the book he was reading, taking care to write only when he thought he was unobserved by the hijackers. But it was a dangerous game, and there were moments when he felt his scalp tingling with fear.

The nearest the passengers got to an explanation of the hijackers' conduct was a short statement from Max. "You all know why this is happening. Your government sowed the wind, you reap the whirlwind. Anyone who wants to be a hero will be shot." Then his tone became more conciliatory. "If you want to use the toilet, you can ask. You'll be allowed to go to the toilet one by one." Max was tightening and relaxing the psychological pressure, giving the corrective touch on the controls.

As the sun climbed overhead, the atmosphere in the closed carriage became suffocating and the passengers sweltered. Even the girls wearing cool summer dresses felt their clothes sticking to their backs. "Can I open a window?" asked Mini Loman. "All right, just a little." A light breeze fanned her face as she opened one of the transom windows and she took a delicious breath. "That's enough. Back to your seat."

How stupid these people were! She longed to say to them, "We've done nothing to harm you. Why don't you leave us alone?" But she remembered their guns and controlled her tongue.

Bimmel could not help recalling his boyhood experience of the Ambonese. Near his village in the province of Zeeland, there had been a Moluccan camp, and he remembered how volatile they had been, how quick to anger. Fights between Dutch and Moluccan boys had been frequent, and a game of football had often ended in a fist fight. For all Max's apparent control, Bimmel feared that, if things went wrong, those guns would be fired.

Seeing the trepidation of the young people around him, he started joking with them, rolling cigarettes for them, making the best of it. Next to him was Mini Loman, and he saw how low she was in spirit. "Would you like a cigarette?" he asked her. Since dedicating her life to Christ, she hadn't smoked, but now, moved by her companion's kindness, she accepted his offer. Inhaling deeply, she suffered a wave of dizziness, but she finished the cigarette. Why did God allow things like this to happen? She didn't even have the heart to pray.

Forty-year-old Rien van Baarsel, an architectural consultant and a lecturer at the technical high school in Delft, was on his way to the University Hospital to discuss the design of a new building. A tall, good-looking man, married with two young children, he was suffering at the moment from hyperventilation, breathing too rapidly and too deeply, a nervous condition stimulated by the climate of fear deliberately induced by the hijackers and aggravated by the stultifying, polluted atmosphere. There could be serious complications if the bout was not relieved. Max, who thought the man was having a heart attack, showed his concern by asking if there was a doctor in the train. This was Rosemary's cue, and she came forward, her dark, straight, shoulder-length hair and country-girl freshness focusing everyone's attention. There was a second volunteer, twenty-two-year-old Marijke Drost of Zwolle, a tall, blonde, friendly girl with blue eyes, but she was at a much earlier stage of her medical training, and Max chose Rosemary. "You can take him into first class," said Max, indicating van Baarsel, and Rosemary left to start work on her first patient.

Still the hijackers marched menacingly up and down, and few of the passengers dared look at them. Instead they averted their gaze, and tried to read items in the sheets of newspaper covering the windows. The temptation to see what was happening behind those windows was severe, and passengers in window seats took an edge of newspaper between thumb and forefinger and peeked. The railway embankment raised them sufficiently above ground level to hint at a panoramic, bird's-eye view, and they found themselves surveying what at other times they would have classed as an idyllic pastoral scene. Horses and cows were grazing in the middle distance between the train and the road. Wild flowers were choking the slopes of the embankment. On the wooded side, the serpentine curve of the river and the straight lines of the dikes emphasized the contrast between the work of nature and that of man. It was evidence of the intervention of man that they sought, but they were disappointed. The only signs of human life were the cars that drove in maddening slow motion on the distant highway, their occupants lingering to prolong their view of the hijacked train, now shimmering and miragelike in the heat haze.

As though these tantalizing glimpses of the outside world were known to him and might inspire a bid for freedom, Max's voice came over the public address system with a warning. "May I have your attention please. If anyone tries to escape, they'll get a bullet in the chest. If anyone does escape we'll shoot two more." True to form, these threats were succeeded by a broadcast of tapes of Ambonese music, presumably intended to soothe.

First to warn the authorities of the stationary train was a dairy farmer named Koops, 800 meters to the south. Soon afterward, the hijacking was confirmed by driver and conductor. However, the chances of a speedy solution were not enhanced by a mishap for which neither hijackers nor authorities could be blamed. The man entrusted with the hijackers' demand notes duly hitchhiked into Groningen. After thanking the driver, he reported to the police station only to find that he'd left the documents on the back seat of the car. All efforts to trace the driver failed.

At the same time the train was seized, Willem Soplanit and his group entered the modern, single-storied, glass-fronted building that housed the primary school at Bovensmilde. The ground plan, a straight, shedlike structure running northeast to southwest, with a T attachment at either end, held no surprises for them. (For annotated photograph, see page 191.) After approaching across the paved area to the southwest, they walked through the entrance doors unchallenged and fanned out left and right toward the classrooms. One of the children, returning to a classroom after being excused, saw them coming. "There's someone in the hall," he reported, but before anyone could investigate, the classrooms were invaded and guns were brandished. "Sir, this is a hijacking," the principal, tall, slim, bespectacled Eef van Vliet was politely told. "Will you please take your class to assembly."

For a moment van Vliet thought it was a joke. The illusion was soon shattered as the intruders hustled everyone into the main assembly room at gunpoint. The fifth-grade teacher, dark, bearded Simon van Beetz, twenty-five, had the barrel of a gun aimed at his temple. With responsibility for 120 children between the ages of six and twelve and five staff besides himself, van Vliet's instinct was to cooperate and order staff and pupils to do exactly what they were told.

Thirty-six years old, van Vliet was a man of quiet confidence who had been appointed headmaster four years previously and who had worked hard since then to build bridges between the Dutch and South Moluccan communities. He himself was married to a girl of Indonesian descent. The tragic death of a South Moluccan child on the way to school had paradoxically aided him in bringing Moluccan children into the school. The South Moluccan school was some distance away, and some Moluccan parents, fearing further accidents, had sent their children to his school because it bordered their homes. He now had fifteen South Moluccan children attending his school.

He and his young and enthusiastic staff were learning Malay so as to get closer to the Moluccan community and especially to the children, and they were teaching South Moluccan culture as well as Dutch. They had won the support of many South Moluccan parents, one of whom had been appointed to the school management committee. Thus it was that van Vliet found it incomprehensible that his school should be singled out for an action of this kind. But he recognized the futility and even the danger of protest. However, one of his two female teachers, Sjaan Abbink, small but plucky, scolded the leading hijacker, Willem Soplanit, when they got to the assembly room. "How could you do this to children?" Both Eef van Vliet and Sjaan Abbink had children of their own in the school.

"Keep quiet and draw the curtains." The assembly room and theatre, nearly twice the area of any of the classrooms, was just about big enough to accommodate the school. The curtains were drawn, and to be doubly sure, the hijackers began papering over the windows. Few of the children realized what was happening, but because they had been taken to assembly, some of them thought the Moluccans were going to stage a play for them. This notion evaporated as the hijackers cocked their guns and stood guard at the windows, fearing interference from outside more than trouble from within. "Tell the children we're here to protect them from being attacked," they told the teachers. But the children were puzzled by this. Who was likely to attack them? Instinctively they knew they were being lied to. Besides, they had seen hijackings on TV. With their teachers outwardly calm and acquiescent, however, they gradually settled down.

One of the first acts of the hijackers was to single out and release the fifteen South Moluccan children in the school. They did this hurriedly, fearing their elders in the Moluccan community more than they feared the Dutch. They knew well enough that, if they retained Moluccan children, the parents would march on the school and humiliate them by taking the children away.

The fourth grade teacher, Harrie Woldendorp, had taken his class to the gym, a separate building on the west side of the school. With him, he had a young visitor from a teacher-training college. He stayed to talk to the trainee while the children got dressed, then followed them back to the school. The first children to reach the school entrance collided with the South Moluccan children as they trooped out in single file. To their right, they saw that the curtains were drawn in the assembly room. On either side of them, they noted empty classrooms with chairs and tables overturned. At first they thought it was a prank by the senior class. Some of them had already been forced into the corridor of the school when one of the released Moluccan boys shouted, "Teacher, there's a man in the school with a gun."

After a few seconds' hesitation, Woldendorp guessed what was happening and shouted to the rest of the class, "Run home as quickly as you can." As the children stood for a moment uncertainly, he began running himself and they followed his example. One of them was Sjaan Abbink's daughter Alice, whose brother Arjan was still in the school. Woldendorp's immediate concern was to warn the teachers at the nearby nursery school to evacuate the children there before it was too late. Meanwhile, he sent the trainee teacher to the principal's house to warn the police by telephone.

One mother who lived near the school was alerted by some workmen running across her garden. She went outside to see what was the matter, but they had gone. "Is your son at the school?" asked a neighbor. Nodding, she hurried toward the school. As she approached, a window opened and a gun was pointed out. "Go away. Go away or we'll shoot." When a shot was fired over her head, she turned and ran back to her home to raise the alarm.

In the next half hour, husbands and wives were alerted at their places of work in surrounding districts and began converging on the school. At first sight, the village looked much the same as usual, with no more than a handful of police blocking the streets, but they soon learned that the school was closed right off and the hijackers were shooting at anyone who tried to approach.

A group of male parents, getting as near the school as they could, worked themselves up into a lather of frustration, debating whether or not to make a rush in a body in an effort to free their children. Others, desperate for a glimpse of their children, stared at the school from the upstairs windows of their houses, less than 100 meters away.

What were they made of, they asked themselves? What would their wives and children think of them if they didn't take some forthright action? Meanwhile the wives, already half-frantic with fear, were assailed by a greater dread—that their husbands, driven by humiliation, might be goaded into some rash and precipitate action that could only bring disaster.

South Moluccan children could be seen playing football over in the Moluccan enclave, and this the fathers resented. Seizing some of these children and using them as a shield to advance on the school was one of the wilder proposals made. The realization that they lacked both the courage and the ruthlessness to risk such a plan and that the police would certainly intervene if they did only increased their frustration.

Most of the children realized that something was seriously wrong when they were not allowed home for lunch. The provision of food was obviously going to be a problem, and about noon three Moluccan women, one with a baby at her hip, approached the school perimeter with a request to be allowed to deliver food and drink. Despite warnings from police, they continued toward the school, pleading for the release of the children. But again the hijackers opened windows and fired shots into the air. The women withdrew, but at 1:50 PM a South Moluccan schoolteacher named Fien Sihalasy—she taught at a primary school in Assen—asked on her own initiative for 110 lunch packs from the civil authorities. The packs were duly produced, and in midafternoon they were delivered to the school by Miss Sihalasy and her sister.

A management center had meanwhile been set up in the provincial civil defense shelter in Assen. Built in 1968, it was twelve meters below the surface of the ground. Bomb-proofed and air-conditioned, it housed a modern operations room and communications center and was completely self-contained. As at Beilen, the attorney general took the chair, but in this case he came from outside the province. Baron W.A. van der Feltz had once been attorney general for the northern provinces, but in 1970 he had been transferred to South Holland and Zeeland. Thinning gray hair, gray eyes that peered modestly from behind spectacles, and a flair for crumpling a new suit in twenty-four hours, made him an unimpressive figure, but his open mind and wide experience, especially his handling of the French embassy and Scheveningen Jail incidents, had earned van Agt's confidence. He had not been called in originally at Beilen because van Binsbergen had been already in control. Supporting him was the queen's commissioner for the province and the chief of the state police, Mrs. Schilthuis and Colonel Bergsma, as before, together with the burgomasters of Vries, the nearest town to De Punt, and Smilde. Dr. Mulder led a team of psychiatrists which included Dr. Henk Havinga, one of the psychiatrists who had advised the police and military at Wijster.

With the school six miles to the southwest of Assen and the train nine miles to the north, the advantages of having one center to handle both sieges at local level soon became clear. Police command posts were established at the technical school in Smilde for the school and at the North Netherlands Golf and Country Club, conveniently hidden in the woods, for the train, but a major difference resulting from experience at Wijster was that communication with school and train would be direct from the management center, cutting out the filter through the command post. The telephone line from the school was switched straight through to the bunker, where Mulder was soon ready to get the talking going. However, no demands of any kind were received from the school, where the hijackers seemed deliberately uncommunicative, and there was no contact as yet with the train.

With the letters to the media still in the mail, and the documents from the train missing, the aims of the two sieges remained unknown, although Joop den Uyl was already forecasting that there would be a demand for the release of the prisoners from 1975. Fortunately, the hijackers were not committing the same error of impatience as before. They had learned from Wijster that it would take several hours for proper communications to be set up and for their demands to be digested and that everyone would stall until then.

The main crisis center was established as before at the Ministry of Justice in The Hague. With the election only two days away, election rivals den Uyl and van Agt had already extricated themselves from the coalition of which their parties formed the major part, but they called an immediate halt to electioneering and appealed for calm. A caretaker cabinet would continue to exercise control, and the election would go ahead. "We will not allow terror to influence the working of the constitution," declared den Uyl. Nevertheless, the calculated kidnapping of more than a hundred children—at the Indonesian Consulate the capture of children had been incidental—introduced a new form of blackmail. "Our first priority," said den Uyl, "is to get the children out." This was gratifying to the hijackers, who this time were well provided with radios. In the school there was even TV.

An innovation was the establishment of a South Moluccan crisis center at Capelle aan den Ijssel under Manusama's vice-president P.W. Lokollo, for coordination and to save Manusama excessive traveling. Like Manusama, Piet Lokollo was an elder statesman who had been a minister in the original 1950 government. Unlike Manusama, he had condoned the recent approach to Vietnam. The group that met in his flat on that Monday morning after hearing the news of the hijackings on the radio included Manusama's minister of interior affairs and representatives of RMS and Badan Persatuan. Frieda Tomasoa, one of the leading members of the Free South Moluccan Youth, acted as secretary. The group's ambivalent attitude was well expressed in a short policy statement that was broadcast later that day.

As head of the crisis center of the RMS, I deplore the latest happenings in Bovensmilde and Haren.

In the first place, because innocent children, women, and, in short, civilians are involved.

But on the other hand, I believe I can declare some sympathy for the motivation that brought these boys to that deed.

Only the way in which this has found expression we cannot concur with. We therefore make ourselves available to help search for a solution to this problem in case we are asked to do so.

Capelle aan den Ijssel,
23 May 1977
P.W. Lokollo

Soon after drafting this statement, Lokollo was telephoned by Henk Zeevalking and asked to go immediately to see the minister of justice at The Hague. All five members of the group traveled, and they went full of hope that they would be able to contribute something positive. The first thing to be done, in their view, was to find out what the boys wanted so that negotiations could begin and the problem could be solved in a satisfactory way. They were quite prepared to take on this task themselves, since, as they told van Agt, they knew the boys best. They were greeted in a friendly manner, but there the courtesies ended, van Agt making it abundantly clear that he expected them, as representatives of the South Moluccan community, to call upon the hijackers, in person and on radio and television, to surrender forthwith. Angered by this uncompromising attitude and feeling that they had not been called as equal partners to discuss a problem but as subjects to be dictated to, the Lokollo group, although condemning what had been done, refused the invitation. Van Agt pointed out that the siege couldn't last for ever and that moderate force might have to be used, but this made no impression, Lokollo and his group believing that the use of force would have little chance of success and expressing that opinion. At this, the meeting broke up.

The actions of the hijackers, especially the abduction of children, were rejected by the South Moluccan community as a whole. But, like Lokollo, they understood what was behind them and would not condemn them out of hand. For a long time some such action had been expected. Parents of the hijackers, as surprised and shocked as anyone—as Hansina's letter suggests they would be—could not suppress a feeling of pride that their children had committed themselves so totally to the battle for freedom. They were not doing it for themselves or for their parents, but for the

whole nation, those in Holland and in Indonesia. Because of their knowledge of the South Moluccan character, in which love of children had a
high place, they did not believe that the children would be harmed. In any
case, there was nothing they could do about it, so they took a fatalistic
attitude.

It was not easy for the Dutch to accept this attitude. They had no
comparable insight into the South Moluccan disposition and could not
draw comfort from it. Thus the Moluccan population, especially of Bovensmilde, was subjected to mounting abuse and threats of violence. Police and military combined to keep the two communities apart.

The assumption among the parents was that the children would be
released by nightfall. It must be so, since there were no facilities for an
overnight stay in the school. At the very least, they would release the
younger children; surely they couldn't be so inhuman as to keep six-year-
olds overnight. But when seven o'clock passed without any progress being
made, the parents had to adjust to the realization that their children were
being cruelly exploited. Most of them found it impossible to think clearly
or logically, and the need for some emotional outlet became urgent. The
situation was relieved to some extent when a psychiatrist and social
worker smashed a window to get into the locked school library, situated
in an old farmhouse at a comfortable distance from the school, and Red
Cross, Salvation Army and social workers opened up the building as a
social, first aid, and information center for the parents. The press were
excluded; coffee, so important a punctuation to Dutch life, was made
continuously available; and the parents flocked there to talk out their
tensions, to vent their anger in criticism of the authorities, and to share
their anxieties and frustrations.

At 9:20 PM, van Vliet phoned his wife to say that the hijackers would
accept food and blankets. The news reached a parent named Dr. Adrian
Pen who had two children in the school and who, as a psychiatrist, found
himself speaking for the parents as a group. He rang the management
center and spoke to Dr. Mulder, whom he knew personally. Blankets, he
found, had not been thought of, and they would take some time to provide.
The delivery was further delayed by a car breakdown, and Pen phoned
Mulder a second time to find out where they were. "Tomorrow morning,"
he suggested, "don't wait until breakfast time to organize their breakfast."
It was a deserved rebuke, not for Mulder so much as for the management
center as a whole, but Pen regretted the outburst. Typical as it was of the
emotional atmosphere that surrounded him, he felt it disqualified him

from playing any representative role. From now on, he would stick to being a parent.

The hijackers had stipulated that only Fien Sihalasy would be permitted to deliver the food and blankets, so there was more delay when she could not be found. It was 10:30 P.M. when she was located, and then the hijackers said they wanted no more food and were only worried about blankets. She duly supervised the delivery.

Dusk had meanwhile shaded into night, and the younger children, after hours of fretful exhaustion and homesickness that not even bouts of TV could relieve, curled up on the bare floor. They were cold and uncomfortable, and some couldn't sleep. The older children, conscious that they were having an adventure, were not so miserable or afraid. They were together, and they had been allowed to stay up late. The hijackers had treated them kindly, even explaining to them why they were being held. It was, they learned, to secure the release of twenty-one of their friends who had been wrongly sent to prison.

For the parents, too, there was a sense of comradeship, of safety in numbers. Many of them stayed all night in the library, waiting for news.

From noon onward, the situation on the train had stabilized, and the passengers became resigned and silent, most of them striving for invisibility. Some were asleep; others were reading. Nelleke Ellenbroek was knitting—baby clothes, thought van der Struik. The carriage was uncomfortably full, but he realized that a lot of people must have been released, perhaps thirty or forty. Lucky devils. He glanced sidelong at his neighbors, trying to gauge their thoughts. Were they as scared as he was? Did they remember, as he did, that the last train hijacking had lasted 13 days and three people had been murdered, two of them in cold blood? His restless temperament rebelled against his utter helplessness. Surely there was something they could do. Then he thought of his wife. It must be even worse for her, knowing nothing of what was happening on the train.

The hijackers, parading up and down with their motley assortment of weapons—one even carried a *klewang*—suddenly looked ridiculous. Fear was still the dominant emotion amongst the passengers, but some of the younger ones, bursting to show their spirit, risked a few stage-whispered taunts, and smirked among themselves. That the hijackers even *felt* ridiculous was clear from their reaction; they could not bear being laughed at. "So you think it's funny, do you?" "There's nothing to laugh at." Two of the offenders, blond, athletic André Schager, a student teacher in physical training, and the rustic but irrepressible young waiter from the restaurant, eighteen-year-old Joop Hoogenboom, were to suffer for their levity. George Flapper could see that they were getting on the hijackers' nerves. "Don't do that," he said, "it's dangerous." There was a warning, too, from Max. "Be careful. Remember Wijster."

By early afternoon, the passengers felt hungry, and those who had brought sandwiches began rummaging for them. The hijackers promptly ordered them to share with their neighbors. Bread was brought from the restaurant to augment these meager supplies, but no one got more than a few mouthfuls. Drinks were supplied on a similar scale—one small can of soda or lemonade between four.

Having established contact with the school, the management center elected to play a waiting game with the train. It would do no harm, it was thought, to leave well enough alone for the moment. But as nightfall approached with no contact made, some effort at communication seemed prudent. At 7:30 PM, a policeman armed with a bullhorn left the command post at the golf club and emerged from the woods to the east of the train. When he judged that he could be heard he began shouting.

"Stick your arm out of the window and wave if you can hear me."

Excitedly, the passengers peered through the holes they had made in the newspapers. But the policeman, under strict orders to keep out of gun range, was almost out of earshot as well, and the metallic distortions of the bullhorn made him inaudible.

"What do you want? We can't understand you."

"If you want to have contact, if you want to have a field telephone, stick your arm out of the window and wave."

Attentively as the passengers listened, they could not decipher the message. Nor could the hijackers. "Replay," they shouted. "Replay." Eventually they seemed to understand that they could have a field telephone if they wanted one. "I want two policemen to bring it, but they must be wearing swimming trunks to show they're not armed," said Max, when the policeman came within earshot, "and don't try any tricks."

The passengers had hardly got over the thrill of this first contact with the outside world, showing that at last someone was taking notice, when one of the hijackers shouted, "Everyone stand up!" What were they up to now? Then came the explanation: "Move, exercise, gymnastics! Move your arms and legs! Bend your knees! Move!" The bizarre scene that followed had its reassuring aspects, in that the hijackers evidently had the welfare of their hostages in mind. A selfish interest, reflected some cynically, since sick hostages would be a liability. Soon afterwards they were allowed to stretch their legs and take an airing on one of the entrance platforms, two at a time.

Max appeared and asked, "May I have your attention please?" He always addressed them in this way. "Who needs medicine? I'm making a list." Several of the passengers knew their prescriptions, and Max noted them down. Van der Struik was one of them; he needed pills for his angina. Then he pointed out Nelleke Ellenbroek. "That woman's pregnant. Can you do something for her?" He had intended to ask Max to release her, but when it came to it he did not dare. Max glanced at the woman, then shook his head. "Pregnant? I don't think so." He went over to her and put the question, and she denied it. "She's not pregnant at all," he told van der Struik.

Later, when she passed him on the way to the toilet, van der Struik queried her denial and she admitted she was five months pregnant. "I didn't want to be an exception," she said. "Don't be silly," he answered. "You must tell them." When she did so, she was moved to the first-class carriage with Rien van Baarsel. A second woman, thirty-one-year-old Annie Brouwers, two months pregnant, was allowed to join her. Later Max beckoned to Saskia Sein, and she wondered what she was in for. The oldest of the women, she had been a nurse for nine years, and Rosemary wanted some help.

The first-class carriage offered much greater comfort, not only in uphol-stery—mock velvet against imitation leather—but also in layout. In the front half, instead of a center aisle with two seats on either side as in second class, there was an aisle offset to the right that made room for double seats of much greater width on the left. The remaining space on the right was taken up by single seats under the windows. The double seats or couches—there were eight of them in all—would enable the women to stretch out fully at night. In the rear half of this carriage, there was an even more luxurious layout. Here the seats were closeted into four com-partments that occupied the whole width of the train apart from a corri-dor. The rear two of these compartments were generally occupied by the hijackers, but the other two were later used by Rosemary as hospital wards and came to be known as the "royal stables." The two carriages of the second train-set were the exclusive preserve of the hijackers.

It was dusk when they heard the bullhorn again from the direction of the woods. "The field telephone is coming. Please close all the windows." At this curt order from the hijackers, the passengers jumped to obey.

Two men in swimming trunks were walking across the fields with landlines and equipment, which they passed through the transom window of the first study compartment, where Max had already established his own command post. The instrument was then installed on the front entrance platform. "That's better," said Max. "Now we can talk like civilized people." Puzzled that no one had yet referred to their demands, which they imagined had been delivered that morning, the hijackers handed copies to the two policemen.

Suddenly Rudi announced, "It's half past ten. You have to sleep." The passengers protested that it was only ten o'clock. "What's the time?" Rudi asked Max. "Ten o'clock," said Max. He turned to the passengers. "Don't worry. Rudi was at the fair in Groningen this weekend, and he won a cheap watch."

Max's intervention served two purposes. It humiliated Rudi, showing clearly who was boss, and it reassured the passengers. It's all right, Max seemed to be saying, you can sleep soundly. Nothing is going to happen tonight.

George Flapper thought this was good psychology. Keep them in a state of fear, but don't frighten them so much that they act out of desperation. In essence, they were being treated like children. The threat of punishment was held over them, but they were in safe hands provided they did as they were told. It was a dependent outlook that should have been conducive to sleep. But could the hijackers be trusted? Few people thought so, and the majority could do no more than doze. Weary of sitting upright all day, they sought relaxation in vain. Tingling and fidgety, they stretched this way and that, sliding involuntarily with the slant of the train and jostling each other. The continual patrolling up and down of armed Moluccans was equally disturbing.

The transfer of the patients in Rosemary's care to the first-class carriage enabled one or two passengers to stretch out, but even Ton Kroon, small enough to curl up on the benchlike seats, found it impossible to maintain a static position against the slope. The remedy of jamming himself into one corner only resulted in cramp. All sorts of grotesque attitudes were adopted in an effort to relax, and when it became obvious to the hijackers that sleep under these conditions was impossible, Max ordered several other women into the first-class compartment. Mini Loman was not one of them, but she asked if she could go, and her request was granted. Changing from the neat white blouse and black skirt she was wearing into T-shirt and jeans, she tried to settle down, but after the heat of the day the night had turned chill. She had developed a headache of migraine proportions, and this was aggravated by the continual clattering of the door behind her as it slid to and fro. Every time anyone passed through, it crashed back heavily because of the tilt of the train. One of the hijackers saw how distressed she was and asked what was wrong. "I'm so cold," she said. "Here you are," he said, "have my coat." And he wrapped his black leather zip-up coat round her shivering body.

All day she had felt the atmosphere of mental cruelty that the hijackers generated, with the ever-present threat of violence behind it. Now this simple act of kindness shocked her, and she hardly knew what to say. The hijackers, it seemed, were human after all.

In the second-class carriage, the young waiter, Joop Hoogenboom, had a similar experience. The hijackers had picked on him all day, making him do all the menial tasks. But when he complained of the cold, Max lent him his jacket. To the outside world, however, the hijackers remained inscrutable, and they made no effort to use the field telephone that the authorities had provided. Let them come to us was Max's attitude. He had acted; the government must react. And at eleven o'clock that night they did. "Max! Telephone!" shouted the other Moluccans excitedly as the bell rang. But Max showed no disposition to hurry. Walking through the aisle with his usual measured tread, he rebuked his colleagues. "Quiet. People are asleep. What's the hurry? We have all the time in the world."

Max did not close the door leading to the front entrance platform, and the passengers sitting nearby heard one half of the ensuing conversation. No doubt this was Max's intention. Already, the passengers were feeling that everything he did had a motive.

"Why do you call us?"

It was not difficult to deduce from Max's replies what was being said at the other end. The passengers didn't know it as yet, but the voice at the other end of the line was that of Dick Mulder. They could only guess at his method of approach, but they heard it being summarily rejected by Max.

"Don't try any of your psychological tricks on me. We learned a lot at Wijster. We have better things to do."

When Mulder tried to hint that a reasonable dialogue between attackers and management center might oil the wheels of negotiation, Max snapped, "No! You must do what we want." Adjusting to Max's tense, autocratic manner, Mulder tried a temporizing reply, but Max responded with a threat. "Then I take my measures."

"What measures?"

"Hard measures."

"Then you are a killer?"

"No, I am not a killer."

This sharp exchange was followed by a final word from Max. "You may call tomorrow morning at half past eight. Not earlier." And he smashed the phone down.

Mulder's initial aim was to get the terrorists talking, to establish a relationship, and to gain their confidence. He was not put off by Max's abruptness. Somehow, by reasonable methods that would stand up to public scrutiny, the hostages had to be got out alive. To that end, he would put himself in the shoes of the hijackers, try to see the outside world through their eyes. His task would be to smooth over the peaks and valleys of their moods, to lower the temperature and slow down the tempo, especially at this early stage when they would be anxious to demonstrate their power. Although the recent Spaghetti House and Balcombe Street sieges in London and the Dr. Herrema affair in Ireland had established new and more sophisticated techniques, the South Moluccans, too, had learned their lessons.[12] The leader of the terrorists on the train, whose identity was soon known, was going to set fresh problems for the government; that much was clear. There were no cast-iron prescriptions to be followed, no psychological blueprints for success; every incident had its distinctive features. As on previous occasions when he had been called in to conduct negotiations, Mulder prepared for surprises.

He did not need to remind himself that he would be dealing with human beings, with young people, mostly, who were fighting for an ideal. He might not regard their methods as acceptable, but at least he found them understandable. Working for a solution was not merely his job as a government employee. It was his human duty.

He did not equate terrorism of this sort with criminal hijacking. The terrorist had the psychological support of a cause, something for which he was willing to die. That was something, however misguided, that commanded respect. And it was on the basis of mutual respect that he hoped to establish the relationship he needed.

To detach the terrorist from his sworn resolve could be a long-drawn-out process, requiring much patience. Mulder was not short of that. When called in to this sort of incident, he put all thoughts of routine business and domestic matters out of his head and prepared for a long confrontation. He began by thinking that it might last six months; then, anything less than that was a reprieve.

---

[12]For the Dr. Herrema affair, see footnote on page 36. Similar techniques of firm, psychological pressure were successfully employed by the British police in the Spaghetti House and Balcombe Street incidents.

Most important of all, he would endeavor to build up a picture of the man at the other end of the line, to imagine what kind of person he was and, from that, what he might do and how best to exert an influence over him. Just as Montgomery had kept a photograph of Rommel in his caravan in the Libyan Desert, so Mulder would carry a likeness of Max Papilaya, as he had already been identified, in his head.

CHAPTER 16

The Second Day

"**Y**ESTERDAY I TOLD YOU to call at half past eight, and it's now fifty minutes later. I don't want to be kept waiting by the telephone."

Part of the government's tactics at Wijster had been to keep the terrorists waiting. Although the hijackers were encouraged to believe in the early stages that they were dictating the terms, they were subtly reminded by minor delays and frustrations of their ultimate dependence on the authorities. Now, on the second morning at De Punt, the telephone call that Max had stipulated should come at 8:30 AM was not made until 9:20.

Mulder did his best to get a dialogue going, but Max cut him short. "No, I won't accept food or blankets. Not until our demands are agreed upon. And when I say call at 8:30, you call at 8:30. If you call me again at twelve o'clock, I will listen to what you say. If you don't call then, you can call at six. We won't accept any food in the meantime."

Mulder did not give up easily. "We don't understand your message. Please repeat."

"I won't repeat it. Ring at twelve o'clock." With that he hung up.

The document that had been handed to the two policemen the previous night had since been delivered. So too had the letters addressed to the Ministry of Justice and the news media, written and mailed before the hijackings. All these messages bore the signature Free South Moluccan Youth. As Joop den Uyl had foreseen, the messages requested the release of the twenty-one South Moluccans serving jail sentences for previous terrorist incidents. The document addressed to the government listed the practical steps that must be taken to effect the release and escape of both prisoners and hijackers, and it ended with an ultimatum:

1. We demand a bus or buses for us and the hostages.
2. We demand that the bus shall have blinds pulled down and all seats removed.
3. We demand that the bus be given a full tank, and there must be a driver to take us to Eelde.
4. We demand a plane to take us to_____[The destination was left blank.]
5. We demand that there must be a crew. They will go on board when we tell them to. We shall take the hostages with us.
6. We demand that this all take place within forty-eight hours. Otherwise there will be victims.

The deadline was set at 2:00 PM, Wednesday, May 25. Because of the mislaying of the original demand note, the government had less than thirty hours in which to find a solution. "What we do depends on you," the Ministry of Justice was told. "We will tolerate no mediators or attempts at interference. Otherwise, people will be killed." The letters to the newspapers also warned that, if mediation were attempted, there would be deaths. If the government ignored the demands, there would be deaths. If any attempt were made at armed intervention or capture or any reprisals were taken against South Moluccans elsewhere, then they would kill.

After the experience of Wijster, these threats were bound to be taken at their face value, as, of course, the hijackers intended. The Dutch Government had no insight into the personality of Max Papilaya and no knowledge of any pact not to kill, and they would have been unlikely to place much reliance on it if they had. Indeed, the impression was that they were dealing with a group likely to prove even more dangerous than the last one. It was felt that ominous signs were the well-phrased communications that had been sent and the uncompromising telephone performance of the leader. "Last time we were dealing with kids," said den Uyl, "this time with professionals." Van Agt agreed that the terrorists had obviously learned from the incidents of 1975.

As soon as the sun came up on that Tuesday morning, Berend van der Struik, who had once worked as a telegraph operator, began signaling toward the edge of the wood, using a piece of foil at first and then an empty soda can. Two of the hijackers were continually patrolling the carriage, but Joop Huismans and André Schager warned him whenever they approached. There was no reply from the woods, and van der Struik hardly expected one. It would only arouse the suspicions of the hijackers. Some of them were already outside the train, firing their guns at real or imaginary targets. "Where are those damned marines?" wrote van der Struik in his diary, another clandestine activity that he pursued defiantly and with much trepidation, knowing how serious discovery might be. But that was typical of van der Struik—he could not just sit there and do nothing. The risk he was taking was underlined when Hoogenboom, the young waiter, attempted to emulate his diary-keeping and was apprehended by Rudi.

Rudi took the diary away to show Max, returning a few minutes later. Hoogenboom had written contemptuously of the hijackers and implied that their guns were loaded with blanks. "Come with me," said Rudi. Hoogenboom, showing plenty of spirit, took his time about putting on his shoes, permitting himself a minor show of insolence; but eventually he was taken forward to Max. "Stand there, and we'll shoot you," said Rudi, pointing a gun at him. "Then we shall see about blanks." As the terrified waiter put his hands up in mute appeal, Rudi put the gun down. "Okay, we won't do it. But you're lucky we don't want to." Hoogenboom was sent back to his seat, where he put his head in his hands, momentarily overcome. Soon afterward he was told, politely but firmly, "If you have the time, you can clean the toilets."

Already the stench from the toilets was abominable, and, as the sun rose, the flies multiplied. One by one, feeling half-drunk because of the tilt of the carriage, the passengers went for their morning constitutional. But first they had to raise their hands as in a school classroom and ask permission. Marc Hustinx suffered a further humiliation. He had saved some water in a glass from overnight to clean his teeth, but his foresight drew a reproof from Rudi. "What are you doing? Did you ask permission? Don't do it again."

Most of the hijackers, although often acting aggressively, still seemed nervous and lacking in confidence. It was clear that they relied a great deal on Max. They avoided contact with their hostages as far as possible, from which Ton Kroon drew the inference that, if there had to be killings to force the government's hand, this would make it easier. Having seen that they were capable of inflicting mental cruelty, he concluded that they would probably be capable of physical cruelty as well, and might kill without scruple.

During the morning, Max called for attention, and the women from the first-class carriage were brought in to hear what he said. When silence was not immediate, Hansina fired a round through the roof. "Freedom is five meters away," said Max, "but anyone who tries to escape will be shot." To emphasize the point, another round was fired through the roof, and as splinters from the ceiling fell into the lap of a woman passenger, any lingering doubts of the effectiveness of the hijackers' weapons were removed. "You have to be sensible," continued Max. "Don't move without permission. Don't do anything stupid, or you will be shot immediately." They had no reason to doubt his word. He still told them nothing of his plans, his demands, or the ultimatum, and with the explosions still reverberating in their ears and imaginations, no one asked questions.

There was some further reorganization, as more of the women were moved to the first-class carriage and those that remained were placed in aisle seats, because they were thought to be less likely to cause a disturbance. Max again went around with paper and pencil asking about medicines, after which he conferred with Rosemary.

At noon the telephone rang, and, as Max walked forward to answer it, the passengers heard him say: "Very good. Twelve o'clock. Exactly on time. That's better." He had won the first round of his psychological battle. But there was no reply yet from the government to his demands, and he called for Rosemary to come to the phone. "We are going to play the following game," he told her. By appointing her as doctor and bringing her into the conspiracy, he was subtly drawing her to his side. "Your government has not accepted our demands, so tell them we shall continue to refuse food, blankets, and anything else until they do. That is the message. But between ourselves, we are not inhuman, and we shall share everything we have here in the train."

Rosemary repeated the message, then passed the list of medicines to Dr. Havinga. She also asked for sleeping pills, tranquilizers, and a stethoscope. The Moluccans then distributed bread, beer, and even vermouth and sherry from the restaurant.

The passengers began to develop the same feeling of isolation and abandonment as their predecessors of 1975, but for the second day running, a cabinet meeting was in progress at The Hague to consider their plight, along with that of the children. Netherlands Railways was inundated with telephone calls from people who feared they might have relatives on the train, and offers of help from social workers and others were almost as numerous. The process of elimination eventually suggested that there were fifty-four hostages on the train, and, once they were positively identified, relatives were contacted and a families center established in the staff clubroom at the railway station at Groningen, with night accommodation available at a Groningen hotel. The response to this was mixed, some feeling that their place was as near as they could get to their loved ones, others that the sensible course was to stay where they belonged and continue as normally as possible. This was the reaction of Ton Kroon's wife, Marianne. Ansje Monsjou's father went to Groningen, while her mother stayed to look after the home.

One who was torn between the two choices was George Flapper's wife, Coby. After the initial shock, her first preference was to stay in familiar surroundings with friends nearby. Then she changed her mind and traveled from her home in Zwolle to be near George. A girl of fair, placid beauty, she and her husband had always promised each other that they would share their experiences in life as far as that was possible, learning from them and from each other. Only by being on hand in Groningen would she be able to live through the experience and the separation hour by hour, day by day.

When she got to Groningen, her fears of finding herself in an atmosphere of highly charged emotion, even hysteria, proved unfounded; talking to people with similar anxieties to her own was a relief. Generally, the absent relatives were highly idealized, but this made their descriptions vivid, and interest in each other's relatives became a source of mutual solace.

One who found the professional help of the psychiatrists and social workers overwhelming was Jan Cuppen's wife, Marie José. She was irritated at being made to feel like a psychiatric patient. She felt perfectly normal, but she was a fighter, and passive acceptance of her situation was foreign to her. "It's cozy in here," she was told by the other families on her first visit. "You get coffee and sandwiches free, the hotel is free, and we have a good relationship with each other. We even get plenty of laughs. If you feel like crying, you go behind that curtain and get sedatives from a doctor." She could not share the blind confidence in the authorities from which others appeared to take comfort, and she was impatient with what seemed the general abandonment of personal responsibility. Some, she noticed, found consolation from being in the limelight and were eager to be photographed and to give interviews. Others seemed to have lost their fighting spirit and to have delegated their problems totally. To ask questions, as Marie José did, was to risk being regarded as neurotic. She got the most help and information from the other professionals who were sometimes in attendance—officials of Netherlands Railways, the police, and the Red Cross, who somehow struck the right note.

Some relatives were unable to travel because of other responsibilities. Vera Nijmeijer's anxieties were intensified by her husband's occupation. "If they find out that Victor's a policeman," she thought, "he'll be the first to be shot." But she kept her fears to herself. With a small daughter to look after and the added worry of a chronically sick mother, she was forced to stay at home in Rotterdam.

There were about seven family groups who settled down to stay in the hotel and spend most of the day in the center. Some living in the Groningen area used the center daily; others living at no great distance dropped in regularly on the chance of some extra morsel of gossip. The remainder —about half—kept in daily contact by telephone.

Whereas the site of the train hijacking was remote and unseen, far removed geographically from relatives and friends, the school was in the center of a populated area in which the parents, the relatives of the teachers, and even the families of the hijackers lived. As anxious parents huddled in small groups in the streets surrounding the school or gathered nervously in the library, the inhabitants of the Moluccan enclave were uneasy eyewitnesses of the agonies of their Dutch neighbors. The tensions in Bovensmilde thus remained at fever pitch, the emotions of hatred and fear being almost palpable, while the Moluccans stayed in their enclave for fear of reprisals.

While the male parents were oppressed by feelings of guilt, the women seized on the smallest item of news and tended to exaggerate both its content and its significance. Eventually, the rumors and counterrumors became so demoralizing that they were very sensibly outlawed, the parents resolving to listen to official pronouncements only, which were made at regular intervals at the library. This became more than ever a sanctuary, a place where no press reporter dared to venture. One photographer who did so was physically roughed up.

To divert their minds and to give time for proper rest while maintaining a twenty-four-hour vigil, parents divided themselves into groups and held discussions. Their main preoccupation was to persuade the authorities that nothing must stand in the way of the release of their children, and that any action against the kidnappers would only precipitate violence. Knowledge of the ultimatum coupled with memories of Wijster convinced the parents that their children were in mortal danger, and only the rhythm of a routine saved them from being driven to distraction.

Official South Moluccan organizations continued to condemn the hijackings, and many important Moluccans expressed their disgust at the involvement of children. South Moluccan women had been the first to try to get food to the school, and a group of fifteen South Moluccan teachers spoke of the actions as "completely without honor" and offered to take the place of the hostages. Theodoor Kuhuwael, the educator who had acted as a mediator in 1975, was asked by Zeevalking with the approval of Lokollo to go to Bovensmilde to ask the occupiers of the school, all of whom he had taught in their younger days, to release the children, and he agreed to do so. A man of high moral standing, Kuhuwael was trusted by the Dutch Government because of his frankness. He freely admitted to a stronger allegiance to the RMS than to law and order in the Netherlands, but he was ready to mediate.

Many South Moluccans, perhaps the majority, while unhappy at the seizing of children, condoned the action as one born of frustration with the aftermath of 1975. Why had children been taken? Because, said young South Moluccans with cruel logic, the pressure put on the government was more effective when the lives of children were at stake.

A grotesque incident the morning of that second day had its value as a distraction. A psychiatric patient who had escaped from a mental hospital at Den Dolder near Amersfoort and made her way to Bovensmilde by train managed to slip through the outer and inner security rings established by the police. In her white mental hospital dress, she was taken for a Red Cross nurse. Walking boldly up to the school, unnoticed by the hijackers, she tapped on one of the assembly room windows. "Hey. I've got something to tell you." Van Beetz saw her first and called to Willem Soplanit—"Fat Willem," as he had been dubbed by the teachers— "There's a woman standing out there. I think she wants to ask you something." The other kidnappers panicked, opening a window and shooting over the woman's head and past her feet. They thought she was a policewoman in disguise, trying to create a diversion. While aiming to scare her off, they kept a keen lookout elsewhere. "Don't shoot," called the teachers, "she isn't well." But when she persisted, more shots were fired. Isaac Thenu lost his nerve completely, yelling at the teachers and screaming at the children, some of whom were terrified. Others, peeking excitedly through holes they had made in the paper covering the windows, were thoroughly enjoying the show.

Fat Willem was the first to recognize the woman's garb. "She's a mental hospital patient! Stop shooting!" The woman took fright and made for the bicycle shed, and Willem agreed on the telephone that two policemen in their underwear could come and collect her.

As Willem was aware, the incident had highlighted the ineptitude of the group. How could the woman have gotten so close without being seen? If she could get through the police cordon, others on less harmless errands might do the same. Guilt and confusion at their combined carelessness abounded, and it was not until evening that the teachers were able to soothe them. Isaac then apologized for his behavior. "I didn't know what I was doing."

Unlike their colleagues in the train, the kidnappers were accepting food. Meals were delivered at intervals, and medicines were accepted for a girl with a congenital heart complaint and for a diabetic. The children were encouraged to find something to do; there were plenty of books in the classrooms, and games like halma and checkers were allowed to be brought in. But the kidnappers were undergoing a bewildering experience, one they hadn't bargained for. They hadn't stopped to think what the occupation of a school containing more than a hundred children might mean, and there were times when the children had them completely in their power. Controlling them would have been a hopeless task had the help of the five remaining teachers not been readily given. The other teachers, in addition to van Vliet, van Beetz and Mrs. Abbink, were Dinie Harkink, a girl who drew strength in a mother-and-daughter relationship from the courage and poise of Sjaan Abbink, and Andreas Weijnholt, who had only recently joined the staff.

The children were not allowed to move freely from classroom to classroom and were supposed to ask permission for everything, but their natural high spirits overcame their timidity, and sometimes they forgot. Excited by their favorite TV program, they got up in a body and began to dance on the podium. The so-called terrorists, unable to make themselves heard, nearly went mad with the noise. Tommy Polnaya, the "little comrade," trying in vain to keep order, seemed to the children to have only two Dutch words in his vocabulary: "Shut up!"

"Please shoot your gun!" said a twelve-year-old to Fat Willem. Another asked: "Can I see the bullets?" Flattered and excited by their interest, Willem took some of the sixth-grade boys into a classroom and explained the function of the various parts of the weapons he and his colleagues had brought and how they were loaded and fired. The boys had never had a more fascinating lesson. The long-haired Guustav Tehupuring displayed genuine talent as an artist when he drew a portrait of one of the children, Ena de Groot, to celebrate her birthday, and she was delighted with it. Some of the children responded by drawing likenesses of their captors and offering them up for approval. They were hardly flattering, but they were accepted graciously. Difficult as it was for the teachers to believe, it was clear that the hijackers genuinely loved children.

During the evening, the hijackers helped to serve supper and make beds. At nightfall, some of the children became fretful and showed signs of homesickness, tormenting their captors with the poignancy of their questions. "Sir, when are we allowed to go home?" Trying to comfort them, the hijackers urged them to wait a little longer. "We're having so much fun here." When the soft answer failed, they tried a harsher tone. "Now you must stop all this noise and coughing at once." Some of the children seemed to cough all night. Out of the darkness, a small voice would pipe up with: "But, sir, if I have to cough, I can't help it."

The children were in familiar surroundings, and they had the constant reassurance of the presence of their teachers, who were able to urge restraint on the hijackers when a child misbehaved or became fractious. They cooperated as best they could for the children's sake and acted even more positively than they usually did in the role of substitute parent. The principal, van Vliet, conducted many of the telephone conversations with the management center and pleaded for decisions to be taken that would bring about the children's early release.

This, as the hijackers had expected, was the government's first priority, and to achieve it, they seemed prepared to make concessions. In a TV broadcast that evening, den Uyl said that the government would not allow any of the hostages to be taken out of the country, but he refused to comment when asked whether the terrorists themselves might be allowed to leave. The possibility that some sort of compromise might be in the government's mind was enhanced when van Agt, also speaking on TV, said that no discussion of safe custody for the terrorists could take place until they had freed the children. These pronouncements, directed as much at the hijackers—who were known to have radio and/or TV—as at the Dutch public, implied the government's acceptance that the terrorists had hit on a weak spot, and that a guarantee of safe custody might be the government's contribution to a bartering deal. But in a direct answer to the terrorists that evening, van Agt took a somewhat firmer line. The demands would only be discussed when all the children had been released. This kept the government's options open, while promising nothing.

The general election, set for the next day—the day the ultimatum expired—had been completely overshadowed by the hijackings, but the government was determined that it should go ahead and so were the Dutch people, who were preparing to go to the polls in an angry mood. After recording his hatred of extremism, den Uyl warned against any temptation to answer violence with violence. But he added, "We cannot give in to terror." This defiant attitude, taken in conjunction with the apparent hints of a compromise, was calculated to make the hijackers pause.

That night on the train, the tense atmosphere generated by the aggression of the younger hijackers still dominated the second-class carriage, where the prisoners were now mostly male. The morbid apprehensions of the hostages were matched by the hijackers' fears of retaliation. Kept in ignorance of government reaction, the hostages floundered in a morass of uncertainty. Only once, when the radio was left on by mistake, did they hear a reference to "the hijackings in Drenthe and Groningen" and realize that some other group of hostages was suffering too.

In this atmosphere, the Moluccans did not find it difficult to pursue their policy of avoiding personal contact. But in the first-class, largely female section, this policy was not so successful. Once again, the inequality of the sexes was demonstrated. The hijackers were not afraid of the women, and this was the decisive factor. Passing from one carriage to another, their relief and relaxation were visible. Perhaps they had no stomach for terrorizing women. And the women themselves proved more adaptable than the men. They knew instinctively that it was the men who were in the greater danger. Intuitively they saw through the mask of brutality that the hijackers wore.

Any or all of these factors may have persuaded Max, at nine o'clock that evening, to give the women an assurance calculated to soothe their anxieties and raise their morale—if they believed him, and they did. The assurance he gave them was that no one was going to be shot. He added that, when the marines came, they would fight to the death outside the train, but they would do the passengers no harm. These promises were not given to the men. Wim Fakkert, the priest turned social worker, had been allowed to move into the first-class carriage with the lad in his charge, who was present at the time, and passed the news on, but it scarcely reassured them.

Even during the night, the atmosphere in the second-class carriage remained tense. Those who let their minds dwell on home and family suffered most. Van der Struik, expecting to derive comfort from thinking about his wife and daughter, experienced a nightmarish attack of insecurity, as though he were falling into some yawning chasm of the mind. Flapper, thinking of Coby, was tantalized to find that, concentrate as he might, he could not bring her face into focus.

Until a late hour that night, Kuhuwael talked with influential residents of the Moluccan enclave at Bovensmilde and tried to establish communication with the kidnappers through their parents, but he found no possibility of any fruitful contact.

CHAPTER 17

The Third Day

IT WAS NOT UNTIL AFTER 9:30 on Wednesday morning, May 25, with the margin before the expiration of the ultimatum narrowed to little more than four hours, that contact between the train and the management center was renewed. To the hostages, it seemed that they were being forgotten. Then at last came the call.

"Max, telephone!"

Max left the door of the luggage compartment open, and as before those within earshot were able to pick up much of his side of the conversation. It was clear that he was trying to establish himself in the government's eyes as the overall leader, essentially moderate but utterly determined, the man with whom the government would be wise to deal. "747 here," they heard him say. He had taken to identifying himself with the code name 747, the number of the train. "On this train," he went on, "my men listen to me. I have them under control. But we know a lot about the fellows in the school. Be careful. Those guys are killers." He proceeded to elaborate on the demands that had already been made.

First, the South Moluccans and their hostages must be taken by bus to Eelde and from there to Schiphol by plane. Second, they must leave from Schiphol by jumbo jet for an unknown destination, leaving the children behind at Schiphol. The adult hostages would be released elsewhere.

The government's attitude to these requests had already been framed, and Mulder's task, in a situation where the government was not prepared to concede very much, was a difficult one. He had to put the government's terms faithfully, yet he must not leave the terrorists without hope, or they might act in desperation. So he adopted the role of adviser, a role in which he hoped to gain the terrorists' confidence. He could not recommend going back to the government on these lines, he said. The government's position was that all the children must be released before the demands could be discussed, while "under no circumstances would hostages be allowed to be taken in the plane." This mention of a plane implied a tacit acceptance that, on the right terms, a plane might be provided. Max refused to accept this advice and requested that his demands be passed to the government immediately. When Mulder demurred, Max insisted. "You will do that on our behalf." Mulder, in his role of impartial go-between, agreed to do so.

Shortly after this conversation, the hijackers at the school asked if they could talk to Kuhuwael. The government, scenting the possibility of mediation, agreed, and Kuhuwael expressed his readiness to try again. At ten o'clock that morning, he talked on the telephone to the hijackers in the school, but it was at once apparent that they only wished to use him as a mouthpiece for their threats. "What is more important?" he was asked. "The will of the Dutch people or the lives of the children and teachers here and the people on the train? The ultimatum of two o'clock applies both to the train and the school."

Whereas on the train the hostages were aware of the buildup of tension without always knowing the reason for it, the teachers in the school were more in the hijackers' confidence. They knew about the ultimatum, and they were manipulated by the kidnappers into increasing the pressure, particularly in the making of telephone appeals. The children, too, were about to be exploited in an effort to scare the government into submission. On the blackboard, a sentence had been written by the hijackers that the children, rehearsed by their teachers, were to shout in unison. "Van Agt, we don't want to die!" was the chosen phrase. As soon as van Vliet saw it, he protested.

"You can't do that with children. You can't make them say that."

"Then what do you suggest?"

"They could say something like, 'Van Agt, we want to live!' "

The kidnappers accepted this, the chalk on the blackboard was wiped off, the new phrase substituted, and the children were rehearsed in their role. To them it seemed like a party game, and they practiced enthusiastically, conducted by their teachers. Shouting a slogan in unison, as it does with a football crowd, made them feel they were playing a part in the action. Their carefree attitude, however, was not easy to interpret when, at 10:45 AM, the windows of the school were thrown open, letting in a welcome blast of fresh air, and the shrill voices of the children took up their chant.

"Van Agt, we want to live! Van Agt, we want to live!"

The effect on the crowd outside the school was traumatic. People in northern Holland don't show their emotions easily, but the parents suffered a paroxysm of fear and frustration. Some of the men talked again of storming the school; some of the women were almost demented. The teachers had guessed there would be a commotion when the voices of the children were heard, but the reaction was so violent that the hijackers feared an immediate attack. Simon van Beetz grabbed the megaphone and shouted a message. "This is van Beetz speaking. Please withdraw from the school as soon as possible for the sake of the children. Please get back."

The incident confirmed the impression already gained by the government and fostered by Max that the leader of the school hijackers was an oddball, and that it was with the level-headed Max that they would have to do business.

The knowledge that the kidnappers came from the local community exacerbated the atmosphere in Bovensmilde, and it was as well that the police had thought to seal off the South Moluccan enclave to protect its occupants from the expected backlash. There were so many telephone calls threatening vengeance if any harm befell the children that the residents of the enclave began to organize themselves into vigilante groups. South Moluccan attitudes on the whole remained ambivalent, but in Bovensmilde, at least, a defiant loyalty to the cause still underlay the surface. "We support them in principle. We must not forget that this offense stems from dissatisfaction among our people."

A further attempt at mediation by Kuhuwael brought no change in the hijackers' attitude. With less than three hours to go the government still stuck to their position of no negotiation until the children were released, while the hijackers, although still ready to trade the children for concessions, rejected any possibility of their premature release on the grounds that they represented their best assurance of safety. The critical stage in the first round of the drama was about to be reached.

In desperation, van Agt decided to bring four of the terrorists whose release had been demanded to the bunker at Assen, so that, if negotiations broke down completely as the deadline approached, they could be put in touch by telephone with the train and the school in an effort to get the dialogue going again. Most of the 1975 hijackers had since expressed remorse at the killing of hostages, and it was hoped that they might be prepared to make an appeal for moderation. Some of them were also expected to refuse the chance of being freed to fly to some unknown destination, preferring to sit out their sentences.

At this critical point, the hijackers asked for a telephone link between train and school. While this had its dangers, since communication between the two groups would enable them to concert their plans and might be mutually sustaining, it was conceded after consultation with van Agt. The longer the talking continued, the better, and the line could be tapped. There was also Max's hint that he could exercise some influence for good over the group in the school.

The extent of Van Agt's desperation may be gauged from his agreement to allow a South Moluccan preacher named Dr. Rutumulessy and twenty-eight of his flock to hold a religious service outside the school, singing hymns and songs and reciting biblical texts denouncing the killing of children. The preacher thought he and his flock could influence the kidnappers, and the risk of a clash was accepted. The impending service was publicly announced, and when the party arrived by bus at about noon, they were allowed through the police cordon. Their singing and their intonation of prayers and supplications, punctuated by a volley of threats from the hijackers, presented a bizarre spectacle, and the climax was reached when a woman with a megaphone approached the school and began talking to the kidnappers. Threatened with shooting, she retired to a discreet distance, and the party knelt down and prayed in the street. The only immediate result was a marginal improvement in racial tensions resulting from this public display of South Moluccan sympathy. Van Agt hoped it would "serve to dampen any understandable but mistaken animosity that threatened to arise in Holland against other Moluccans," and he appealed to the Dutch for restraint.

During the morning, the management center tried several temporizing ploys. "The government wants to negotiate," Mulder told the group in the school, "but first I want to talk to the boys in the train." The train hijackers, however, were absorbed in other matters. "We are going to search you," they announced to the male hostages, "to look in your clothes and your luggage for weapons." Strangely, they hadn't thought of this before. Covered by the terrorists' guns, the hostages had to go one by one to the first-class carriage. "Here are two automatic guns," said Max, "and we have thirty-two bullets in each. So don't try anything. Don't make any suspicious move or we'll shoot." Then his manner changed as he told them a story. "My father was in the KNIL. He was a loyal soldier of the Dutch. They had one principle—they never stole, plundered, or looted. Once there was a friend of my father's who looted. Two or three days later he was dead. So we never do anything like that."

The women watched the men being brought into their compartment, most of them looking awed and submissive. The men knew Max had been having talks with the outside world, they had heard by this time about the ultimatum, and many were trembling. With loaded guns pointed at them, they feared they might find the "search" a euphemism for something more dramatic. The Moluccans had killed last time, and sooner or later they would surely kill again.

Max searched each hostage individually, then went through his luggage. No one was more apprehensive than Victor Niemeijer, who had tucked his identity card into his belt. But they were only looking for weapons. They borrowed a camera from his luggage but promised to return it. They did not find his briefcase.

Before he sent them all back to their seats, Max said, "Look in your clothes and in your luggage to see if there's anything missing. People at Wijster and in the Indonesian consulate said the South Moluccans stole from them. We don't want you saying something is missing later. Check your possessions now." The accusations of petty theft had wounded South Moluccan pride. Hijackers yes, but not thieves. "No, Max," said the hostages in turn, "we are not missing anything."

Soon after the search was completed, Max passed through the second-class carriage on his way to his "office." Sensing the agitation that the search and the news of the ultimatum had caused, he changed his tune completely. "We don't intend to hurt a hair of your heads."

What were they to make of this? Although they didn't know the details, they were aware that an ultimatum had been issued and that it was due to expire at two o'clock that afternoon. As the hour approached, the tension mounted. Conversation ceased; people consulted their watches every few minutes; and the atmosphere became electric. Despite Max's assurance, some act of violence to justify the ultimatum seemed certain.

Preoccupied as they were with personal survival, the male hostages nevertheless felt humiliated by their fears and by their dependence on the whims of a handful of terrorists. They deeply resented their loss of freedom and even hoped that the election might be postponed on their account, so that they could vote.

Overshadowed as the election was in the media, the Dutch people were turning out to the polls in record numbers, as though every vote expressed their support not so much for any one political party as for the constitution. In the final tally both coalition parties, Labor and Christian Democratic Appeal, increased their total vote, their percentage of the vote, and their number of seats in the Second Chamber, confirming public confidence. When the new cabinet was formed several months later, van Agt was appointed prime minister. But, as the terrorists' deadline approached, the polling booths emptied, and the whole nation stood by their radios, hungry for news.

In the school, Willem was walking about with a hand grenade, and, unlike the explosives laid in the train and the consulate in 1975, it was real. He promised the teachers he would explode it at two o'clock if the demands were not met. In what sounded like a final call to the management center, the teachers heard him say, "You know what you have to do, and we don't want delay." The teachers feared that, if that hand grenade were thrown in the crowded assembly room, there would be terrible carnage, and they discussed what they could do to protect the children. They planned to get them together as the time approached and shelter them under tables and desks. When the hijackers enlisted the help of van Vliet in making another appeal to Mulder, he took the opportunity to hint at the threatened danger. *"The situation here is very explosive,"* he said, *"literally and figuratively."*

By 1:45 PM, the teachers were wiping the sweat from their brows. At 1:50 PM, there was a call from Mulder. He was trying to spin out the time, trying to overrun that dreaded moment of two o'clock. Before the hijackers cut him off, he said he would ring again at half past two.

When the deadline passed without incident, it brought little relief. Remembering how deadlines at Wijster had been allowed to expire only to have killings take place soon after, the hostages' agony was merely prolonged, and the nation at large remained anxious and subdued. But after an hour, there was a gradual if cautious relaxation. Queues formed again at the polling booths, and crowds gathered in bars and cafés, becoming more animated as time passed.

In Bovensmilde, the vacuum left by the complete cessation of the normal tenor of life was not easy to fill, and the expiration of the ultimatum left a sense of anticlimax. After two days of sickening anxiety and two sleepless nights, it was borne in on parents that the initial crisis was dissolving into a war of attrition. Their ordeal might last a long time yet, and they began to pace themselves, if only subconsciously. Despite the strain they were under, they had so little to do that they were fighting boredom for much of the time. The playing of games to pass the time struck a discordant note, and few parents did more than talk, smoke, take Valium, listen, and wait.

Part of the defense mechanism was to substitute a new routine. Red Cross and social workers had absorbed most of the jobs that parents might have busied themselves with, but help was offered and sometimes accepted. There was comfort, too, in getting themselves organized, appointing working parties for tasks of no real importance, drawing up rosters for night attendance at the library while the remainder slept. One of the shared tasks was entry control at the library, which was completely unnecessary since no outsider had the courage to come anywhere near the place.

At a loose end on that Wednesday morning, Adrian Pen, the psychiatrist with two children trapped in the school, called at a neighbor's house for a chat and a beer. The neighbor was an old friend, but he was not directly affected by the kidnapping, and for once they could find little in common. Overnight, they had become strangers, with nothing to say to each other. Drawn in the course of the morning to the library, Pen met people there whom he hardly knew but to whom he found he could talk on the most intimate terms.

The village was sharply divided, not only between Dutch and South Moluccan but also between Dutch and Dutch, those who had children in the school and those who did not. The former were enjoying a precarious importance, the latter felt isolated. Parents of children who had stayed at home that day for some reason or who had escaped from the gym felt deprived, cheated of the experience and the limelight. They almost wished their children back in the school.

Parents of both sexes were finding that their partners were reacting untypically, revealing traits that had lain unsuspected for years. Couples who would have expected to stand together against the world in such an emergency found that, rather than uniting them, the strain was raising barriers which might be hard to remove. How, they were asking themselves, could I have lived with this person for so long and known so little about him—or her? Husbands saw their wives cracking the cruelest sick jokes about the plight of their children and appearing to revel in them; some wives became so cynical that they wrecked the composure of others. Husbands who had been repeatedly restrained by their wives from taking precipitate action found themselves despised for not doing so. Eventually, partners turned the searchlight in on themselves, fearing that many of their reactions were conditioned rather than instinctive and that they were mostly doing what was expected of them.

Paradoxically, the hijackers seemed to have attached no great importance to their deadline. They were still concerned not to rush their fences. They were more interested in the telephone link that, by midafternoon, enabled them to talk to each other for the first time. When it was connected, they were as excited as children. "Hey, hello! How are you there? What's going on at your end? What's the news?" Eventually they settled down and started discussing their future plans, going into much more detail than anything the government had heard hitherto.

Gathered together in the corridor near the principal's office, with no children present, the teachers put a proposition to Willem. "We'll go with you in the plane if you'll release the children." Willem insisted that twenty children must go with them to Eelde and in the plane to Schiphol, and he stipulated that they must be some of the youngest children, because they would be the easiest to manage. "You can't do that," said van Vliet. "Take twenty boys from the sixth class, and we'll look after them." "No, it has to be the youngest." The teachers were then told to write down the names of the twenty youngest children who were behaving the best, the children who didn't cry and who didn't keep saying they wanted to go home. It was an unenviable task.

At four o'clock that afternoon, Willem contacted the management center and presented a fresh list of demands. Max's dominant role seemed to be confirmed in the preamble, which made the demands "in the name of the train hijackers." The demands read as follows:

1. We shall depart only with the twenty-one Moluccan detainees.
2. We must be brought to Eelde airfield and so must the detainees from the north. [The Moluccan prisoners were distributed over various jails.]
3. The five teachers and the pupils of the first and second class will go with us to the Eelde airfield and in the plane to Schiphol.
4. The children will only be released at Schiphol.
5. From the train, twenty hostages will go with us via Eelde to Schiphol. Fifteen of them will be released at Schiphol, but five will go with us to some other destination.
6. No weapons will be given up.

No deadline was set but the impression was given that the demands must be met by eight o'clock that evening.

These proposals represented a substantial reduction from the original demands. The hijackers were sticking to their request for the release of the twenty-one prisoners, but they were asking for no more than twenty children to go to Schiphol. Of the train hostages, twenty would be required to go to Schiphol, but fifteen would be released when they got there, leaving five adult hostages from the train and the five teachers from the school to accompany the hijackers abroad. Both Max and Willem felt that this arrangement would give them reasonable protection, while fulfilling the government's priority condition.

The teachers heard Willem ask Mulder for a Boeing 747 for the journey abroad. Van Beetz had read something before the hijacking about South Moluccan political contacts overseas, and now he said, "I know where you're going—to Benin, in West Africa. And if not there, then to Vietnam." But the hijackers wouldn't be drawn out. "Perhaps we will go to Indonesia," they said, "to the South Moluccas." Van Beetz gained a strong impression that they weren't sure where they were going themselves.

Presentation of the hijackers' demands coincided with the arrival at the crisis center at The Hague of the Lokollo group, and they too brought proposals for a government compromise. These proposals proved to be almost exactly similar to those made from the school on behalf of those on the train, strengthening the impression that the demands of the terrorists, even if not previously known to the Lokollo group—and collusion was certainly suspected—had their support. The proposals were immediately discounted for that reason.

The total lack of mutual understanding was now distressingly apparent. The Lokollo group had imagined that they would be negotiating from a position if not of strength then certainly not of weakness, and they expected concessions. The government expected the South Moluccan leadership to call their young hotheads to order, as Manusama had done in 1975. The absence of the relationship of confidence and trust that had been built up with Manusama in 1975 was greatly missed now.

Zeevalking restated the government's position, so that there would be no further misunderstanding. There could be no negotiating until all the children were released. No hostages would be allowed to be taken in the plane under any circumstances. Then he added a third condition, obliquely at this stage, but prefaced by a subjunctive which confirmed a readiness to take part in a bartering deal. Supposing the government decided to allow the hijackers to leave the country, the destination of the aircraft would have to be known in advance.

The government was again hinting that they might be prepared to consider a compromise. Providing their own position was protected, the full process of the law might not be invoked and the hijackers might be allowed to go free. But the first two conditions would have to be fulfilled beforehand.

The release of the children, then, remained paramount, and in view of the failure of Kuhuwael to make any impression, Zeevalking asked Lokollo for an alternative. Lokollo suggested the South Moluccan doctor Frans Tutuhatunewa, who had been a minister in Manusama's government and a member of the action committee chaired by Karel Wielenga. Van Agt had met Tutuhatunewa at the conference on January 17, 1976, and liked him. Indeed, the doctor, with his white hair, coffee-cream complexion, and open, friendly manner, was an attractive personality. Like Kuhuwael, he was well known to the hijackers, in his case as the family doctor of their childhood. Van Agt telephoned him, and Tutuhatunewa drove to Assen that evening to meet Mulder. But since Kuhuwael had made two abortive attempts that day and the atmosphere in the school had quietened down and there had been no further reference to an eight o'clock ultimatum, Mulder advised leaving well alone for the moment. He gave Tutuhatunewa a list of five young South Moluccans believed to be involved in the hijackings, which proved only partly accurate, and Tutuhatunewa suggested contacting their families to find out whether any help might be enlisted from them. The South Moluccan doctor met two of the male parents, but they were not prepared to intercede.

That evening van Agt described the situation as still very serious, but he added that the fact that no calamity had followed the expiration of the original ultimatum gave some reason for hope. He believed that the establishment of direct contact between the two attacking groups was proving of value. Den Uyl, with the possible solution put by Zeevalking to Lokollo in mind, thought that a "basis for negotiations" was developing. Meanwhile, whatever role had been planned for the four prisoners who had been brought from Assen, it was evidently regarded as having been overtaken by events. Their possible mediation was no longer considered, and they were returned to their jails.

It was not only the Dutch Government and people who were worrying about the hijacked children. The hijackers themselves, having underestimated the problem, had obtained a delivery of air beds to make the children more comfortable, and had helped the children inflate them. But their uneasiness was increased during the day when a child named Madeleine Witges, not a very robust girl at the best of times, contracted a stomach upset. This may have accounted for an offer Willem made that evening to let the children go in exchange for replacement hostages. The idea was immediately rejected.

The hostages in the train were suffering greater discomfort rather than less, especially those in the second-class section, where the upholstery was harder and the tilt greater than in the first. The men sweated profusely in the suffocating heat, throats became parched, and there was insufficient water to slake thirsts or allow the refreshment of a wash or the luxury of cleaning the teeth. Subjected to a degree of mental and physical cruelty unknown among the women, they were aware that another crisis was approaching. Following the tension of the search came the expiration of first one ultimatum and then another, and the hijackers assured them that the government had abandoned them. "They won't give you food," Max told them, blaming the authorities for the privations he was himself inflicting. "There's your government for you. They don't know how to handle the problem, so they're not bothering about you. All they think about is the election and forming a cabinet." To the hostages, there seemed some truth in this, since the timely operation by the hijackers of the on/off switch on their radio, which was plugged into the public address system, expunged all news of the hijackings.

Soon after the expiration of the eight o'clock deadline, Max decided that the time had come for a tougher line. He and his fellow hijackers had promised that there would be victims if their demands were not met within a set time, and action could be delayed no longer. Something had to be done to break the government's nerve, and at about half past eight, with the light still good, the door of the men's compartment was flung open and Max entered, followed by some of his colleagues. Max was carrying a rope, and he approached the blond student teacher André Schager and called him from his seat. Kees Bimmel, who was sitting next to Schager, saw how he was forced to go with two of the hijackers, and there was such menace in their manner that he hardly dared look. Inwardly he resolved that if they came for him he would resist.

The moment had come which in their various ways they had all anticipated, the moment that for three days had filled them with a dull, smoldering dread: the repetition of the Wijster murders, the killing of hostages in cold blood. "That's bye-bye to André," thought Bimmel, but there was nothing he could do about it. Few of the other passengers realized what was afoot until someone saw Schager standing outside the train, blindfolded and covered by the terrorists' guns. "Hey! André is outside! What's going on?"

From the edge of the woods, even with dusk approaching, it was alarmingly clear what was happening. As the watchers recalled all too vividly the shooting of Bert Bierling, they saw a blindfolded figure standing outside the train with a rope round his neck.

Following up the visual threat, Max called Mulder on the telephone and translated it into words. The government was to give in or the bound and blindfolded victim would be shot. "I'm afraid I can't help you," said Mulder calmly. "You're in charge. You have the might. You also have the responsibility. I'm not talking about law and order so much as your responsibility for the impression this will make on the outside world, the effect it will have on your ideals and your aims for fulfilling them."

"We can't fulfill our aims without violence. If the government doesn't give in, there will be victims."

"You may tell me this, but what must I do with the information? I've given you the government's answer, so it's up to you. Let's talk about other things."

If Mulder appeared to be shrugging his shoulders at the prospect of killings, playing poker with the lives of the hostages, this was inescapable in his view. What was actually happening he didn't know, but he had to sit tight and keep his nerve. It was not that he was insensitive to the plight of the hostages. Rather, it was that he feared that revealing any hint of alarm or intimidation would only encourage the terrorists.

The threat of being hauled off blindfolded, to be shot down like a dog outside the train, sent a shudder of horror through the men's compartment. Max was staging a macabre tableau, the finale of which would be the shooting of André Schager. To the hostages, that much seemed certain. Once they heard Schager protest, followed by Max's sharp retort— "Shut your trap!"—so different from the facade of politeness he presented in the train. When no shots came, van der Struik, for one, imagined that André might have been hanged.

When Schager was being taken away, however, Max had seen how frightened he was and had whispered soothingly to him. "You've only got to stand outside the train for a time. It's only for the outside world. We just blindfold you, bind your hands behind your back, and tie a rope round your neck. The rope is only for show. When you've been outside the train for an hour, you come in again." To his surprise, Schager found that he trusted Max, and without resisting he allowed them to put the rope round his neck and lead him outside.

So it was to be a repetition of the balcony scene at the Indonesian consulate—that was if Max was to be believed. More than one hostage recalled the many thousands of Jews who had queued willingly to go to the bathhouse only to find themselves in the gas chamber. Later, when Max called on Rosemary Oostveen to join Schager, imaginations conjured up an execution in which Rosemary would be made to certify that the victim was dead.

Rosemary herself reacted vigorously. "I will not die for your ideals—or for van Agt." If they wanted her to go outside the train, they would have to force her. But Max turned on his most gentle, persuasive manner. "It's only for show."

"Why me?" In her single-minded devotion to her calling, she had done her best to cooperate with Max.

"Because we know you'll be susceptible to reasonable arguments. You'll understand that we have to do this to convince the government, and you won't make a fuss. We won't hurt you. You're too useful to us and the passengers, because of your medical knowledge. It would be very foolish of us to shoot *you.*" At this, somewhat reluctantly, Rosemary agreed to go.

Also bound and blindfolded and sent outside was the young waiter Joop Hoogenboom. He too was assured that he would not be harmed. All three were warned that under no circumstances were they to give any hint that they were unafraid. "Don't smile when you look toward the cameras," Max told Rosemary, "but you can smile when you look at us." The advice was hardly necessary, since none of them knew for certain whether or not their captors were telling the truth. As for Mulder, his attitude remained the same.

Schager's ordeal lasted the longest. He was a fit young man, but through standing still for so long he developed cramp in both legs, and gnawing pangs of hunger accentuated his weakness. For a time he shivered with cold, and then he found he was sweating. He was visualizing himself falling to the ground unconscious when he was replaced by a young student in underwater engineering named Peter Blankert. He whispered something to encourage Blankert and was taken inside in a state of collapse. After being allowed to sit for a minute or so, he was led by Hansina to the zigzag connection, where she rubbed his body with balsam, pounding it so vigorously that when she finished his whole being was aglow. Despite the hunger he had felt outside, he went straight to sleep when he got back to his seat.

The effect of these charades, traumatic enough while they lasted, was to bring a slight relief of tension in the front carriage. When other hostages were subjected to a similar ordeal, their absence was taken more philosophically. But at no time was humor extinguished entirely. "They'll have to let me out soon," someone was heard to say at a tense moment, "my ticket is out of date."

Another revelation to the male hostages was the news brought to them from the first-class carriage by the capricious but extroverted Ansje Monsjou. Cuppen likened her to a butterfly, with contacts everywhere, fluttering from one to another. Bimmel summed her up with the Dutch expression, *"Jangje lacht, Jangje huilt"* ("Little Johnny laughs, little Johnny cries"). But she had lost her fear of the Moluccans, and, finding the religious talk in the women's section overdone, she came through to talk to the men. From her they got a clear picture for the first time of how differently the women were treated. The men did not even know for certain how many hijackers there were. Ansje was able to tell them not only the number but also their names and ages and occupations. The Moluccans had been nothing like so successful in keeping their distance from the women.

Thanks to the ebullient, motherly presence of Saskia, who stood up to the hijackers whenever necessary, and the calm reassurance radiated by Rosemary as she went about her role of doctor, a much more relaxed atmosphere was developing in the first-class section. Saskia learned how to roll her own cigarettes, and she tasted beer for the first time in her life. "Better than nothing," she thought. But after one sip, amid great amusement, she decided she'd had enough.

Saskia made it her business to establish a good relationship with Max, although she always kept her distance. She talked to him about his beliefs and motivations, which she attacked on religious grounds. If any of the hijackers behaved in a thoughtless or threatening manner, she complained to Max and he dealt with them. When Thys's habit of swirling his pistol on his forefinger got on her nerves, she told him to stop. "Would you like to hold it?" he asked. "No," she said. "Put it away or I won't talk to you." She never saw him with it again.

Whereas the men found it hard even among themselves to drop the formal method of address usual in Dutch society, the use of forenames was soon established among the women and extended to the hijackers, though the latter were always punctilious in using the formal Dutch pronoun when addressing their hostages, correcting themselves when they forgot. Barriers, however, were soon broken down in the first-class section, where the hope among the hostages was that they would not be easy to reerect.

CHAPTER 18

Both Sides Take a Gamble

T HE HIJACKERS had been confident that the seizure of the school would bring a swift surrender. By the fourth day of the hijacking, Thursday, May 26, the responsibility was weighing heavily on them. However, they still believed that the holding of the children must place an even greater strain on the government, and they were not disposed to release them without firm guarantees that their objectives would be met. At four o'clock that morning, they revealed their mounting anxiety by calling the management center. Somehow the government's stand of no discussion until the children were released must be altered.

After a lifetime of indoctrination in the legend of Dutch duplicity and with the incident of the bus at Wijster still very much in mind, the hijackers, like most of their kind, feared a double-cross. To protect themselves, as they thought, against some piece of trickery that might later be passed off as a misunderstanding, they demanded that before they released the children the government must publicly commit itself on the national radio and TV networks to guaranteeing them a free departure. And they stuck to their plan—again fearing a double-cross—to take some of their hostages with them in the plane, which was still for the same reason (or so they said) to have an undeclared destination.

The hijackers demanded an answer by 7:30 AM, and at precisely that time the telephone rang in Max's command post, to which the instrument had been moved from the front entrance hall. Once again the government reiterated that none of the hijackers' demands could be discussed until the children were freed. The result was a repeat performance of the tableaux of the previous night outside the train. The first victim, eighteen-year-old Roelie Brinkman, was the girl whose South Moluccan friend had pleaded for her release before being sent out of the train on the first day. So again, the hijackers had chosen someone who they had reason to believe would understand their motives. "I want to do it for you," said the girl, "but I want to be sure I come back."

"How old are you?"

"Eighteen."

"That's too young to die." Half an hour later she was brought back in, and others then went through the same ordeal.

Although the government had made release of the children its first priority, it was aware that conditions in the train were much worse than in the school. A stationary train in hot weather, unventilated, with a diminished supply of water and choked, overflowing toilets, was horrifying enough even to the imagination. The actuality of it must be almost intolerable. The unsanitary conditions, the lack of opportunities for personal hygiene, the claustrophobia, and the disorientation resulting from living on the slant were quite sufficient to cause mental and physical breakdown. When added to this were hunger, thirst, and the lowering threat of violent death, there was an obvious limit to the endurance of those subjected to it. Nevertheless, with the stamina shown by the captives at Wijster to sustain them, the government was determined to use force only as a last resort. Meanwhile it was emotionally committed to securing the release of the children.

This was the policy that was guiding Dr. Mulder in his conversations with the hijackers, although, as it happened, it did not have his unqualified approval. He believed that, so long as there were children among the hostages, their presence must exert a humanizing influence. But the government had to consider the emotive impact of the abduction and possible death of Dutch children on existing racial tensions. It also had in mind that, so long as there were children among the hostages, the military option would be extremely difficult to exercise. An attack on the train in which a number of hostages were almost certain to die might be justifiable. An action by the government that led to the death of even a single child seemed unthinkable. This of course was the premise on which the hijackers were working.

At 9:00 AM on Thursday, the occupiers of the school stepped up the pressure by issuing a new ultimatum, to expire at eleven. This time the threat that accompanied it was more subtle. There was no mention of victims, but they threatened that, unless the government gave way, the children would get no more food.

Food was also still being refused by the train group, and liquids of all kinds remained scarce. With the hot weather persisting, Saskia, ignoring the hijackers, opened a window to get some fresh air, then sang a phrase from a song of the 1950s: "Brandend Zand en nog geen water" ("Burning sand, and water nowhere"). The Moluccans thought this was a song from a more recent period, sung on Dutch TV by an ample, dynamic woman named Tante Leen who specialized in songs about the prewar Jewish quarter of Amsterdam. They promptly christened Saskia Tante Leen— Auntie Leen—and this somehow cemented their relationship.

In the war of attrition that was developing, the withholding of food and water seemed likely to be a powerful weapon. Van Agt's reaction was that, if the hijackers persisted in this, the government might have to break off negotiations. "These are dangerous people who have to be taken seriously. It is clear they are capable of anything." Den Uyl said he saw little hope of the early release of the children, and police and army believed both groups were preparing for a long siege. This display of pessimism seemed to suggest that the government might after all be preparing public opinion for a violent solution.

The Moluccans, however, had guessed right—they had found official-dom's Achilles heel. Unknown to them as yet, the government *was* prepared to make exceptional concessions to secure the release of the children. After further consultations, they confirmed the decision they had been contemplating the previous day. If they were driven to it, they were prepared to concede as the ultimate limit unimpeded departure for both groups of hijackers, allowing them to take with them those South Moluccan prisoners who had not been involved in actions during which hostages had been killed. Counting the death of Mr. Abedy as accidental, this meant that fourteen of the twenty-one prisoners would be free to go. "The prospect of this could be offered," the management center was told, "if the putting into effect of it depended on the government." This circumlocutary phraseology was intended to cover the government against the failure of the Moluccans' chosen haven to cooperate. For instance, if the hijackers elected to go to Vietnam, as it was strongly rumored they would, and the Vietnamese Government refused to accept them, the Dutch Government's responsibility would be ended. If any of the hostages were killed in the meantime, there would be no further question of unimpeded departure. All the other conditions already laid down by the government would have to be fulfilled.

The terrorists had been told many times that their demands could only be discussed when all the children were released. On Wednesday morning, when the situation was first discussed between Max and Mulder, Mulder had repeated this condition and added another: in no circumstances would they be allowed to take hostages in the plane. But he made no reference to the "basis for negotiations" under which the hijackers might be allowed a free departure. And when he rang Max at 7:30 on that Thursday morning, he still kept this offer in reserve and confined himself to the bare statement that the demands could not be discussed unless the children were released.

Called to The Hague that afternoon, the Lokollo group was confronted this time by van Agt, who told them of the hijackers' refusal to accept food. "You have to do something about this problem," he said. "That's an order."

"It's impossible for us to help to resolve it," replied Lokollo, "while we have nothing to offer these boys. We must have one or two demands met first."

"The attackers know that their demands can't be seriously discussed until the children are released."

Lokollo still refused to order the release of the children, and the talks had no tangible result, unless it was to increase resentment on both sides. Van Agt knew from experience that the terrorists were not likely to be diverted from their purpose unless their leaders intervened, while Lokollo, incensed at being given orders, did not think that the offer of a free departure with no other concessions would satisfy the boys.

There was nothing for it but to pass the government's suggested "basis for negotiations" to Max, and this Mulder proceeded to do, adding that any killings in the meantime would invalidate it, and that all other conditions already stated by the government must be fulfilled. He did not restate what these conditions were.

The government's offer represented a substantial surrender to terrorism on the part of the government and a significant victory for the hijackers. The Lokollo group appeared not to have recognized this, but Max certainly did. In his talks with Mulder, however, he learned that the teachers would have to be released as well as the children and that the adult hostages would have to be left behind in the train. If he agreed to this, what guarantee would he have that the government would keep their word? For him, the lessons of the past suggested that they would not. Feeling perhaps that he had the government on the run and that all he had to do was stand firm, he repeated the formula he had put forward the previous day. The two junior classes of children, about twenty in number, together with their teachers, would be required to accompany them to Schiphol, where the children would be released. Of the fifty-four train hostages, thirty-four would be left behind in the train. The remaining twenty must accompany them to Schiphol, and five would be required to go with them in the plane. This remained Max's minimum insurance against a double-cross.

Unknown to Max or to Lokollo, the government was taking a gamble, and in doing so they were keeping an ace up their sleeve. From their experience of 1975, they did not believe that the hijackers would have a prearranged destination, and from recent soundings they thought they would have the greatest difficulty in finding one. When the time came, they would insist on having a destination that could be properly checked and confirmed, so that plane and crew would not in their turn be taken hostage. If the hijackers refused to name a destination, the government would regard themselves as released from their part of the bargain.

It was a piece of casuistry to which the government had been driven by the threat to the lives of more than a hundred children. Provided their hunch was right, they would avoid making any concessions. The dilemma would come if their bluff was called and a destination was named and confirmed.

For most of that day, both groups of hijackers continued to refuse to accept deliveries of food. But that evening, Max was in optimistic mood. "There's been some progress," he told the passengers, "and it might go well. So we're celebrating by sending for some food. You can choose what you want. Chops, potatoes and greens, or *nasi goreng.*" Most people went for a traditional Dutch meal, but some found it difficult to choose. Two who agreed on a compromise were Rien van Baarsel and Saskia Sein. "You take the meat, potatoes, and salad," said van Baarsel, "and I'll take the *nasi goreng,* and we'll have half each."

Kees Bimmel, who as befitted an embryo restaurateur was always talking about food and wines, produced a nice piece of drollery to go with his *nasi goreng.* "The Indo-Chinese restaurant that served this must be getting a nice line in publicity. Can't you imagine it? *'Eat the same food here as they eat on the train.'* I'll bet he's even having it served by armed South Moluccans."

Max's decision to feed his hostages was partly self-interest; for what might still be a long siege, he needed to keep them healthy. But although the conditions of hygiene in the school were far superior to those in the train, it was the seven-year-old Madeleine Witges who had fallen ill. It had not been the terrorists' intention to harm the children, and their concern was real. They allowed van Vliet to take the child's temperature and pulse and describe her symptoms on the telephone to a doctor, and later they agreed to her release. That evening, after van Vliet had carried Madeleine to a waiting ambulance, a government spokesman described her as "very ill with an internal disorder which might be serious." When a second child, eleven-year-old Jannette Hynen, also developed a fever, Sjaan Abbink was not slow to test the hijackers' nerve. It was very hot in the assembly room, so she took the child into the corridor and sat there with her. When Fat Willem appeared, she said, "This is all wrong. This child has to go too. Her pulse is racing, and her heartbeat isn't right either." Willem was so shocked that he agreed. Later Sjaan admitted to her colleagues that, although Jannette had certainly been unwell, she had exaggerated her symptoms. With several other children showing signs of a similar malaise, the teachers agreed that, provided they didn't overdo it, more children might be released in this way.

While the atmosphere on the train that night changed from hungry depression to cozy, romantic, almost sensuous conviviality as the passengers settled down to savor their meal, the sickness in the school threatened to become prevalent. Breakfast on Tuesday had been the last proper meal in the train, and everyone was so ravenous that even the aroma of food as it was handed up to the train, after being pushed along the rails on a trolley from the nearest level crossing 1200 meters to the north, sent them into ecstasies. As Max distributed candles, and the half-light flickered on eager faces, van der Struik felt he was watching some surrealist play. The euphoria in the train as rumors of an early release gained credence was in stark antithesis to the sickroom contagion at the school, where, both before and after eating, children were being laid low in rapid succession with stomach pains, fever, headaches, vomiting, and diarrhea.

A third child was released at 11:40 PM, and a fourth at midnight. By this time, a preliminary diagnosis was reported to the hijackers. It was a virus infection that, it was said, "might be meningitis." This so frightened the hijackers that they wrapped towels over the lower half of their faces to try to escape infection and insisted that the children take the pills that were sent in for them, whether they had developed symptoms or not. They did not neglect to take the pills themselves.

By one o'clock on that Friday morning, May 27, three more children had been freed, and the visitation truly threatened to reach epidemic proportions. One of the classrooms—van Vliet's—was turned into a hospital ward, and some twenty children were lying on the floor there on airbeds. As Dr. Mulder stepped up the pressure for the children's release, two-way conversations between train and school, train and management center, and school and management center, became almost continuous.

Max offered to abandon the demand that twenty children from the two youngest classes accompany them to Schiphol and, indeed, to release all the children, provided the remaining demands, including those previously unacceptable to the government, were agreed upon. This offer was debated in a long session at the crisis center during the night. While the ministers were deliberating, a protracted and tortuous conversation was taking place between Mulder and Max.

In earlier talks with Mulder, Max had taken and kept the initiative, briefing himself thoroughly beforehand so as not to get sidetracked, and being careful not to be caught off his guard. Mulder's objectives had been different. The basic rule was to keep the terrorists talking. Deciding at an early stage that Max was the main intellectual force to which he was opposed, he had endeavored to seek out his strengths and weaknesses, starting with the assumption that any hijack leader must be suffering from some form of megalomania and endeavoring to lead him slowly and gently back to reality.

Mulder had listened attentively to everything Max had to say, ignoring anything abrasive, trying to give an impression of sincerity. He had avoided using the code number 747 because of its impersonal nature, but he never started conversations with "Hello, Max," which would have trespassed too far into Max's supposed anonymity. What he did was to use Max's name in the middle of a conversation as though it had involuntarily slipped out. This zoomed him in closer without alerting Max to the danger.

Mulder had gained the impression, in his talks with Max, of a man with a psychologically narrowed mind but, within these limits, an intelligent one. Max for his part, while treating Mulder as an equal and even addressing him as "colleague"—"You are a psychiatrist, but I am a kind of psychiatrist myself," he had said—generally accorded him the respect with which he himself liked to be treated. By the small hours of Friday morning, Mulder was in a position to exert an influence on Max of which the latter may not have been fully aware.

The precise details of what passed between Mulder and Max, and later between Havinga and Max, during that Friday morning are unlikely to be revealed unless and until the Dutch Government decides to release the tape recordings that were made. Since these recordings would presumably expose much of the strategy and tactics employed in dealing with the hijackers, they are unlikely to be released in the near future. One must go to the accounts given by Dr. Mulder and Dr. Havinga, to the actions and subsequent reactions of Max, and to the evidence of the train hostages and of the teachers in the school.

Mulder has said that these talks were part personal, part political, part racial, part philosophical, part medical, and that they were directed, from his side, at developing an intense psychological pressure on Max's personality as he had assessed it over the first few days. However blinkered and egotistical Max may have been, he regarded the kidnapping at the school as an ugly conception in which the ends barely justified the means. With the outbreak of sickness, he was prepared to end it, subject to assurances from Mulder.

Called to the phone by Max, Rosemary was given a diagnosis of the illness by Mulder from which she could only conclude that the infection must indeed be meningitis. This conjured up such a horrifying vision of pestilence in the school that she immediately transmitted her fears to Max.

Sooner or later, Max had to trust somebody, and he decided to put his faith in Mulder and try to do a deal through him. Mulder reacted confidently. "I am sure that, on the release of the children, the government will do its best to solve the problem of a safe conduct passage. That is what they have said." Again, no other conditions were stated and no other assurances given. Max had to take it or leave it, and he decided to gamble. "I will in one minute call the school and tell them to let the children go."

At 3:45 AM, Max called Willem and said he had agreed to the release of the children, repeating the assurance he had received from Mulder. On the one hand, he was convinced that the children were in serious danger; on the other, he had pinned the government to a promise. Willem for his part was as keen as Max to get rid of the sick children, but he had heard nothing of the conversations between Max and Mulder, and he had no intention of releasing the healthy children as well. Thus he was extremely angry when an announcement on the radio revealed that the government was making this assumption.

The evacuation of the sick children was allowed to go ahead, and, shortly after four o'clock, the first ambulance drove up to the school. When the teachers began loading the children two to a stretcher, Willem objected that they might kick or otherwise injure each other, and they were carried out one at a time. The children who were well enough to walk then filed out in batches of three or four, using blankets as cloaks. The evacuation had to be discreetly organized so that it offered no threat to the occupiers, and the ambulance men were not allowed to enter the building. One of the terrorist group stood at the door with an Uzi, a white hood masking his face.

Van Vliet and Mrs. Abbink plotted to get their own children attached to the sick group. "You take Arjan and I'll take Eveline," said van Vliet. "Then at least they'll have someone out of the school back home." They took the two children to the corridor and sat them on chairs near the door. While they were waiting there, Willem spoke to them. "You are very ill?" The children, aware of a touch of irony, grinned. It was obvious they were only pretending. Willem knew who they were, and he let them go.

The incident showed clearly that the teachers in the school, although aware of the radio announcement, were resigned to the fact that only the sick children were going to be released.

At five o'clock, with the evacuation still in progress, Max put to Mulder the same demands as before. The school group, excluding the children, would be accompanied to Schiphol and into the plane by the teachers, while the train group would take twenty of their hostages, of whom five would be required to board the plane. He added that the hijackers would not surrender their weapons.

The ministerial council had meanwhile confirmed its decision. The government was prepared to do what was in its power to give the hijackers the possibility of leaving Holland, provided three preconditions were met. These were:

1. Release of all the children.
2. Release of all the remaining hostages at Schiphol [this was a compromise between Max's position and the government's].
3. Only those prisoners whose activities had not caused deaths would be allowed to accompany them.

The government afterward contended that there had been a fourth condition—that the hijackers' destination must be known beforehand. But, while the government regarded knowledge of destination as implicit in any promise of a free departure with safe conduct, they avoided mentioning this to the hijackers at this stage. To have done so, as they well knew, would have enraged them and almost certainly have ruled out the evacuation of the school.

At about six o'clock that morning, when the ambulances returned for a further load, waiting parents saw the male nurses being called across to the school entrance by the terrorists. They watched in anguish as the nurses were turned back and the ambulances drove away empty. Willem had called a halt.

Most of the messages from the school to the management center were being passed by van Vliet under Willem's direction, but contact on both sides had been brief. Max was the acknowledged spokesman, and Mulder found communication with the school dried up when it got beyond routine. But now Willem took an independent line. The idea of releasing the rest of the children, he felt, was a government trick. In any case, from his point of view, it would be irresponsible. They seemed perfectly healthy, and many of them had slept right through the chaos and panic of the night. It was all right for the group in the train. They were still holding over fifty hostages. The school group, with hostile forces in close proximity, would be especially vulnerable if they gave up the remaining children. So the ambulances were sent away.

The government's promise had been conditional upon the release of all the children, and Havinga, who had taken over temporarily from Mulder, soon reminded Max of that. He also spoke of the danger that the virus would spread further, affecting the healthy children too.

Havinga talked a lot about responsibility, especially for the health and lives of the children. He said this must ultimately devolve on the overall leadership, and he reminded Max that he had given the impression that he was responsible for both operations. Havinga emphasized the desperation of the parents, and the cauldron of unrest in Bovensmilde. Humanitarian considerations demanded the immediate release of all the children. "You can't keep them any longer." Max seemed to listen, and Havinga felt he was making progress. Later Max rang back and agreed to use his influence on the group in the school. Questions of safe conduct and the naming of a destination were still not discussed.

Max was then heard advising the school group to cooperate. "Let the children go, and we'll get a bus," he said. He also gave them additional details of his agreement with the government. "No hostages will go with us to foreign countries." He had evidently accepted that. "How many prisoners will go with us we don't know yet." This, in Max's mind, was the only point that was still not settled.

The management center had already held out the prospect to the school group of a "free release and safe conduct." This had been confirmed by Mulder in a talk with van Vliet. Again, there was no mention of naming a destination. Willem asked, as he had done once before, that the promise be repeated on TV and radio, but this apparently reasonable request did not commend itself to the government and they ignored it.

At this point van Beetz, a sensitive, highly-strung young man who had worked himself to a standstill in the four days of occupation, collapsed from exhaustion. He looked so ill that Willem thought he might die.

Willem didn't want anything like this happening in the school, so he decided to release him. "You can go," he told van Beetz. "I've sent for an ambulance."

But van Beetz refused. "I'm not leaving until the rest of the children are out of here. Then I'll think about it."

"That's not possible."

"You promised, and I won't go until you keep your promise."

"We didn't promise. We promised only that the sick children could go."

Max had staked everything on releasing the children, and he managed to convince Willem that this was their best chance. "Very well, Simon," said Willem when he returned from the phone, "all the children can go. A bus is coming for them, and you can go too."

Still van Beetz refused. He felt he would be letting his colleagues down. He was determined to go with them to the bus and the plane even if he had to crawl there. But Sjaan Abbink convinced him otherwise. "You don't realize how ill you are." Then she added in a whisper, "You can give valuable information to the government if you go."

As he left, all four hijackers embraced him. "It's going to be all right," they said. He felt they meant it as a promise. The other teachers felt it too. A promise from a South Moluccan, thought Sjaan Abbink, means a great deal. As the stranded teachers waved a cheerful good-bye from the doorway, the children in the bus waved back.

Willem then rang Max. "Now you have to take over. We have lost our lever, our trump card. We can do nothing. It's up to you."

That night the exhausted school hijackers fell into a deep sleep, leaving no guard. The teachers had the key to the front door and could have escaped, but they feared reprisals against the hostages in the train. In any case, with the last of the children gone, they confidently expected to be home next day.

Just as Mulder and Havinga had regarded it as implicit in the phrase "free release and safe conduct" that a destination must sooner or later be known (one could scarcely arrange a safe conduct passage for anyone unless one knew where they were going), so Max and all the hijackers regarded it as implicit in the release of the children that a free departure, accompanied by at least some of their friends, must be within the government's power to grant and must therefore be guaranteed. The seeds of misunderstanding had been sown.

CHAPTER 19

"They Have Made Fools of Us"

"THIS IS NO TIME for rejoicing."

The government's ambivalence was nicely summed up in this phrase of Premier den Uyl's. Relief at the freeing of the children was tempered by the knowledge that many of them were in hospital, while the lives of some sixty adult hostages were still at stake. That the government was looking for a speedy end to the train action too seemed likely from the intense activity by police and military in and around De Punt. Barbed wire barriers in woods and fields were being lifted; rails were being cleared to allow another locomotive to approach the train, presumably to shunt it to the level crossing to the north; and eight ambulances were drawn up on a country road close by. All this seemed to presage the evacuation of the train. But a request to the media not to report these preparations suggested that they were no more than provisional and that final arrangements had not yet been made.

If rejoicing was regarded as premature by the government, this was not so in the train, where Max was radiant. He was confidently expecting to get away that day. "It's all over," he told the women. "We have won. There's been an agreement. We have let the children go, and we shall be leaving Holland by plane later today. A bus with its windows and seats removed will come to take us to Schiphol, where a plane will be waiting for us, and where you will be exchanged for our friends in prison. When they are in the plane you can go free. It may be cold in the bus, so wear some warm clothes. Here is some paper for labels. Write your names on your baggage so it won't get lost."

Eighteen-year-old student Ineke Rijstenberg, knowing that the men were often kept in ignorance of what was happening, slipped into their compartment to tell them. "Pretend you know nothing," she said. She understood that the hijackers were going to Vietnam.

Max did in fact pass the news on to the men. "Are you pleased?" asked George Flapper. "I was very optimistic when I left my home," Max replied, "and I was even more optimistic when at the start no one was killed. Now I know we shall get what we want."

The Moluccans began to share out the remaining stocks of food and drink. No sense in frugality now. Janneke Fransen, a student from Meppel, who was celebrating her twenty-fifth birthday, was called to Max's office and presented with 200 Dutch guilders—more than $110. "Do take them," said Max, when Janneke hesitated. "We won't need the money, because we're either going abroad, or for some other reason we shall have no need of it." The reservation was a sign that he was not entirely convinced of the outcome even now.

There had been so much talk during the night that some confusion in the minds of the protagonists was excusable. Mulder and Havinga believed that, apart from the limited assurance that the government would do all in its power to facilitate a safe conduct passage, the children had been released unconditionally. Max interpreted "doing all in its power" as a firm guarantee. According to Mulder, Max was suffering from a familiar mental aberration known as "partial perception." He heard the phrases he wanted to hear and was deaf to the rest. For Max, it might be argued that he sometimes found the verbal sophistications of the psychiatrists a trifle obscure. Fatigue too must have played a part, causing the impairment of judgment and understanding. Later, even Mulder could be no more than "almost sure" what was said.

Behind all the government's thinking, unrevealed as yet to Max, lay the escape clause of the naming of a destination, and they still relied on that to confound the hijackers' hopes. Behind Max's thinking lay the uneasy suspicion that he had released the children without adequate safeguards. Therefore he sought to make good his error.

He could get nothing out of Mulder that morning, and he insisted that the government must now play its part. Again he took a gamble. "I have assured the passengers they will be released today," he said. "I shall tell them that the bus will come between three and six this evening. That should give you plenty of time. Then we will see what you are going to do, and whether you will keep your word."

In vain did Mulder protest that the assurance given had been in the most general terms and that much had to be done before a plane and a crew could be found and a time of departure considered. "We made a deal,

Max," he said. "The deal was that we would play honestly. We have always talked with respect for each other. But you'll understand that if you do this, I shall have difficulty in retaining my respect for you." At this, Max became abusive, and all the bitterness at past treacheries, real or imagined, came flooding out. "Do you know how they treated us when we left Ambon? Do you know what they told us? That we would return to an independent republic!" The tirade went on and on. At length he repeated, "I'm going to tell them we're leaving between three and six today."

"There's no basis for that," said Mulder. And when Max's reaction was again one of impatience, Mulder said soothingly, "Max, I have the feeling that this can go on for weeks." "For weeks?" echoed Max angrily. "For months!" It had been his resolve from the start that it should not be the South Moluccans who gave in this time, and he was determined to make that clear.

He had already made it clear to the women hostages. Perched on the arm of Mini Loman's seat, with several of the women grouped around him —among them Saskia, Ansje and Rosemary—he had talked about his plans and his people. "If my demands are not met," he said, "I'd rather kill myself than go to prison. I don't want to fall into the hands of the Dutch police. I'm going out of this country, or I'm going to kill myself. I'm quite willing to give my life for this." Mini, having herself dedicated her life to a belief, wondered if she would be prepared like Max to die for it. It was a challenge to her, and she was impressed. Some of the other hijackers, she felt, were too juvenile, too immature. They seemed more like frightened boys. But Max was serious. He looked honest, and he sounded sincere. This was her first real contact with him, and she found it comforting to feel that he too was motivated by a high ideal.

Mulder had always regarded continuity as of special importance in his dealings with terrorists, and this meant that he was almost always on call. But now he was forced to rest, and it was to Havinga that Max developed his campaign for a satisfactory ending that day. Max made the assumption that a bus was coming, and Havinga did not contradict him lest he precipitate some act of violence. He talked in a general way about the bus without saying whether it was coming or not. But he warned that the fulfilment of the government's assurance would not be easy. The bus would have to be of an appropriate size, and it would take time to find the right one, and to recruit a driver. Then there was the question of making an aircraft available, and finding a volunteer crew.

To Max this was reminiscent of the stalling tactics used at Wijster, and he said so. But when one of the hijackers telephoned at noon and demanded that the bus arrive within half an hour, Havinga again protested that there were difficulties and that, for practical reasons alone, a bus in half an hour was impossible. Asked when the bus might arrive, he said: "Six PM at the earliest."

Havinga agreed to talk to one of the hostages to discuss the arrangements, and the hostage Max chose was Rosemary. Continuing the pretense of cooperation, Havinga asked about the health of the hostages and whether ambulances would be required. All that was needed, said Rosemary, was a bus. She then asked for confirmation that the bus would arrive at six o'clock. "Don't get pinned down to that exact time," said Havinga. "Because of technical problems, it may be somewhat later."

So there were technical problems too. It all seemed to add up to a policy of prevarication, as though Havinga had been told, "Keep stalling for the moment while we try to work something out."

When three o'clock came and there was no news, then four o'clock, then five o'clock, the hijackers became sullen and irritable, and the hostages apprehensive and subdued. Max, determined not to be disappointed, went through the train asking if there was anyone qualified to drive it. He fancied he saw the bus at the level crossing, and he wanted to move the train up there. He asked fifty-year-old Ton Meulman, who was a conductor, if he could help, and Meulman, surprised that Max would know he was a railway employee, explained that the overhead connections were collapsed and that he could do nothing. (Max had his own dossiers on the male hostages, compiled with the unconscious aid of the women and filed away in his head.) After drawing a blank with another railway employee from Utrecht, fifty-two-year-old Hans Oude Elberink, he accosted thirty-eight-year-old Mart Kuiper, a construction engineer. "You too work for the railways." The cool, immaculately dressed Kuiper (Flapper wondered how anyone could turn himself out so sprucely in such conditions) went forward to the driver's compartment after being urged on by the ever-active van der Struik, who accompanied him. But he too pronounced it hopeless. Max also asked for someone to drive the bus, if and when it came, and Victor Nijmeijer, who had otherwise kept an understandably low profile, volunteered.

When the bus failed to arrive at six o'clock, the government was roundly cursed, by hijacker and hostage alike. The hostages, of course, only knew what Max told them, and he had not mentioned his ploy of fabricating a time and calling on the government to honor it. Now he decided to try another tack. "Rosemary," he said "we must exaggerate the discomforts in the train, tell them things are much worse than they really are. Then they may do something."

Rosemary's position, in relation to both the hijackers and the hostages, was a complex one. She had to have a foot in both camps. Wielding power as she did only by courtesy of the hijackers, she had to keep on good terms with Max. Her youth and the fact that she was not fully qualified reinforced a natural diffidence in her dealings with her patients, and her social attitudes helped her to cultivate a modest approach. She did not feel or radiate any sense of superiority because of her profession. Normally a purposeful, ambitious, single-minded girl, she found herself adapting to circumstances and people, altering her personality to suit her situation. Respect for her calling made her generally acceptable to both groups, but her loyalties were bound to be divided. Like everyone else, she knew only what Max told her—although he confided in her much more than in the others—and to dispute what he said might endanger her special position, with all it meant to the health and morale of the hostages. So she agreed to do what he said.

Max needed someone to talk to on an intellectual level, and Rosemary, distanced from her fellow hostages by her role, needed someone too. This threw them together. She discussed his problems and his political convictions with him and expressed an understanding of South Moluccan ideals that was genuine, but she made it clear that she objected to his methods. Nevertheless she was bound to identify to a more than average extent with the immediate aims of the hijacking. She had the medical responsibility for more than fifty patients, including two pregnant women.

In appointing her to talk on his behalf to the control center, Max was undoubtedly using her, and Mulder and Havinga were bound to keep in mind that she must be under pressure from the hijackers, overt or covert, to follow their line. Now, as she called the control center for news, her complaint that a bus had been promised, that the hostages had sweated all day in the train with the sun beating down on them, hoping to be home by nightfall, and that the women especially could not stand it much longer, was guardedly acknowledged by Mulder. Indeed she felt that he replied evasively, and she accused him of beating about the bush. Her apparent identification with the hijackers goaded Mulder into retaliation. "Rosemary, the only thing you have to worry about is passing your exams. You are a well-meaning but stupid girl."

Both hostages and hijackers was oppressed by the fear that the government was backtracking. As usual, morale plunged deepest among the men. Van der Struik, still brooding over his enforced inactivity, toyed with the

the idea of setting fire to the train. Then they could all escape. He got as far as putting a match to the newspaper covering his window, then quickly extinguished the flame as he thought of the consequences. It was impossible to do anything. There would only be victims.

It was different in the first-class carriage. After five days in second class, where she had felt frequent surges of resentment at the laughter and jollity emanating from the women's section, Joke Winkeldermaat had been allowed to move back there and had found the atmosphere infectious. Saskia, particularly, with her stories about her life, her children, her operations, and her pregnancies, kept them continually amused. Now Saskia tried to lift them out of their despondent mood. "There's no need for us to worry. Either they get a plane or they will die here fighting. If there's a raid, they'll fight it outside the train. They've promised us that." This was not what the hijackers were telling the men.

A cynical view had meanwhile been taken by the press and public of the virus that had emptied the school. The government denied that they had introduced it deliberately. "Nature merely gave us a helping hand," declared van Agt, and he explained that the symptoms were perfectly consistent with the confined conditions, the unaccustomed diet, and the hot weather. Since a total of twenty-six children were admitted to the Wilhelmina Hospital in Assen, it seems unlikely that any government would risk such an epidemic deliberately. No one could have forecast how the terrorists would react. Once having gotten the children out, however, the temptation for the government to capitalize on its good fortune proved irresistible.

Between 6:30 and 7:00 that evening, Mulder called Max with bad news. The government was indeed backtracking. There could be no question of releasing the hijackers in the school until all the children under observation for meningitis were cleared. There would have to be a period of quarantine, probably three or four days. This was a staggering blow. Mulder added that the lack of a declared destination was a further impediment. It was unlikely that any country would accept them during the incubation period. In any case, it would be difficult to get a crew. The school group, too, were told that it was impossible to give them a free passage until after a period of quarantine. Yet there had been no attempt to isolate the children when they were released from the school. Tearful parents were allowed to meet and embrace their children, and although all the children were given a medical checkup, "it was very superficial" according to a parent with expert medical knowledge, and they were not recalled for tests. Those admitted to the hospital were given a more thorough examination, but the majority were soon released. So it does not seem that the threat of meningitis was being taken very seriously. But for the government, it was a godsend. It gave them what they wanted: a cast-iron excuse for delay.

Max passed through the second-class carriage on his way back to fetch Rosemary. She was the only one who could advise him on a matter like this. "Something has come up," he said as he passed through the second class, and he used the Dutch expression: *"Er is een kink in de kabel"* ("There's a kink in the cable"). His face was contorted with emotion. When asked what he meant, he could not control his anger. "They have made fools of us, just as they made fools of our parents twenty-seven years ago." Somehow he recovered his composure. "I won't say any more now."

All that the hostages had endured in previous days, the rekindling of hope that morning, and the gradual return to a deeper depression as the hours dragged by, had left them outwardly apathetic but inwardly turbulent. The terrorists, their buoyancy punctured, were equally agitated. On orders from Max, the windows were screened with blankets, and the guard, which had been relaxed during the day, was reposted. Hansina, who had shown she could act aggressively, maddened them by cocking and uncocking her gun at her post in the entrance hall, until suddenly she fired it involuntarily, shattering the silence. Fortunately the bullet went out of the train.

Max was well aware that the pressure on the government would now have to come from the train. But in building up that pressure he was not conscious of the explosive atmosphere he was creating. Already Hansina's nerves had been affected by it. It wanted only the spark of some careless remark to set off the detonator, and it was van der Struik who supplied it. Restless as ever, he was chafing at his helplessness. "If I were ten years younger," he said, loud enough for those around him to hear, "I'd do something about it, I can tell you."

Men like Joop Huismans and Mart Kuiper, sitting next to van der Struik, were normally quick to scotch his more preposterous notions. But they did not foresee the effect of his sally on a twenty-nine-year-old Dutch Chinese named Syer Kong Yong. Already in a state of agitation, Yong had the added incitement of the barrel of a rifle sticking out across the aisle almost in his face. The rifle was being nursed by Rudi Lumalessil's younger brother Ronnie, who had proved the most aggressive of the group.

Provoked beyond endurance by van der Struik's innuendo, Yong seized the barrel of Ronnie's gun and tried to wrest it from him. He fully expected the other male passengers to rally round and overpower Ronnie. They would then be ready to deal with the other hijackers. But as Yong fought for possession of the gun, most of the men around him dived under their seats. Only a handful, of whom, to do him justice, van der Struik was one, shouted at him to desist and moved quickly to restrain him.

At that moment Rudi burst into the compartment, Uzi at the ready, drawing a chorus of agonized cries. "Don't shoot! Don't shoot!" Furious at the threat to his brother and evidently bent on revenge, he leapt forward with the clear intention of settling accounts with Yong. As the passengers screamed, van der Struik hurled Yong to the floor, while Joop Hoogenboom, who had been sweeping the aisle, tried to drag him to safety.

Max was sitting in the first-class section talking to the women when Rosemary called him. "Max! Quick! Something's wrong!" Max showed at once that he could move with feline swiftness when he wanted to. Gliding forward as though on skates, he was through and into the front carriage in a moment. Taking up the cry of "Don't shoot!" and using the supports of the luggage racks for leverage, he sprang like a Tarzan through the air onto Rudi's back, locking his legs around Rudi's neck.

Most of the hostages believed that Max was just in time to save Yong's life. It was a desperate moment, but at least it confirmed Max's determination to avoid bloodshed if he could. But there were one or two, among them Mart Kuiper and George Flapper, who thought that Rudi, for all the brotherly instincts that the assault had aroused, had had a definite span of time, perhaps two or three seconds, in which he could have shot Yong without danger of injuring his brother if he hadn't held back.

Some of the hostages also gave a high mark to Ronnie. Very upset and sweating profusely, he actually sought their approval. "Did I do right?" During the attack he had deliberately thrown his gun out of reach.

Max blamed the incident on the government, and he lost no time in turning it to advantage. "If the bus had come this afternoon," he told Mulder, "this wouldn't have happened. Several passengers might have been killed." His voice rose to a scream. *Is that what you wanted?*

The effect of Max's outburst was not quite what he intended. The incident was interpreted by Mulder as the first sign of group disintegration among the hijackers—a situation fraught with danger for the hostages.

Max was puzzled as to why, after several days in which he had feared some violent reaction from the men—and found them almost unbelievably passive and apathetic—trouble should have erupted when they were not under immediate threat. Rosemary explained that frustration and anger had been smoldering for days, reaching a flash point when, after a period of tantalizing uncertainty, the prospect of early release had evaporated. Whereas Max had taken the women more into his confidence, he had kept the men under threat and maintained his nonfraternization policy with them, with the result that the second-class carriage was a hive of anxiety and rumor. "Come and help me explain it to them," he told Rosemary, and she accompanied him forward.

"May I have your attention please. There's something I have to tell you —but perhaps it's better if Rosemary tells you." And Rosemary described how the children in the school had fallen ill and been released, but that there was a danger that some of them might be suffering from a dangerous infection called meningitis. "They are having blood tests," she said, "but it will be three or four days before the doctors can be sure. Meanwhile the South Moluccans in the school will be kept in quarantine."

Max then intervened. "If our friends in the school have this illness, we shall leave them behind. But we will wait for the tests. If they are cleared of infection, they will go with us."

This was reassuring, and the male hostages, in a more relaxed mood— some of them with the aid of tranquilizers distributed by Rosemary— settled down to wait. Van der Struik appealed to Max to disarm his guards, pointing out that their weapons had proved more likely to cause trouble than to prevent it. "Next time there really will be an accident. We all want to come out of this alive." Max said nothing, but they saw no more guards that day.

Max was also scared by the prospect of an epidemic in the train, and he asked the management center for clean clothes and underwear for the hostages and soaps, brushes, and disinfectants to sterilize the train. He had already shown his awareness that sick hostages as a weapon could turn into a boomerang. It was not long, however, before captors and captives alike began to suspect, like the press, that the meningitis scare was a government ruse to extricate themselves from their promises. For Rosemary Oostveen the feeling of doubt and distrust was reinforced when, in a discussion with the management center on the medical implications, an alternative cause of the sickness was suggested. The government, she feared, was hedging its bets.

CHAPTER 20

The Whitsun Weekend: Talks About Talks

HOPES THAT THE RELEASE OF the children would bring a speedy solution, one that could be activated as soon as the quarantine period was over, degenerated in the course of what proved a frustrating Whitsun weekend. The attitude of both sides had hardened. Government pronouncements spoke of "talking over" the situation with the hijackers, the word "negotiation" being discreetly dropped. Government requests that a destination be named were rejected by the terrorists. Mulder reiterated the difficulty of recruiting a crew without a destination being known, but this did not convince the hijackers, who recalled that in 1974 the Dutch Government had succeeded in raising a volunteer crew for the Japanese Red Army group although flight plans had been vague. Mulder said the government was not prepared to dispatch a plane on a mystery tour. The crew of such a plane would themselves become hostages. Max, fearing that, as soon as he named a chosen destination, the government would pressure the country concerned into refusing them entry, would not answer. The result was deadlock, and the talks stagnated. "There is no workable solution in sight," said van Agt, adding that in the course of the talks the terrorists often got highly emotional. Contacts reverted to mundane matters of food, clothing, blankets, pillows, sheets, and washing and cleaning materials. There were substantial deliveries on that Saturday, Max doling them out like a Santa Claus. A huge milk churn of warm water was brought, and, for the first time, the hostages were allowed to wash. Meanwhile the hijackers still refused to speak to any of their own community leaders and were impervious to all appeals for the release of the pregnant women, frequently reacting by hanging up the telephone.

The line between the train and the school was severed, the excuse offered being that it had broken down. It had served its purpose, and it was not repaired. Further communication between the two groups, it was thought, could only stiffen resolve. And with Max so clearly in charge, negotiations with the school group virtually ceased. A barbed wire fence surrounding the school area isolated them still further.

Inside the school, the hijackers' first task was to clean up the mess. Assembly room and classrooms were swabbed out and disinfected. With water flooding the corridors, the teachers were locked in the stock room, Fat Willem accompanying them as guard. He began to tell them about his life in jail, and all the time he was talking, he was leaning against a shelf on which he had placed the hand grenade he had earlier threatened them with. That hand grenade so fascinated Sjaan Abbink that she couldn't concentrate on what Willem was saying. Why had he brought it into the stock room? What did the hijackers intend? Willem always frightened her; she could never be sure what he would do or what he was thinking. If he wanted to blow them up, the confined area of the stock room was the ideal place.

When, more than an hour later, the door was unlocked and the teachers were ordered out, they were obviously still under strain. The hijackers looked at them in surprise. "Why are you frightened?"

"What are you going to do to us?"

The hijackers sat down on the floor and motioned the teachers to squat beside them. "We can't do you any harm," they said. "We've been talking too much with you. We can't hurt you any more."

Despite the many setbacks, the government was avoiding pessimism. "In our opinion the hijackers never intended to kill," said Toos Faber, speaking for the Ministry of Justice. "On the contrary, they have been very afraid of harm befalling their hostages. They know very well that if any harm does come to them, they will never get out of the country." A more specific warning, that if any hostage was harmed the train might be rushed by troops and police, was passed to Max. Van Agt still felt that the best bet was that the hijackers would get tired and give up their hostages when they found that no foreign country would accept them.

Mulder came back again and again to the question of naming a destination. "You will understand," he told Max, "that the Dutch Government can't agree to sending an air crew into the air just to replace the existing hostages. That is what it would amount to. They may have to fly over blocked airspace, or attempt to land at blocked airfields. I don't even know whether they can find a crew willing to do it. One can't exclude the possibility that they can't." In fact, the Dutch Airline Pilots Association was refusing to cooperate. "But it's very clear to me that whether they find one or not, the government won't allow them to go. When we have your destination, then permission can be asked for you to land."

"That's just a trick."

"I can understand that you will think it's a trick. But I can guarantee that it isn't. The government can't send a plane in the air to just nowhere."

"We have a destination, and we'll let you know what it is when we're in the air."

"That's just what the government won't allow."

At the South Moluccan crisis center, disappointment and even indignation at the continuing stalemate was intense. The significance of the use of the phrase "talk over" when applied to the demands of the hijackers was not lost on Lokollo. And on Whit Sunday, May 29, he and his group sent a letter of warning to van Agt with a request for an interview. The government's attitude, they wrote, had been that there could be no negotiation until the children were released. Now that the children were free, the term "negotiate" had been changed to "talk over," and the besiegers felt betrayed. While the hostages deteriorated mentally and physically, the pressures on the besiegers would be increased to such an extent that they might take ill-advised steps against them. Outside intervention would then become unavoidable. The obvious solution—that the Dutch authorities and the besiegers reach an agreement satisfactory to both sides—was seeming more and more unlikely, yet that was the solution that must still be hoped for. The quickest way out of the impasse was to guarantee the besiegers a free pardon to go abroad, leaving their hostages behind. Such a solution would enhance the authority of the South Moluccan crisis center and enable them to work for the restoration of good relations between Dutch and South Moluccans.

This was a balanced review of the situation, but to Dutch ears it sounded too much like a repetition of the threats of the terrorists, and van Agt, when he received the Lokollo group later that day, expressed himself as not happy with it. Lokollo pointed out that the prime minister himself had used the phrase "talk over" in a statement, and that it was becoming clear that the government had never really intended to negotiate at all. Van Agt's reply confirmed his fears. "We don't negotiate with terrorists."

"You said you could only negotiate when the children were free. Now that they are free, you won't negotiate."

This was how it looked to South Moluccans. In fact, what the government had said was that the demands of the terrorists could only be *discussed* when the children were free. But the word "negotiation" had certainly been used during talks with the Lokollo group. It was a deliberate piece of ambiguity that, like the "preparation" of a bus at Wijster, was forced on the government by the threats of the terrorists.

The Lokollo group was not told anything of the progress of talks with the hijackers, and they did not know that an offer of a free departure to a named destination had been made. This omission inevitably reduced the chances of a destination being found. Instead, van Agt tried once again to persuade Lokollo and his group to throw their weight into the scales to get the hijackers to surrender.

"We can't do that. What can we tell them?"

"There are fifty-four people on the train and four still in the school who must be freed," said van Agt. "The Dutch Government has the responsibility to enforce law and order, and it can't accept a situation like this. As for accepting the demands of the hijackers, that would only hurt the state." It was this continuing problem, the fear that any sign of weakness would only stimulate fresh outbreaks of blackmail and terrorism, that the South Moluccan leaders, Manusama excepted, never seemed to grasp.

The whole machinery of government in Holland had now been virtually halted for a week. Following this meeting, and with the growing danger of permanent damage to the hostages in mind, van Agt decided that it must be made clear to the hijackers that the concession that had been offered of unimpeded departure was of limited duration, and that, unless a destination was named, it would be brought to an end. Mulder did his best to get this across to Max as gently as possible. "If you don't mention your destination, something that can be properly checked and agreed so that nothing can go wrong and so that it can be announced in the press, it means in effect that while you refuse to name it you can keep this stalemate situation going indefinitely, without the government having the right to intervene. You would have carte blanche for continuing your action. So I must tell you that it is in the government's mind that, ultimately—and I don't know when, this is not an ultimatum, it's just for information—they've got to know within a reasonable time, for the reasons I've mentioned, and they will put a limit on it.

"You and I want to finish this in the best possible way, retaining our respect for each other. You may even tell me that you don't have a planned destination and ask me not to tell the government that, and I won't. But, if you really have a destination, the government must know what it is, otherwise the whole basis of a free departure will be null and void, cancelled, abandoned, gone."

Rumors from South Moluccan sources that the hijackers might be granted asylum in Vietnam or Yemen were discounted after the Dutch foreign minister, Max van der Stoel, had made discreet inquiries. They did not wish to get involved. Recognizing the difficulty of getting a blanket assurance beforehand and the delay that might ensue while he tried, Max had placed his hopes in the supposed contact with Vietnam. But the thought of setting off like some latter-day Flying Dutchman did not deter him. Others had done it before, and it would be an adventure. Once they were airborne, the pressure would be on their sympathizers to accept them. It was even possible that a destination might be found for them by the Dutch.

Max's reaction to the threat of a time limit was one of wrathful indignation, rising to a crescendo of vituperation. Uncharacteristically, he lost his temper. The government in general, and den Uyl and van Agt in particular, all came in for abuse. "The government promised us a free departure," he reminded Mulder, "and we let the children go. We are honest, but they have cheated and betrayed us, just like they always do. We insist on a free departure. That is what we were promised. Only then will we give up our hostages. We will not name our destination. If we do, they will only betray us again."

The delicate fabric of trust and respect that Mulder had tried to reweave since Friday had fallen apart, and there was little more he could say. Max stormed back into the second-class carriage and repeated his tirade of two days earlier. "Your parents betrayed us, and now they betray us again. For twenty-seven years they have fooled us, and now they fool us again." In the face of Max's righteous anger, it was impossible for the hostages not to believe that the government had deliberately deceived him.

Signs that the terrorists were preparing for a long siege now became visible from outside the train, as Max no doubt intended. Some of the girls, among them Joke Winkeldermaat and eighteen-year-old trainee kindergarten teacher Wilma Mann, volunteered for the duty of cleaning under the train, accepting the unpleasantness for the chance of some exercise and, ultimately, a breath of fresh air. Ostentatious covering by the guns of the terrorists and an order to screen their faces did not deter them; they knew it was only for show. They dug a hole to cover the excrement and piled up the rubbish for collection. Male volunteers were not accepted; they might try to escape. Windows were then opened and blankets aired. Max asked for a cake to celebrate André Schager's birthday on Sunday, making up to him for past indignities. And books, magazines, games, crossword puzzles, and materials for needlework and embroidery were all delivered in the course of the weekend. For the hostages these comforts, welcome as they were, confirmed that release was likely to be further delayed.

For Mini Loman, already simmering with impatience at being denied her freedom on this special day—the Day of Pentecost—the realization stimulated her into stalking angrily down the aisle to Max's command post. She had listened with interest to his arguments and reasoning. Although, like Rosemary, she couldn't approve of his methods, she understood the utter desperation of the South Moluccans in trying to get wider recognition for their independence struggle. For the moment, though, her own helplessness was the spur. Sliding open the door of Max's compartment, she confronted him angrily.

"How long is this game going on? Because I'm fed up with being kept here for nothing, fed up with having nothing to do. I want to go home. My parents will be worried about me. Why don't you let us out of this train?"

Her voice sounded harsh and unpleasant. Already she was ashamed of her outburst. That was the effect Max had on her. He looked at her calmly, and his manner was gentle, his voice soothing. "Mini," he said, "you are a Christian, aren't you?"

"Yes."

"You are always complaining that you have nothing to do. If you don't want to make yourself ill, you have to be patient, and wait. Read your Bible. Maybe you will find something there to help you."

She tried to maintain her stand. "Why can't we go?"

"You complain that you are being kept here for nothing, but you ought to realize that it means a lot to us."

She felt his answers as a reproach. "I suppose it does."

"If you really are a Christian, Mini, you will come through this. Now, come and sit down and let's talk."

She felt herself relaxing. To her, Max seemed more like a friend than a captor, and she was almost happy to be with him. She curled up on the floor at his feet.

"I'm a Christian too," he said. "But perhaps a little different from you."

"If you're a Christian, you shouldn't do things like this. You should try some other way, not using violence."

At this Max surprised her by bringing out his personal Bible. "I read it every day," he said. "I probably know it as well as you do. It's just that my interpretation is different from yours. You say God doesn't want violence, but didn't he allow David to kill Goliath? Those heroes of the Old Testament were fighting for a just cause, and God was with them. I'm fighting for a just cause, and I believe God is with me."

Mini tried to explain that the coming of Jesus Christ had changed Old Testament conceptions. They talked for over an hour, and eventually Max asked if she would come and talk to him every day.

At three o'clock on Whit Monday afternoon, with the siege entering its second week, the hijackers in the school were informed by Mulder that they must name the destination of the aircraft without further delay. Otherwise the opportunity for unimpeded departure would be considered to have lapsed, and the government would be faced with an entirely new situation. This important ultimatum was withheld from the train in case Max should react violently. Even the threat of a time limit had infuriated him. The government was perfectly well aware that the initiative had passed to the group in the train, and contact with the school group had been deliberately restricted in order to isolate them, but with their telephone line to the train severed, it was hoped that they might be caught off their guard. If an admission could be got from them that no sure destination existed, Max could be faced with it. But the school group avoided the trap.

The following morning, Tuesday, May 31, Max showed he had taken the time limit warning seriously by asking for two members of the Free South Moluccan Youth, Pieter Tuny and Jack Ririmasse, to be allowed to come to the train as contacts. Since up to this point he had refused all attempts at mediation and even threatened shootings if anyone so much as approached the train, this looked like a victory for the government's tactics. In fact, Max wanted these two, whom he trusted, to check and confirm which country would accept them. He was especially relying on Tuny's supposed connection with Vietnam.

While the government met at The Hague to discuss the mediation request, and took their time in answering, a statement from the Ministry of Justice announced that all negotiations about a getaway plane, the freeing of jailed compatriots, and the naming of a destination had been suspended. The government was studying plans for a military assault, although this was kept secret, and an armored train was being prepared at Onnen, three miles north of De Punt, in case a rescue operation was required. However, if mediation could prevent the use of force, the government was anxious to keep the possibility open, and a search for suitable "contact persons," as they came to be known, was begun.

On the same day, a group of young people calling themselves the Free Moluccan Youth of Bovensmilde, Assen, Elst, Gennep, Hatert, Heerde, and Tiel and the Liberation Front of the RMS published a letter in which they demanded political concessions from the government and unimpeded departure for the hijackers in exchange for the lives of the hostages:

> We know our young people, and we fear that a violent end will ensue if the government continues to concentrate on the release of the hostages to the exclusion of the wider issues. These boys have a lot to offer—namely sixty human lives. The government will have to set something positive against this to be considered realistic.

No threats from the hijackers had been received for several days, and van Agt denounced this letter as "infamous." The young people then claimed that their letter had been misinterpreted. It had not been meant as a threat. The incident was a reminder of the political naïveté of young South Moluccans and of their difficulty in expressing themselves accurately in Dutch.

Talks about talks continued. The South Moluccans mentioned by Max were not acceptable to the government. They were too close to the hijackers' own group. Manusama's group and the Badan Persatuan were not acceptable to the terrorists, whose action was directed as much against their own leaders as against anyone. Max issued a clear statement that he blamed the government-in-exile and wanted nothing to do with them. He nominated Mrs. Soumokil, and suggested that the Dutch Government should nominate one other. The government was not enamored of Mrs. Soumokil, who was believed to have criticized the consulate hijackers for giving up too soon, but they appreciated her status among South Moluccans as a figurehead, and eventually they accepted her as a contact person. They also agreed to her proposal that she be accompanied by a man named Dr. Hassan Tan, a fifty-six-year-old pulmonary specialist who some years earlier had worked as a general practitioner in Westerbork camp and in Assen and who knew the local people. A man of integrity and urbanity, with no axe to grind, he was a surprise choice, to none more so than himself, but subject to the presence of Mrs. Soumokil, he was prepared to accept. The choice was approved by the Lokollo group, who promised him a free hand. Born in Ambon, but of Chinese extraction, Tan had gone to Holland in 1946 to study medicine and married a Dutch woman. From 1967 to 1973, he had been minister of public health in Manusama's government. He had not been considered for a mediation role in 1975 because he had been out of the country at the time. A Muslim, he had been on a pilgrimage to Mecca. Max turned him down, partly because of his association with Manusama, partly because he doubted whether Tan could help him over a destination, but Tan had done useful work as a mediator in minor disputes in the past, and van Agt insisted. "It's either Dr. Tan or none at all," Mulder told Max. "That's the point of view of the government." Thus the talks about talks dragged on.

CHAPTER 21

The Psychiatrists Prepare

O F THE SEVENTEEN CHILDREN who had remained in hospital, ten were released over the Whitsun weekend, while the child with the symptoms of meningitis was making good progress, and it was soon established that she had not contracted the disease after all. Dr. Gottlieb Neddick, who treated the children at Assen Hospital, believed that they would all recover fully from their physical illness, but that the psychological condition of some of them might be serious.

Government determination to give better psychological support to the hostages than last time had been given prominence within forty-eight hours of the hijacking when Dr. Willem van Dyke of the Psychiatric Clinic at Groningen University Hospital said in a statement that many lessons had been learned from 1975, and when the train passengers were released they would be brought at once to a reception center at his clinic, where they would first have a two-hour screening before meeting their families. "They will stay here for the first night, and with their comrades they will be able to get accustomed to freedom. This we now know is very important."

This process was partly a precaution against the tendency of hostages to blame the authorities for their misfortunes. It would allow for the true position of the government to be explained to them, so that they could be disabused of false impressions. (Some saw it as a preplanned brainwash.) It was also important, said van Dyke, that they shouldn't go straight home, to be confronted by families who, according to the evidence of 1975, might be shocked by their reactions. "During the past week, we have been telling the relatives what to expect and how to cope with the problems that will doubtless arise. Previous sieges have proved the breaking point in

265

marriages and the cause of considerable personal problems within individuals and between loved ones."

At the families center in Groningen, stiff upper lips were discouraged. "I have been told by the social workers," said one girl in her twenties, "that I should give vent to my feelings because it would make me less tense, and I have cried bitterly." On their own initiative, some of the wives found a visit to a local bar in the evening, although frowned on at first as frivolous, was more effective than a tranquilizer.

The problems confronting the child psychiatrists were especially complex. "We want to help the children to overcome the fears and anxieties they have experienced," said one of them. "These are manifesting themselves in the fact that the children have built up a defense mechanism against them. They just want to forget what happened. Many of the parents want to do the same." This was not regarded as a healthy reaction. "When terrorist victims try to forget, they find out within a few months that they have symptoms in which their problems manifest themselves—symptoms such as loss of concentration." The danger came from repressing unpleasant memories only to have them return when the victim least expected them and could not cope with the repetition. "They think that the best thing is just to forget about it. But we don't agree."

Justification for these views seemed to come from those hostages who were still suffering the aftereffects of Wijster and Amsterdam. "They are still experiencing things that relate to those events. For many of them, emotions are coming to the surface now that should have been encouraged to come to the surface at the time." Gerry Vaders, a severe critic of the intervention of psychiatrists immediately after Wijster, now denounced laissez-faire attitudes, realizing that the experience had changed his life. He had found it difficult to immerse himself in the daily routine of running a newspaper. Others reported recurring bad dreams and psychological fears. Jan Bies, one of the two surviving soldiers, dreamed repeatedly of the black faces of terrorist gunmen; he couldn't believe that he had actually shaken hands with them when they surrendered. Harsoyo confessed that he feared the approach of South Moluccans when walking in the street. Children, it was thought, might retain such symptoms for years. Irma Martens, the youngest of the hostages at Wijster, said she thought she had shaken off the effects until the new hijackings occurred. "This brought it all back to me. I lie awake in bed at night and go through it again in my mind. I just couldn't believe such a thing could happen again."

Whereas parents were anxious to keep the press at a distance, psychiatrists thought it would be a good thing to let the children talk. Parents were inclined to take their children away for a holiday; psychiatrists thought they should first be allowed to settle back into their environment. "You must consider your child has been on a school trip on which something has gone wrong."

To what extent had the children suffered, and to what extent might they suffer in the future? Few, perhaps, had been fully aware of their situation. Yet it was noticeable that they followed news bulletins closely to see how their teachers were faring. "In the beginning we thought they [the hijackers] were rather rude," said eleven-year-old Paul Leertouwer, "but later they were quite nice to us." Seven-year-old Wim van t'Hoog said he had had a wonderful time. "We had a lot of fun in the classrooms. It was just a big party, and we played lots of games. I wasn't frightened, not even of the rifles they had. We were friends with the Moluccans. It was good." Wim's parents said he came home at the end of the ordeal as from any normal schoolday and went off to his bedroom to play with his electric car.

Psychiatrist van Dyke, who kept many of the children under observation, concluded that they did not seem to have been terrorized by their ordeal. "Although many are suffering from bad dreams at night, during their games they astonishingly portray the terrorists as smiling, gentle people, not as menacing villains. Clearly a relationship based on trust rather than fear was built up."

"It was not frightening at all," agreed a boy of twelve. "In fact, we got to like the South Moluccans. It was all like one big game." A ten-year-old girl said, "We were afraid, but not a lot." No one said they had been threatened. Twelve-year-old Roelof Snippe had played his mouth organ for his friends to help pass the time and keep their spirits up. The worst thing that happened to one fifth-grader was a loss of status. He had to sleep in the fourth-grade group, "with the little ones." The psychiatrists, however, still warned of trouble ahead.

One embittered father said that, after this, it would be impossible to live among the South Moluccans any more. But the majority of parents disagreed, and so did the children. Ronald, nine, and Ferdinand, seven, still wanted to play football with the Moluccan boys, and their mother rejected the idea of keeping Moluccan children out of the school. "You can't destroy the Moluccan quarters. That is no solution. And if you move them, you only pass the problem to someone else. The Moluccans wouldn't benefit from it, and they have to live somewhere. I don't approve of all they do, and I suppose the weapons will have to go. If they keep to decent standards as they used to, they must be given a chance. We have never had any trouble with them, and my husband, who is an upholsterer, has done a lot of work in the Moluccan quarters."

After being talkative at first, Adrian Pen's two boys became more introverted. They settled down slowly, rather as they would on return from a holiday. The old toys and books were brought out; they surrounded themselves with familiar things; they were clearly picking up the threads. With the sieges still in progress, their favorite game inevitably became Hijackers, which Pen thought was probably therapeutic. They became so steeped in communiqués and press releases that Herman, the older of the two boys, composed one of his own:

> Bovensmilde, ANP, Reuters. Yesterday night the Prime Minister, Joop den Uyl, came to Bovensmilde to help organize the streets. "As prime minister of this country I might just as well hold a rifle for once in a while." Thus said Joop den Uyl as he got his wish. In one day he had controlled 234,567 motor cars. "I think," said Joop, "this is because I am a prime minister." He stayed till 8:10 PM to drink coffee with the policemen.

This delightful piece of fantasy, stemming as it did from the hourly radio presentation of nonevents as hot news, suggests that the emotional atmosphere the children breathed after their release may have made a deeper impression on youthful minds than the experience itself. Parents, too, had been advised not to bottle up their emotions but to let their children know they had been frightened, and some may have overdone it. In any case, it soon became clear that the parents had been much more frightened than the children. The children seemed to have come through their experience well adjusted and mentally unscathed. It was the parents who needed medical and psychiatric attention. Van Dyke's warning about the breaking point in marriages, indeed, was proving true.

Meanwhile, for the train hostages, the most elaborate after-care operation ever devised for an international hijacking was being prepared. After Wijster the government had set up a Central Steering and Guidance Committee[13] to advise on the after-care of hostages and to conduct a scientific investigation into their physical, psychological and social health over a period. But this investigation did not begin until March 1977, and meanwhile, doctors, psychiatrists and social workers rather left it to ex-hostages to come to them. Despite strong feelings of isolation and aban-

---

[13]*Centrale Beleids en Ondersteuningsgroep* (CBOG).

donment that even extended to their home life, few had sought psychiatric help, feeling that their anxieties and phobias were irrational and a sign of weakness. The policy of the psychiatrists this time was to be more active, while still being careful not to intrude. By overemphasizing their belief that the hostages must expect to have psychiatric problems, the psychiatrists might be making a self-fulfilling prophecy.

After one or possibly two days at the reception center, hostages who were otherwise fit and well would be referred to their family doctor and the social psychiatric service. Medical dossiers on each individual hostage were compiled with the help of general practitioners, and letters were sent by the Department of Health to the relevant doctors with advice on how to treat long-term psychiatric problems attributable to hijackings. Despite some brilliant exceptions, many family doctors, according to one critic, had shown little imagination with hostages of the 1975 sieges and last time had tended to "rely on the Valium pot and a pat on the shoulder." Yet each of Holland's eleven provinces operated its own fully-staffed social psychiatric service, and, with better organization, it was intended to keep track this time of the health and well-being of every surviving hostage.

CHAPTER 22

The Second Week

A FTER MAX'S REQUEST for contacts on May 31, the hostages in the train settled down, under Max's direction, to a life of routine. Early reactions of awe and submission became attenuated, and much that had hitherto seemed haphazard became predictable. One of the hijackers, generally Thys, the first to go about unarmed, would enter the carriage with, "Good morning, gentlemen, did you have a good sleep?" And the answer would come: "Excellent, Thys." The men's compartment was surprisingly quiet during the night, no snoring, no nightmares, no disturbances. Most people by this time had managed to compensate for the slant of the train by the use of pillows. There were some who found difficulty in sleeping, but fifty-one-year-old Arie Dijkman, traveling to Groningen from Eindhoven for the Philips Electronics Company, slept better than he did at home. He also showed a natural skill and diplomacy in coping with the emotions of others.

One young man, twenty-year-old student Daan Peter Pot, scandalized everyone in second class by sleeping round the clock. Jan Cuppen, the painter, noticed as he lay half-awake how verticals retained the illusion of being upright, until two hijackers, talking together in the entrance hall, appeared to be standing at an angle, like clowns who have nailed their shoes to the floor. For him, sleep was an occupation in which he could fancy a bond with the outside world.

Breakfast arrived at 8:30 AM, just bread and tea, which nineteen-year-old Janneke Wiegers, a trainee teacher from Assen, served to the men. Some of the women slept till eleven o'clock, and the hijackers took them their breakfast in bed.

Most people found it distasteful to be continually dirty, but only the fastidious really managed to keep up appearances. One who did was Rien van Baarsel. Mini Loman was sitting next to him, and she admired him for it. Many of the men let the stubble grow for two or three days, and some grew beards, but van Baarsel was always well turned out and clean shaven.

Water was brought to the train daily by handcart, but it was rationed, and washing in the restaurant kitchen was allowed only on alternate days. Max saw his hostages as prisoners of war, to be kept healthy, under some imagined hijackers' convention, while being subjected to a fairly strict regime. Rosemary ministered to their physical and mental wants and weaknesses and organized daily exercises.

The midday meal was much the same as breakfast—bread and coffee. It was the hot evening meal, rounded off by a substantial dessert, that everyone lived for. Before going to sleep, they got a cola or fruit juice, and then they settled down for the night, in a sleeping bag or blankets. In the second-class section, their feet and ankles stuck out over the edge of the seat, or they rolled up like mummies on the floor. Lights—candles—were put out at ten, with a final word from Max. "Good night, sleep well, the RMS is watching over you."

A regular visitor to the men's carriage was Saskia. "Good morning, everyone, beautiful morning. Having a good holiday?" And when her ebullience was greeted with mock groans: "Rise and shine! I'm here to cheer you up!" One day she brought in a Bible that had been delivered by the Red Cross. "There! Isn't that a nice gesture!" Hans Oude Elberink had survived several months in a Nazi concentration camp, and he knew the practical value of a Bible. His cynicism affronted Saskia. "Good. We can use it for cigarette papers."

Most of the men were glad of Saskia's bright, vivacious personality. But one who couldn't stand what he saw as her forced cheerfulness was Cuppen, who would murmur to his neighbor Marc Hustinx, "Here's that dreadful woman again!" He could well imagine her in her nursing days, entering a children's or old people's ward in much the same way. To annoy Cuppen, and because he liked Saskia, Hustinx would sometimes invite her to sit down beside him and talk.

Cuppen was much happier when the visitor was Ansje Monsjou. Then he would get her to sit next to Hustinx and mischievously lead Hustinx on. Like George Flapper, Cuppen had his likes and dislikes. He invited some of the hostages over to sketch their portraits, but others who were eager to "sit" for him found his attention suddenly wandering. His greatest animosity was directed against those who had caused this interruption to his life. To a man of his Bohemian tastes, liberty and privacy were sacrosanct, and to lose them was a humiliation. The trouble was that any action aimed at restoring these freedoms could only endanger the group. Not that he itched to take such action—he was honest enough to admit that he lacked the courage. But to be forced to embrace cowardice as a means of survival was the worst abasement of all.

In a defiant attempt to assert his individuality, Cuppen sought to demonstrate the absurdity of the daily routine by wearing his pajamas all the time and refusing to shave. Why should he dress when he couldn't go out? He was determined to have something to show for his days of captivity, if it was only a beard. Yet he didn't think that the vacuum in which they were living, a kind of hibernation, was likely to induce any deeper change.

Flapper had come to the same conclusion. One didn't find out what others were really like in this sort of situation. Everyone tried to behave normally, to present the familiar facade to the world. Men who had always been fastidious about their appearance continued to be so. What was there to be learned from that? Only that the barriers were still up. Perhaps because the depths of fear that had been plumbed at Wijster had scarcely been reached, people didn't talk so much about themselves. One thing Flapper noticed about his fellow hostages, some of them, was a sudden access of greed. When quantities of clothing, tobacco, and other comforts were delivered, there were always people who grabbed them whether they needed them or not. Something was going for nothing, and they were afraid of missing it.

The male hostages were not a homogeneous group. They consisted rather of a honeycomb in which the cells were curiously isolated from each other. Individuals moved around during the day, and some went as far afield as first class, but superstition—or the territorial imperative—was strong, and they moved back to their original "pad" for the night.

The relationship between hijackers and hostages had fallen far short of the emotional levels of Wijster, but it matured a little in that second week, although the contrast between first and second class continued to be marked. The hijackers took their guard duties less seriously, keeping their firearms unloaded or on safe, or discarding them altogether. Ben Boevink, an insurance colleague of Joop Huismans who had moved into the women's section, had to call Mingus back after a game of checkers. "Here, come back. You've forgotten your tools." In this section, the atmosphere sometimes resembled a holiday hotel in wet weather when no one can go out. Even among the women, though, tensions and despondency were never far from the surface. Almost every day, one or more of them broke down and had to be comforted by Saskia or Rosemary, and only a handful had any real contact with the hijackers. Those who made such contact played games and cards with them, to the hijackers' delight, and even helped them to embroider RMS emblems on their T-shirts, with colored wools sent in from outside. Ineke Rijstenberg was one of those who schooled them in the art. The spectacle of a Moluccan slouching through the train with an automatic pistol slung round his neck, begging male and female hostages alike for a particular color of silk thread for his T-shirt, became one of the more incongruous sights.

Junus painted a picture on one of the T-shirts and gave it to Saskia. The train, with an armed hijacker standing outside on guard, the trees, the sunshine, and the highlighting of the RMS colors, were beautifully done.

The men were more interested in the political side of the Moluccan question than the women and more impatient to know the hijackers' plans, but attempts by Max to involve them in discussions about South Moluccan problems and motivation generally failed. Books on Moluccan political history were circulated, and one who scanned them briefly was Bimmel. "I understand something of your motives," he told Max, "but it's no reason to keep us hijacked. I don't mind discussing it and involving myself in it in my own back garden, but not in prison with a pistol at my back." In the improved atmosphere, he could say this openly to Max.

Without wishing to become over-friendly, the male hostages, following the incident with Yong, sought a better understanding, and Max, who first set out to avoid contact, now seemed to resent its absence. "I talk to a lot of people in the first class," he said, "why none in the second? Anyone can come and see me at any time." The men greeted this cautiously. If they talked to Max individually, the chances were that they would all say something different. Then they would argue afterward among themselves, and the united front they wanted to present would be undermined—which might be just what Max wanted. They decided to appoint one person to represent them, to be a liaison with Max on their needs and to disseminate what news Max was ready to reveal. There were several people in the train who might have performed this task adequately, but the hostages were wary of anyone of too volatile a temperament, like van der Struik, or too extroverted a nature, like Flapper. Their choice fell on the social worker Wim Fakkert. The reverse of flamboyant, Fakkert was respected for the role he had assumed of guide and mentor to the lad from Eindhoven, and he had already shown what van der Struik called "the patience of a monk" in giving comfort elsewhere when it seemed to be needed. Capable of drawing others out without revealing his own reactions, he was discreet, competent, objective, and self-effacing. If some found him the typical social worker, he was an unemotional link between hostages and hijackers and a more or less unanimous choice. Even when it came to the Bible, which the South Moluccans were so fond of quoting, he was not at a disadvantage. His appointment confirmed rather than bridged the gap between the men and their captors. Instead of making general announcements for all to hear, Fakkert moved quietly through the carriage and related what Max had told him to groups of four or five, sometimes just to one or two, varying his approach each time, judging his audience, telling the same things in a different way to different people. In this way he avoided alarming or upsetting anyone. Flapper asked him once if he hadn't found the life of a priest a lonely one, and Fakkert, blushing with embarrassment or perhaps annoyance, clearly indicated that he wished to keep his distance. For his temerity Flapper was rebuked by other hostages. "That's not the sort of question one asks."

When Thys asked Victor Nijmeijer if he could borrow his sunglasses (they were special pilot's glasses), Nijmeijer risked asking if he could go back and retrieve his briefcase; he had feared discovery all along. Thys was as eager to acquire the glasses as Nijmeijer was to regain possession of the briefcase, so the deal was struck. Nijmeijer was immensely relieved to find the briefcase still there under the seat.

Boredom affected everyone, but the hostages soon learned to space out their day. Some, like Bimmel, resented the vegetable existence. Others, like Cuppen, while still nettled by the loss of their liberty, felt no sense of timeless monotony; every day seemed different. Many, like Joop Huismans, carefully husbanded every task, stretching it out, never doing two things at once. If he decided to light his pipe, he put his book away. It then became a fresh thing to do later.

Most people found difficulty in concentrating, whether they were reading (the standard of literature delivered to the train in the first week or so was appalling), playing games—cards, checkers, and monopoly—or doing crossword puzzles. They ate, played a bit, read a bit, talked a bit, waited, and wondered. Perhaps it would all end tomorrow. Few thought it could last more than a fortnight. They heard from Fakkert and Rosemary that the talks with the authorities were deadlocked through Max's refusal to name a destination, and that the mediators put forward by Max had been rejected. But, if they got depressed, there was always someone on hand to console them.

Boredom among the hijackers held more dangerous possibilities, but for the moment the results were harmless. When they saw anything move outside the train, they shot at it, whether it was a crow, a helicopter, or a fleeting glimpse of a marauding marine. When they discerned the slightest movement in the woods three to four hundred meters away, they shot at that too, despite the distance. The hostages knew the marines were over there in the woods, and once or twice they saw movement close to the train and guessed that listening devices had been planted underneath them, but they were not unduly worried at the firing. "They can't hit a crow at five meters," said Bimmel. "They won't hit the marines at four hundred."

Day after day, there was nothing to be seen, no tanks, no armored cars, no troops. It seemed that the world had deserted them. Perhaps because of this, they became especially sensitive to sound. They welcomed the friendly clatter of the helicopter and imagined the crew taking photographs. At least it was evidence of movement. Natural sounds affected them differently. The lowing of cattle depressed them, and the call of the cuckoo, which mocked them throughout that second week, proved maddening in its monotony. But a doe whose track took it close to the train excited their interest. They watched it step cautiously through the high grass, drink nervously from a ditch, then disappear with an elegant leap behind the bushes. In its sudden movements, it seemed to suggest a poignant awareness that its freedom, too, might be transient.

Squinting through the holes in the coverings—in places the newspaper had been reinforced with blankets—they could see, if they had a mind to, the hordes of motorists who stopped or dawdled on the highway. Cuppen felt degraded by their morbid curiosity and hoped they felt degraded too.

Max still radiated confidence and seemed sure of ultimate success. Appointing himself as President of the South Moluccan Government on the Train, he walked around with a conductor's cap on his head and Rosemary's stethoscope round his neck as badges of office. He also appointed a minister of environmental hygiene and a minister of food, and, when the hostages wanted anything, they had to apply to the appropriate "minister." These jokes, which seemed out of tune with Max's dignity, did not last long.

Of the other hijackers on the train, art student Junus—he was learning to be a sculptor—proved the shyest and most gentle, although he acted the disciplined soldier and was studiously obedient to Max. Hansina, who had been a loved member of the family of the dentist for whom she worked, seemed sullen and withdrawn, giving the impression of being hard and unapproachable. Jo's shaved hair was beginning to grow, giving him a spiky look that made him more frightening than ever in appearance, but the terrorist who really made them uneasy was Ronnie. His elder brother Rudi proved well versed in the history of Dutch perfidy, but Ronnie exuded a smoldering animosity that was far more frightening. Once, when Ansje Monsjou was sitting with Marc Hustinx, he had to ask her to go away, "because I get a really nasty feeling, he's looking at us with such hate." Later, when Rosemary was sitting with Hustinx and Ronnie was standing in the doorway, it was Rosemary who quailed before his gaze. "I'm going away. He's looking so mean at me, as though he's going to do something to me."

Mini Loman, during one of her visits to Max, fell afoul of Ronnie. As she slid open the door of his command post, Max ordered Ronnie out. "We want to talk, Ronnie. We want to be alone." Ronnie scowled, and as he slung his machine gun over his shoulder, Mini said jokingly, "Yes, Ronnie, clear off. On your bike." Ronnie's eyes flashed, and he swung his gun as though he would smash it into her face. "Ronnie! Stop!" yelled Max. "Don't do it!" Ronnie glared at her, then sullenly withdrew.

Mini felt shaken, but Max said, "Don't let Ronnie worry you, Mini. He's had some bad experiences with white people, and he's very bitter about you all."

That night, as Mini lay awake worrying about her clash with Ronnie, he came into the carriage, as she had hoped he might, and she called him over. "I'm really sorry if I hurt you, Ronnie. I only meant it as a joke. I hope you're not still angry with me." He looked embarrassed, but he muttered, "It's okay now," and smiled.

Wilma Mann thought all the hijackers, Ronnie included, only threatened for fun. Marc Hustinx thought the other hijackers were jealous of both Mini and Rosemary, because of their friendship and influence with Max. Max placed his confidence more and more in Rosemary's judgment, and once Hustinx heard him say: "She's my second mother."

This was the relationship between them, rather than that of brother and sister, or anything physical. Contacts in the train were strangely sexless. In the evenings, at what had come to be known as the "joke hour," the humor quickly degenerated into the ribald, whether women were present or not, but it went no further than that. Among the women, dressing and undressing went on without embarrassment, despite the presence of men. A kind of hospital atmosphere prevailed—plenty of jokes, but no contact.

A change in the sleeping habits of the hijackers gave Bimmel a chance to make himself more comfortable. Some of the Moluccans had slept in the second-class entrance hall immediately forward of the zigzag passageway connecting first and second class, but after a few days they moved to the first-class entrance hall on the far side of the connection, leaving the second-class hall empty. Bimmel had been sleeping on the floor in the men's compartment, and he asked Max, "How about three of us sleeping in that entrance hall? It's no problem for you, because none of you sleep there now, and it would give more room for the other guys here. They'll sleep better too." After thinking it over, Max agreed.

Helped by André Schager and Peter Blankert, Bimmel spread out some of the big cardboard cartons in which the underwear had been delivered and found they made excellent floor insulation. There was no shortage of blankets, and they soon made themselves comfortable. The women's compartment, which was much smaller than the men's, was also crowded, and the rotation system they had inaugurated under Saskia, in which they took turns sleeping on the eight couches, although fair, was far from ideal. One girl whom Bimmel had struck up a friendship with and who needed a good night's sleep more than most was Rosemary, and Bimmel invited her to join them. Again, sex did not enter into it. "You can sleep with us," said Bimmel, "there's room enough. In first class, there's a lot of movement at night. They're often restless and coughing. Come and sleep with us, and you'll get a good rest."

Most evenings, Rosemary went forward for a talk with Max, then joined them in the entrance hall. On that first night, Bimmel heard her sobbing, reacting to all the tensions of the day. Even some of the more stable characters approached the breaking point at times, and Rosemary, while helping them through their troughs, had to keep her own guard up all the time. The pregnant women, she felt, were her responsibility, but she could not persuade Max to release them. If she goes on like this, thought Bimmel, she'll break down, and we won't have a doctor. So he lit a candle, and, with the other two boys asleep, he and Rosemary talked for more than an hour about the day and about all the things Max had told her. For Rosemary, the entrance hall became a sort of decompression chamber, where she could be her natural self and where she unburdened herself, in confidence, of all her cares.

Max would not even agree to a visit by a gynecologist, and he also refused to release an engineer named Theo van Hattem who was taken ill in that second week, but he did allow the delivery of a blood-pressure gauge for Nelleke and oxygen for van Baarsel. On Wednesday, van Hattem, who had been on his way to a hospital for treatment for a jaw complaint, fainted, and Rosemary persuaded Max to call for an ambulance. But after drawing up close to the train, it was ordered back. Max promised to call Mulder again in ten minutes, but it was another hour and a half before Rosemary reported on Max's behalf that the sick man was better and that the ambulance was no longer required. It was difficult for Mulder to gauge to what extent Rosemary was under duress, but the incident led to one of the most heated exchanges between Mulder and Max so far. "You're seriously endangering the health of the hostages," said Mulder, "especially these three." Max's response was to hang up on him. Max thought that van Hattem had made a fuss about nothing, and he did not wholly exonerate Rosemary. "You must not simulate."

Mini Loman's relationship with Max was on a different plane. Rosemary shared his practical problems, Mini his spiritual. When he greeted her, she would ask him about the negotiations and he would say, "I think we are maybe one millimeter nearer." But they did not discuss the siege itself, nor did she attempt to question him on it. The influence she hoped to have was of a different kind. She was concerned above all that he should believe in Jesus Christ as his personal savior. Her talks with Max, she found, helped her as well. For the first time, she was really witnessing for her religion.

Max asked if she thought it was possible for a person to hear the voice of Jesus, and she told him in great detail of her own conversion, when she felt that God had spoken to her. "He can speak to *you*, Max." She could see that he was moved. But he couldn't believe that God could change people overnight. "It can happen, I accept that, but it has to be slowly."

During one of her talks with Max, Mini asked him what he would do if she tried to escape. He lifted his revolver and put the barrel to her temple, then pulled the trigger. "Don't worry," he said as he did it, "it's not loaded." But she flinched just the same. "If you try to escape," he said, "I can assure you that you will be shot. I like you a lot, but I would still do it." This was at variance with the impression he had given Saskia and Rosemary and several of the girls. Which was the real Max? What did he really intend? The time might come when that question would be crucial.

In his talks with Mulder, Max always maintained that he was only one of a group and that there were at least two others whom he always had to consult who had the power of veto. But on a personal note, he told Mulder what he had told the women: "Of one thing I'm certain, I will not go to prison. If I don't get away, I won't survive." This could only mean that he envisaged a violent end. Yet so deep was the impression he had made both inside and outside the train that the assumption was that, as long as he remained in control, there would be no killings. If, as time passed and the pressures rose, the terrorists quarreled and Max lost control, others in the group might prove more ruthless. It may well be that Max fostered this notion, as he had encouraged the belief, demonstrably erroneous, that the group in the school were killers. He wanted the government to conclude that they might do far worse than settle with him.

Throughout that second week, Max remained under continual pressure from Mulder and Rosemary to let the pregnant women go. Seeing them as his strongest bargaining point, he still refused. Mini did not ask how a man who professed to want to know God could use children and pregnant women to enforce blackmail, but Max himself referred obliquely to it. "Do you know, Mini," he said, during one of their talks, "I pray every night for forgiveness from God for this siege. Every night. God is righteous, but I'm sure he understands my motives. I'm glad no human is my judge, only God." This last sentence was exactly what Paul Saimima had said after Wijster.

Toward the end of that second week, on Friday, June 3, with a visit to the train by Mrs. Soumokil and Dr. Tan at last agreed upon and due to take place the next day, George Flapper asked one of the hijackers, "Can I have some tobacco for my pipe?" "Go to Max," he was told. So he went forward, and he had an extraordinarily frank and friendly talk with Max that lasted an hour. Although loquacious and opinionated, Flapper had a direct and engaging manner and an inquiring mind. The aptitude that had suggested a career in psychology had not been channeled narrowly, and he found in Max a warm personality not very unlike his own. "Come in," said Max. "Sit down. Have a cigarette." Almost at once Flapper was asking questions naturally and directly, as he might have done in his normal environment.

First he wanted to know the reasons for the hijacking. The object, said Max, was to get the release of the imprisoned South Moluccans and to go away with them, also to publicize the RMS ideal. He talked of the history of his people, how they came to Holland, and how the young were rebelling against the passive acquiescence of their elders in the absorption of South Moluccan independence and culture, both in Holland and in Indonesia. Flapper said he thought this was the wrong way to go about it. In the long run, such action could only rebound on the South Moluccan people. With a good public relations and information service, they would achieve much more. "I don't understand how you can do this as an intelligent man." Max's answer, misconceived though it might have been, sounded logical. "Enlightenment by information doesn't come easy to South Moluccans, because they don't know how to do it. They aren't fluent enough in the Dutch language. Many South Moluccans still find difficulty with the gender of words. They haven't got to that point yet, let alone to being able to convince people by argument." As for the use of violence, Max pointed to the Dutch action against the camp at Vaassen in October, 1976. This, he said, showed that the Dutch also used violence when it suited them.

Max complained that Dutch people would never understand the South Moluccan soul. Even among the hostages at Wijster, who had shown compassion at the time, only Karel Wielenga had done anything for them. This was not quite true. Although many of the 1975 hostages had expressed a revulsion against what they afterwards saw as their weak-mindedness on the train, two at least—Hans Prins and Wientje Kruyswijk—had kept in touch with their captors by visiting them in prison, and others among them—including Gerry Vaders and Walter Timmer—had campaigned for their cause. Currently Hans Prins had offered his services as a mediator but had been refused by the government, since they thought he might be in physical danger.

Max went on to explain that some of the younger South Moluccans had been to Ambon and made contact with RMS sympathizers there. They were turning to communist countries for help, to Russia and East Germany and other republics who were following the socialist road. Flapper asked if this didn't make for problems with their parents and their religion. "Yes, it does," said Max, "but the most important thing is to free the South Moluccas. That must come first, and we have to use all methods to achieve it."

Max spoke of what he called the primitive conditions, the oppression and the persecution that were suffered in the Moluccan islands, and he told of the guerrillas who were still operating there. "When you get away," asked Flapper, "are you going to join the guerrilla struggle?" "I don't want to tell you," said Max, "but when we are in the plane, I will tell you. I will also tell you the country of our destination."

"Why won't you tell the government now?"

"We were promised a bus and a plane if we released the children, but the Dutch Government hoodwinked us. They want first the destination, then the bus, then the plane. We want first the bus, then the plane, then the destination. That's what it hinges on. I don't want to give them the final clue, because they have already cheated us once, and I don't trust them."

"Where is it you want to go to? Is it Vietnam or the Yemen?"

Max started to laugh. "There is also a small country called Benin."

CHAPTER 23

Dr. Tan and Mrs. Soumokil

A T TEN O'CLOCK ON FRIDAY morning, June 3, the twelfth day of the siege (the Wijster train hijack had lasted thirteen), Max finally accepted Dr. Tan as the second contact person or mediator. Piet Lokollo and his group were then called to The Hague for a briefing, and the minister of culture, recreation, and social work, Harry van Doorn, with Henk Zeevalking also present, put the government's view forcefully to them. Indeed van Doorn's manner, cultivated no doubt in his days as a prosecutor in criminal courts, was resented, the South Moluccans complaining again that they were given nothing but orders. Because of the length of time the hostages had been held, said van Doorn, law and order must be restored, and there could be no further question of unimpeded departure. This must be made absolutely plain to Dr. Tan and Mrs. Soumokil. The government was determined to speed the matter to an early conclusion because of its great concern for future race relations in Holland.

The two contact persons visited the bunker in Assen that afternoon. Since they were not strictly negotiators or mediators, it was not thought appropriate to brief them. However, the attorney general, Baron van der Feltz, explained that the contact was at the specific request of the group in the train and that the school group was not involved. He stressed the seriousness of the situation and emphasized that no solution would be accepted that did not correspond with the maintenance of law and order. He then referred to the deteriorating health of the hostages. "Time is of the essence. The situation cannot be allowed to last much longer." No reference was made to the possibility of military action. The two mediators replied that they would do their utmost. "God will guide us and bring a solution," said Dr. Tan.

Mulder gave Tan his opinion of the psychological aspects. He described the hijackers as acting from diminished responsibility and attributed to them a restricted horizon and a narrowing of consciousness. "In this situation, the mind compensates with a certain illusion of power. The danger is that this can lead to megalomania." Mulder added that he believed he had already detected such symptoms in Max Papilaya. He described how Max had taken to addressing him as "colleague" and said he appeared to identify himself with the revolutionary leader Che Guevara.

Tan promised again to do his utmost to find a peaceful solution, but he would have to do it in the South Moluccan way. "You've got to give me time. You can't expect us to find a solution in a few hours or even days. You've been trying unsuccessfully yourselves for nearly two weeks." It was a valid point.

That evening, Mrs. Soumokil spoke to Max on the field telephone. "When are you prepared to receive us?"

"If Dr. Tan comes by himself," said Max, "he'd better stay at home. He can come if you are present, Mrs. Soumokil."

Tan took the phone. "Would it be possible to meet tonight, if only because we as mediators would very much like to meet the boys?"

"We need time to prepare for your visit. It will soon be dark. Go home, take it easy, and get a good sleep. We will receive you at 2:00 PM tomorrow."

When the mediators arrived at the hijacked train the following afternoon, Saturday, June 4, the formalities of South Moluccan ceremonial were punctiliously observed. Mrs. Soumokil's progress from the car that drove her to within 200 meters of the train was hampered to some extent by her sarong and her high-heeled shoes, but at the top of the embankment she was met in traditional style by a woman, Hansina, who was accompanied by Jo and Thys. An attempt to fashion steps from empty crates had failed, but the indignity of lifting Mrs. Soumokil bodily into the train was avoided by the use of a ceremonial staircase, brought on a hand trolley with the day's delivery of food. Towels of an appropriate color had also been requested by Max, from which replicas of the South Moluccan flag had been hand-sewn. A wooden rod had been wrenched from the train fittings to serve as a flagpole.

If the scene had its element of comic opera, it was nonetheless a colorful and emotional occasion. Josina Soumokil, the mother figure from the mother island of Ceram, widow of the most revered of South Moluccan freedom fighters, had come to talk to her sons. They were young men occupying a tiny strip of territory on behalf of the RMS, flying the RMS flag, and prepared to give their lives for the cause. However strained the circumstances, for hijacker and contact person alike, it was a proud moment.

According to Moluccan tradition, the meeting, which was held not in the command post but in the rear part of the first-class section, began with a prayer. Standing before the improvised flag, Mrs. Soumokil prayed first for the South Moluccan people and for an end to their sufferings whether in Holland or in Indonesia. Then she prayed for forgiveness for the boys who had taken part in the actions—naughty boys, she called them—actions that had involved innocent people, but actions in which they had participated not for themselves but for all South Moluccans, out of love for their country.

After saying how honored they were to see Mrs. Soumokil, Max defended himself over the retention of innocent hostages. "The hijacking need not have lasted so long if the Dutch Government had kept its promise. It should have been finished a week ago. Then there would have been no need for you to come."

Tan, who was received less warmly, actually had to submit to a weapons search. "Why did you bring him?" asked Max. Mrs. Soumokil gave a thumbs-up sign. "He is good." Tan explained that he came as a doctor and elder brother to give a helping hand. He felt it an honor, one he had done nothing to deserve. But the boys needed contact with people outside the train, and he hoped to help fulfill that need. At the mention of the people outside the train, Max bridled. "They've made fools of us. We've been betrayed. We don't trust them any more."

Tan was out of his depth, and his diffidence was not alleviated when Max indicated that he wanted a word in private with Mrs. Soumokil. He wanted to ask her to pass a note to Pieter Tuny requesting him to find out whether the Boeing 747 he had asked for could land in Vietnam. If not, could they go to Hanoi as passengers on a special flight? Max still believed in the integrity of the Vietnam contact. Failing one of these alternatives, could they go to Yemen? A third possibility mentioned by Max was Benin (formerly Dahomey). The government of this Marxist state had shown an encouraging sympathy for the South Moluccans in their struggle for independence, and the president had received a delegation from the Tamaëla faction (rival to Manusama), allowing them to set up an office in Cotonou. If not an ideal haven, it would solve the immediate problem.

Up to this point, Max was still not aware that the period for naming a destination had been arbitrarily ended. In vain did Tan explain to him that the government had withdrawn its offer. Max could not and would not accept it. He rehearsed the circumstances of the government's promise in great detail and convinced his visitors of his sincerity.

Despite the urgency expressed by the Dutch Government, the talks took on the gossipy recapitulation of a family gathering, entirely consistent with Moluccan tradition. How were things in the villages? Not much change. And in Manusama's government? Not much change there either! For Tan, this meeting was precursory, to establish personal contact, and he was feeling his way. But in the five hours and forty minutes that the talks lasted, he had ample time to observe the state of mind of the hijackers. He regarded them, physically and mentally, as normal. They laughed, joked, chatted, and reasoned, and showed no sign of mental imbalance. Their morale was high, and he found no evidence of the group disintegration sensed by Mulder. Rather he was impressed by their solidarity. He talked to the boys individually and found no hint of their consciousness being narrowed or their sense of responsibility being diminished. The only point on which he agreed with Mulder was that Max saw himself in a sort of Che Guevara role. The whole thing would have been over days ago, he felt, if the government had kept its promise. But it had been made abundantly clear to him that that solution was no longer available, and he had one more go at Max before he left.

"As Mrs. Soumokil has already mentioned, you have been naughty boys. As naughty boys at school, you expect punishment. But there are many kinds of punishment. If you have not killed anyone, your punishment will be less."

"We have no intention of killing anyone," said Max. "Even if someone tries to escape, we shall not kill them. But there must be a bus and a plane."

"Give me a letter with your demands that I can take to the Dutch Government."

Max went and wrote the letter, and when he returned he said, "I want you to give that letter not to the management center but personally to van Agt."

Returning to the bunker in Assen, Tan reported that the hijackers had interpreted the government's assurance at the time of the release of the children as a promise of a free passage and could not accept that such a promise could be withdrawn. It was impossible, he said, to forecast what the result of his contact, which was still in the first phase, might be. He had with him a letter for van Agt, which he wished to deliver personally. His refusal to hand it over there and then occasioned some surprise. "It is my moral duty," he said, "I have given my promise. It is to prevent further communication problems. It doesn't mean that I don't trust you. The boys in the train are prepared to give their lives, so there must be no more misunderstandings."

Aerial view of the train at De Punt, showing the curve of the track as it heads toward Groningen. *Air Division of the Rijkspolitie*

Aerial view of the primary school at Bovensmilde. The South Moluccan section of town lies at the top of the picture. *Air Division of the Rijkspolitie*

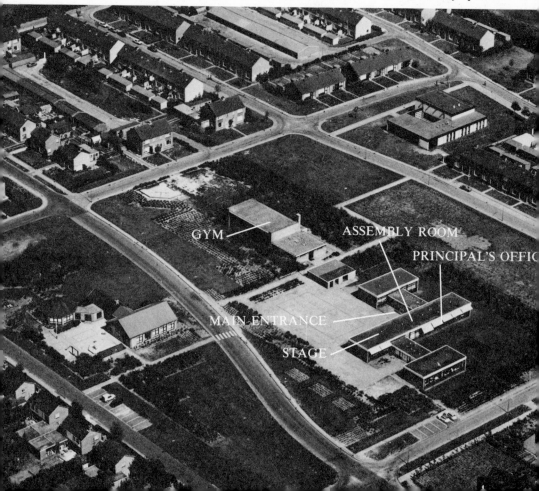

GYM

ASSEMBLY ROOM

PRINCIPAL'S OFFIC

MAIN ENTRANCE

STAGE

Andre Schager, bound and blindfolded, standing outside the train at De Punt.
Rob Brijker Press

A delivery of food is made to the school while a masked terrorist stands
guard. *ANP*

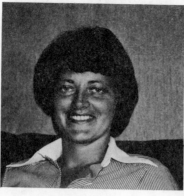

Some of the hostages from the De Punt train: Top (left to right)—Ansje Monsjou, Mini Loman, George Flapper (shown with his wife after rescue). Middle (left to right)—J.W. Fakkert, Jan Cuppen, A.L. Bramer. Bottom left (left to right)—Berend van der Struik, J.W. Fakkert, A.J. Dijkman, G.J. Hogervorst. Bottom right—Joop Hoogenboon. *ANP* and *ANEFO* and *Private Collections*

P.W. Lokollo, vice-president of the self-styled South Moluccan government-in-exile. *Photo by Tjerk S. de Vries*

Mrs. Josina Soumokil and Dr. Hassan Tan surrounded by journalists after a visit to the De Punt train. *ANP*

CHAPTER 24

The Third Week

F OR THE SECOND WEEKEND in succession, the flat fields of Zuidlaren
became a place of pilgrimage for thousands of sightseers, many of
whom arrived with binoculars and picnic baskets as in the Noel Coward
satire of a family outing on an English Bank Holiday. ("Let's go down to
that park where that girl was murdered." "I'll cut some sandwiches.")
Many took up their vigil near the canal running alongside the Assen–
Groningen road. But none were allowed within a mile of the train. All they
could see, beyond the pastures where farmers carried on working uncon-
cernedly and Friesian cows grazed, was the dim yellow outline of the train.

Throughout the visit of Dr. Tan and Mrs. Soumokil, the train hostages,
under orders from the hijackers, were obliged to sit still and keep quiet.
They could talk only in whispers, and they were not allowed to go to the
lavatory. This enforced inactivity, over a period of nearly six hours, added
greatly to the atmosphere of uncertainty and suspense.

The mediators saw nothing of the hostages, so they were unable to
express any opinion on their condition—a matter that was greatly exercising the government. As for the hostages, they heard on the radio that there
were to be negotiations that afternoon, and some of them had been told
by the hijackers that the government was ignoring their plight. Now at
last it seemed that things were moving.

The news that reached the Dutch Government that evening, however,
was that the talks had produced nothing new, and they at once invited
Lokollo and his group to The Hague in order to restate their position in
the clearest possible terms. The lives and work of many thousands of
people were being disrupted. There could be no more discussion of any
kind about the hijackers' demands. Release of all the hostages and a return

to law and order were urgent requirements, and a second meeting with the two contact persons must take place as soon as possible at which all this must be stated. The group was asked to convey this at once to Dr. Tan and Mrs. Soumokil, and this was done next day at a meeting at Ede. Curiously enough, nothing was said at this meeting about a destination for the hijackers, Dr. Tan being unaware of the problem, Mrs. Soumokil relying on the help of Pieter Tuny, and the Lokollo group assuming that the hijackers knew where they wanted to go and had made the necessary arrangements.

Invited to go to Mrs. Soumokil's home in Assen for a meeting, Pieter Tuny took his friends Jack Ririmasse and Pede Metekohy, both of whom were related to one or another of the hijack groups. Although Tuny had had a brother in the Wijster train and now had another at De Punt, neither had ever hinted to Pieter of his involvement. After the Wijster incident, Thys had said, "When you say you will never surrender you don't give in," but that had been his only comment. Junus Ririmasse had told Tuny sometime earlier that he might be involved in some action, but Tuny had stressed the pointlessness of it. "You saw what happened in 1975." Junus had said he thought they had a country to go to this time, but he had added that he intended to withdraw from the group. "Don't count on negotiations with Vietnam," Tuny had warned. "They have never been official."

Confronted now with Max's note, which mentioned three possible havens—Vietnam, Yemen, and Benin—and asked him to do his best to confirm one of them as a destination before Mrs. Soumokil's next visit to the train, Tuny expostulated. "This is ridiculous! What are they thinking about? Do they expect us to go shopping for them at this stage? It's not so easy!" Next day he visited the Moluccan crisis center in Capelle, where the impression he got was that, although no official approaches had been made, he could write down Benin for sure.

Meanwhile the government, while debating the possibilities, was still holding back from a military assault. Tan, for his part, having declared that he could only deliver his message to van Agt, waited to be contacted. As for the group in the train, they still believed that, as long as they stood firm, the government would give in.

Contact with the school was still confined to routine matters. Any queries of a sensitive nature were countered by the hijackers with a blank: "I don't know." Conditions in the school were far more comfortable than in the train. The entire building was occupied; sleeping and washing facilities were adequate; and movement was not unduly restricted. The teachers accepted the hijackers as idealists rather than criminals, and for long periods they sat and talked with them, while the management center attempted no contact. As for the children, most of them were now attending an improvised school, though the parents had insisted on police protection for them. The South Moluccan children were kept at home.

The psychological battle between Mulder and Max continued. Mulder's aim was to insinuate a disciplined routine into domestic matters that would bring home to the hijackers that their role was being reversed. Instead of issuing commands, they were obeying them. Meals were delivered at fixed times. Special meals were no longer allowed, everyone having to eat the same food. Crockery was substituted for the paper plates, cups, and bowls supplied hitherto, the hijackers being warned to take care of it and return it for further use. When Mulder suggested another delivery of clean underwear, Max agreed and casually asked for sixty pairs. Mulder said this was too vague. He had to know individual sizes, which Max then had to provide. Mulder's methods introduced a pattern and rhythm into the day-to-day living situation, and the hijackers found themselves cooperating. Even the night's rest somehow came under Mulder's direction. "Well, fellers," he would say at about 9:30 each evening, "I'm off to sleep. If you need me, then of course I'm available, but we've had a tiring day." This was generally accepted by the hijackers, although Max always laid down the next time of contact.

The government's policy did not meet with unanimous approval. It was one thing, said one of its critics, to keep the situation off the boil and try to insure that events ran smoothly for the hostages and quite another to allow the hijackers to become complacent. Pressure ought to be applied continually, and the gunmen should be repeatedly told that their position was hopeless. It should be made clear to them that, if there was any shooting, they themselves would be the first victims. It could be hinted that, if they gave themselves up, they might get lighter sentences (Tan had already done this). Otherwise their fate would be either death or a lifetime in jail. There should be no restful letups or useless conferences.

Dutch public opinion, which up to this point had approved a policy of firmness with caution, began to show show signs of impatience. Ministers sometimes faced harassment when they appeared in public. One man even grabbed de Gaay Fortman by the coat. "You coward!" he said. "The marines could finish this in five minutes—and you don't dare do anything!" De Gaay Fortman's explanation that it was no good getting angry, and that the lives of the terrorists also had to be considered, only increased the man's fury. A Dutch group from Zwolle offered themselves as replacement hostages, but this sort of palliative had never appealed to the government, and it did not do so now.

The one hopeful sign came through Rosemary Oostveen's repeated warnings to Max of the physical and mental strain the delay was imposing on the two pregnant women. Although both women had remained defiantly cheerful and had even been an important focus of morale, Rosemary feared that they might be nearer to mental and physical breakdown than they pretended. Both were suffering from minor debilities that could be due to inactivity but might be more serious. "They could become desperately ill if you don't release them," she told Max. "And where would that leave you? You will be to blame, and your whole action will be discredited." She was also urging the release of Theo van Hattem, the man who had suffered the collapse the previous week. Some of the hijackers were resentful of her urgings, and there were times when it seemed that she might be jeopardizing her position, but she persisted, finally accusing Max of being a sadist. "Rosemary has called me a sadist for not releasing the two women," Max told the hostages, "and as I don't want to be a sadist I'm letting them go." This was on Sunday, June 5, and the only condition Max made, when he called Mulder, was that the women be exchanged for an RMS flag. They must not be collected by ambulance as that would give a false impression of their state of health and mobility. Mulder offered the help of Dr. Tutuhatunewa, who could examine the women before their release and pronounce on their fitness to walk from the train, and Max accepted. Mulder managed the whole operation discreetly and unofficially, lest news that an RMS flag had been delivered to the terrorists give offense to Indonesia. The Dutch Government wanted nothing to do with it.

Tutuhatunewa collected a flag and staff from Bovensmilde and, after a talk with Mulder, left in a police car for the train. Because the flagstaff might attract the notice of journalists, he left it behind in the bunker. Tutuhatunewa left the car one kilometer from the train and set off with his medical bag and a plastic bag containing the flag, accompanied by one of the food-delivery men carrying boots and raincoats for the two women. The hijackers formed a guard of honor, and the doctor boarded the train at the rear and was introduced to his charges. They seemed perfectly well, as did the hijackers themselves, each one of whom he examined. But when he inquired about the health of the other hostages, Max said, "We have a medical student for them."

"Take care that no blood flows," said the doctor, "otherwise we shall be left to pick up the political splinters."

"I guarantee that nothing will happen to them," said Max. "All their wishes will be granted except their freedom. They are only suffering the same lack of freedom as the people in occupied Ambon."

There was a round of hand-shaking before the doctor left with the women. "I hope," said one of them to the hijackers, "that your case will soon come to a good end."

Back in the bunker in Assen, Tutuhatunewa reported on his visit. He had found the hijackers balanced, frank, and straightforward, and he was satisfied that no harm would come to the hostages. But he added that the hijackers had been adamant that they had been promised a safe-conduct passage. "I have never made such a promise," said Mulder. In a subsequent conversation with Tutuhatunewa, he appeared to concede that someone else might have done so.

When news of their forthcoming release was first given to the two women, van der Struik observed that they showed no great elation. They had never wanted special treatment. "Remarkable proof of solidarity," he noted in his diary.

The superficial verdict on the two women when they reached Groningen was that they looked surprisingly well and seemed in excellent shape, but a more considered opinion had to await a fuller examination. Everyone in the train, said Nelleke Ellenbroek, was suffering extreme mental stress, and many were troubled by minor ills, such as sores and constipation. But the hijackers had treated them "correctly."

Annie Brouwers said, "The people in the train are in reasonable physical condition, but the main problems are boredom and lack of exercise." They needed more games and books, and more wool for their embroidery, for which there had been an unexpected demand. "Even some of the men have started needlework because of the boredom." On the whole, apart from the reference to mental stress, the impression given was that the health situation was tolerable. It looked as though the hostages could probably stand many more days of captivity. Satisfying as the news of the release was, it carried no suggestion that the hijacking might soon be over.

Dr. van Dyck said he believed that up to a point the longer the sieges went on, the greater the hostages' chance of survival. "There is another risk, however. If you wait too long, you may have to contend with exhaustion and loss of control. The hijackers may start doing dangerous things. It's an extraordinarily difficult thing to evaluate, just where the line is drawn between one phase and the next. The man dealing with them by telephone has to be highly skilled." He drew attention to a difficulty that had been encountered from the beginning. "They will have learned from the tactics used by the government at Wijster and become wary of being talked down by psychiatrists." Gerry Vaders wrote on the same subject in his newspaper, *Nieuwsblad van het Noorden.* The loser in a war tended to learn more than the winner. Experience might produce a brand of terrorist immune to the subtleties of psychiatry. There was even a feeling in police circles that an averagely intelligent policeman might after all be the best direct contact.

The released women were able to confirm that there were thirty-six men and sixteen women still in the train, and they carried reassuring messages from many of them. They were also able to give the precise disposition of hijackers and hostages, where they congregated in daytime and where they slept—information that would be invaluable if it came to an assault.

The likelihood of such an assault grew daily. Max stuck to his demands despite assurances from Mulder that the government was no longer willing to concede unimpeded departure, and van Doorn and Zeevalking impressed on the Lokollo group that, if an end didn't come soon through a return to law and order, it would come by violence. There remained the letter from the train that Dr. Tan had declared he could only deliver to van Agt. After the ministerial council had consulted on Tuesday, June 7, about the line to follow, van Agt got in touch with Tan by telephone.

"You have a message for me?"

"Yes."

"Can you tell me what it is?"

"No. You will understand that I can't do that on the telephone."

"It's now about 4:30 PM. Could we meet at the Provincial Assembly House in Assen at 8:30?"

"All right."

Mrs. Soumokil was alerted, and the two contact persons, together with Frieda Tomasoa, secretary to Lokollo's crisis center, delivered the letter personally to van Agt. By that time Tan had had the letter in his possession for more than three days. But it contained nothing new. No doubt Dr. Mulder, through his contacts with Max—he had had a long talk with him the previous afternoon—had foreseen that. After restating his version of the promises given before the release of the children, Max repeated his demands for a bus, a plane, and the release of the Moluccan prisoners in exchange for hostages. There was still no mention of a destination. The letter continued: "Have we gone one step further? No. The Dutch Government has betrayed us, Moluccans and hostages. It has not kept its word. Can you blame us that some of us have lost their trust because Jopie [Joop den Uyl] and Dries [Andreas van Agt] and their colleagues have not kept their word? Are our demands unreasonable? Once before we have been raped by the Dutch Government. We won't let it happen a second time."

Van Agt read the letter in front of them, then shook his head. "We have never made any promise." Tan was in no position to argue. "My function is simply as a contact person. I cannot discuss this point with you."

Van Agt said the government completely rejected the demands of the hijackers. "So many people have now been held hostage for so long that the government's view is that the law should follow its course." The government was bracing itself for the military option.

In a last effort to avoid this solution, Dr. Tan and Mrs. Soumokil declared themselves ready, despite their disappointment, to pass the government's answer on to the hijackers. Van Agt accepted gratefully, and it was agreed that they should go to the train a second time. "Keep yourselves in readiness," said van Agt.

Tan appreciated that if he went back to the train empty-handed, Max and his group would hold out stubbornly, and a catastrophe would follow. In desperation, he went back to his home in Rolde and worked all night with his family on the composition of a face-saving solution that would, he hoped, offer a way out for both sides. Early on Wednesday morning, June 8, he drove to the bunker and showed his plan to Mulder. Mulder supported its submission to the Dutch Government, and Tan for his part announced his intention of taking a copy to the South Moluccan crisis center at Capelle. At 2:40 that afternoon, he and Mrs. Soumokil left Assen by helicopter for Rotterdam and Capelle, where his plan was backed unanimously. Among those present were Manusama, by invitation, and Etty Aponno. Mulder, called that day to report to The Hague on his contacts with Max, took a copy of the plan with him.

Tan saw the essence of his plan, which contained twenty-two points in all, as: (1) the restoration of law and order, which meant that the hijackers must lay down their weapons and release their hostages, and (2) the avoidance of loss of face by both parties. In general, the aims and sentiments of the plan, involving a willingness on both sides to find a new way to a harmonious society in the Netherlands, were wholly admirable. But the manner in which the second objective—the avoidance of loss of face —was to be achieved asked too much of any government. The hijackers were not to go to prison, or even to stand trial. Instead, they were to be sent to a "positive" approved school exclusively for South Moluccan accused. Punishments meted out to those accused of murder in 1975 were to be remitted, and other punishments for past acts of terrorism were to be "adjusted." In return, there was to be no more disorderly conduct by

South Moluccans, who were to work with the Dutch in a number of ways toward the harmony envisaged. How this was to be guaranteed was not stated. The plan was kept secret, but, to anyone who knew the details, it must have been painfully obvious that it was a nonstarter.

The possibility of a military assault had been increasingly discussed by the hostages in the train. Some favored it and even thought it long overdue, but the majority were firmly against it. All without exception feared it. Those who favored it pointed to the suitability of the terrain for a surprise attack via river, dike, and ditch and believed that if it had to come, then the sooner the better. Flapper thought a decision must come soon one way or the other. Either the hijackers would give in, or there would be an attack. But many believed that a successful attack, without killing a large number of hostages, was impracticable. Rosemary, for one, thought there would be far too many casualties to justify such action. What did the hijackers think? This was likely to be the decisive factor.

Again and again, Max had assured the women that he would not be taken alive and that he would never go to prison. It seemed like an invitation to the military to come and get him. "Remember what it says in the Bible," Saskia told him. "Those who live by the sword shall perish by the sword. Realize what you are doing. You're carrying a gun, and if the marines come, there's a good chance you'll be shot."

"We know that," said Max. Hitherto Max had believed, with Rosemary, that the government would hold back because of the likely cost to the hostages. Now he was not so sure. This drove him to a drastic change of policy. "We are only living for the Moluccas," he told the men. "For us, it is departure or death. And if we die, you die. Either they meet our demands or we will all die, you included." The men could scarcely believe he would do it. He did not make this threat to the women.

Several of the men, among them van der Struik, Fakkert, Flapper, Kroon, and others, tried to reason with him. "If somebody wants something, they want to live for it, not to die. What can you do for the Moluccas when you are dead? A dead warrior isn't a warrior any more. You want to die for your ideals, but isn't it better to live for them?"

"That's true," said one of the hijackers.

But Max said, "If we die, there will be others to take our place."

Kees Bimmel was one who took the threat of an assault seriously. The windows in the second-class entrance hall where he slept were left uncovered, and every night he stood up and undressed by candlelight, making sure that his silhouette would be visible from a distance. He reasoned from his own brief military experience that the marines would come at night, and that they would have to find some point, probably one of the entrance halls, to break into the train. He wanted to make sure they knew where he and his friends were sleeping. Others, Joop Huismans among them, thought that Bimmel and his group were taking an unnecessary chance. In the face of the confident predictions of his neighbor van der Struik that the marines would come, he had always argued that it was impossible, but he could never quite convince himself.

In fact, the marines had a pretty accurate idea where hostages and hijackers lived and slept. In addition to bugging devices, infrared photography, infiltration, and the evidence of the pregnant women, there was a moment almost daily, just before sunset, when the light penetrated the covered windows and revealed a breakable code of assorted heads.

To the hostages, there seemed no way of protecting themselves in the event of an attack, and they began to think about alternatives. Bimmel decided that he could escape quite easily. On a dark night, wearing his dark green coat, he could squeeze through a window, dash across the rails, and dive into the bushes, where he could hide. No one would come after him in the darkness. All he then had to do was negotiate one or two dikes and ditches, and he would be clear. But he was inhibited by Max's threat to kill two for every one who escaped. He still hadn't made up his mind whether or not Max would kill, but he knew the uncertain temperament of South Moluccans and did not dare take a chance. Van der Struik's ideas were more ambitious. "Why don't we take over the train?" He believed the Moluccans would show no more than token resistance. It might even be a relief to them. "There are some nice chaps among them," he argued. Or perhaps they should all walk out. He doubted if the Moluccans would do anything to stop them. But no one took him seriously. He contented himself by continuing his signaling by heliograph: COME AND GET US OUT OF HERE.

Once, during a delivery of food, van der Struik turned his window down and shouted, "Tell those buggers out there we're getting fed up in here. Some are going nuts. Suggest to van Agt that he change places with us for a while." His outburst was received by his fellow hostages with a mixture of merriment and disapproval.

In the fight against depression and boredom, the hostages were doing rather better than their captors. Jan Cuppen, finding that his role of tatterdemalion was unpopular, took his share of the latest delivery of underwear and ended his pajama game; it had not been his intention to irritate his fellows. But his satirical good humor remained proof against

ennui. The boredom of the terrorists took various forms. They fired specu-
lative shots at distant observation posts; they strayed outside the train to
pick wild flowers; they fell asleep on guard, letting their Uzis fall from
their laps; they played cards, checkers, and monopoly with their hostages;
they vandalized unoccupied parts of the train. Finding that the men still
mostly ignored them, they baited the women, chalking up slogans like:
"Your government is letting you die," and "Tomorrow you will all be
dead." At this, some of the women became almost hysterical, and when
Saskia complained to Max, he gave the culprits—it was mostly Ronnie
and Jo—a dressing down. But to Saskia, he excused them. "My men must
do something. It is better that they work off their aggression like this than
in some other way."

One of the greatest fears of the hostages remained that Max might lose
control and be overthrown. The same risk was continually being assessed
outside the train. Max himself seems to have been aware of the danger,
and during the third week the hostages discovered that he was calling
daily meetings in a rear carriage, presumably to maintain group identity
and bolster morale. The hostages, guessing the purpose of these gather-
ings, dubbed them "courage sessions."

Early on that Wednesday morning, Max called for the two contact
persons to come to the train at two o'clock in the afternoon; he hoped by
then that there would be an answer from Pieter Tuny. Newspapers carrying reports unfavorable to the hijackers' chances of being offered asylum
had been diligently sent to the train, and Max was getting anxious. But
with Tan on his way to Capelle and Mulder to The Hague, the second
Tan/Soumokil visit was put off for twenty-four hours.

At The Hague, Mulder expressed his confidence that his methods would
get results in the end. As for Tan's criticism of his assessment of the
hijackers' mental state, Mulder protested that no one who had been in the
management center throughout could evaluate the actions and behavior
of the hijackers any differently. It did not need a psychiatrist. Common
sense, he felt, supported the view that the hijackers had acted from a
narrowness of perception, and that they were living in a world bordering
on fantasy. This was the chasm he was trying to bridge, and he appealed
for more time to continue the attempt. But he had to admit that he had
very little to show for sixteen days of talk, except in the negative sense that
no one had been seriously hurt. Even this was arguable. The government
had to evaluate the cumulative effect on the hostages, and Mulder, believing as he did that the psychological results of the 1975 sieges had been
greatly underestimated, understood their concern. It was clear to him

that, unless the situation changed dramatically in the next few days, the government would act.

Returning to Assen, and picking up the threads of his conversations with Max, Mulder was faced with a further dilemma. He did not feel able to pass on his sense of imminent crisis to Max, except indirectly. Otherwise it would sound like a threat. The possibility of military intervention, he felt, had been implicit in the situation from the beginning and must increase as time passed. The hijackers would know about the preparations that had been made for an attack on the consulate in 1975, also the attack on Scheveningen Jail, and in their comments they had let Mulder know they were prepared for anything. "We are ready to go to the limit," Max had said. But to face them with a direct threat would undermine the atmosphere of mutual confidence he had tried to rebuild since the events of the first Friday.

It was no part of his job to scare the terrorists into submission. Frightened terrorists could be doubly dangerous. He indulged in no preaching, no recriminations. "Max," he said, "let's face the different possibilities . . ." One of those possibilities was an assault on the train. That was as far as he felt he could go.

He had pointed out repeatedly his belief that Ambon was overromanticized and that South Moluccans, accustomed to life in Holland, would find it intolerable, but this made no impression. Now he tried to help Max extricate himself from his quandary over a destination. "As far as I can judge, there is perhaps one country—and here I'm not speaking officially, but purely as Dick Mulder—that might accept you, and that is Uganda, the country of Idi Amin. Would it really be consistent with your ideals to go to such a country, not being sure what purpose they'd use you for and whether or not you'd be alive next day?" But Max would not be drawn out on this subject.

Theo van Hattem's swollen jaw was giving him more and more discomfort, and he was scarcely able to eat. The previous night Rosemary had consigned him to the "royal stables." He had been there no more than an hour when he complained of a pain in his chest. Rosemary gave him a pill to ease the pain and slept on the opposite couch to be near him, but the pain persisted. On Wednesday morning, Saskia told Max that if he didn't let the man out at once he'd have a death on his conscience. Rosemary, less dramatically, told him much the same thing. "Please, Max, let him go. It's dangerous to keep him here. He's very ill."

"Are you convinced of that?"

"I really am. Letting him die won't help your cause. You'll be held responsible."

Max never made instant decisions, always saying he needed time to consult the others, but about 9:30 he called the management center and asked for an ambulance. When he returned to the compartment, he announced his decision. "Our Theo is going out of the train to the hospital." Everyone *clapped*. "We hope," added Max, "that he'll soon be out of the hospital too."

By this act of humanity, Max virtually sealed his fate and that of his group. Van Hattem spoke well of his captors after his release, saying, "They are not bad boys." He revealed that the greatest fear of the hostages was an assault from outside. They would rather stay in the train another three weeks. But Professor Jacob Nieveen, head of cardiology at Groningen University Hospital, where van Hattem was taken, warned that many of the fifty-one remaining hostages might not be able to stand what he called "the intolerable strain" much longer. Of van Hattem, he said, "Although this man has no history of heart trouble, he developed a definite abnormality on the train. He was in pain and in fact had what amounted to a very small heart attack." The hostages on the train were exposed to continual stress, lack of exercise, and a fatty diet that might soon bring more of them down with heart problems. His fears, he explained, were based on van Hattem's description of conditions on the train and on his own assessment that many of the hostages, those of forty and above, were in an age group prone to cardiac illness under stress situations. "From what we know of this patient, I no longer rule out the worst for the health of the others."

If Professor Nieveen was exaggerating the risks, it was from the best of motives. The terrorists might be persuaded to let the hostages go. But the effect was different. Max, with the help of Rosemary, could make his own firsthand assessment of the dangers he was running so far as the hostages were concerned. He saw no reason to panic. The government could only evaluate the situation from firsthand knowledge in three exceptional cases. For the rest, they had to rely on past experience and psychiatric and medical advice.

When it came to weighing up the advantages and disadvantages of an assault on the train, such advice suddenly became scarce. Many experts to whom the government turned refused to answer, other than in the vaguest terms. Every individual had his or her breaking point, that much was admitted. But to evaluate when that point might be reached in a given situation was pure guesswork. The government was approaching the point where fear for the many was inclining them to risk injuring the few, but they were not reaching this conclusion on medical or psychiatric advice. Should they wait for just one of the hostages to become physically or mentally crippled, or for 10 percent or 20 percent or 50 percent, before taking action that might result in many deaths and would certainly have political consequences? A medical man who gave advice on a matter of that kind might find his reputation for professional objectivity sullied. It had to be a political decision.

CHAPTER 25

The Second Tan/Soumokil Visit

A T ELEVEN O'CLOCK on Thursday morning, June 9, Dr. Tan telephoned Dr. Mulder to confirm that he would be calling at the management center at about 1:00 PM preparatory to going to the train. Would Baron van der Feltz and Dr. Mulder cast their thoughts in the meantime over the first two points in his plan, namely the restoration of law and order, and the prevention of loss of face for both parties.

When he arrived at the management center, Tan was given the government's replies to these two points by Mulder. Dealing with them in reverse order, the government said it could not accept the second point, as it could be interpreted in various ways and might lead to misunderstanding. On the first point, although the government backed it 100 percent, they also felt unable to give an answer in black and white as this again could lead to various interpretations. "Dr. Mulder," said Tan bleakly, "you hand us a sentence of death."

Mulder did not reply, and Tan continued, "You won't give us anything concrete. I must have an alternative. We have to meet the boys empty-handed. What can or must we tell them?"

The government's position had already been made clear to the mediators by van Agt, and they had agreed to communicate it to the hijackers. Now they were reminded by van der Feltz that, in view of the deterioration in the hostages' health, the government wanted an early end to the siege and would not yield to any demand that was contrary to the law. Unless release was swift, serious consequences would follow. Military intervention was not specifically mentioned, but van der Feltz felt that the two contact persons must be well aware that a termination by force was

303

a serious possibility. For Tan, after his efforts to find a solution, the government's rigid attitude was a bitter rebuff.

The intention had been for the mediators to be accompanied this time by Frieda Tomasoa, so that some record of the conversations could be made, but Max insisted on receiving them alone, and at 2:30 PM they went to the train. After the formalities of the welcome and prayers, Tan conveyed the Dutch Government's message. The health of the hostages was now the overriding anxiety, and the law must follow its course. Max then withdrew briefly with Mrs. Soumokil, and she handed him a note from Pieter Tuny. It said simply: "Vietnam—no, Yemen—no, Benin—yes."

Max returned to the compartment in an uncompromising mood. "Our attitude remains the same. We shall not depart from it. An aircraft or death."

"Van Agt says you have never been promised a plane," said Tan. "He regards the matter of a free departure as closed, because you failed to avail yourself of the opportunity by naming the country of destination within the set time limit."

"We know nothing of a set time limit." This was substantially true. Mulder had explained to Max that the government would have to set such a limit, but the final warning had been passed not to Max but to the school. "We have been betrayed," repeated Max. "We have been promised a free passage, and it would be madness to reveal our destination. No other hijackers would do that."

Max still would not accept that the offer of a free departure could be withdrawn. He still believed that, if he called the government's bluff, he must win. Tan tried in vain to disabuse him. "A plane at government expense? Forget it. It's finished." But Max would not let go.

Despite the note he had just received from Pieter Tuny, Max again mentioned Vietnam as a possible destination. Mrs. Soumokil said, "You will be branded as terrorists, and Vietnam won't want you." "Then we'll go to Benin," said Max.

Tan reminded the hijackers that, if they persisted, the next stage would be some act of controlled violence by the government, following which the best they could hope for, assuming they survived, was a prison sentence. "Let them come," was the reaction. "We are not afraid." And Max said: "None of us is prepared to go to prison, not even for one hour of our lives. The first RMS president gave his life for our ideal. Who are we to do less?" When Mrs. Soumokil demurred, Max said, "Maybe it is necessary that we sacrifice ourselves. Perhaps then we shall get recognition."

"Let's talk about the pros and cons if you're killed," said Tan. "We don't want to lose young people like you. What will your death mean? I have great respect for your ideals, but it will mean a loss in the fight for independence. You are needed to build up the South Moluccan community. We shall benefit more from young lives than young deaths, especially of youngsters like you who have pledged your heart and soul to our mother country."

"For each dead South Moluccan," countered Max, "others are ready to carry on the fight."

Tan said he had produced an alternative plan. Perhaps it might yet form the basis of a compromise. "Whichever way the situation develops, we have to live in the midst of and with the Dutch population. The relationship between the Dutch and the South Moluccans is now so strained that daily contact has become dangerous for both groups. We advise you to give up the battle." He stressed again that, as no one had been killed, their punishment would be less.

To this the hijackers remained silent, until Max said, "We haven't yet heard your alternative plan." After Tan had outlined it briefly, Max turned to the other members of the group and put the question to them one by one. "What do you think of this plan?" All those present declared without exception that they were unanimous in sticking to their previously adopted attitude. "Departure or death. For us there is no other way."

There was nothing more Tan could do. Whether the presence of Mrs. Soumokil, with its poignant reminder of the guerrilla struggle waged by her husband, influenced the hijackers is an imponderable. She seems to have supported Tan. But evidence that Tan's persuasive arguments made some impression came before the two mediators left the train. Whether it was anything more than a moment's remorse for the dejection of the worthy Dr. Tan is doubtful.

It was Rudi who spoke. "The idea of Dr. Tan is a humane one, and we are human beings. Although at this moment we all agree about the stand we have taken, we cannot and must not exclude the possibility that at another moment God can order us to act differently."

Tan looked questioningly at Max. "We will think it over," said Max. "Each of us has the right to think it over."

"God has the last word," said Rudi. "We will follow His will."

For Tan, if it was not a ray of light, it was at least a glimmer. "We have no direct telephone line to you. Please tell Dr. Mulder if you want to see us again."

Tan was given a letter to take with him, addressed to the government, and he was also asked to convey the hijackers' point of view to the management center in writing. When he asked if he could include mention of the "glimmer of light" shed by Rudi, he was told that he could. Reporting this to van der Feltz and Mulder, he admitted that he was clutching at a straw. But it had given him hope. "We expect an important message," he said. "Please call us at once if we're wanted. We're quite prepared to go back to the train a third time." But the government regarded Tan's optimism as misplaced and saw no grounds for hope, and Tan was not to know that the letter he was carrying from Max would effectively extinguish his "glimmer of light."

The letter read as follows:

We shall not depart from our attitude. We demand compliance with the demands you received from the two mediators Mrs. Soumokil and Dr. Tan. We have only two things in view. Either departure or death.

We South Moluccan Youth who are at present on the train will not die alone, but all the passengers will follow us, if the Dutch Government is unwilling to agree to our demands.

Do not think that this is some kind of game. Exactly what is more important? An aircraft or the lives of the passengers?

It had been the government's hope that the terrorists did not have the stomach to allow serious physical harm to come to their hostages. Their threats that there would be victims had not been carried out, and they had shown their concern for the health of their hostages in various ways. But Max had repeatedly said that he was prepared to hold out for six months or a year, that they would never take him prisoner, and that he was prepared to go to the limit. The military option had always been regarded as a last resort, but Max's latest letter seemed to leave no alternative.

The problem facing the government was to choose the method and the moment that would insure maximum preservation of life. It was a critical and self-searching exercise. The aim was to release the hostages before they suffered irreversible damage, with minimum danger to the hostages themselves and to the forces employed. The hijackers would be expendable. Indeed, to fulfill the objectives, it would be necessary to eliminate them, before they could carry out their threat.

The two contact persons had talked to the train hijackers for ten hours in all. They had not succeeded in changing their attitude. All that had emerged was a new and more desperate threat. Subject to some last-minute development on the lines hoped for by Dr. Tan, the assault on the train appeared likely to take place at the earliest feasible moment.

CHAPTER 26

The Plan for the Assault

WHILE DR. TAN and Mrs. Soumokil were preparing for their second visit to the train, contingency plans for an assault were being carefully rehearsed at the air force base at Gilze Rijen in Brabant—in case this last attempt at mediation should fail. The tentative plan to approach the train in armored railway trucks manned by marines had been tested and found wanting, and a much more sophisticated scheme, involving the use of sharpshooters and a commando attacking force, backed up by jet fighters, had been substituted. This was the plan that was being rehearsed on that Thursday morning. With the cooperation of the media, news of the rehearsal was kept secret. But government sources confirmed that plans were being considered to use military force to seize the train rather than allow the hostages to undergo further weeks of terror. "The government has made it clear that it considers the hostages will be mentally and physically damaged by an indefinite prolongation of the siege. We cannot tolerate the situation much longer. If the talks fail, you can guess what action we would take."

Essential requirements were that the precise conditions obtaining at De Punt should be known and reconstructed. At Gilze Rijen, Netherlands Railways supplied an exact replica of Train No. 747, while two and a half weeks of observation, aerial and ground reconnaissance, and infrared photography, backed up by the evidence of the released hostages, helped to convince the government of the practicability of the scheme. The flat, dike-veined terrain around De Punt, although unsuitable for armored vehicles, had proved compatible with the nocturnal sorties of the marines. Because of the difficulty of identifying friend from foe in complete darkness, however, the attack was to be timed for first light.

Above all, the plan had to insure surprise. Quite apart from the danger of return fire, the initial assault had to preempt any opportunity for the hijackers to turn their guns on their hostages. This was to be achieved by sharpshooters, who were to open the attack by riddling the areas where the hijackers were known to be sleeping, especially the command post at the front of the train. The sharpshooters were to move in under cover of darkness and establish themselves at a point 200 meters north of the train on the east (golf club) side of the track. Simultaneously, marines would be moving in from the same northerly direction, but on the other (highway) side of the track. To gain entry, some of them would carry explosive charges on lances to blow off entrance doors. To confuse the hijackers, a small force of frogmen would plant noisy but harmless fireworks under the train.

It had to be anticipated that, as soon as the firing started, the hijackers would attempt to move through the train, either to congregate for defense or to kill their hostages. Therefore, while the marines shouted at the hostages to keep their heads down, the compartments where hostages were sleeping were to be penetrated by gunfire at shoulder height. But when the firing started, the hostages' instinct might be to jump up and try to escape, which would be fatal. By the time the plan was practiced at Gilze Rijen, the military commanders had requested a refinement involving the use of jet aircraft, designed to make doubly sure that the hostages kept their heads down. Six F104G Starfighter jets of the Royal Dutch Air Force would make a succession of mock attacks on the train, diving down to twenty meters at a speed of 750 kph. By using their afterburners, the fuel-consuming system from which jet engines get extra thrust, they would emit a noise from the rear part of the engine casing that was known to be paralyzing in its effect. When it was practiced at Gilze Rijen that morning, troops representing hostages sitting in the train found that although they knew what was coming it was impossible not to duck.

While the plan for the train was being tempered and proved, a parallel plan was being produced for the school. Here there was no impediment to the use of armored vehicles, giving greater protection to attacking troops. Two or three vehicles were to plow into the flimsy, semiglass structure to gain entry, and marines would rush through the openings thus created, while marksmen prepared to pin down the terrorists and forestall any attempt at resistance. Again, the sleeping quarters of hijackers and hostages were known. Two additional precautions were necessary at the school to achieve surprise. A high level of mechanical noise was to be maintained beforehand in the area of the school, to camouflage the sound of the attack. And the assault on the train would be anticipated by a minute or so, otherwise the occupants of the school would be alerted by the mock air attack on the train.

CHAPTER 27

Friday, June 10—Eve of the Attack

A FTER THE LAST VISIT of the mediators, the atmosphere in the train underwent a subtle change. The boredom and despondency of earlier in the week were replaced by periods of deeper depression, sometimes acute with foreboding. Everybody knew it, though not all of them admitted it—the impasse could only be resolved by violence. "We have burned our bridges," Max told Saskia. And she realized he was at his wits' end. But he still did not tell her what he had told the men.

The contagion of fear had already spread to the families center at Groningen, where relatives, alarmed by rumors that an assault was imminent, demanded some say in the government's policy-making. Marie José Cuppen, accompanied by Peter Blankert's father and with a psychiatrist in attendance, had a meeting with Mrs. Schilthuis, queen's commissioner for the province, but the latter's advice not to try to interfere with decisions on which they did not have the facts to base a judgment came as a rebuff. The rebuff was echoed in a statement by Ministry of Justice spokesman Willem van Leeuwen, who said that the government could not be influenced by third parties. "We share their anxieties, but it is impossible to take them into account if the government is faced with the need to take a vital decision." The crisis team sat until 3:30 that morning without passing judgment, then resumed deliberations after a few hours' rest.

Den Uyl admitted that the situation was critical, but otherwise he was noncommittal. "Yesterday's attempt at mediation produced no concrete proposals that could lead to a breakthrough. Consequently, there will be measures connected with security." The public was left to guess what these might be. A full-blooded attack still seemed unlikely. "Our aim is restoration of the legal order," said de Gaay Fortman, "if possible, without loss of life."

A second letter to the government from the Free South Moluccan Youth and RMS Liberation Front angrily rebutted van Agt's accusation that their earlier letter had been "infamous" and claimed that it had given a true picture of affairs. They asked again for a political approach and demanded to know whether van Agt was a politician or a policeman. They warned against a policy of attrition; it would not bring the hijackers to their knees. "We know our young people, and we know this is the wrong way to go about it. . . ." The Dutch provided a vast budget for South Moluccan affairs, employing many social workers specially engaged to operate among young South Moluccans and well aware of their problems. Why hadn't some of these people been asked to take part in the management of the crisis? The government said they wanted to negotiate, but they did it through completely unrepresentative persons. Dr. Tan, too, had drawn attention to this, believing that South Moluccans should have been continually present in the management center. The government's answer was that suitable South Moluccans were simply not available; it had taken long enough to find two acceptable "contact persons."

The letter again ended on a bitter note. "Different solutions will call for new actions, and these will call for counteractions. This is not what we want, and it is not what the Dutch people want. Does the Dutch Government want it? Perhaps political and economic relations with Indonesia are more important than the lives of sixty people and the suppression of people in Indonesia and a peaceful life in Holland."

Shortly after midday, Mulder called Max in an effort to get the talks moving again, but Max still demanded that the hijackers be allowed to leave the country with the imprisoned South Moluccans. Only on that basis could talks be resumed. When Mulder tried to direct an appeal personally to Max, the South Moluccan insisted that the decision was a corporate one and that he was bound by it. "The government must decide which is more important, an aircraft or fifty-one people. If they play with the lives of these people, they must be out of their minds." Mulder warned Max that the government was "fixed in its point of view." "Think, Max," he urged, "think what the result can be." This was as near as he got to a direct warning that the government was being driven to seek a violent solution. Max replied that he wanted no more contact with Mulder "or anyone else." Max had threatened before to break off the dialogue for good. This time it seemed that he meant it. Mulder reported the conversation to van Agt by telephone. The news finally convinced van Agt that military intervention was unavoidable.

Meanwhile Mrs. Soumokil's efforts to provide the hijackers with a destination had run into difficulties. Rumors that Benin was ready to accept them were denied in the press, and on that Friday the subject was discussed by the Lokollo group at the home of Dr. Tan. The meeting was also attended by Reverend Metiary. A complication was that Benin had no diplomatic representative in Holland, and all communications had to go through the ambassador for Benin in Brussels. Lokollo showed Tan a letter he had written to the ambassador requesting asylum for the hijackers and asked him to take it to Brussels, but Tan refused. He had no diplomatic status and was not even a member of Manusama's government. He would simply be acting, he said, as a messenger boy. The Benin contact was dominated by the Tamaëla faction, and someone should be appointed who had been involved from the beginning in the attempts to secure sanctuary, of which Tan had known nothing. In any case, he wanted to be on hand in case of a change of heart on the part of the hijackers.

After trying various ways of getting the letter to Brussels that night, Lokollo postponed further discussion of the proposal until the next day. He was not to know that Max van der Stoel, the Dutch foreign minister, had already sought and received an assurance from the ambassador that Benin was not willing to accept the hijackers.

A suggestion by Lokollo that the mediators should issue a statement to the press was approved, subject to agreement by van Agt. "It's up to you," said van Agt when Tan telephoned him. "You can make a statement if you wish." Work on the text was begun.

That afternoon van der Struik asked Max if they might be allowed to hear the news. "We are also in this game," he reminded Max. "We are a part of it. Why can't we know what's going on?" "I'll think about it," said Max. And at four o'clock, instead of the usual irritating shutdown at news time, the bulletin was allowed to come through. No progress had been made, they heard, in the talks that had taken place between the two contact persons and the train hijackers, and there had been no developments since. The situation was critical. The government was watching the position carefully. And there was more in this vein—not much to bite on. Yet, to the older hostages, it was reminiscent of broadcasts they had heard in wartime on the eve of great events or when armies were on the move. The platitudes had an air of finality about them. The end must come soon.

In the management center, it was suggested that the hijackers might be given a final warning and a last chance to surrender. Since they would almost certainly be annihilated in the planned assault, this seemed no more than a minimum act of humanity. But the whole success of the operation depended on surprise. Max's letter had promised that death for the hijackers would mean death for the hostages. To warn the hijackers would be to invite them to make the assault as costly as possible, for the assault forces as well. Very likely the hostages would be used as shields. That was something that the planned operation was designed to prevent.

On radio and television that evening, important statements were made from both Dutch and South Moluccan sides. De Gaay Fortman, questioned in the street on his way to the crisis center, asserted that law and order must come first and the lives of the hostages second, a sequence that was reported that evening and received at the families center with dismay. Others who drew the conclusion that an attack was imminent were the teachers, who turned the volume down and somehow contrived to keep their jailers out of earshot during critical moments.

The statement compiled by Dr. Tan and Mrs. Soumokil sounded equally doomlike. "We have failed completely to make the boys on the train change their minds. Unfortunately, we have also not succeeded in convincing the Dutch Government of the seriousness and resolution with which these boys intend to reach their goals." The statement appealed for a compromise and spoke of "the seriousness of the situation, which has now developed because of the obstinate attitude of both sides. The Dutch and South Moluccan peoples must know how fatal the consequences could be." A civil war between white and brown could break out in Holland if the conflict was not resolved. "We appeal most sincerely to the Dutch and South Moluccan peoples to go forward together peacefully."

That evening, the hijackers ordered the recovering of the windows, suggesting a heightened fear of attack from outside. The covering in some parts had become torn and frayed. But they showed no real awareness that an attack might be imminent. Over a period of eighteen days they had seen nothing to indicate preparation for an assault, and they still gambled on the protection offered by their isolated situation and the vulnerability of their hostages. An attack might come soon, but they would be bound to get some warning. A night raid was something they hardly considered. Selective firing in darkness was not thought to be feasible.

There were other events on that Friday, contrived or fortuitous, that conspired to put them off their guard. Tubs of water were delivered for bathing, and the hostages took turns, two at a time, to splash about naked in the entrance halls. A delivery of clothing—new trousers, new T-shirts —and a fresh selection of books, requested that morning, arrived by truck that evening. If these events were not intended to allay suspicions and encourage complacency, they had that effect.

Governing the hijackers' thinking, however subconsciously, was a faith in double standards. Whatever treacheries or deceits they themselves might practice, governments must always play fair.

When the order to recover the windows was given, Marc Hustinx was painting, using art materials sent in from outside. The best covering available was sketching paper. As he flattened a sheet over the window above his seat, he heard the rumbling of thunder and noticed that the distant sky was an ocherous yellow, bilious and malignant. But by the time he had painted flowers on the paper—after asking permission—he felt better.

The same storm was lurking in the area of the school, where the terrorists, standing on guard at the windows, were silhouetted against jagged flashes of lightning. "It's very dangerous," van Vliet told them, "to stand there with your guns in your hands. They may conduct the lightning." After wrapping towels around their guns, the hijackers resumed their vigil. But as twilight deepened into night, they relaxed. They too believed there was safety in darkness.

For the men in the train, the evening brightened up when Ansje Monsjou came in to join them. She was in high spirits and talked of her plans to go to India with her swimming-instructor boy friend. She was impatient to travel and see the world, but her father wanted her to finish her studies first. Arie Dijkman, who had traveled a good deal for Philips, asked, "Why go to India? It's a poor country, there's nothing much to see there." But to Ansje, India with its temples and its mystics and its hippie communes was magic. She was saving up for the journey.

The men had planned a joke session that evening, and Jan Cuppen had noted down a few phrases to jog his memory. He could never remember the best jokes otherwise. But for once, he fell silent. It was the first time Hustinx had seen him moody or depressed. Ansje Monsjou, however, soon stimulated him into his usual jocular frame of mind. "You are always sitting next to Marc," he said. "I think you're in love with him." "Okay," she said, "I'll sit next to you." Some jokes were told, they played Mastermind, then Jo Franken, a jovial fellow from southern Holland, amused them with his conjuring tricks, with the aid of an accomplice. Suddenly the unpredictable Ansje pretended to take offense at something and got up and walked away. When she came back, she sat next to Hustinx. "So I'm too old," said Cuppen. "You don't like me any more." The leg-pulling, which Ansje never tired of, continued, and the jokes got more and more colorful. From the women's carriage, too, came shouts of laughter as the hijackers joined the girls in their games. The contrasts in this community, thought van der Struik, were unbelievable.

Joke Winkeldermaat played cards with one of the Moluccans, and then she and three other Moluccans played dominoes against Rien van Baarsel. The Dutchman had sometimes taken on four or five of the hijackers at a time. When it got dark, she borrowed a cigarette lighter from one of the Moluccans to shed a flickering light over the checkerboard. As they sat there in a little group, heads together, with the Moluccans treating her so kindly, she couldn't think of them as terrorists.

Max had not neglected his talks with Mini Loman, and early that evening she went forward to his command post. This time, she took with her the young medical student Marijke Drost. As they sat down together opposite Max, Mini thought she had never seen him look so tired and dispirited. His eyes were bleary and bloodshot, his nerves were on edge, and his slight frame looked astonishingly frail. When she asked her usual question about progress, he shrugged his shoulders. "Mini," he said wearily, "this could last another six weeks."

Mini knew he had never expected the siege to last so long. The government, he told her, wouldn't budge an inch, and his own resolve was unchanged. They talked a little longer, and then the two girls were called to dinner. As they left, Max kept Mini back for a moment. "Can you come back at 7:30? By yourself?"

When she returned, he started asking her questions, questions that had been stimulated, perhaps, by Rudi's remark that if God showed them the way they would follow it. "What am I going to do? Do you think God will give me the answer if I pray first, and then ask him what to do? Do you think fasting will bring me the answer?"

She didn't know what to say. All she knew was that she had to be honest. Surely she could find some comfort for him from her religion? "If you are a Christian," she said, "you don't always have to have answers." She had often told him that she believed in fasting, that it had helped her to sharpen her senses and enable her to hear God's voice. "I believe that God can work miracles. But first you have to stand right with the Lord. You have used violence to take this train, and that surely can't be right before God."

"Can't I fast?"

"It's not just a physical thing. It affects the whole being. You must first have a personal relationship with Jesus Christ. Then you can fast."

Max's disappointment was painful to see. He was searching for an answer, something that would make up his mind for him, point the way to what he must do. The burden of responsibility for the lives of others was crushing him; he wanted desperately to find a way to God. While the other hijackers had become increasingly restless and bored, Max had made the decisions. Mini thought the only really mature young man other than Max, and the only one who might help him now, was Junus. Yet Junus's loyalty might be a drawback; he would do what Max said. Max was alone, and in his loneliness, he was crying for help.

He knew about God intellectually. Mini understood that. It was just that he was unable to take the final leap of faith that was demanded of the Christian. "You must commit your life to Christ. You must make a personal decision. Don't think about the other boys. They can't help you in this. It's something you have to do by yourself." She saw the agony in his eyes. "I'll pray about it," she said, "and you must pray too. Perhaps we can find a solution."

"Perhaps we can fast together?"

Much as she longed to find some way of helping him, she could not deceive him. "If you really want something from God, you have to get your priorities right."

"I want an answer from the Lord on what to do about this siege." He kept repeating this.

"You must first commit your life to Christ."

The time was eleven o'clock and she was afraid she would disturb the others back in the carriage if she stayed longer. "I'll pray for you, Max. Now I really must go."

"Can you give me something to remember you by? When I'm out of the country?"

She thought, when he spoke, that he was looking at her gold bracelet. She felt an urge to give it to him, but something held her back. She would give it to him tomorrow. Or perhaps there was something else she could give him. She wanted time to think about it. "Of course, I'll give you something, something I treasure." There was a bond of real affection between them. She felt desperately sorry for him, and the tears welled up in her eyes. He looked so forlorn. The situation had evolved beyond him, and he could no longer control it, yet he wanted to bring it to a good end. She said again, "I'll pray for you. I promise you that."

"Thank you, Mini. I do need your prayers."

In the men's carriage, too, it was half an hour later than usual before Ansje laid her head on Marc Hustinx's shoulder for a moment, said goodnight, and went back to the first-class section. She had in fact moved into the first-class entrance hall, which the hijackers, who had occupied it for a fortnight, had vacated. But she hadn't wanted to sleep there alone, and Rosemary had moved back through the zigzag connection to join her.

This had left room for one more in the second-class entrance hall, and Bimmel, Schager, and Blankert had been joined by Ineke Rijstenberg.

Victor Nijmeijer, who was never able to sleep comfortably in the men's compartment because of his height, asked that evening if he could move to the first class, where he could lie full length. Permission was granted, and, before he went to sleep, he said to Saskia, "This is the right moment to attack the train. We've been here three weeks now, and they must know where the hijackers are sleeping." He hadn't been able to imagine it until this moment, but suddenly he saw that it had gone on too long. "Yesterday," said Saskia, "I made a list of all the people in the train, because I thought it must end soon."

Mini Loman, back in her place, found Marijke Drost awake. "I have a strange feeling tonight, Mini," whispered Marijke, "the atmosphere is so tense."

"I have the same feeling—of foreboding. We must pray about it. Are you a Christian, Marijke?" Marijke did not answer. "Our lives are in their hands," said Mini. "What would happen to you if they killed you, Marijke? What would happen to your soul?"

Marijke did not speak for some time. "All I can say, Mini, is that if I come out of this alive, I will change my life. I will do things in a different way."

"Do you believe in prayer?" When Marijke nodded, Mini said, "Then pray as you have never prayed before, because if the others find out that they may have to spend another six weeks in here, they'll go crazy."

After the usual Friday cabinet meeting, which ended on this occasion at 3:45 PM, the principal ministers moved on to the crisis center. Present were den Uyl, van Agt, de Gaay Fortman, van der Stoel, van Doorn, and Zeevalking. For the first time at one of these meetings, van Agt followed his general review with a policy statement. A position of utter stalemate had been reached, he said. The aggressors, so far from being exhausted, appeared able to continue their action indefinitely. They had refused further contact. Medical advice indicated that the hostages had reached the limit of stress that ought to be imposed upon them. They were now under a more serious threat than ever before. Finally and conclusively, the restoration of law and order could be delayed no longer. The timing of military intervention against aggressions of this kind involved a delicate balance, but the time had now come. "I am of the opinion that we shall have to make an end of it tomorrow morning, and the only way open to us is force."

Van Agt had considered slowly and with foresight. Now he was acting swiftly—too swiftly, perhaps, for some. "Do we not need more time?" asked den Uyl.

No one wanted to risk the lives of the hostages in an attack while there remained a reasonable chance of getting the hijackers to surrender. The hijackers, too, had rights as citizens, as de Gaay Fortman had pointed out, and their lives were of consequence. But continuance of their action greatly magnified the risk of permanent damage to the hostages, making the gamble of inflicting death or injury on the few to release the many daily more acceptable. On the other hand, the hijackers had closed the door on a change of heart with depressing finality. Then there was Max's letter. Above all was the need for a normalization of the affairs of state and a return to law and order.

The inertia of military operations may also have been a factor, however subconsciously. With an attack planned and prepared and troops standing by, the pressure to set the action in motion built up. It had come to the notice of ministers that senior South Moluccans were saying, "The Dutch Government will never attack the train." If the hijackers were allowed that degree of complacency, they could keep their siege going for months.

A suggestion that a decision be delayed another twenty-four hours was resisted by van Agt, because it would mean attacking on a Sunday. That might have advantages of surprise, but it was abhorrent to him on religious grounds. In effect, it would entail a delay of two days, in which time the situation was likely to deteriorate still further. Discussions revealed a consensus in favor of attack on the morrow.

Again it was den Uyl who, while not opposing the decision, provided a steadying influence. "I think every one of us should go back to his ministry and think it over. We will meet here again at eight o'clock."

That evening, as the skies over northern Holland blackened and a gale rattled the windows of both train and school, the Dutch ministerial council reassembled to confirm their decision. It took them just fifteen minutes, and it was unanimous. They then discussed the merits of the plan and the possibility of giving the hijackers a warning.

Once the decision was taken, no one held stronger views than den Uyl on the form the attack should take. It must mount sufficient power to crush resistance. As for giving the terrorists an ultimatum, that would compromise security and endanger not only the lives of the hostages but also those of the men being sent by the government into action.

The atmosphere in the crisis center when this decision was taken was sepulchral, something that those present would never forget. Everyone knew what it meant. A period of extreme danger for the hostages, some of whom would almost certainly be killed or wounded—and certain death for the terrorists.

The executive order for the assault would be given by the military commanders at 4:00 AM the next day, Saturday, June 11, the nineteenth day of the siege. Action would begin at first light.

CHAPTER 28

The Assault

A T 2:30AM ON SATURDAY, June 11, an assault force of forty marine commandos, bullet-proof vests bulging under their camouflaged, light-weight clothing, faces blackened to merge with the darkness, left their tented encampment in the grounds of the North Netherlands Golf and Country Club 400 meters from the train and boarded the trucks that were to take them on a wide circuit before depositing them on the far side of the track. The assault was timed to start at 4:48 AM. Heading first to the north, away from the train, they followed the road as it turned abruptly to the left to cross the railway line at the level crossing 1,200 meters north of the train. Beyond the crossing, they turned left and left again until they had backtracked to a point 1,000 yards north of the train on the highway side of the track. Parking their transport in a country lane near a farm and riding school, they prepared to cover the remaining distance on foot, using the shelter of hedges and dikes. It was necessary for them to approach the train obliquely from the highway side in order to be clear of the line of fire of the sharpshooters. Meanwhile, on their right flank, a group of eight frogmen with similarly blackened faces were pursuing a tortuous course across meadow and swamp that would bring them up under the train to lay their explosives. This was the group that had reconnoitered the train night after night in the previous eighteen days.

Last to leave the wooded area protecting the golf club were the thirty-six sharpshooters, drawn from the state police and the army. After walking 200 meters through high, wet grass to a point where the river approached the railway before passing underneath it, they positioned themselves against the top of the dike on the train's starboard bow, bringing the whole length of the train within their line of fire.

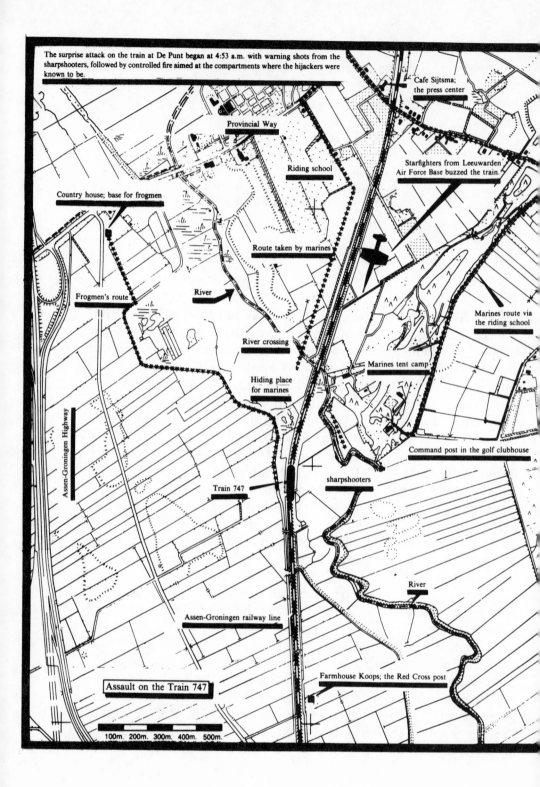

The surprise attack on the train at De Punt began at 4:53 a.m. with warning shots from the sharpshooters, followed by controlled fire aimed at the compartments where the hijackers were known to be.

Cafe Sijtsma; the press center

Provincial Way

Riding school

Starfighters from Leeuwarden Air Force Base buzzed the train.

Country house; base for frogmen

Route taken by marines

River

Frogmen's route

Marines route via the riding school

River crossing

Marines tent camp

Hiding place for marines

Command post in the golf clubhouse

Assen-Groningen Highway

Train 747

sharpshooters

River

Assen-Groningen railway line

Farmhouse Koops; the Red Cross post

Assault on the Train 747

100m. 200m. 300m. 400m. 500m.

Although they would be firing to keep heads down in other parts of the train, they would be concentrating their fire on those sections thought to be occupied by the hijackers—the front section, the first-class entrance hall, which, unknown to the sharpshooters, had been occupied for the past two nights by Rosemary and Ansje, and the last two cabins of the rear first-class section. As the early morning mist lifted, the ugly snout of the train loomed into focus at an angle of 45 degrees to their position, leaning a little toward them on the slope of the bend. Fixing their telescopic sights, they waited for H-hour.

The marines, having trekked southward along the railway line, forded the river, using boats positioned there earlier by the frogmen, then continued south until they reached the cover of a clump of bushes surrounding a small fen less than a hundred meters from the train. The time was 4:00 AM—forty-eight minutes to wait.

At 4:20 AM, the six Starfighters took off from their base at Leeuwarden in Friesland and set course for the prearranged waiting zone over Zoutcamp, thirty kilometers northwest of De Punt. There they circled, waiting for the operations officer accompanying the marines to transmit the signal to attack. As a safeguard against signals failure, Colonel Harry Arendsen, the squadron commander, was airborne in a helicopter close to the target area, ready to relay the signal if necessary. There was a second backup signals link on the ground at Zoutcamp.

At 4:45 AM, the two ground commanders, marines and sharpshooters, conferred by radio. A gray dawn was breaking, but a check with the air force liaison link revealed that the Starfighters had just started another circuit. It would be three minutes before they could line up on the correct approach path for their timed run to the train. After a short consultation, H-hour was put back to 4:53 AM, so as to synchronize the opening barrage of the sharpshooters with the Starfighters' initial dive on the train.

Marc Hustinx usually woke up with cramp about 2:00 AM. But when he awoke the time by his watch was 4:30 AM. As usual he had pins and needles, and he turned over to relieve them, but he was pleased at having slept so long. The usual early morning traffic to the toilet had started, and he was still half-awake, like several others, when the firing began. Ton Kroon, he knew, was still in the toilet.

Most of the hostages had tried to imagine what an attack from outside might be like. They were utterly shattered by the reality. Nothing of such savagery had seemed remotely possible. Although the timed run of the Starfighters from Zoutcamp was somehow miscalculated, so that the rifle and automatic weapons of the sharpshooters exploded unaccompanied out of the night, everyone immediately dived for the floor. Bullets penetrated walls and windows and ricocheted around the hostages' heads, while the harsh, urgent voices of the marines shouted at them through megaphones. "Lie down! Lie on the floor! Keep down! Keep your heads down." Someone on the floor next to Hustinx, driven by claustrophobia, panicked and tried to reach the door. "I must get out! I must get out!" Hustinx grabbed him and pushed him down. Then the thunder of the jets rocked the train on its axles and sheets of flame from the afterburners rolled along the windows like a forest fire. Eardrums throughout the train were numbed or punctured, horses and cattle in the fields stampeded with fright.

Kees Bimmel was asleep in the second-class entrance hall, and his first thought was that the hijackers were firing at something outside the train. Then he heard the yelling of his fellow hostages and knew the attack had come. There was an explosion from somewhere under the floor (produced by the frogmen), then a stream of bullets tore through the wall above his head. For a moment he lay flat on the floor with the others, and then he thought of Rosemary. For a fortnight, they had talked intimately every night, and they had been very close. Reaching up to the handle of the sliding door leading to the zigzag connection, he pulled it open and shouted, "Rose! Come to us!"

Rosemary had already made up her mind she must get to Kees. But as she jumped up from the floor, she was hit in the legs. Looking down, she saw in the dim light that her sleeping bag had been perforated by bullets. Had she not moved at that moment she would have been riddled.

Bimmel saw the door on the far side of the connection slide open, and then Rosemary dived through and crawled across to him. Frightened and confused, she was calling, "I've been hit! I've been hit!" As Bimmel pulled her towards him, the door on the far side of the connection swung to under the force of gravity, leaving Ansje on the far side. In the same instant, Bimmel felt a bullet graze his scalp, literally parting his hair, and he was forced to duck down, leaving Ansje where she was. Spreading his body over Rosemary and Ineke, he calmed them down. "Lie still. It'll soon be over, and we'll be free. Everything's going to be all right."

"I've been hit here," said Rosemary, indicating her legs. Both had been grazed, one badly. Bimmel felt them but couldn't locate the wounds. Bullets were still piercing the area above his head, and he decided they must move further forward. The marines would be sure to know that the second-class carriage was full of hostages. "Open the door as quick as you can and get forward," he told Schager. "I'll bring the girls." As he spoke, he heard a muffled cry behind him, coming from the first-class entrance hall. "I've been hit in the eye. I'm blind. I'm going to die." He knew it could only be Ansje Monsjou.

Bimmel pulled Ineke over the top of him and pushed her into the carriage. "Move forward and hide." Rosemary couldn't walk, but he took her in his arms and crawled forward, dragging her by his side. Someone was still shooting through the roof, and the voice from the bullhorn, audible only intermittently between the thunder of the returning jets, was still shouting, "Keep down, keep down." He laid Rosemary on a vacant couch and dived for the floor.

He had only just settled when he saw the doors of the front entrance hall collapse. Suddenly, the hall was full of marines. The first thing they did was fire a volley through the doors of the toilet. Van der Struik saw them too and feared for Ton Kroon. In fact, Kroon had been back in his seat less than a minute.

Behind them, the rear entrance hall was also filling up with marines. There was pandemonium as shots were exchanged between one end of the carriage and the other. "Stop it!" yelled Bimmel. "They're friends!" A diminutive marine dived through a broken window above him and landed on top of him. "Any hijackers here?" "No," said Bimmel, "no hijackers here."

In the back of the train, Rudi grabbed his Uzi at the first sound of shots and began to run forward through the train, closely followed by Hansina. Somehow they got as far as the restaurant, where Hansina was hit. Rudi bent over her, muttering a prayer. "Pray for a good end to it all," he told her. "I must go on." His intention was to shoot as many hostages as he could before killing himself.

Despite the firing that was still being kept up from outside, Rudi got through the restaurant into the first-class carriage and entered the corridor on the right leading to the women's section, passing the "royal stables" where four of his comrades had been sleeping. He did not stop to investigate, but kept moving forward, finally bursting open the door of the women's section. The screams of the women were now audible above the din, yet the carriage seemed empty at first glance, most of them having dived under the seats. Some who had tried to get out had been grabbed and pulled down by others. There were some, though, for whom there was no room on the floor, and they lay flattened face down on the seats. Among these was Saskia, who was trying to protect her head with a pillow. Others could find nothing more substantial to shield themselves with than blankets.

"Stand up!" shouted Rudi. Like several others, Joke Winkeldermaat didn't know what to do, but she got ready to obey, until the woman next to her held her down. "The safest thing we can do is lie still." She did so, fully expecting to die. The train was still shuddering with the noise and air displacement of the jets, so much so that she thought it must soon fall apart. That would be the end for them all.

Rien van Baarsel, the man suffering from respiratory trouble, was fighting for breath. Lying on the floor beside him was Mini Loman. Often he had talked to her about his wife and two small children. Now, in a moment of near suffocation, he stood up to get some air and was immediately hit, falling back on the couch where Mini had been sleeping a few moments earlier. "Help me," he called. But, with bullets still streaming through the windows, no one could move.

Ahead of them, the first-class entrance hall, where Ansje was lying wounded, was blasted open by marines. Rushing in, they confronted Rudi from the opposite end of the carriage. The nearest hostage to Rudi was Marijke Drost, and he grabbed her, holding her in front of him as a shield. "I surrender," he called, "but I'm not going alone." The marines did not dare shoot, but one of them lobbed what everyone took to be a hand grenade—it was a smoke bomb—down the corridor, and it hit Rudi on the ear. This shocked Rudi into firing his Uzi. A bullet entered Marijke's chest and shot out through her ribs. "Don't shoot, don't shoot!" shouted Rudi in panic. "I surrender!"

The firing of the gun had been involuntary. When it came to shooting women and turning the gun on himself, Rudi's courage had failed him.

Marijke was clasping her chest, and Mini thought she would die. "Are you injured?" It was all she could manage to say, and it sounded so lame. "I think so, I think so." Showing great coolness, the girl applied her medical knowledge at once, tearing off her blouse and binding the wound.

Two weeks earlier, Rudi had held off with his Uzi when he seemed to have time to shoot the Chinese boy before anyone else could intervene. Now his life was spared by the marines. But van Baarsel lay dead across Mini Loman's seat. And under the door of the first-class entrance hall, which had been blown in by the marines to gain access, lay the lifeless body of Ansje Monsjou.

Mini Loman was hoping against hope that Max had survived. Why hadn't she given him the memento he had asked for? Somehow she must find a way of giving it to him. But Max had taken his last gamble. In the front study compartment of Train 747, Max and two of his comrades, Mingus and Kojak, lay dead.

Of the hijackers in the "royal stables" behind the women, Junus and Thys were together in one compartment, Andreas and Ronnie in another. Junus and Thys had finished guard duty at 3:00 AM and were asleep. Junus was badly wounded, and Thys was dead. In the adjacent cabin, which was drenched with bullets, Ronnie was dead, but Andreas miraculously escaped unhurt. Not one of the four was able to return the sharpshooters' fire. The only one of the hijackers who may have fired back was Hansina. But when the marines found her, she was dead.

Many of the women hostages, scarcely able to believe they were alive, were sobbing in terror. In addition to Rosemary and Marijke, several had sustained minor injuries in the shooting, as well as burst eardrums. The men had fared better. "It's over, fellas, they're getting us out," said van der Struik. He was the first of the male hostages to speak. In previous days, he had often been terrified, but he had always believed the marines would come, and during the attack, he had been too elated to feel afraid. His reaction now was one of triumph, a reaction that Flapper, for one, found distasteful. "Here they are all very dead," he heard one of the marines say from the front, and van der Struik called out, "Beautifully done!" Yet, a few minutes later, when they took him out of the train and he saw the bodies of the six dead South Moluccans lined up alongside the track, and the three survivors—Rudi, Junus, and Andreas—face down and arms spread, trembling with terror and shock, all the elation drained out of him, and he felt a surge of pity. He could not get over it, he was so deeply moved. All this damned playing at soldiers. What in God's name had been the point of it? Even the sight of Ronnie, the most militant of the hijackers, affected him deeply.

Within three and a half months van der Struik too was dead, from a heart attack, a victim of the hijacking as surely as were Rien van Baarsel and Ansje Monsjou. Marijke Drost, who had had such a fortunate escape, recovered. Later she received a letter from Rudi. "You may hate me," he wrote, "that is your right. But I'm sorry." He was honest enough to say that he didn't really know whether he meant to shoot her or not. She accepted his apology.

A minute or so before the attack on the train, armored personnel carriers converged on the school, ramming the external structure in three places and disgorging a force of marine commandos, while other troops gave covering fire. The teachers, alerted by the broadcasts of the previous evening, had gone to bed fully dressed, the two women in the principal's study and the two men in the corridor. Of the hijackers, one was on guard and the other three were sleeping in the stock room. When the attack began, the women heard Willem shout: "Come here! Come to here!" They thought at first that the call came from van Vliet, and they hurried out into the corridor, then realized it was Willem. Van Vliet called to them to stay where they were, but they had no idea what Willem planned and felt bound to obey him. Otherwise he might shoot them. Van Vliet shouted "Get down!" But, with Willem still screaming at them, they crawled to the stock room, which Willem had earmarked as the strongest part of the building. He was only anxious to protect them. As the armored vehicles crashed into the building, one wall of the stock room collapsed, but no one was seriously hurt. The hijackers offered no resistance, and in a very short time they were spreadeagled on the paving outside the school and the teachers were free.

The interior of the school, partly demolished, strewn with dust, rubble, and broken glass, presented a sorry spectacle. Still chalked on a blackboard in the assembly room was the sentence the children had chanted on the third day of the siege. "Van Agt, we want to live!" Underneath it, one of the children had chalked an impromptu caricature of Tommy Polnaya. Beside the blackboard was a Ministry of Education poster that struck an unconscious note of irony. "Not separately, not apart, but together in the public school."

CHAPTER 29

Post-Mortems

T HE JOURNEY OF THE HOSTAGES by bus to Groningen turned into a triumphal procession as cheering thousands lined the streets or waved from their balconies, many of them still in their nightclothes. Suddenly the hostages were heroes, a role they were quite unprepared for. As Dutch flags were waved at them and the jubilation rose to a crescendo, many of them wept unashamedly. It was a natural and spontaneous reaction on the part of the people of northern Holland, free from political undertones. To the hostages, it was a warming demonstration that they had not been forgotten after all.

Taken as planned to the Psychiatric Clinic at the University Hospital, they arrived half-stunned by the turmoil of the assault, yet emotionally stimulated by their rapturous welcome. They could hardly have seemed more in need of psychiatric protection. The staff of the clinic encouraged them to give vent to their feelings, and most of them were soon talking in an animated and often excitable manner. Physical checks showed them to be in surprisingly good condition, but the psychiatrists, assuming that reactions would be similar to last time, strongly advised them to stay in hospital for at least twenty-four hours.

After Wijster, anger on the part of the hostages with what was seen as official ineptitude, coupled with overidentification with their captors, had prompted attitudes and criticisms that many hostages had afterwards recognized as unfair. This time, the intention was to protect them as far as possible from indiscretions of that kind. Better to avoid the press altogether for the first few days, van Dyke told them, than to make comments they might subsequently regret. They were encouraged, however, to sign a joint statement registering their gratitude for their release

327

and their sympathy at the death of two of their number. The statement made no mention of the deaths of the hijackers, and several of the hostages, among whom George Flapper and Kees Bimmel were the most vocal, objected. They were overruled on the grounds that such an expression of sympathy was a symptom of the overidentification against which they were being warned.

Flapper was furious—as if normal human fellow-feeling could legitimately be suppressed for fear of some psychological hangup. South Moluccans would be bound to interpret the omission as a studied piece of callousness. Dutch deaths mattered. The deaths of South Moluccans did not. This was certainly not the intention of the psychiatrists, but the statement went out.

The efforts of the psychiatrists to avoid the mistakes made after Wijster met with no more than partial success. Few of the hostages took kindly to the suggestion that they stay in hospital. They saw it as a kind of quarantine. Although the psychiatrists pleaded the wisdom of an overnight stay, nearly everyone wanted to go home.

Anxious to burst the dam of inhibition and see the pent-up emotions flow, the psychiatrists held on to their patients as long as they could, but their very presence may itself have been inhibiting. "I don't want to say anything of that kind," protested Flapper. "If I have emotional things to say, I will say them to my wife." He was taken to an anteroom, where Coby was waiting. After a tearful reunion, he talked with her for a minute or so, and then van Dyke interrupted them. "It's better for you to stay here for twenty-four hours," he told Flapper. Flapper's attitude was typical of his fellow hostages. "I don't want to do that. I don't want to be a hostage a second time."

It was natural that after nineteen days the hostages would feel that they couldn't get back quickly enough to home and family. The reaction had been the same after Wijster. Which was worse, they asked themselves, to be hijacked for three weeks or to be delivered into the hands of the psychiatrists, the occupational therapists, and the social workers? That was the attitude. "When I hear the experts," said Jan Cuppen, "I can't avoid the impression that they consider a hostage normal only if he behaves abnormally." Debarred from emphasizing the phenomenon of late sequelae because of the dangers of making a self-fulfilling prophecy, the psychiatrists were similarly tongue-tied over the aftereffects of Wijster and the Indonesian Consulate. All they could do was hope that their long-term plans for aftercare were not thwarted.

Many of the hostages did achieve considerable release of tension before they left the hospital that night. After coffee and sandwiches, during which they were kept under observation and encouraged to talk, they were given the opportunity to shower. On the way to the shower room, Mini Loman found one of the girls sobbing her heart out. Mini went to comfort her and lost control of her own emotions in the process. Together they cried for several minutes. All the pent-up feelings of nineteen days came out in a waterfall. This was just what the psychiatrists wanted. Having recovered their composure, they reveled in the delicious hot water flowing over their bodies. X-rays followed, and then they were allowed to meet their families.

All but two of the hostages who had not been wounded went home that night. Home for them was to be reborn. Janneke Wiegers, back with her parents in Assen, expressed the general mood. "Everything looks and smells so good."

After his day at the clinic, Flapper made the cynical comment that hostages only existed for the benefit of psychiatrists. That was how it seemed to him. Yet for the psychiatrists, the dilemma was an impossible one. They understood their patients' resistance, yet they had in mind the oft-repeated complaint of the 1975 hostages, who had felt abandoned at the time of the hijackings and deserted afterwards. "I wasn't just isolated once," one of them had said, "I was isolated twice."

One who, far from being isolated, had to fight for her privacy was Rosemary Oostveen. Headlines that described her as "the Florence Nightingale of the train" embarrassed her, and she refused to be photographed or interviewed. She did not wish to be recognized and pointed out to others for the rest of her life as, "That's the doctor who was in the train."

Rien van Baarsel, to whom she had ministered throughout the hijacking, had proposed that on their release the hostages should club together and buy her a golden rose. There was a chorus of agreement at the time, but sadly the idea died with him.

As for the schoolteachers, although they attracted less of the limelight, their problems of resettlement far exceeded those of their counterparts in the train. The latter were shaking the dust of De Punt off their shoes and scattering to the four corners of Holland. The teachers were remaining in Bovensmilde. Ahead of them lay the task not only of living in peace with their neighbors, but also of reconstituting healthy nonracial attitudes within the school. Despite calls in some quarters for separate education, this was a task that they expressed themselves as positively in favor of attempting. It would not be without its defeats and disappointments. Already some of the younger Dutch children had suffered a psychological relapse and were hiding behind their mother's apron strings at the sight of South Moluccans.

In justifying the government's action, den Uyl said the decision was taken "because in the end we saw no other way." He appealed to both Dutch and South Moluccans not to let feelings of revenge get the upper hand. "That violence proved necessary to put an end to the hostage seizure is something that we feel as a defeat." Van Agt joined in the self-justification. "I beseech you to believe that there was no other way. We tried everything. Every path of dialogue there might be, we followed it. We found them all closed."

Criticism of the government for authorizing the attack and for perpetrating what some saw as a disastrous overkill was not confined to South Moluccans, but it completely ignored Max's threat to kill the hostages. Whether or not the threat would have been carried out, had the hijackers been given the opportunity, remains an imponderable, but the government had to assume that it might be. How long they could have afforded to delay the attack was another imponderable, but most people thought they had waited long enough.

Other imponderables were the accusations of duplicity on the part of the government that were subsequently made. These covered three main points:

1. That they introduced the virus into the school.
2. That they fabricated the suspected case of meningitis.
3. That they never had any intention of letting the hijackers go.

In the absence of firm evidence, the government's integrity on these points must be taken or left according to the individual viewpoint. On points 1 and 2, the probabilities are that the epidemic in the school was spontaneous, but that the government took maximum advantage of it. On point 3, the government, like Max, took a gamble. Bitterly opposed to offering any kind of concession, they took a chance for the sake of the children, backing their hunch that the hijackers had no fixed destination and would be unable to find one.

The dominant reaction of the Dutch public was relief that the ordeal was over and the loss of life no worse than it was. Terrorists could not be talked to indefinitely, otherwise society would be disrupted on a grotesque scale. Therefore they backed the military operation and admired its execution, which in view of the risks was considered successful. As for the terrorists, they had got what they asked for. Many Dutch people had reacted with sympathy after Wijster, despite the killings, but a second outbreak was seen as counterproductive. The hijackings seemed pointless, directed at the only friends the South Moluccans had. Yet the soul-destroying experience of the South Moluccans since 1950 and their poignant vision of a promised land were not forgotten. In a society that, like most Western societies, was riddled with social guilt, many felt that they and their government must somehow be to blame.

A less complicated reaction came from the children who had been taken hostage. After years of mixing naturally with South Moluccan children, they had acted naturally with the hijackers. But when the school group was captured and the teachers were released, they rejoiced. Accustomed to accepting punishment philosophically, they had no compunction about the expected imprisonment of the hijackers. And whereas their parents felt compassion for those killed in the train and for their families, the children reacted with crude logic. "Why do you worry about those killed in the train? Have you forgotten the three they killed at Wijster?"

South Moluccan reaction was typically split between the generations. Young people believed that violence by the oppressed was legitimate. Radicals spoke of the "cowardly way" the sieges had been ended, and how the government must accept responsibility for the consequences. "They should have ended it in a peaceful manner," said Etty Aponno. But he did not say how. On the other hand, Manusama agreed that the Dutch Government had had no alternative but to use force. "I hope, too, that Dutch people will realize that the vast majority of South Moluccans deeply regret what happened." He urged South Moluccans to "express our independence ideal in a much better way from now on." Another sober comment came from Lokollo. "A bomb has fallen on the centuries-old bridge of confidence between the Netherlands and the South Moluccans. This bridge must now be repaired."

At the trial, the school group was unanimous that the immediate cause of its action was disillusionment with the Köbben Commission. Rudi, on behalf of the train group, said: "Do not look at our deeds, look at the reason for them, because our rights have been denied us." Nevertheless the sentences passed on both groups were severe. Willem Soplanit, for taking the initiative in the actions, was sentenced to nine years. Isaac Thenu and Guustav Tehupuring, who were considered to have taken the initiative equally with Soplanit, also received nine years. Tommy Polnaya got seven years. For the train group, the court took into account that they had lost six of their comrades. Rudi Lumalessil, who had lost his brother and his girl friend, and Junus Ririmasse, who was wheeled into court on a stretcher, were given eight years, and Andreas Luhulima, six.

Among the more penetrating comments made in the course of the trial were those of Max's cousin, Pieter Papilaya. After proclaiming that Max was neither a terrorist nor a murderer, and that in his life he had earned the respect of everyone, he said he couldn't explain how he had come to this action. "Something higher must have moved him." But if the causes of discontent were not removed, young South Moluccans would identify with the figure of Max. He added a comment of even more potential significance. "We older ones have some guilt. We have moved our young people to such an extent that these actions are the result."

Here for the first time was an admission that the fault might not lie all on one side. If the Dutch, too, could face up to their own shortcomings, a worthwhile compromise might yet be achieved.

On January 26, 1978, the Ministry of the Interior summarized a government memorandum tabled in the Dutch parliament on the problem of the South Moluccan community in the Netherlands.[14] The summary came to the point in a paragraph headed "The New Approach: Right to Own Identity." For the first time in history, said the summary, Dutch society found itself confronted by a minority whose orientation and ideals lay elsewhere and to whom the preservation of its own social and cultural identity was paramount. Development within Dutch society had thus been rejected and isolation preferred. This forced Dutch society to examine what the rights and duties of cultural minorities in Holland were and what elements existed to advance or hamper their objectives. "As regards the Moluccan desire to remain themselves," continued the summary, "the government now feels that the Moluccans have the right to the preservation of their own identity as expressed in their habits and customs, their religious organizations and language." *The government now feels.* This was the vital admission, with its revolutionary implication that the government had been wrong and had changed its mind.

Progress toward a new era in Dutch/South Moluccan relationships was to be governed by two principles: (1) The government could not and would not force the Moluccan minority to relinquish its own identity and integrate into Dutch society; (2) The Moluccan community must respect the values and rules of that society and keep channels of communication open

---

[14]*Bulletin No. I 15, Ministrie van Binnenlandse Zaken.*

with it. "These two principles are also incorporated in the 'International Agreement Regarding Civil and Political Rights' issued by the United Nations, which the Netherlands will ratify shortly." Ratification duly came in December, 1978.

The memorandum went on to lay down important new measures in the fields of education, housing, employment, and participation in local affairs, for all of which government grants would be forthcoming. The long-standing grievance of the nonpayment of KNIL pensions between 1956 and 1964 was to be rectified. These were intended as rough outlines, and the Moluccan minority were encouraged to involve themselves as widely as possible in the formulation and execution of all policies that concerned them. As a start, full consultation with Moluccan agencies was sought before the memorandum was debated in Parliament.

There remained the situation of South Moluccans in Indonesia. Here the Dutch Government could offer no help. Historically, however, the subject was covered by a report of the Köbben-Mantouw Commission, which concluded, after an exhaustive study of documents, that the Moluccan fight for independence had been initiated by the Dutch Government itself, that everything possible had been done to secure self-determination for the various countries of the old Dutch colonial empire, but that the objective had already been lost by the time of the Round Table Conference of 1949. "The Commission is of the opinion that the establishment of these facts may promote understanding and possible respect on both sides."

It was not to be expected that the realism of the memorandum would satisfy everyone. Soon after its publication, in March, 1978, the modern building housing the offices of the Drenthe provincial government on the outskirts of Assen—where Max Papilaya had worked as a registry clerk —was occupied by three young South Moluccans. Seventy hostages were taken, one of whom was killed at the outset "to encourage the others." This time, in addition to the release of South Moluccan prisoners and a free departure by plane, a ransom was demanded amounting to $13 million. The siege bore the stamp of criminal extremists, using the RMS as a rationalization. Marines stormed the building successfully within thirty-six hours, suggesting a harder government line for the future, but this was disclaimed by the new prime minister, Andreas van Agt, who had succeeded Joop den Uyl four months earlier. Van Agt revealed that, through a secret contact inside the building, the government had been warned that there would be many victims if action was not taken within minutes. Van Agt afterwards conceded that the Dutch would simply have to learn to live with the siege problem, but consultations with prominent South Moluccans on the new policies put forward by the government went forward as planned.

Inevitably over the years, more and more young South Moluccans have found their way into regular employment and have started homes and families of their own and become anchored in Dutch or mixed Dutch/Indonesian society. A similar dilution has taken place in the South Moluccas themselves because of the Indonesian government's policy of transmigration. These changes pose the most serious threat of all to the South Moluccans as an ethnic group. It is likely that growing fears of integration and assimilation and of the disappearance of a separate identity and culture fanned the embers of the RMS ethos and produced the militant nostalgia of the 1970s. For the future, South Moluccans are unlikely to relinquish their dream of Ambon, but things that seem impossible in one decade can sometimes be feasible in another. In the meantime, the preservation of a separate identity, language, and culture now seems guaranteed.

The second group of hijackers set out to correct and atone for the mistakes of the first, and to succeed where they failed. The 1975 hijackers had gone badly wrong when they killed, and the murders, however much some tried to justify them, lay on the Moluccan conscience as a blot on their good name. The 1975 hijackers had surrendered; that rankled even more. Max was determined to avoid killing, and never to surrender. The rest of the group supported him.

By their zealotry, Max and his comrades compelled the Dutch to reconsider what burden of injustice, real or imagined, of the body or of the soul, could inspire such a sacrifice. By killing for a cause, the 1975 hijackers had sought to convince. By dying for one, Max and his comrades made the greater impact.

Max was not a man with a deathwish. He had experienced a call, one he regarded as sacred, and he had responded. As his cousin had suggested, something higher had moved him. The objectives set by the group were limited, but Max, as he showed in his talks with the hostages as well as with Dr. Tan, was conscious of the wider issues. "Maybe it is necessary that we sacrifice ourselves," he had told Mrs. Soumokil. "Perhaps then we shall get recognition."

The 1975 hijackers had understood this too, and Paul Saimima had been ashamed of the surrender at Wijster and had spoken of his own survival with anguish. There was a postscript to this when, on the first anniversary of the death of Max and five of his comrades, that unhappy, tortured soul Eli Hahury hanged himself in his cell.

Hans Oude Elberink leaving
the hospital. *ANEFO*

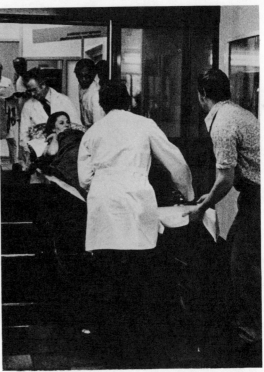

Rosemary Oostveen being wheeled into
the hospital after the assault on the
train that freed the hostages. *ANP*

After the assault: Max Papilaya's shattered "command post."

The six hijackers who were killed during the assault on the De Punt train: Left to right (top)—Max Papilaya, Hansina Oktoseja, George "Kojak" Matulessy. (Bottom)—Domingus "Mingus" Rumamory, Ronnie Lumalessil, Mattheus "Thys" Tuny. *Private Collection*

Scene from the funeral of the six South Moluccan hijackers killed in the assault. *ANP*

APPENDIX A

DECLARATION OF INDEPENDENCE OF THE SOUTH MOLUCCAS

To grant the real will, wishes and demands of the people of the South Moluccas, we hereby proclaim the independence of the South Moluccas, de facto and de jure, with the political structure of a republic, free from any political connection with the Negara Indonesia Timur and the Republic of the United States of Indonesia, on account of the fact that the Negara Indonesia Timur is unable to maintain her position as a part of the United States of Indonesia, in accordance with the "Denpasar Settlement," which is still valid at present, and concerning the resolution of the Council of the South Moluccas of March 11, 1947, while the Republic of the United States of Indonesia has acted in a way which is incompatible with the resolution taken at the Round Table Conference and its constitution.

Ambon, April 25, 1950

> The Government of the South Moluccas,
> the President J.H. Manuhutu,
> the Prime Minister A. Wairisal.

APPENDIX B

ROYAL ARMY DEMOBILIZATION COMMAND IN INDONESIA—NETHERLANDS DISTRICTS IN INDONESIA COMMAND

No. AC-363   Djakarta, February 2, 1951

Re: Instructions concerning the discharge of Ambonese ex-KNIL soldiers

1. The Netherlands Government has in principle decided on (temporary) dispatch to the Netherlands of the Ambonese ex-KNIL soldiers and their families, who do not wish to be demobilized in any place located in the territory of the R.I., provided written assurance is obtained from the R.I. Government that the Ambonese soldiers, who wish to return to Indonesia from the Netherlands, will again be admitted in Indonesia.

2. In anticipation of the aforementioned assurance and in order to be able to make the necessary preparations, the Ambonese ex-KNIL soldiers who opted for "discharge South Moluccas" should now—under withdrawal of all therewith conflicting instructions—make their choice from one of the following alternatives:
   (a) Discharge within Indonesia
   (b) Temporary dispatch to the Netherlands

3. *Discharge within Indonesia*

   For those who after all state the wish to be discharged within Indonesia, the following regulations apply:
   (a) For the administrative completion and the dispatch to the place of destination, the rules contained in my instruction of December 11, 1950 . . . apply in principle.
   (b) Every soldier (regardless of family composition) will moreover be granted immediately upon discharge a sum of R. 5,000,—in order to facilitate his transition to civilian life.

   A relevant instruction will be issued to the military cashier.

338

4. *Dispatch to the Netherlands*

The Government wishes to give this dispatch a temporary character in so far, that every soldier removed to the Netherlands, if he states the wish thereto, can return to Indonesia again, to which end consultations are in progress with the Indonesian authorities. Furthermore the following provisions apply:

(a) On the day of embarkation all will be placed on pension or as case may be, standoff pay.

(b) In the Netherlands, they will be accommodated in encampments, where the costs of care, etc., will be deducted from their income.

(c) For the administrative and transport arrangements for carrying out this dispatch, the same rules apply in principle as for the dispatch of ex-soldiers who opted for "Transition to Royal Army" or "Discharge in the Netherlands"; for this, further provisions will be determined in consultation with D.D.M.V.

The Commander of Netherlands
Districts in Indonesia
The Chief of Staff
J.G.M. Smit, Lieutenant-Colonel

APPENDIX C

MOTIVES OF THE SOUTH MOLUCCAN FIGHTERS—MEMORANDUM OF EXPLANATION

The fundamentals of our South Moluccan battle for independence are:

By fundamentals we mean that one day, before the RMS was proclaimed, we first asked God the Almighty for his help. This was on April 24, 1950.

The day after, on April 25, 1950, the proclamation of the Republic of the South Moluccas took place, and this was totally in line with both the law *and the wish of the people.*

1. On this basis and this foundation we fight for the independence of the Republic of South Moluccans (RMS).
2. We South Moluccans fight because the identity of our people is in danger of being destroyed by the Indonesian Government and its imperialism. By identity we mean the morals, the habits, and the culture of our people, which compared with Western cultures is many times more humane, and doesn't occur anywhere else in the world.
3. We South Moluccans fight because it is impossible for us to live freely and happily in a country whose government has betrayed our ancestors, our parents, and our young people, while fellow countrymen now languishing in Indonesian prisons etc. are suffering and according to our sources of information are being tortured. In the South Moluccas our brothers and sisters live in dreadful and inhumane conditions.
4. In this type of action we are repeating what happened on August 31, 1970, in Wassenaar. The thirty-three people then involved surrendered, after which the Netherlands Government promised them that they would work positively for their cause. These thirty-three persons made it known that they were open to reason.

   Alas, that which the Netherlands Government had promised was never fulfilled and so the government has again betrayed these thirty-three people

340

and through them the whole of the South Moluccan people.

5. We are sad and regret that the Netherlands Government by acting negatively toward our cause has left us nothing else but this form of protest, since all other channels that might have been used for a peaceful settlement or a positive solution have now been blocked. Therefore we South Moluccans declare that the Netherlands Government is guilty of an attempt to destroy our people.

6. We South Moluccan fighters are nevertheless ready to fight for our rightful independence struggle, although we regret very much that innocent blood may be spilled (in this case of hostages). If that proves to be the case, then we will have acted in those moments under an overpowering compulsion *(vis compulsiva)*. This is because the habits, morals, and cultural interests of our people for us is of a higher value than our own lives and those of our hostages. So if any blood of the hostages flows then the Indonesian and also the Dutch Governments are responsible. The attitude of the police will decide the destiny of the hostages.

7. We South Moluccan fighters have come to this form of battle because for twenty-five years our attempts at peaceful methods of struggling for our rights, amongst others by petitions and protest marches, have all been ignored by the Indonesians and especially by the Dutch Government (since all this peaceful form of struggle has taken place on Dutch soil).

We came to the decision that taking hostages would be our next step because this is permitted according to the rights of peoples if it serves the purpose of preventing acts of injustice by an enemy and/or forcing the fulfilling of obligations one toward another.

The Indonesian Government, through its imperialism, and the Dutch Government, through its complicity, have been correspondingly responsible for the plight of our people and form in our view the enemy. Besides this the Dutch Government has many obligations toward the RMS cause.

If the taking of hostages occurs, then it is in any case also God's will, because His will be done, not only in Heaven, but also on earth.

Signed : Free South Moluccan Youth
MENA MURIA

Index